Praise for *One Day in August*

'A lively and readable account'
The Spectator

'[A] fine book ... well-written and well-researched.'
Washington Times

'A fast-paced and convincing book, *One Day in August* ... clears up decades of misinformation about the ignoble raid and should provide comfort for the few remaining survivors of that notorious massacre ... Building on the work of previous historians who didn't have access to the documents he had, O'Keefe has provided meaning to what has always been seen as a senseless massacre. And for Ron Beal, who witnessed the slaughter 71 years ago as a bewildered and terrified private, that is everything. "Now I can die in peace," he told O'Keefe. "Now I know what my friends died for." Amen to that.'
—*Toronto Star*

'Based on extensive original research ... O'Keefe's landmark new book presents a new and original explanation of what happened on that fateful August day in 1942.'
—*The Globe and Mail* (Best Book)

'This is a valuable, well-researched, and thought provoking book. The author has uncovered new evidence and cleared up a lot of questions ... I have known for years that there was an intelligence-gathering element in the plan; but not to the extent revealed by David O'Keefe. O'Keefe's book is a must read if one is to really understand the Dieppe raid.'
—Julian Thompson

'Highly original and bracingly revisionist, *One Day in August* is that rare book that is able to say something new about something so familiar. Based on extensive research in official records in Canada and Britain, many of them previously undiscovered or long-forgotten, *One Day in August* is historical writing at its best: engrossing, revealing, and enlightening.'
—Citation, RBC Taylor Prize

'O'Keefe has definitely made the biggest breakthrough of the last twenty years in our understanding of the raid ... His principal research achievement is to have kept digging in the British archives with such persistence that the keepers of the British code-breaking secrets conceded that there was no point holding back the remaining records linking Bletchley Park, Ian Fleming and the Dieppe raid.'
—Peter Henshaw, Dieppe scholar and intelligence analyst,
Privy Council Office

'In the same way that intelligence in the Second World War had to be based on multiple sources rather than a single thunderclap moment or dramatic source, David has built this case through a whole series of small pieces of evidence ... [He] has certainly changed our view of Dieppe into the future; he has added a new dimension that we really weren't aware of before.'
—Stephen Prince, Head, Naval Historical Branch, Royal Navy

'The most important work on the [Dieppe] raid since it occurred in 1942.'
—*Rocky Mountain Outlook*

'O'Keefe tells a masterful story of the intrigue and cryptology behind the fighting forces ... I will be among the first to say that any subsequent book on Dieppe or Ultra intelligence will have to take into account his stunning new research and bold claims ... For years, popular histories were derided, especially by academics, as all story and no analysis, and for offering few new contributions to understanding the past. But that seems to be changing in recent years, as the best popularizers find new hooks and angles for their histories, and employ new evidence – usually oral histories, or, in O'Keefe's case, deep archival research – in innovative and revealing ways.'
—*The Globe and Mail*

ONE DAY
IN AUGUST

ONE DAY IN AUGUST

IAN FLEMING, ENIGMA AND THE DEADLY RAID ON DIEPPE

DAVID O'KEEFE

ICON

This edition published in the UK in 2022
by Icon Books Ltd, Omnibus Business Centre,
39–41 North Road, London N7 9DP
email: info@iconbooks.com
www.iconbooks.com

Previously published in the UK in 2020 by Icon Books Ltd,
and in Canada in 2013 by Knopf Canada

Sold in the UK, Europe and Asia
by Faber & Faber Ltd, Bloomsbury House,
74–77 Great Russell Street,
London WC1B 3DA or their agents

Distributed in the UK, Europe and Asia
by Grantham Book Services, Trent Road,
Grantham NG31 7XQ

Distributed in Australia and New Zealand
by Allen & Unwin Pty Ltd, PO Box 8500,
83 Alexander Street, Crows Nest, NSW 2065

Distributed in the USA
by Publishers Group West,
1700 Fourth Street, Berkeley, CA 94710

Distributed in South Africa
by Jonathan Ball, Office B4, The District,
41 Sir Lowry Road, Woodstock 7925

Distributed in India by Penguin Books India,
7th Floor, Infinity Tower – C, DLF Cyber City,
Gurgaon 122002, Haryana

ISBN: 978-178578-899-4

Typeset in Adobe Text by Marie Doherty

Maps by Andrew Roberts

Printed and bound in Great Britain by
Clays Ltd, Elcograf S.p.A.

Contents

About the author

Professor David O'Keefe, a former officer in the Black Watch (Royal Highland Regiment of Canada), is an award-winning historian, author, film-maker and leading authority on Canadian military historical research. He currently teaches history at Marianopolis College in Quebec.

List of Illustrations

Maps

05:20. Infantry and tanks land on beaches and destroy road blocks

Approx. 06:00. HMS *Locust* enters the inner channel (the 'Gauntlet')

06:10–06:40. Royal Marine Commandos and IAU obtain intelligence booty

06:30–07:00. IAU depart Dieppe with intelligence booty

Plate section

For those like Ron Beal who never knew;
and for those like Paul McGrath who did.

Note on Sources

An Ode to C.P. Stacey

'No respectable historian would dream of writing a Naval history of the late war unless he was given access to our sources of information,' mused John Godfrey at the end of the Second World War. His successor as Director of Naval Intelligence, Rear Admiral Edmund Rushbrooke, elaborated on the system adopted in the United Kingdom. 'The Head of the Historical Section (Royal Navy) had been indoctrinated into Special Intelligence,' he wrote, and 'it may be found necessary to indoctrinate others of the Historical Staff, such as the writer of any history of the U-Boat Campaign which was influenced in a dominating way by Special Intelligence.'

The British realized that skilled historians would question the multitude of inconsistencies, open-ended questions and all-encompassing excuses for various events – including Dieppe. Fearing that their curiosity would lead to unintended revelation of the source – one that continued to be used in the Cold War – both the British and the Americans adopted a hybrid approach: historians would be indoctrinated into Ultra, but the use of the material would be severely restricted. Official army, navy and air force historians were then instructed to use this knowledge to sidestep any historically dangerous areas – a process similar to the way the Admiralty used Ultra to reroute convoys from the clutches of U-boat wolf packs. This privilege was not made available to the official historians in Canada, although Canadians took part in Ultra-inspired missions, worked at Bletchley Park, and were indoctrinated in and used the material in the field.

When the brilliant patriarch of Canadian military history, Colonel Charles P. Stacey, set his official historical team to work on Dieppe in the days following the raid, he was fighting a historical battle with one hand tied behind his back. The story line fed to the war correspondents to protect the true intent of the raid spilled over into the historical realm, creating an impenetrable fog. Forced to rely on the personal testimonies of men sworn to secrecy to lay the cornerstone for our understanding of the raid – sanitized after-action reports, official communiqués, war diaries and snippets of message logs – Stacey lacked the essential ingredients and contextual knowledge to achieve a firm understanding of Dieppe. But Stacey was no fool: as the war went on, he realized that the Allies did have something up their sleeve, but he had no clue at that time about the nature of Ultra, how pervasive it was, how it was used, or the sources and methods used to maintain the flow. Regardless, he was able to cobble together a truly accurate 'human' account of the battle – one that will never fade from history.

After the revelation of Ultra in the late 1970s, the initial expectation that it would rewrite the history of the Second World War soon faded as the British government released only a tiny portion of the millions of pages of material created under that security stamp during and after the war. On the fiftieth anniversary of the war's end, in 1995, both the British and the American governments embarked on a protracted release of these documents, which continues to this day. Although I began my research that same year, the story has emerged slowly and I did not have a single 'eureka' moment as such, but rather a string of significant and exciting finds, and countless hours of dead ends, that in the end allowed the pieces of the puzzle to fall into place. It was the painstaking assembly of minuscule pieces of evidence – balanced, sorted and weighed against other evidence – that has finally allowed me to tell the 'untold' story of Dieppe. New technologies such as the internet, the microchip and digitization – ones that would have delighted Charles Babbage, Alan Turing, Frank Birch and Ian Fleming – have allowed me to consult more than 150,000 pages of documents from archives on two continents and over 50,000 pages of published primary and secondary source material for this book.

The methodology I employ is straightforward, based in large part on the sage advice of a multitude of mentors in the historical realm and, perhaps rather ironically, on the musings of Colonel Peter Wright, the man who served as General Ham Roberts's intelligence officer aboard the *Calpe*. After the Dieppe fiasco, Wright went on to become the highly respected and Ultra-indoctrinated intelligence master for General Harry Crerar's First Canadian Army throughout the battles in Normandy and north-west Europe. On his return from the war, he resumed his legal practice and was eventually appointed a judge on the Ontario High Court of Justice. He believed that the primary job of the intelligence officer is first to assess what the enemy *is* doing and then what he *should be* doing – sage advice I adopted as my general approach to historical inquiry. In other words, the evidence must drive the story. In this case, because there is much 'white noise' surrounding the Dieppe saga, I placed greater weight on the documents created before or during the raid than on those written later. Because the Dieppe scholarship is vast, much of this material had to be left on the 'cutting-room floor,' though I used it during my research phase to eliminate possibilities, myths and conjecture, and to provide a litmus test for my analysis.

On the fiftieth anniversary of the end of the Second World War, one historical commentator proclaimed that nothing more could be said about this war and that it was time to move on to the history of the Cold War. The remarkable revelations in this account are but one example of the short-sighted nature of that comment. As long-classified materials on Ultra and on other conflicts make their way into open archives around the world, we realize that the book never closes on history and that only now can the real history of the Second World War begin to be written.

I have decided to adopt a hybrid approach to writing this treatment, and I employ an unfolding narrative as the vehicle to deliver the goods. Unlike strict academic studies where one can simply read the introduction and conclusion to get the main points down, I have decided to peel the layers back chapter by chapter not only to inform and enlighten but hopefully to captivate the reader with the truly miraculous world of historical investigation. Likewise, explanations and qualifications of evidence considered too detailed for the main narrative are dutifully tucked away in the endnotes to satisfy and amplify traditional scholarly demands. As such, *One Day in August* unfolds page by page, like a grand mystery that requires it be read from cover to cover for full historical impact and enjoyment.

Although this new interpretation answers many of the old questions surrounding the intent behind the Dieppe Raid, it also raises a slate of new ones that organically emerge as a direct result of the evidence unearthed and the constantly evolving nature of historical understanding. Essentially, it provides a firm foundation from which to build a more complete picture of the Dieppe Raid and the reasons behind it. In the coming years, more information will undoubtedly grace the vast wealth already available. The various agencies responsible for SIGINT material – the Government Communications Headquarters in England, the National Security Agency in the United States and, to a lesser extent, the Communications Security Establishment Canada – along with the respective arms of the ministries or departments of defence – continue to release documents into the public domain year after year.

Like the generations of skilled historians who passed the torch to me many years ago, I turn this interpretation of Dieppe over to a new generation of young scholars. I hope they will be as inspired as I have been to dive into the realm of historical research – regardless of the subject or the challenge.

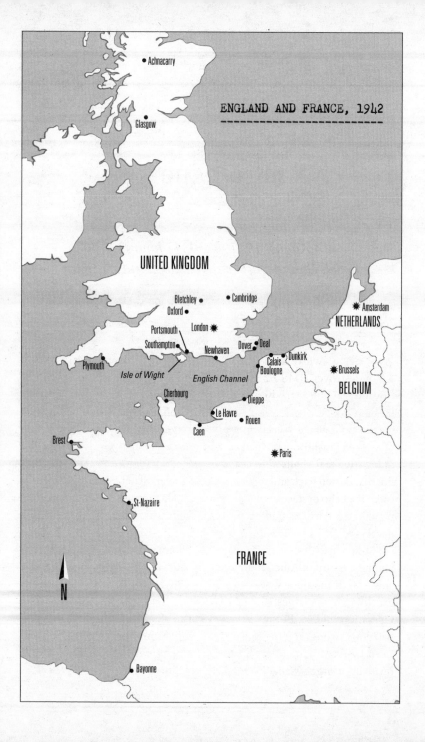

Prologue

August 19, 1942, 0347 hours,
English Channel off Dieppe, Normandy, France

Moving swiftly across the slick deck of the drab grey British destroyer HMS *Fernie* and up onto the bridge, a peacoat-clad Royal Naval Voluntary Reserve officer from Special Branch discarded his hand-rolled cigarette and pressed his binoculars to his eyes, adjusting the focus wheel to account for the darkness. In the distance, a series of fire-red mushroom-shaped explosions merged with the silver glow of bursting star shells and a carnival of red, orange and green tracer fire that darted back and forth just above the ink-black waterline. Then came the echo of staccato machine-gun and high-powered cannon fire, punctuated at irregular intervals by the whiplash crack of larger-calibre naval gunfire.

Straining to discern friend from foe, Commander Ian Fleming stood among a group of Allied journalists, broadcasters and photographers and American military observers expecting to witness the successful execution of the largest amphibious raid of the war to date, known as Operation Jubilee. But it was now clear to all aboard that something had gone wrong, and that the carefully synchronized raid, planned by Lord Louis Mountbatten's Combined Operations Headquarters and involving a largely Canadian force, had begun 63 minutes prematurely.

1

Ian Fleming – who a decade later would write *Casino Royale* and launch his immortal James Bond dynasty – was listed innocuously on the ship's manifest that day as a 'guest.' For years, historians and biographers have asserted that the normally desk-bound member of the British Naval Intelligence Division played no role other than that of observer, and that Fleming's natural desire for action and adventure, fused with an innate talent for bureaucratic machination, had landed him a prize seat on the *Fernie*, the back-up command ship.

But this 'guest' was in fact present in an official capacity – to oversee a critical intelligence portfolio, one of many he handled as personal assistant to the Director of Naval Intelligence, Rear Admiral John Godfrey. He was on board to witness the launch of a highly specialized commando unit that had been created specifically to carry out skilled and dangerous operations deemed of the greatest urgency and importance to the war effort. Fleming's crack commando unit was set to make its debut under cover of this landmark raid on the coast of German-occupied France.

With the dawn, however, came the sober realization that the raid had gone off the rails in truly epic fashion. As the sky lightened, Fleming could see heavy German fire coming from the hotels that lined the beachfront and ribbons of flame flaring out from the towering clifftops. Below, the main beach – which had hosted generations of English vacationers, including Fleming himself, who had won and lost at the tables of its seaside casino before the war – had become a killing field for the assaulting troops. Catching quick glimpses of the scene through the swirling smokescreen, he could make out small black, motionless dots on the rocky beach where countless Canadian soldiers now lay dead and wounded, and scores of tanks and landing craft sitting abandoned or burning alongside them. Above the town hung an ominous black, acrid cloud, periodically pierced by German and British fighters swooping down to search out quarry, while rapid-firing anti-aircraft guns from both sides swept the sky with bright yellow and orange tracer fire. The roar of aircraft engines, the sounds of machine-gun and cannon fire, and the explosion of artillery and mortar shells shook the air, as British destroyers attempted to assist the men pinned down on the beach, and now holding on for dear life.

2

Just 700 yards offshore, Fleming watched helplessly as his fledgling commando unit headed through the heavy smokescreen in their landing craft towards the deadly maelstrom. Tragically, what was about to occur was not simply the final act in the darkest day in Canadian military history but the beginning of one of the most controversial episodes of the entire Second World War. This one day in August – August 19, 1942 – would haunt the survivors and leave the country struggling to understand why its young men had been sent to such a slaughter on Dieppe's beaches.

But what was known only to the young Commander Ian Fleming and a few others was that the raid on this seemingly unimportant French port had at its heart a potentially war-changing mission – one whose extreme secrecy and security ensured that its purpose would remain among the great mysteries of the Second World War. Fleming's presence on board HMS *Fernie* connected the deadly Dieppe Raid with the British codebreaking effort (commonly known as 'Ultra'), one of the most closely guarded secrets of wartime Britain. And understanding exactly why Ian Fleming was on board the *Fernie* that day was a key that helped me finally to unravel the mystery behind the raid.

Over almost 25 years and through two editions of this book, I combed through nearly 175,000 pages of primary sources and interviewed participants in the raid (as well as filming them for the documentary *Dieppe Uncovered*, aired simultaneously in England and Canada on August 19, 2012).

Locked away until now in dusty archives, the story unfolded and took shape over time as intelligence agencies and archive facilities in Britain, the United States and Canada released long-classified documents withheld for seven decades from public view. Slowly, each piece was added to the puzzle until, at the end of my journey, I found a story that rivalled a Tom Clancy or a James Bond thriller – although this saga was all too true. And this stunning discovery, kept under wraps until now, necessitates a reconsideration of this phase of the Second World War and a reassessment of the painful legacy of Dieppe.

As Ron Beal, a Dieppe veteran, said to me after I laid out the story for him: 'Now I can die in peace. Now I know what my friends died for ...'

CHAPTER 1

The 'Canadian' Albatross

This was too big for a raid and too small for
invasion: What were you trying to do?
German interrogator to Major Brian McCool, August 1942

During his intensive interrogation in the days following his capture, the exhausted prisoner, Major Brian McCool, the Principal Military Landing Officer for the Dieppe Raid, was subjected repeatedly to one burning question from his German interrogator: 'What were you trying to do?' Still at a loss, the bewildered McCool lifted his head and replied, 'If you could tell me ... I would be very grateful.'

For nearly three-quarters of a century, that same query has remained unanswered despite numerous attempts by historians, journalists and politicians to explain the reasons behind the deadliest amphibious raid in history. The veterans of that fateful day have themselves never understood the abject failure they experienced and the staggering loss of life their comrades suffered on the blood-soaked beaches of Dieppe. Over the decades since, a pitiful legacy of sorrow, bitterness and recrimination has developed to frame the collective Canadian memory of an operation seemingly devoid of tangible purpose and intent.

The cost to Canada of Operation Jubilee, as the Allies' raid on Dieppe on August 19, 1942, was code-named, was appalling: 907 men killed – roughly one man every 35 seconds during the nine-hour ordeal – a rate rivalled only by the charnel-house battles on the western front in the First World War. Adding to that sobering toll, a further 2,460 Canadian names filled the columns of the wounded, prisoners of war and missing in the formal casualty returns. By nightfall, a total of 3,367 men – 68 per cent of all the Canadian young men (mostly in their teens and early twenties) who made the one-day Channel crossing to France – had become official casualties in some form. Units such as the Royal Regiment of Canada from Toronto, which suffered 97 per cent casualties in less than four hours of fighting on Blue Beach at Puys, virtually 'ceased to exist.'[1] To varying degrees, the same was true of the other units of the raiding force: bodies of men from army regiments in Quebec, Ontario, Alberta, Saskatchewan and Manitoba fell in piles alongside men from the east and west coasts who toiled in the signals, medical, provost, intelligence or service corps.

The catastrophe would strike a deep chord throughout Canada, seared into the country's psyche as both our greatest historical mystery and our supreme national tragedy. For decades, Dieppe has been Canada's albatross.

The losses on that day in August 1942 represented a snapshot of Canadian society. The lasting images were stark and unforgiving: the dead – once husbands, fathers, sons, brothers, managers, janitors, students, fishermen, farmworkers and clerks, who had risked their lives in the name of Canada – lay motionless on the pebbled beaches or slumped along the narrow streets of the town, their often mangled bodies used as fodder for German propaganda. Brothers in arms for that campaign, they now rest in the cemetery close by for eternity, bonded and branded by the name 'Dieppe.' For those fortunate enough to be taken prisoner, their reward was almost three years of harsh captivity, their hands and feet shackled night and day for the first eighteen months, and a cruel forced death-march in the winter of 1945 over the frozen fields of Poland and Germany. Only after that did the survivors among them reach home.

For many, coming home did not end their Dieppe experience. By then the units they had once viewed as family had rebuilt, and they found few there who had shared their particular experience. Unlike so many other veterans, they had no 'band-of-brothers' stories to share – of storming the beaches on D-Day, slugging it out in Normandy, liberating French and Belgian towns, or delivering the Dutch from the twin evils of starvation and Nazi Germany – and therefore nothing dislodged the Dieppe stigma. A few of the lucky ones managed to move on, reminded of the 'shame and the glory' only at chilly Remembrance Day ceremonies, on muggy August anniversaries or by recurring night terrors. Without proper care for what we now recognize as Post-Traumatic Stress Disorder (PTSD), some who could not exorcise the Dieppe demons found temporary solace by lashing out in numerous and at times self-destructive ways instead.

The raid, it should be remembered, was not strictly 'Canadian': it was conducted under the overall command of Lord Louis Mountbatten's Combined Operations Headquarters, and close to 5,000 other Allied soldiers, sailors and airmen, mostly from the United Kingdom, with a smattering of Americans, French, Poles, Belgians and Norwegians, shared the same fateful ordeal in Operation Jubilee. They too were left with lingering frustration about the apparent lack of purpose behind the raid, a vexation captured on the web page of the Juno Beach Centre in Normandy – one of Canada's military history ambassadors to the world: 'Dieppe was a pathetic failure,' it reads, 'a bizarre operation with no chance of success whatsoever and likely to result in a huge number of casualties.'[2]

∽

The historical struggle that followed has proven almost as nasty and inconclusive as the battle itself, with the finger-pointing beginning not long after the sounds of conflict faded. Accusations ranged from incompetent leadership to Machiavellian intent after those involved with the planning and conduct of the raid offered up what many felt were deeply unsatisfactory excuses for the disastrous results. The central issue remains, as it has since that raid, the lack of any clear rationale for the intent behind the controversial operation. That absence has left a legacy not only of sorrow but of suspicion, intrigue, mistrust and conspiracy. The common denominator throughout public discourse – that Canadian men had been sacrificed for no apparent or tangible reason

– led to a sentiment of unease that quickly built up steam in historical accounts, in the press and in public discussion.

Attempting to rationalize what has defied rationalization, researchers and commentators over the decades have sought to make sense out of the seemingly nonsensical. Historians have searched valiantly through the Allied planning papers, after-action reports, personal and official correspondence, and other ancillary documents available in the public domain, looking for any scrap of evidence that would lead to discovering the driving force or imperative behind the Dieppe Raid. Although the planning documents revealed a list of desired objectives for the raid, they remained nothing more than a grocery list of targets that offered little clue to what achieving them would actually mean in the end.

Officially, Prime Minister Winston Churchill would maintain that the raid was merely a 'reconnaissance in force' or a 'butcher and bolt raid' – explanations that Mountbatten and others associated with the planning and implementation of the raid expanded upon. Before long, another standard excuse emerged: the Dieppe Raid was simply launched to test Hitler's vaunted *Festung Europa* (Fortress Europe) and, as such, it was the necessary precursor to future amphibious operations such as the D-Day landings. After that came the 'sacrificial' excuses: the Dieppe Raid had been designed by Great Britain specifically to placate its new ally, the beleaguered Soviet Union, by creating the 'second front now' that the Russians were demanding, and thereby drawing German air and land forces away from the East and into Western Europe. From there it moved to questions of deception and intrigue and then on to an attritional contest where the raid was conducted to draw the Luftwaffe out into a great blood match with the RAF. These excuses never satisfied the soldiers involved and led to a healthy scepticism among professional and amateur historians alike. Soon, fingers began to point, with suggestions that the leading players in the Dieppe saga all had something to hide.

They were indeed a motley crew, some highly distinguished, others less so, and the reputations of these men have only added to the furore. Lord Louis Mountbatten, the chief of the Combined Operations Headquarters, is traditionally pegged as the main culprit, not so much

for his headquarters' handling of the planning and conduct of the raid –
as 'inexperienced enthusiasts' – but more for his personality and royal
bloodlines.[3] A vainglorious and ambitious character without a doubt,
'Dickie' Mountbatten is traditionally accused of operating far above
his ceiling, a man primarily interested in courting the press for favourable headlines designed to put him and his headquarters on the map.
But nobody in the chain of command has been spared – all have been
painted to varying degrees with the same brush of suspicion, guilt and
incompetence. Were the force commanders who called the shots from
the distant bridge of the headquarters ship HMS *Calpe*, offshore from
Dieppe, responsible – Canadian Major General John Hamilton 'Ham'
Roberts and Royal Navy Captain John 'Jock' Hughes-Hallett? Or were
the highest authorities in wartime Britain, the Chiefs of Staff Committee
and, ultimately, Prime Minister Winston Churchill, to blame?

It's a truth of human nature that any void in our understanding tends
to force open a Pandora's box of wild, seductive and intriguing theories.
In this case, they span the spectrum from bureaucratic bungling and
inflated ambition to treasonous intent; from impotent claims that the
raid was conducted simply for 'the sake of raiding' to the intentional
tipoff of the Germans as an act of betrayal by the French to gain favour
with their occupiers. Or perhaps, some surmise, Dieppe was part of
a clever game of foxes – an Allied deception to cover the upcoming
invasion of North Africa – or, alternatively, an unauthorized action by
Mountbatten to win praise and secure his place in history. Some commentators, citing the relative lack of firepower in the raid, for instance,
and the overreliance on the element of surprise, coupled with the
unprofessional approach to planning and execution, suggest that the
entire operation was sacrificial in nature, intended to fail right from the
start, to demonstrate the foolhardiness of American and Soviet calls for
a second front in 1942.

Some theories are merely silly and irresponsible, such as the urban
legend making the rounds in the cafés along Dieppe's beachfront today
that the raid was an 'anniversary present' from Winston Churchill to
his beloved wife, Clementine, who in her youth had summered in that
delightful Channel port town – a favourite seaside holiday spot for
English families.

Despite all these efforts to make sense of the Dieppe Raid, however, the mystery has remained intact for over seven decades, taunting us with the pain of its legacy.

That was my own experience long ago in 1995, when I called up a recently declassified file in the British National Archives in London. This wartime British Admiralty file, which at first did not appear to have any connection with the Dieppe Raid, contained an appendix to an 'Ultra Secret' classified report concerning the exploits of a highly secret Intelligence Assault Unit (IAU) that, because of its clandestine activities, was known during the war by a variety of names, most notably No. 10 Platoon, X Platoon, 30 Commando or 30 Assault Unit (30 AU). Until the release of that file, there had been nothing to confirm the commando unit's existence, rumoured to be the brainchild of Royal Naval Volunteer Reserve Commander Ian Fleming. Barely a decade later, Fleming would forge another lasting creation – the super-spy James Bond, the most famous, enduring character in espionage literature. The Intelligence Assault Unit was raised and trained with one specific purpose in mind: to steal, or 'pinch,' the most sensitive of intelligence materials from the Germans, items needed to break their top-secret codes and ciphers, including the Enigma ciphering machine, allowing the Allies to read enemy message traffic and to wage war effectively.

It was a short passage in the fourth paragraph that started me on my journey of discovery: 'As regards captures, the party concerned at DIEPPE did not reach their objective.' The connection was startling: for the first time here was direct evidence that linked one of the greatest and most closely guarded secrets of the entire Second World War – Enigma – with the deadliest day in Canadian military history. Never before had anything similar appeared in the vast corpus of literature dealing with the Dieppe saga. Something that had remained classified as 'Ultra Secret' for over half a century by British intelligence appeared to be lurking beneath the veneer of the traditional interpretations of Dieppe.

∽

In June 1941, British intelligence adopted the term 'Ultra' as a security classification for intelligence derived from tapping into enemy communications, most notably their encrypted radio and later tele-printer traffic. Considered prize intelligence – or, as Winston Churchill called it, his 'golden eggs' – 'Ultra Secret' went above the traditional top-level classification of Most Secret, or, as the Americans referred to it, Top Secret. Logically enough, the term quickly became a security 'catch-all' that not only denoted the end product used by Churchill and his commanders to formulate their decisions on the field of battle, but also extended to the technology, processes, policies, operations and even history centred around the secret British code-breaking facility known as Bletchley Park.

Purchased by the Secret Intelligence Service (SIS, or MI6 as it became popularly known) at the outset of the war, this sprawling Victorian estate in Buckinghamshire, just an hour's drive north of London, was the main site for the Government Code and Cypher School (GC&CS), which was responsible for signals intelligence (SIGINT) and code-breaking. By military standards, it was a most unusual place: the requirements of the job called for the utmost in intellectual prowess, which meant recruiting some of the most 'beauti-ful' minds that Great Britain, and later the Allies, could offer. The head of operations, Alastair Denniston, had served in British intelligence during the First World War, and now he recruited 'men of the pro-fessor type,' as he called them, for the new challenge. Drawn mostly from elite universities such as Oxford or Cambridge, these men and women came from a variety of disciplines – mathematics, the sciences, linguistics, classics, history, to name but a few – literally the best and the brightest of the academic world. In this large mansion, they joined forces with gifted intelligence officers (again British and later Allied) from the navy, the air force and the army to produce something that up to that point no other country in history could boast: a relatively consistent and comprehensive ability to tap into a direct information pipeline to monitor their enemy's strengths, weaknesses, intentions, capabilities, hopes, fears, desires and dreams. As Frank Birch, the head of Bletchley's Naval Section who had served as a cryptanalyst in the First World War, suggested: 'There lingered until the end of the war in certain elevated and rarified atmospheres, several of the old popular superstitions about SIGINT (signals intelligence). A familiar one was the belief that codes and ciphers were broken by a few freakish individuals with a peculiar kink, no help, and very little material except for the damp towels round their heads.'[4]

As those in the 'rarified atmosphere' would soon learn, Bletchley formed the most potent weapon for a nation at war, and as their importance to the cause increased, so too did the size of Bletchley Park. Soon, numerous numbered 'huts' began to spring up around the grounds; these nondescript plywood barracks housed the offices of the naval, air, military and diplomatic sections, which toiled not only to break into, or decrypt, enemy messages intercepted by the many radio intercept stations located around the British Empire, but then to turn what they intercepted and decrypted into sensible and accurate intelligence to be used by the decision-makers to help win the war.

By the end of the Second World War, Sir Harry Hinsley, the official historian of British intelligence, who as a 23-year-old undergraduate in history played an influential role in Bletchley's Naval Section, concluded that Ultra may not have been the 'war winner,' but it was undoubtedly a 'war shortener.' By his reckoning, it shaved at least one year, if not two, off the duration of the war, thereby saving millions of lives.[5] However, the road was not a smooth one. Although victory ultimately prevailed, mistakes were made along the way.

Information is power, and everyone involved in the Ultra Secret process knew it. In all such cases, then, as now, the enemy must never realize that his supposedly secure communications have been successfully penetrated or, better yet, systematically and consistently penetrated. For this reason, signals intelligence and code-breaking, or cryptography, must be conducted in the strictest secrecy, or the enemy will catch on and change the codes and ciphers that guard his message traffic.

Because of its vital military importance and potential, Ultra became one of the most cherished and carefully guarded secrets of the war, surpassing even the development of the atomic bomb in the post-war era. Ultra required elaborate precautions to maintain its security, given that more than 10,000 people played various roles connected with it by war's end. Such was the secrecy surrounding the work in Bletchley Park that all those who worked and lived there – from the clerks and young female secretaries to the brilliant code-breaking 'boffins' – knew that to talk about their work informally, even to dorm mates or colleagues outside their hut, was treasonous and could result in lifetime imprisonment or even execution. Accordingly, the security surrounding Ultra was to be maintained indefinitely.

As things turned out, the very existence of Ultra remained under wraps for over 30 years following the conclusion of the war. In the late 1970s, for reasons that are still unclear today, the British government officially, and some say unwisely, acknowledged Ultra. Even then, it took close to two more decades before the first batches of significant documents were released to the public – a release that began in 1995, on the fiftieth anniversary of the end of the Second World War, and continues in a piecemeal fashion to this day.

Such was the nature of the recently declassified document I had unearthed in the British National Archives. As I continued to scan the pages of the document, the experience reminded me of a miner discovering his first nugget, wondering if he has indeed tapped into a lucrative vein or simply into 'fool's gold.' Thus began my nearly two-decade historical journey in search of the truth behind Dieppe.

The information contained in the document only increased my natural curiosity. What was the 'objective' of this 'party'? What role did the objective play in the overall context of the raid? Could it have been a long-concealed reason for the Dieppe Raid? The document offered nothing more direct than that one sentence – 'the party concerned at DIEPPE did not reach their objective' – but it struck me immediately as a potential game changer. Included in the document was a general 'target list' of items that Commander Ian Fleming's Intelligence Assault Unit had been asked to pinch in the summer and autumn of 1942. Labelled 'Most Urgent,' the items on the list all related to the four-rotor Enigma cipher machine that the German navy (Kriegsmarine) had recently introduced to encrypt its messages before they were sent via wireless. Among these items were 'specimens of the wheels used on the Enigma machine, particulars of their daily settings for wheels and plugs, codebooks, and all documents relating to signals and communications,' as well as anything connected with the German signals intelligence effort against British communications. Given my background as a signals intelligence and Ultra historical specialist for the Department of National Defence in Canada, those lists made perfect sense in the context of the times.

Mid-1942 was the desperate 'blackout' period for the British Naval Intelligence Division (NID). Thanks to the cryptanalysts working around the clock in Bletchley Park, for nearly a year – from the spring of 1941 to February 1942 – the British had enjoyed astonishing success in intercepting and decrypting German navy messages between its head-quarters and its surface and U-boat fleets. During that period, German communications were encrypted on a three-wheel Enigma machine – a complex electromechanical rotor cipher machine belonging to a family of devices (the army, navy and air force each had their own version) first developed by the Germans at the end of the First World War. To do their work, the cryptanalysts at Bletchley Park relied on pinched material – Enigma machines captured from destroyed submarines, for instance, or, more importantly, the codebooks, rotor-setting sheets and instruction manuals used to unravel the German secret transmissions. So great was their success, both in stealing materials from the Germans and in intercepting and decrypting the German messages, that the Naval Section at Bletchley Park euphorically nicknamed 1941 the *annus mirabilis*, the 'year of miracles.'[6]

But the miracle ended abruptly on February 1, 1942, when the German navy ordered its U-boat arm operating in the Atlantic to enci-pher their top-secret messages on an improved and more complex four-rotor version of the Enigma machine that left the expert code-breakers at Bletchley hopelessly in the dark. The next ten months were a frantic and dangerous time for Great Britain – in particular for her Admiralty and Naval Intelligence Division. Due to a combination of factors, all exacerbated by the Bletchley code-breakers' sudden inabil-ity to read the German messages and locate enemy submarines before they attacked, merchant shipping losses in the Atlantic suddenly sky-rocketed, seriously threatening Britain's vital oceanic supply and trade routes.

There was near panic in some circles over the perceived threat to the Allies' command of the vital sea lanes essential to ultimate victory in the war. Fortunately for the Allies, when the Germans introduced their updated four-rotor Enigma, they possessed only enough of these machines to equip their Atlantic fleet, leaving for the moment all the other areas of operation – the Mediterranean Sea, the Baltic, Norway and the German home waters – with the three-rotor machine and still vulnerable to Bletchley's code-breaking skills. But the Royal Navy's Intelligence Division knew the clock was ticking as they discovered early in 1942 that now surface vessels operating in the English Channel and in Norway had been outfitted with new four-rotor machines but had yet to put them into operation. Obviously, it was only a matter of time before they became operational and extended the blackout from the potent U-Boat arm to the entire Kriegsmarine. This growing crisis led directly to the creation of Ian Fleming's commando unit, operating under the aegis of the Naval Intelligence Division and focused solely on 'the pinch.'

As I read on, the document outlined the criteria for the commandos in Fleming's new Intelligence Assault Unit: they should be familiar with the materials targeted in a pinch but not indoctrinated into the mysterious world of Ultra and Bletchley Park in case, God forbid, they fell into enemy hands and cracked under interrogation. In addition, the unit would include a special adviser with experience in 'commando raids' and 'cutting-out parties' to guide in the selection of targets and later compile a list of lessons learned. Here, one cautionary note in the report stood out supreme for me: 'No raid should be laid on for SIGINT purposes only. The scope of the objectives should always be sufficiently wide to presuppose normal operational objects.'[7]

That passage, in light of the Ultra Secret designation, raised some startling new questions: If Commander Ian Fleming's specially raised and trained commando unit was targeting Dieppe, was this pinch the purpose and intent behind Operation Jubilee, the *raison d'être* for the raid? Could the initial motive for the raid on Dieppe be, as that last passage suggested, to provide a cover under which the commandos could raid a specific target in Dieppe and then depart without rousing German suspicions? Could it even be that the pinch of the target materials, under cover of the other objectives, was the driving force for the entire operation – a scenario that seems ripped from the pages of an Ian Fleming or Tom Clancy spy thriller?

Fleming's inclusion in the raid to oversee his nondescript commando unit, which was making its combat debut, had earlier raised no questions. Traditionally, it has always been viewed as a lark or a 'day trip' to Dieppe. But knowing now what his commando unit was targeting opened up an unexpected avenue for a fundamental reassessment of the Dieppe Raid. The potential implications were staggering.

Fully aware of the importance of Dieppe in the Canadian psyche, I realized that my theory required substantial investigation before it could even be proposed – something that proved daunting and near impossible in 1995 for the simple reason that few classified British intelligence files had been released into the public domain. It was true that millions of pages had become available to historians and researchers on the fiftieth anniversary of the war's end, but the British, American and Canadian governments still held back critical intelligence files that they regarded as too sensitive or potentially too controversial to release at that time. So, over the next two decades, as more documents slowly became available, my investigation continued and resulted in the first edition of this book in Canada, which then accelerated more releases of classified material that prompted the writing of this edition.

In 2010, with the vast majority of the research and most of the central pieces in place, it was time to take my journey to another level. I set out my argument to the historians at the Royal Navy's Historical Branch in Portsmouth and the Government Communications Headquarters in Cheltenham. My thesis came as a shock to both groups but they both separately offered that I was indeed 'on to something,' because they too were curious about the Dieppe mystery. The chief historian at the Government Communications Headquarters agreed to a further public release of classified files dealing with the contextual story of pinch operations, including reports of previous similar operations and vital documents on pinch policy or 'doctrine.' These documents provided a series of small but highly significant 'eureka moments' that helped me to round out the Dieppe saga. Many times I felt I was building a complex historical jigsaw puzzle that had begun with just one tantalizing piece and grew year by year until I felt comfortable enough to come forward with the findings.

This work has indeed kicked at the darkness until it has bled daylight. Now, after close to eight decades, we can lift the albatross from our shoulders and move past the initial sorrow, anger, excuses, recrimination, and bitterness to achieve something essential – a genuine understanding of the reasons for the raid on Dieppe. In this way, we can honour those who sacrificed so much on that one day in August 1942.

CHAPTER 2

A Very Special Bond

My job got me right into the inside of everything,
including all the most secret affairs. I couldn't possibly
have had a more exciting or interesting War.
Ian Fleming, the *Playboy* interviews

Many of us love to revel in all things James Bond, so the legend of Ian Fleming's charismatic and unsinkable 007 has fused over the decades with the legend of his creator. Was he a spy himself? Was he a crack commando? Did he or did he not train to become a secret agent in Camp X, outside Whitby, Ontario, under the famous William Stephenson, the 'man called Intrepid'? Speculation and fantasy, all. As Ernest Cuneo, the American Intelligence Liaison officer who worked with Fleming during the war and later collaborated on the early Bond films recalled, 'James Bond is no part of Ian Fleming ... it reflects merely his cynicism.'[1]

Until recently, for the serious historian, it seemed almost inconceivable that Bond's creator played more than an ephemeral role in planning the tragic raid that August day at Dieppe – and so it appeared to me too, initially. Yet the information I began to unearth as I went deeper into this story reveals a very different Ian Fleming *circa* 1942.

It all began three years earlier, in the late spring of 1939, when Rear Admiral John Godfrey, the 51-year-old, silver-haired though balding new director of the Naval Intelligence Division, invited Fleming, twenty years his junior, for lunch at the fashionable Carlton Grill – the restaurant in one of London's most luxurious hotels off Whitehall, once ruled over by the French master chef Auguste Escoffier.*

At that luncheon on May 24, Godfrey was just three months into his appointment, and he wanted to meet Fleming, a former journalist turned stockbroker, with the idea of appointing him as his personal assistant. Godfrey's mentor, Admiral Sir William 'Blinker' Hall, the legendary spymaster from the First World War, had suggested he should hire someone to help him with his overwhelming pressures and responsibilities in a world verging on war, particularly in the now long-neglected Intelligence Division.[2]

John Godfrey immediately reached out for suggestions for a worthwhile candidate.[3] As with most things in the shadowy world of British intelligence and espionage in those days, Fleming's name reached him through the time-honoured old boys' network – specifically Sir Montagu Norman, the longest-serving governor of the Bank of England.[4] Fleming, like Norman, had been tempered at Eton, the prestigious boys' school that had crafted the character of generations of the privileged class, preordained for positions of power within the British Empire. The brief resumé Godfrey received seemed impressive enough: the young journalist had achieved a modicum of notoriety dabbling as an 'occasional informant' for the Secret Intelligence Service while covering the Russian beat for Reuters in the 1930s.[5] And he was made of the right stuff: he was the grandson of Robert Fleming, the founder of Robert Fleming & Company in Dundee, which produced jute-based products during the American Civil War years before moving on to investments in the lucrative American railroad industry. Eventually, he had transformed 'the Flemings' into one of the last private merchant

---

* A year later, the Carlton Hotel itself was nearly destroyed by a German bomb during the Blitz, and today the site is occupied by the New Zealand High Commission (passers-by are reminded of the hotel's previous glory only by a small plaque stating that the young Ho Chi Minh, the Communist founder of modern Vietnam, worked there in 1913).

banks that focused on mergers and acquisitions, putting it on the financial map on both sides of the Atlantic alongside J.P. Morgan, Jacob Schiff, and Kuhn, Loeb & Co.[6]

Robert's two sons, Valentine (Val) and Philip, followed in the family business until 1910, when Val, Ian's father, won a seat in Parliament. A product of Eton and Oxford, Val became a rising star in the Conservative Party, 'a pillar of the landed squirearchy.'[7] On the outbreak of war in 1914, he and Philip joined the dashing Queen's Own Oxfordshire Hussars.[8] After fighting through the second battle of Ypres the following spring, Val was twice mentioned in dispatches and earned the Distinguished Service Order before succumbing to German artillery shells in the autumn of 1917, just one week before Ian's ninth birthday. Val's friend and parliamentary ally, the brash, outspoken Winston Churchill, penned his obituary for the *Times*.[9] Little did anyone know then that the former First Lord of the Admiralty, at that point disgraced for having staunchly backed the Gallipoli debacle one year into the war, would reappear two decades later out of the political wilderness. Less than a year after Fleming's introductory luncheon with Godfrey, Churchill reclaimed the political reins of power at the Admiralty and moved on to even greater heights as minister of defence, and in May 1940 he added the portfolio of prime minister at the darkest moment in British history.

Graced with a 'fine head, a high forehead with a head of thick brown, curlyish hair, parted on the side and neatly combed over to the left,' Fleming exuded sophisticated confidence despite 'a somewhat aloof manner.'[10] His shoulders were 'average large, his waist thickish.' He possessed a 'good, firm jaw' with 'piercing blue eyes' separated by a nose that had been 'broken and unrepaired.'[11] His sad, bony face with its clear blue eyes was strong-featured, despite the disjointed nose he had acquired during his athletic days at Eton, which only added to 'his rakish allure.'[12] Tall and slim, Fleming moved gracefully and with purpose but carried himself 'more like an American than an Englishman' for he did not rest his weight on his left leg but rather distrusted it, with his left foot and shoulders slightly forward, giving him the look of a 'Philadelphia light-heavyweight' that contained 'more of a hint of the boxer's crush than the squared erect shoulders of a Sandhurst man.'[13]

Like many other trust-fund babies who came of age in the wake of his father's 'lost generation,' he lived a carefree life. He had left the Royal Military College at Sandhurst after allegedly contracting a venereal disease; the rumour cast a cloud over his character and general suitability for a King's commission. His distraught mother, fearing for his psychological well-being, sent him to a kind of finishing school for men in Kitzbühel, Austria, where, along with skiing and mountain climbing, he came under the influence of Ernan Forbes Dennis, a former British spy, and his wife, Phyllis Bottome, a novelist. They encouraged Fleming's aptitude for languages and suggested he start writing. Considering a career in diplomacy, he next enrolled in universities in Munich and Geneva but soon developed a reputation as a playboy. He travelled through Europe at his family's expense, trying sporadically to write between visits to taverns, casinos and brothels, chain-smoking and already drinking too much. When he failed the competitive examination for the Foreign Office, his mother managed to secure him a position as a journalist with Reuters News Agency, where he reported from Moscow on the trial of some British engineers accused of spying. Given his charm, Fleming also made friends in influential circles. When he returned to England, he joined a prestigious brokerage firm.

Fleming's ability to operate in French, German and Russian impressed Godfrey, as did his 'talent for spare and simple prose,' developed while writing for Reuters.[14] But there was much more to Fleming than his social, linguistic and writing skills. Like many people who leave an indelible impression on their peers, he was a wealth of contradictions. 'At the first encounter,' recalled his friend William Plomer, who later became his editor at Jonathan Cape for most of the Bond books, 'he struck me as no mere conventional young English man-of-the-world of his generation; he showed more character, a much quicker brain, and a promise of something dashing or daring. Like a mettlesome young horse, he seemed to show the whites of his eyes and to smell some battle from afar.'[15] Indeed, as Cuneo lamented, 'Fleming was as spirited as a warhorse before battle.'[16]

In large part, what attracted Godfrey to Fleming was the young man's intense interest in cryptography – an intelligence source that Godfrey knew all too well had been vital to the outstanding success of Naval Intelligence during the First World War. Fleming had always been a student of the philosophical underpinnings of science and technology and their impact on society, a passion that led him to amass an impressive collection of first-edition works that in one way or another transformed the world.[17] Half in jest, Fleming would later argue that the moniker 'C,' used to denote the head of the British Secret Intelligence Service, did not refer to Sir Mansfield Cumming (its first head) as everyone thought, but to Charles Babbage, widely referred to as the 'father of the computer.'[18]

In 1822, nearly a century and a quarter before Bletchley Park unleashed the world's first computer, Babbage, assisted by parliamentary funding, embarked on the development of his 'Second Difference Engine.'[19] Unfortunately, official patience soon ran dry, leaving the development of 'the computer' on the sidelines until the Second World War, when Britain's very survival demanded assistance beyond human intelligence. The fact that Babbage's invention could have rivalled or even eclipsed Gutenberg's printing press as the most influential technological development in a millennium, affording Great Britain an unmatched industrial advantage, was not lost on Fleming. Babbage and his cryptographic passion became Fleming's own fervent intellectual pursuit: he studied his writings carefully, captivated by passages on the art and science of deciphering, which Babbage had compared to picking locks.[20] Various segments from Babbage's seminal *Passages from the Life of a Philosopher*, published in 1864, were, according to Fleming, the 'most cherished' in his collection.[21]

Apart from his intellectual interests, there was a darker side to Fleming that Godfrey came to appreciate and even foster. Although some viewed him as 'the warmest kind of friend, a man of ready laughter and a great companion,' others remarked that Fleming was 'a totally ruthless young man [who] didn't consider anyone' – a sentiment shared by Godfrey, who said that Fleming 'had little appreciation of the effects of his words and deeds upon others.'[22] Cuneo, to a degree, concurred: 'Moody, harsh, habitually rude and often cruel' described 'some of his actions' but 'does not describe the man.'[23] Cuneo, instead, found him 'quite simple to understand' within the complex class structure of the time. 'He was not English, he was a Scot by his father's line, only third generation in a class structure which reserves its highest accolades for the peerage, and even within ... grades the standings on the length and quality of title. Ian Fleming was not a peer of the realm.'

Cuneo believed that Fleming 'felt no particular discontent with himself. He felt much discontent with the world in which he lived, for he was a knight out of phase, a knight errant searching for the lost Round Table and possibly the Holy Grail, and unable to reconcile himself that Camelot was gone and still less that it had probably never existed.'[24]

He was best at dealing with things and ideas rather than people. 'He was primarily a man of action,' Godfrey wrote, whose 'great ability did not extend to human relations or understanding of the humanities.'[25] Fleming's Machiavellian flair flourished in the Naval Intelligence Division, where an 'element of ruthlessness and perfidy, verging on the unscrupulous, [was] inherent in certain intelligence activities.'[26] As Cuneo, who performed similar functions for the United States Office of Strategic Services, recalled: 'Ian Fleming knew exactly what he was trying to do' with 'not the slightest presumption of innocence.' Although 'Fleming never killed a man with his own hand,' Cuneo recalled, 'during the war, like everybody else, we [were] engaged in helping to kill thousands.'[27]

Fleming was a civilian, quite unlike 'service-trained officers imbued with the instinct to "play the game" ... a maverick who had a gambler's instinct and a taste for adventure.'[28] From Godfrey's perspective, Fleming possessed intellectual flexibility that let him easily transform, engage with and understand any problem, idea or concept with equal ease, whether in a formal work setting or over drinks and a meal. In many ways, Fleming reminded Godfrey of Churchill: he 'had plenty of ideas and was anxious to carry them out, but was not interested in, and preferred to ignore the extent of the logistic background inseparable to all projects.'[29] To Plomer, Fleming 'always seemed to take the shortest distance between two points in the shortest possible time'; to which Cuneo concurred, for 'Ian habitually, almost compulsively, sought in games of chance, the chance in a million.'[30]

෴

And so it happened that, in May 1939, Admiral Godfrey offered Fleming the job of personal assistant to the Director of Naval Intelligence (DNI). He had no obvious training or experience for the role, but neither did most of the men (and fewer women) recruited into the secret services at that time. Rather, his primary traits were initiative, imagination, brains, and a tireless commitment to winning the war, not so much on the battlefield as in the world of intelligence.

Fleming did not begin his work in Room 39 of the Old Admiralty Building until mid-July, almost two months after his lunch at the Carlton Grill, because his employer, the brokerage firm Rowe & Pitman, only then granted him leave. Godfrey wanted all his staff in uniform, so he appointed Fleming a lieutenant in the Special Branch of the Royal Naval Voluntary Reserve (RNVR). He appeared in the dark blue jacket of the 'wavy navy,' with a pair of undulating gold and emerald-green stripes on his sleeves, and Godfrey placed him right outside the green-baize door to his own office (Room 38). The larger space, the 'cave' as its inhabitants called it, was crowded, noisy, blue with tobacco smoke, with telephones before every man at his desk and secretaries clattering along on typewriters or arranging documents in the endless rows of filing cabinets. Every window was adorned with the obligatory blackout curtains. A few years after the war ended, Godfrey remembered the scene fondly:

> The staff in this room, which later developed into the coordination section, grew up from nothing in a very haphazard way. As far as I know, it never had a head, nor would a 'head,' in the way that the word is usually accepted in the service, be tolerated. I believe this has never been said before and may come as a surprise to some. 'Room 39' consisted at one time of two stockbrokers, a schoolmaster, a K.C. relieved by a most eminent barrister, a journalist, a collector of books on original thought, an Oxford classical don, a barrister's clerk, an insurance agent, two regular naval officers, an artist, two women civilian officers, and several women assistants and typists. Ian had a brainwave and some other specimen arrived for trial, and if he did not suit was mysteriously spirited away. There were many transitory types, both male and female, that came and went if Room 39 did not take kindly

to them. But, there were habitués who stayed and stayed and became the elders of this community. The atmosphere was more like that of a commune than one would expect in the nerve centre of an important division. The noise in this room was terrific. It got so bad that I had a green baize door installed between Room 39 and my room [Room 38]. Everyone had a telephone of their own; some had two or three; they used them incessantly and relentlessly – almost savagely. They enjoyed the click and clank of typewriters, and the ebb and flow of humanity, and it was with the greatest difficulty that I persuaded them to banish the typists and to institute some control over the nomadic marauders from other sections who camped out in the narrow defiles between the desks, or crowded round the fireplace. Few of them met outside Room 39 ... They worked like ants, and their combined output staggered the imagination.

To this section of interesting, and incongruous ingredients must be added the fatigue, fog, and frustration of war in an arena where the bad news was always known but could not be revealed, bad working conditions, fuggy rooms during the blackout, night work for some, blitz, and the friction caused by frayed nerves, and unsatisfactory personal relationships.

Given all these stresses and strains ... how was it that Room 39 achieved such phenomenal success, and was so much admired inside and outside the Admiralty[?] The answer may be found in the mutual respect and the close personal friendships which grew rapidly between the naval officer and the civilian, whether in the uniform of the R.N.V.R. or not.[31]

Few of Ian Fleming's close friends thought he would stay more than a month; the mundane administrative side of the work would, they said, 'drive him mad.'[32] It did not. Fleming was in his element and took everything in his lofty stride, later telling an interviewer: 'I could not possibly have had a more exciting or interesting War ... my job got me right into the inside of everything, including all the most secret affairs.'[33] Sitting at his desk piled high with dockets stamped *Most Secret* or *By hand of officer only*, and with folders bristling with sheets of coloured paper to indicate a particular source or a security grading (such as orange for

Ultra), Fleming was at the centre of wartime Britain. At any moment, one or both of his two personal phones – one red, the other green – could connect him internally with all branches of the NID or externally to many corners of the British war effort.

The view he maintained overlooking Horse Guards Parade confirmed his position. From his perch, Fleming could survey the Foreign Office, which also housed the head of the Secret Intelligence Service, as well as the government offices of Great George Street, where the Air Ministry and Bomber Command toiled, and the neo-baroque War Office Building long used by the army and the Chief of the General Staff. Almost directly across sat Number 10 Downing Street, the unassuming official residence of the prime minister, and nearby Richmond Terrace, the eventual home of Lord Louis Mountbatten's Combined Operations Headquarters. In the distance he could just see Big Ben and the great clock tower of the Houses of Parliament, forever a symbol of London and the British Empire now fighting for its survival. In the long shadow of Big Ben, beneath Whitehall, lay the underground bunkers built to house, among other things, the Cabinet War Rooms, where the prime minister and the chiefs of staff (COS) gathered regularly to confer once Luftwaffe bombs began to fall in the summer of 1940. Surrounded by all this expanding power, Fleming knew he was at the hub.

It was an excellent appointment. Fleming had a flair for administration, and he quickly rose to the rank of commander. Although they worked together for only three years, Godfrey became one of his lifelong friends and enthusiastic supporters. 'Ian,' he would later write, 'has achieved a unique worldwide acclaim and more publicity, I believe, than any other human being this century.'[34] He bewailed the fact that, by the time of Fleming's death in 1964, the man himself had been 'overtaken by Bond,' with little more 'than a screen of lampoons and parodies erected around him.' In short, he lamented, 'Ian has disappeared.'[35] And in some ways, Fleming the intelligence officer did disappear, cloaked by his own personal fame as a writer, while rumours, fallacies, half-truths and hyperbole have swarmed around his role in Naval Intelligence, leaving, perhaps on purpose, more than a hint of fantasy attached to all he touched in the discharge of his duties. He has been credited with carrying out dangerous and spectacular missions

– kidnapping high-ranking Nazi officials, facilitating their defection as part of an Illuminati or other nefarious organization, performing political assassinations, sabotage and espionage missions or commando operations ... The list goes on.

So polarized have the stories and arguments swirling around Fleming become that some historians have even denied that he had any knowledge whatsoever of the mysterious world of signals intelligence, and particularly of Ultra. Nigel West, for instance, the renowned historian of the British secret services, wrote that 'Fleming was almost certainly never indoctrinated into the valuable cryptographic source distributed as Ultra.'[36] It is a curious statement likely calculated to downplay Fleming's importance in British intelligence and pre-empt further investigation, for in John Godfrey's words, Fleming 'participated in practically all the intelligence projects' during the Second World War. Clearly, as Godfrey's personal assistant, Fleming was tasked with several responsibilities, including Section 17 (the coordinating centre for Naval Intelligence in which staff used Ultra material in their daily operations), and he helped to plan pinch operations for the code-breakers at Bletchley Park. Fortunately, a document declassified only in 2002 clears up the confusion. According to this list, the only one of its kind in the public record, Fleming was among the fewer than 70 officers in the Admiralty who knew of Ultra's existence, and among the fewer than 50 permitted to use the original messages to accomplish their daily tasks.[37]

One of the sources of this confusion was Fleming himself, who, Godfrey recorded, 'teasingly floated' the idea of James Bond as a veiled autobiography treading a fine line between fiction and fantasy, a notion that immediately raised the alarm in the intelligence community. The concern was real enough: constrained by the provisions of the Official Secrets Act and by the gentleman's agreement among members of Godfrey's staff, Fleming could not reveal the true nature of his work. And without some knowledge of Ultra, it would have been impossible for Fleming to carry out the objectives of his loosely defined job description as Godfrey's personal assistant. Fleming acted as gatekeeper, fixer and principal 'go-to' guy for the Director of Naval Intelligence – historically the senior intelligence service in Great Britain, whose tentacles spread over the entire globe. 'I made a point of keeping Ian in touch with *all* aspects of NID work,' Godfrey wrote. 'He was the only officer who had a finger in practically every pie. I shared *all* secrets with him so that if I got knocked out someone else would, we hoped, be left to pick up the bits and achieve some sort of continuity.'[38] Unlike others in the NID who 'knew a great deal about one subject,' Godfrey maintained that Fleming 'knew a bit (and a big bit) about all.'[39] Any misstep Fleming made with tongue or pen could inadvertently reveal the inner workings, even long-buried secrets, of British intelligence. As Godfrey would later record, had Fleming, who was only 56 when he died, known about the many attempts to write his biography, he would, like most of the senior intelligence operatives of integrity, 'have drawn a veil' over his Second World War activities and been '100% uncooperative' or even 'laid false trails.'[40]

Godfrey too played his role in this obfuscation: when a young author was commissioned to pen Fleming's biography, Godfrey summoned him to lunch and explained firmly that certain aspects of his protagonist's work, 'such as sources of intelligence, cooperation with other intelligence agencies, and anything of a nature which could lead to political embarrassment or controversy ... must never be revealed.'[41] For all these reasons, a realistic version of Ian Fleming *circa* 1942 has remained cloaked in what Godfrey called a 'security smokescreen of deception' where 'reality and fantasy got so mixed up that those who ought to know better became deceived.'[42]

Fleming did not rival 007 – one was a secret service field operative, the other an intelligence officer – but there is much more to Ian Fleming than authorities were prepared to admit in the mid-1960s when he died, and the spotlight shifted to the man who was, and remains, one of the world's most successful, bestselling authors. That is why it is crucial for any understanding of the Dieppe Raid to investigate Fleming's true character and his role within the mysterious world of British naval intelligence.

～

Ian Fleming's boss, Admiral John Godfrey, who was sacked as Director of Naval Intelligence following the failure of Dieppe, is perhaps one of the least known of the remarkable figures of the Second World War.

A leader with wide interests, gifted with 'an exceptionally powerful and original intellect,' he could suddenly 'assume a demonic relenting smile at the end of the grilling that could make a strong man wet in the palms and weak in the bowels.'[43] He cut an imposing figure in his smart admiral's uniform, vigorous, stern in profile, and with steely blue, penetrating eyes. A grammar school boy from Birmingham rather than Eton, a graduate of the British Naval Academy HMS *Britannia* rather than Oxbridge, he was an experienced and respected career naval officer who had already spent all his adult life in His Majesty's Royal Navy when the war broke out.

During the First World War, Godfrey served in the Mediterranean theatre, spending the entire Gallipoli campaign on board a cruiser before joining the staff ashore, where he earned high praise as an exceptional staff officer. He was mentioned in dispatches and awarded both the Légion d'honneur and the Order of the Nile. After the war, he served as the deputy director of the Naval Staff College and also as captain of several fighting vessels in the Pacific and on the China station. His last seagoing post was as commander of HMS *Repulse*, one of the darlings of the British fleet.[44] In short, Godfrey had advanced by his own merit, not privileged birth.

Much like his new protégé Ian Fleming, Godfrey was a maverick, a commander who made it clear he 'did not conform to the usual pattern of senior naval officers.'[45] His abrasive manner, hot temper and intellectual arrogance often led to clashes with those he encountered above him and below, and he had as many enemies as admirers: to some he was brilliant, to others an over-intellectualized bore.[46] After one frustrating session with Admiral Sir John Kelly, Commander-in-Chief, Portsmouth, in 1936, this item appeared in Godfrey's file:

> I cannot call to mind, since I reached Admiral's rank, any Captain who impressed me less favourably. A real 'Heavy Weather Jack.' He is reputed to be very 'Brainy': the only evidence I have had of this is his propensity for seeing difficulties and obstacles which less 'Brainy' people like myself are unable to see ... He is the first Captain whom I have ever had to discourage from coming to see me. He made a habit of coming, almost daily, with questions that a reasonably intelligent

Lieutenant could have answered for himself – till I could stand it no longer. I was extremely glad to see the last of him and, consequently, of his Ship.[47]

Unfortunately, this brusque and uncompromising demeanour eventually turned his colleagues in the Joint Intelligence Committee against him, and after the Dieppe Raid they recommended that he be dismissed from his position.

Personally, however, Godfrey was a highly cultured man. His interests were reading and music rather than public-school games. His wife, Margaret, a capable Cambridge-trained woman, went on to do valuable war work in intelligence herself, serving at Bletchley Park and later at her husband's pet project, the Inter-Services Topographical Department (ISTD) located at Oxford University.

Godfrey would stamp his individual leadership style on the Naval Intelligence Division in the first three years of the war, though he himself had been heavily influenced by two First World War admirals. He worked for five years under the first, Admiral Rudolf Burmester, who was at Gallipoli and served as chief of staff for the Mediterranean fleet. Burmester preached against the dominant 'remote control' style of leadership common in the navy, choosing instead to take his staff and subordinates into his confidence and 'throw on them full power and responsibility, avoiding any appearance of interference.'[48] Godfrey adopted this style too, thinking it the 'only method' likely to achieve success in the current fast-paced, multi-dimensional world of naval intelligence.

The second and more profound influence was 'Blinker' Hall, who had headed Naval Intelligence from 1914 to 1919. Enthusiastically aided by Winston Churchill, who was instrumental in developing signals intelligence within the Royal Navy and whose drive helped put it on the map, Hall turned Room 40 in the Old Admiralty Building into the cryptographic hub of the British Empire where he and his team intercepted and decrypted German diplomatic, military and naval messages.[49] He quickly became a legend when, almost immediately after the first shots were fired in August 1914, they received a codebook stolen from the German cruiser *Magdeburg* and, within days, cracked the code of the German High Seas Fleet.[50] That breakthrough greatly aided the British in their command of the oceans and their efforts to keep the German fleet bottled up in home ports for most of the war. The team then turned to diplomatic traffic and, in 1917, intercepted and deciphered the famous Zimmermann telegram, in which the Germans urged Mexico to declare war on the United States. That invitation so enraged the Americans that they too entered the war, enabling the Allies finally to defeat the Central Powers.

At his first meeting with Blinker Hall, in 1917, Godfrey, then a young staff officer, was taken by the older man's gambling nature. As he later recalled, Hall's mantra 'boldness always pays' struck him to the core. 'Mistakes,' Hall used to preach, 'may be forgiven, but even God himself cannot forgive the hanger-back.'[51] Godfrey shared his mentor's vision that situations were never hopeless. The problem lay, rather, with 'men who become hopeless about them.'[52]

Godfrey soon put this philosophy to use when he was appointed Director of Naval Intelligence in 1939.[53] This division, along with the intelligence arms of the other two services – air and land – had been much neglected in the years since the Great War. The 1919 Treaty of Versailles, which ended the war, had essentially scuttled the German navy, and Britain, exhausted by its enormous war effort, relaxed into passive complacency. With war imminent once again, Blinker Hall urged Godfrey to revive his division swiftly. The two men met regularly, with the septuagenarian Hall playing the role of patron and even lending Godfrey his flat at 36 Curzon Street – well serviced by his housekeeper – for the duration of the hostilities. It was just a short walk across Green Park from his office. As Godfrey wrote later: 'He very unobtrusively offered me full access to his great store of knowledge and judgment on this strange commodity, Intelligence, about which I knew hardly anything.'[54] His counsel would be crucial since intelligence, particularly signals intelligence, would again rocket to the forefront in the new war as England struggled to hold command of the seas.

Although Hall urged Godfrey to pick his own team and shape his division for the new war as he saw fit, he was anxious to help resuscitate his old fiefdom. Never fully out of the game, despite giving up active duty in 1919 and serving as a Conservative member of Parliament in

Stanley Baldwin's post-war government, Hall introduced Godfrey to his old code-breaking team in Room 40 – brilliant men such as Oxford scholar Dillwyn 'Dilly' Knox – who were now in the process of setting up shop at Bletchley Park for the new war.[55] What fascinated Godfrey was the unique position of power and independence that Blinker Hall had carved out for himself during his time as director. His special position as head of Naval Intelligence had been recognized throughout Whitehall and had enabled him to deal directly with Cabinet ministers and high officials in various government departments outside his own. In what turned out to be sage advice, he counselled Godfrey to 'act on his own initiative, obtaining permission, if necessary, afterwards ... the DNI is entitled to enlist the help of anyone inside or outside the country from the Archbishop of Canterbury and the General of the Jesuits downwards,' including leading bankers and corporate heads.[56]

From the beginning of their professional association, it was clear that Hall and Godfrey spoke the same language, sharing a common outlook and a 'strange similarity of experience.'[57] Both had commanded battlecruisers before becoming director; both for different reasons achieved an 'anomalous sort' of independence inside the Naval Staff; both eventually shared anxieties about their respective Sea Lords, felt the adverse impact of hostility from outside the Admiralty, shouldered responsibilities, and sometimes made decisions without the help or knowledge of those in higher authority. Both, too, longed to see the return of the day when the Naval Intelligence Division had been the senior intelligence service and a 'law unto itself.'[58]

But the Intelligence Division Godfrey inherited was no longer the state-of-the-art organization Hall had left behind at the end of the Great War. In what some would categorize as the natural evolution of the trade, and others as an attempt to blunt the strength and influence of the senior service, most of the division's knowledgeable staff had found new homes in other armed branches of the service, in the rapidly rising Secret Intelligence Service or in the Foreign Office.[59] To Godfrey's dismay, he no longer had aerial reconnaissance, human intelligence, and the best British naval cryptographic minds under his immediate control, as Hall once had. Even the man who had run Room 40, Admiral Sir William 'Bubbles' James, had been returned to regular duty as Commander-in-Chief of Portsmouth.[60] Realizing that Godfrey had far fewer of the 'cutting-edge' intelligence sources under his direct control, Hall urged him to forge cast-iron links with rival services and the new government departments – in particular, the Government Code and Cypher School and the Foreign Office – and with foreign dignitaries, paying special attention to the then-neutral American ambassador. It was a tall order that required panache and the appropriate inside 'machinery,' or network, to carry out. As Godfrey saw it, his first duty was to make preparations for war that were at once practical and imaginative – practical in the sense of putting to use the knowledge, facilities and skilled personnel available; and imaginative in the sense that his whole intelligence empire could be adapted to the needs and opportunities of war.[61]

Hall's concept of 'decentralization' proved Godfrey's saving grace – something he learned first-hand in the opening months of the war when two-thirds of his valuable time was taken up with 'press investigations and post-mortems.'[62] To remedy this drain on his time, he got approval from the Chief of the Naval Staff for the Sea Lords, as well as the directors of other intelligence branches, to deal directly with the heads of specific sections of his Naval Intelligence Division rather than with him. It was a smart move: as the war ramped up, his staff grew from about a handful to nearly 1,000 by 1942.[63] He set out to select men with the 'right sort of personality and knowledge ... [and] to thrust responsibility on them even if they were not quite ready for it,' on the principle that it is 'only by experiencing responsibility that one can learn to be responsible.'[64]

The Second World War differed vastly from the First in many respects, among them the executive direction of the war. The new war would be war by committee, where restraint would be imposed on formerly idiosyncratic policies and decision-making. Godfrey, as Director of Naval Intelligence, sat on the Joint Intelligence Committee (JIC), a subcommittee of the chiefs of staff, along with his peers in the military and the air force.[65] To his relief, he soon found that 'neither the First Lord, First Sea Lord nor the Vice Chief of the Naval Staff had time to keep in touch with the DNI's work,' allowing him a fair degree of freedom to act as he liked.[66] He quickly set out to resurrect the division in the Hall tradition, hoping to 'cut miles of red tape' and 'get what he wanted in a few days instead of a few months.'[67] He imaginatively took aggressive steps to recruit 'barristers, dons, journalists and graphic designers, geologists and geographers' to work under him, 'alongside R.N. hydrographs and Royal Marine majors.'[68]

In this respect, Ian Fleming was the ideal personal assistant for Godfrey. He too had no use for pomposity and did not suffer from what his boss termed 'very senior officer veneration.' Godfrey expected Fleming to act as his intermediary with other branches of intelligence, to sort out potentially damaging flaps over policy, and to tackle problems of a sticky or perhaps less than gentlemanly nature, such as covering up the death of French double agent Captain Pierre Lablache-Combier at the hands of British intelligence.[69] As one intelligence officer later remarked, Fleming was Godfrey's 'link with an appalling range of activities inseparable from modern war; from the cracking of codes to the practice of deception, from the preparation of topographical documentaries on the areas we have been driven from and would return to, we hoped, to the interrogation of suspected enemy agents and the training of our own agents. He had to keep an eye on these multifarious aspects of naval intelligence and report frequently to this always demanding Admiral.'[70] Godfrey was vividly aware of all that Fleming accomplished. He later remarked that as the need for naval intelligence 'changes from a sluggish brook to a raging torrent, war ... changes the intelligence officer from Cinderella to the Princess.'[71]

⁓

That summer of 1939, with tremendous efficiency, John Godfrey wasted no time in mobilizing for the expected war. His Naval Intelligence Division quickly grew into a labyrinthine organization. Room 39 was the helm, its workload divided among more than two dozen numbered sections, each one dealing with a range of intelligence duties and located in various rooms within the ever-changing layout of the Old Admiralty Building. Sections 1, 2, 3, 4, 16 and 20 were the geographically organized 'country' sections: Section 1 covered Germany, Scandinavia, the Low Countries and occupied France; Section 2, the Americas; Section 3, the Mediterranean and Africa; Section 4, the Far

East; Section 16 tracked Stalin's Soviet Union; and Section 20 hovered over unoccupied France, and portions of Africa, as well as the neutral countries – Spain, Portugal and their possessions. In addition, there were other sections: topographical intelligence, 5; the production of geographical handbooks, 6; enemy technical developments, 7; communications, 9; the security of British codes and ciphers, 10; the photographic library, 11; the intelligence summaries prepared for the chiefs of staff, the prime minister and the War Cabinet, 12; and propaganda, 19.

Section 14 was Godfrey's secretariat; and Section 8, the Operational Intelligence Centre (OIC), led by Lieutenant Commander Norman Denning, kept control of and disseminated a vast range of intelligence, from sightings of ships and aircraft by paid observers to information derived from captured documents and prisoners of war. Located in the claustrophobic, dungeon-like atmosphere of the Citadel – the concrete, brown bunker awkwardly attached to the Old Admiralty Building – the OIC handled the most vital of all intelligence traffic: Ultra – Signals Intelligence, or 'Special Intelligence' as the navy also called it. Here, via a specifically dedicated underground cable from the Naval Section at Bletchley Park, staff kept their fingers on the pulse of the war at sea, tracking movements of deadly U-boat wolf packs, German raiders, and their super-battleships the *Bismarck* and the *Tirpitz*.

Despite weekly staff meetings and daily conferences of the 'inner circle' of the NID, all these sections operated independently of one another. Section 17, comprising Godfrey's personal staff, including Ian Fleming, was the essential link that connected the whole structure.[72]

The task Godfrey gave Section 17 was to coordinate intelligence internally and to liaise between Naval Intelligence and the other intelligence bodies. Before long, as the demands of war increased, its role began to enlarge in scope and importance as it connected with the multiple arms of the entire Allied intelligence machinery. Section 17 in turn divided into subsections: 17P handled Ultra, the secret intelligence derived from breaking German and Italian naval ciphers; 17M specialized in German agents' traffic; 17Z focused on propaganda; and 17F, under Ian Fleming, coordinated and controlled them all.[73] Godfrey wasn't interested in a passive intelligence-collection body that waited for information to arrive on its doorstep from sources that might magically appear.[74] Rather, he demanded that all his staff move aggressively to develop and maintain intelligence pipelines that provided the raw natural resources vital to the Empire's national interest. To meet that expectation, Section 17, and Fleming, had to maintain close contact with the full range of intelligence departments and committees, ensuring that Godfrey and his inner circle had access to all planning reports, memoranda, operational orders and signals, with advanced warning of all upcoming 'futures,' to use the naval parlance for these operations.[75]

Fleming's role in the NID quickly evolved into much more than that of personal assistant or liaison officer, with Godfrey increasingly counting on his dauphin to represent him officially on various interdepartmental committees and to put his operating vision for a decentralized intelligence division into action. Fleming handled both general and highly sensitive portfolios such as the Joint Intelligence Committee, which sent its advice to the chiefs of staff, the prime minister and the War Cabinet. He also maintained an intimate working relationship with the nascent Political Warfare Executive (PWE), designed to attack the German economy in particular, and the highly trained Special Operations Executive (SOE), which had been established by Cabinet in July 1940 'to coordinate all action, by way of subversion and sabotage, against the enemy overseas' and, as Churchill instructed, 'set Europe ablaze!'[76] Likewise, he was required to meet with Sir Stewart Menzies, who had taken over as the new head, or 'C,' of the Secret Intelligence Service and the Ultra pipeline it provided. In addition, Fleming kept in touch with the Inter-Services Security Board (ISSB) and various joint operations and planning staffs – the Chief of Combined Operations (CCO), the Geographical Handbook Section, and one of Godfrey's beloved personal projects, the Inter-Services Topographical Department (ISTD).[77]

As Fleming's responsibilities evolved, he took on more than his pay grade demanded, fulfilling in many ways what Godfrey hoped to take from the Blinker Hall tradition. According to Norman Denning, 'Ian had enormous flair, imagination, and ability to get on with people ... He could fix anyone or anything if it was really necessary.'[78] This talent was not lost on Godfrey, who strangely confided in his memoirs that

'Ian should have been DNI and I his naval adviser,' and that 'if he had been ten years older and I ten years younger, this might have had the elements of a workable proposition.'[79]

Godfrey enlisted Fleming to act as his intermediary with Winston Churchill, but even then, the strained relationship between the PM and the DNI continued to deteriorate throughout Godfrey's tenure. Churchill's determination to add 'master strategist' to his role as 'master statesman' led him to intrude on other people's responsibilities, and Godfrey had little patience with his constant interference or with his habit of massaging or intentionally misconstruing intelligence to fit his policy and public relations schemes.[80] Early in the war Churchill inflated the number of U-boats sunk to boost public morale; and he regularly flooded Naval Intelligence with his 'prayers' – nightly letters that began 'Pray tell me ...' or 'Pray, why does this have to be?' – for which he insisted the explanations and answers must be provided the following day. Making matters worse, these requests usually came in the form of pointed, harshly toned attacks that Godfrey found condescending and challenging to answer. To placate the prime minister and keep him at arm's length, he turned the task over to Fleming, who, with his writer's skill, accomplished it with great aplomb.

⟊

The first eighteen months of the war were desperate times for Great Britain. Starting in September 1939, Hitler's Nazi Germany over-ran Poland in just six weeks; then in April 1940 invaded Norway and Denmark, followed by her shocking, lightning victories in Holland, Belgium and France in just six weeks. By the end of May, in the legendary 'Miracle of Dunkirk,' some 330,000 British and French troops were hurriedly evacuated from the beaches around the French Channel port and brought back to England in more than 700 vessels, large and small, many of them pleasure craft, fishing smacks, barges and even paddle steamers. These dramatic and historic events culminated in the collapse of the French army, followed by surrender, occupation and collaboration, transforming the complexion of Europe, with Germany now in firm control on the continent. Immediately, Hitler turned his focus to the British Isles, planning to defeat the defending Royal Navy and Royal Air Force as a precursor to a cross-Channel seaborne invasion of England known as Operation Sea Lion. Great Britain would be the final – and triumphant – point in his expansion west. By August 1940, the Battle of Britain raged as the Royal Air Force tangled with the Luftwaffe over the Channel and southern England. On September 7 the first German bombs fell on London, and the terrorizing year-long Blitz began. Meanwhile, Italy had entered the war in the spring and announced a blockade of Britain's Mediterranean and African territories and, one month later, invaded Egypt. The tough, long-drawn-out campaign in North Africa began late that year and only grew in intensity throughout 1941.

The question on the mind of the new Prime Minister, Winston Churchill, was straightforward: how far could Britain's armed forces be stretched? Already fighting to the death to defend the Empire at its core, he faced protecting strategic imperial interests in the Mediterranean, the Middle East and North Africa – all without the support from France and its navy. British prosperity, and indeed her survival, depended on her ability to command an extensive network of sea lanes that brought in food, oil, raw materials, tanks, aircraft and manpower, a network now threatened and harried by Hitler's menacing U-boats and surface raiders.

Then, in the summer of 1941, Hitler turned east and launched a massive invasion of Russia. This momentous event, which thrust Britain into a marriage of convenience with Joseph Stalin's Soviet Union, meant the Empire would no longer have to go it alone. This shotgun arrangement, however, came at a price, as Stalin demanded a steady flow of crucial supplies – and in vast quantities – to support his Red Army locked in a death struggle with the German invaders. Fearing that the Soviets could make a separate peace with the Germans (as they had in the First World War), Churchill sought to seal this fragile new alliance by fulfilling Stalin's demands with regular dispatch of merchant convoys that would deliver essential military hardware and critical industrial goods to the northern ports of Archangel and Murmansk. As such, British command of the sea lanes, already stretched, now took on another burden. In these dire circumstances, with Great Britain pressed to draw blood from a stone, Churchill, always intrigued by the bold and the daring, reached out to a varied collection of imaginative and Machiavellian characters including John Godfrey and Ian Fleming.

↬

Godfrey had early on allowed Fleming the freedom to exercise his initiative and his creative abilities. Before long, the young assistant took over intelligence planning within the Naval Intelligence Division, 'for which he had a marked flair.' To Godfrey, Fleming was, above all, a classic 'ideas man.'[81] In truth, however, Fleming's original and creative approach to intelligence planning and gathering bounced between the professional and the amateurish. He believed in being open to 'the unexpected' or 'the chance remark' that might provide a shortcut to answer some unsolved riddle.[82] As Dennis Wheatley, the bestselling writer of thrillers and adventure stories, who was also one of Churchill's 'Deception Planners' charged with developing ways to deceive the enemy, recalled, 'I had quite a number of dealings with Fleming ... he was full of ideas not only for helping to stop the invasion, but for our eventual plans to land on the continent.'[83] Their relationship included the planning period for both the Dieppe Raid and Operation Torch, the Allied invasion of French North Africa in November 1942, where Lieutenant Alan Schneider, an American officer specifically attached to Fleming from the US Office of Naval Intelligence, recorded that 'we were both ideas men and would come up with all sorts of harebrained schemes, making sure that someone else would have to carry them out.'[84]

In the desperate and wild atmosphere of the war, schemes that today seem absolutely fantastic were regularly hatched by men and women – many of them very young – striving by any means to derail the Germans. Some were remarkably successful. Fleming began with modest yet devious ruses, such as employing an actor to create a character who would appeal to the vanity and snobbery of a particular highbrow German naval officer during interrogation, or disguising an officer as a priest to extract vital information from a U-boat captain during confession.[85] He then went on to more creative schemes, such as his plan with another writer, Aleister Crowley, an occultist and self-proclaimed 'wickedest man in the world,' to take advantage of the credence some in the Nazi hierarchy gave to astrology and the occult. He had two objectives in mind: to lure a high-ranking Nazi official to defect, and to buy time for Britain to recover from the fall of France by persuading German authorities through deliberately placed deceptive horoscopes that an invasion of England in the summer of 1940 was not in the stars.

In another scheme designed to hide the code-breakers' work at Bletchley Park and the signals intelligence funnelling into the Operational Intelligence Centre, Fleming introduced the cover story that British intelligence employed 'Pendulum Practitioners' to find U-boat positions at sea by swinging pendulums over a map.[86] Encouraged, he initiated other, far more exotic plans that were approved by the admiring Godfrey and developed right through to the final planning stages. They never came to full fruition, however, or were scrapped at the last moment because the circumstances changed.

Operations Goldeneye and Tracer were two such plans from 1941. They were designed to enable Britain to keep monitoring what was happening in Spain and especially in the Mediterranean should Germany invade that country or General Franco enter into an alliance with Hitler. In February that year, as Fleming developed plans for Goldeneye, he visited Madrid, seeking ways to establish liaison offices in that city and also across the sea in Tangier with secure cipher leads to London. This operation seems to have had special meaning for Fleming: when the war was finally over, he bought an estate in Jamaica that he named Goldeneye, and there between 1951 and 1964 he wrote all twelve of his spy thrillers featuring the fictional MI6 officer James Bond.

Operation Tracer was far more elaborate, planned to cope with a possible takeover of the strategically important British colony and military base of Gibraltar – the island guarding the entrance to the Mediterranean Sea. Fleming had an underground bunker constructed there, carved into the towering rock face. If the Germans did manage to invade the island, a specially trained team of agents, including doctors and wireless operators, would be sealed into the cavern, with no chance of escape for at least a year and possibly much longer. Outfitted with provisions, wireless sets, and observation posts camouflaged from view, the team would report on Axis naval traffic squeezing through the narrow Strait of Gibraltar until the Allies could invade the island

and rescue them. If time ran out, however, the agents would be left to their own devices. As things turned out, both Operations Goldeneye and Tracer were cancelled in August 1943, after the threat of a Nazi invasion of Spain had evaporated.

As the urgency to win the war intensified, Fleming became ever bolder in his schemes. 'It was an atmosphere,' Donald McLachlan wrote in his account of James Bond's origins in Naval Intelligence, 'in which ordinary ideas of fair play and morality were not so much exploded as subtly and indeed pleasantly corrupted.'[87] Fleming had found his niche: dreaming up intelligence-driven operations fostered by desperation and opportunity, harnessed to action with Godfrey's blessing and the formidable decentralized authority that came with it – all within a Churchill-inspired atmosphere that permitted and indeed encouraged the implementation of ruthless special operations.

According to one observer, writing about this urgent climate where the British desperately strove to keep their sea lanes open and protect them from attack by Germany's navy, including its deadly U-boat fleet:

> The Chiefs of Staff, anxious to obtain further information about the enemy, started casting about for sources whence such intelligence might be obtained, and became conscious of the potential importance of documents captured from the enemy. The immediate result of these various endeavours was a series of directives and the proper way to handle them.[88]

As such, the focus of the Admiralty took a new twist: to steal, or 'pinch,' materials – whether from the Kriegsmarine's ships at sea or, later, from their shore-based facilities – that were crucial to the code-breakers at Bletchley Park.

CHAPTER 3

A Ruthless Start

*Public opinion seems to regard incendiary bombing, napalm
and propaganda as respectable activities that can be indulged
in by civilized powers without loss of face. Murder, arson,
eavesdropping and the use of noxious gasses are not quite U.
Where should the line be drawn, is there a moral issue, or are
our perceptions of right and wrong permanently blunted?*[1]
Admiral John Godfrey, Director, Naval Intelligence
Division (Retired), 1966

A solitary German Heinkel He 111 bomber, camouflaged with grey-green and sky-blue wash, dropped from the clouds to under 1,500 feet, trailing a long cone of smoke from what appeared to be its port engine, before levelling out temporarily, allowing the crew onboard to prepare for a dicey crash landing midway across the murky, frigid English Channel. The sight of a German bomber in obvious distress over the narrowest part of the Channel, near Dover, was not uncommon: during the previous eight weeks, beginning in September 1940, the Battle of Britain had shifted into its Blitz phase, which would last more than a year, with RAF fighters or British anti-aircraft gunners on the ground slowly racking up 'kills' of German intruder aircraft with increasing frequency. Any German bomber unlucky enough to suffer damage over England, as this one surely had, might possibly be able to limp out to sea and into the waiting arms of a friendly German R- or M-boat – minesweeping vessels whose crews were generally on the alert to pluck downed men from the treacherous mid-Channel waters. With British cities ablaze, civilians dying or uprooted, the nation's children and some of its cultural treasures evacuated inland or abroad, and the spectre of an imminent German invasion looming over England, the fate of falling into British hands was not the preferred option for any enemy personnel.

On board the bomber, the crew of five prepared to 'pancake' the wounded 'bird' just as the second engine cut out, leaving the plane gliding silently in a permanent but gentle descent towards the water. At 1,000 feet, one member threw caution aside and, abandoning the usual coded procedure, dispatched a distress call in plain German to any vessel in the area. A German patrol boat swiftly appeared. Crashing through the waves, it ploughed towards a position just a few hundred yards from what it expected would be the touchdown point of the falling bomber.

Breaking the near silence, calls to 'hang on tight' joined the whistle of the wind snaking through the bullet-riddled fuselage and the cracked panes of the nose canopy. The plane bounced once on the water and spun clockwise almost 90 degrees in a slow-motion pirouette before settling with its nose pointing towards the oncoming rescue craft, just 1,500 feet away and closing in fast. In no time, it seemed, the crew regained their senses and, with clockwork precision, following the drill they had rehearsed in training, popped off the cover of the escape hatch and deployed the tiny dinghy. Clad in regulation khaki Luftwaffe flight suits, sporting bulky yellow Mae West-style flotation devices, and with flight goggles hung around their necks, their wedge caps replaced by bloodied bandages, the men rowed hard towards their rescuers, waving frantically, shouting phrases in excited German clipped by the wind. The *Räumboote*, or R-boat, crew responded with the obligatory toss of a towline to draw them to the rescue craft.

Just as their deliverance seemed complete, a siren blared, summoning the R-boat crew to action stations, followed by shouts of '*Jabo! Jabo!*' (for *Jagdbomber*, fighter bomber) and the ripping sound of 20 mm and 37 mm flak guns on the aft deck discharging shells skywards. The rising stream of yellow tracers picked out a tiny black speck descending rapidly from 4,000 feet above, revealing within seconds the distinctive mono-winged shape of an RAF Lysander reconnaissance aircraft making straight for the scene, firing all the while. With the attention of the R-boat crew fully engaged in fending it off as it swooped down, the Lysander suddenly banked left to drop its bomb load hundreds of yards from its intended mark. On cue, the 'German' bomber crew sprang into action to launch their Trojan Horse ploy.

Pulling out weapons hidden on the rubber dinghy and tucked into their Luftwaffe flight suits, the British commandos boarded the R-boat, surprising the crew of seventeen and killing or capturing most in the first few seconds. After a cursory search of the boat to ensure they had subdued everyone on board, they located and seized their target: a three-rotor version of a German naval Enigma machine with its associated codebooks and setting sheets. Only then did they turn their attention to the captured crew members, whom they quickly ushered to the aft deck. In unison, the commandos raised their weapons and opened fire, eliminating all witnesses to the pinch, before unceremoniously tipping the bodies overboard and setting course for the nearest English port. This move indicated to the circling Lysander pilot above that the ruse, appropriately code-named Operation Ruthless, had succeeded and that the intelligence booty was en route to Commander Ian Fleming, the author of the scheme, waiting in the port of Dover to deliver the machine and its associated cipher aids safely into the hands of the cryptanalysts at Bletchley Park.

In reality, Operation Ruthless never came off as planned. Fleming, with cooperation from the RAF, had indeed drawn up a highly detailed 'script' for the mission, as outlined above – one that demonstrated his characteristic flair for the dramatic. At the time, Operation Ruthless was highly secret, and it has long been believed that the operation never took place; even in the context of what was becoming Britain's fight for survival, Ruthless crossed the line into the uncomfortable realm of war crimes. Some accounts have suggested that an official further up the chain of command at Admiralty intelligence than his boss John Godfrey reined him in and forced the abortion of the mission. But those accounts are wrong: recently declassified files reveal that Ruthless did go ahead, following the script devised by Fleming, but twice it came up empty.[2]

Ruthless was conceived in early September 1940, in the wake of Winston Churchill's 'finest hour' speech, in which he warned that the very survival of Western civilization now rested with the British, who stood alone against Nazi tyranny. In this context, there can be little doubt that the 'intelligence booty' Fleming sought in Ruthless was akin to the Holy Grail for Bletchley Park. Fleming had dreamed up the operation to assist the gifted cryptanalysts who worked in Bletchley's Naval Section – brilliant mathematicians, physicists and classical scholars such as Dillwyn 'Dilly' Knox, Alan Turing and Peter Twinn. These men now found themselves stymied in their critical struggle to break into German naval communications enciphered on a specially designed Enigma encryption machine. Despite their impressive intellectual efforts, they desperately needed 'cribs,' or 'cheats' – plain-language German text – that they could match up with a stretch of ciphertext and thus discover the daily 'key' setting, or password, which would unlock the contents of the top-secret German messages. Depending on how quickly they could complete this process, they would provide Godfrey's Naval Intelligence Division with access to real-time enemy naval communications. That breakthrough would give a priceless advantage to an island nation facing German invasion – one increasingly forced to rely on its overseas empire and on troops drawn from its far-flung dominions for the raw materials and manpower necessary to fight on in the war.

Dilly Knox, the great Oxford classicist who had been recruited to work for the Royal Navy's First World War cryptographic bureau housed in Room 40 of the Old Admiralty Building in London, had suggested to Fleming that he send a bogus signal to the Germans asking them to resend the upcoming keys for the Enigma machines – keys that changed daily. Politely rejecting the idea, Fleming informed Knox that 'the possibility should be examined and something got ready and kept ready for use in an emergency.'[3] In fact, Fleming considered the idea foolhardy: not only would it alert the Germans to what they were after, forcing them to strengthen their signals security, but it would reveal how much the Allies depended on this intelligence source and their potential method of decryption. Rather, he thought, the material had to be pinched, and with a velvet touch so the Germans would never catch on that their encryption system had been compromised in any fundamental way. It was one thing for the Germans to suspect the British of attempting to crack their codes and ciphers, or even succeeding on a limited and temporary basis; it was another to have clear proof of systematic success or the likely method of achieving it. As long as the British could continue to cover or camouflage their pinch operations and any breakthroughs they made, they could benefit from a steady stream of bona fide intelligence drawn from the proverbial horse's mouth. The fundamental trait of any pinch operation is the need to 'fox the enemy,' and that in its extreme form is what Fleming planned by engaging in wholesale murder for Operation Ruthless.

On September 12, Fleming had outlined the plot for Ruthless in a memo to John Godfrey, who eagerly approved the plan. He then approached Mountbatten's predecessor at Combined Operations, Admiral Sir Roger Keyes, and asked him to organize Ruthless under the auspices of his headquarters. Fleming was quickly rebuffed: Keyes deemed the size of the operation 'too small to come within their charter.'[4] Undaunted, Godfrey decided to carry out the plan as an Admiralty operation and presented the scheme to the nascent Joint Intelligence Committee (where he sat as the navy's representative), which quickly sanctioned the endeavour. Godfrey then obtained full approval from Admiral Dudley Pound, the First Sea Lord, and from Air Chief Marshal Sir Cyril Newall, the head of the Royal Air Force, who offered support from No. 11 Fighter Group – which, two years later, would support the Dieppe operation. This cooperation was crucial because the RAF agreed not only to clear the vital airspace over the Channel needed at the height of the Battle of Britain but to provide the captured German bomber – the decoy – with a pilot to fly it. In addition, it would train the commandos who made up the rest of the crew and supply their German uniforms and weapons. Newall also offered an operational base, a wireless network to track the events, and an RAF Lysander reconnaissance aircraft, plus a specially sequestered hangar to harbour the crew and the cover rumour that the team were a special 'spy party' set to land soon in Germany.[5]

The mission would start at dawn, when the captured bomber would take off and join the tail of other German aircraft making their way home across the Channel from their nightly raids on British cities. With German rescue boats working on a grid pattern, it was more than likely that the 'German' crew or the Lysander would find a lone victim not long after getting airborne. Once spotted, the reconnaissance aircraft would vector the bomber onto a collision course with the vessel, and the ruse would unfold: in quick succession the crew would send a distress signal, cut one engine, light a smoke candle to simulate a fire on board, dive quickly, and crash-land the plane in the Channel in the path of the advancing rescue boat. Once down safely, they would deploy their raft, load their weapons, and scuttle the bomber so it would sink quickly and remove any temptation on the part of the rescue boat to call in additional reinforcements for salvage purposes.

With commandos in full paddle towards the rescue vessel, the Lysander would dive out of the sky, drawing the crew's attention, and make a half-hearted strafing run, just missing the ship. Taking full advantage of this diversion, Fleming's commando unit would then board the vessel, capture and kill the German crew, commandeer the vessel and its Enigma machine and cipher aids, and hightail it back to the nearest British port, shadowed by RAF aircraft to prevent prying eyes from spotting the results of the privateering operation. In case things went wrong, Fleming prepared a cover story to obscure the pinch imperative of the mission and prevent suspicion that the special party sought more 'valuable targets than simply a rescue boat.'[6] Should the commandos fall into German hands alive, their story – confirmed by follow-up communiqués dreamed up by Fleming – would be that the mission was 'a lark by a group of young hot-heads who thought the war was too tame and wanted to have a go at the Germans. They had stolen a plane and equipment and had expected to get into trouble when they got back.'

Contrary to historical accounts that claim Fleming's flight of fancy never passed beyond the planning stage and was curbed in utero, Ruthless did, in fact, go into operation on October 16, 1940. However, with no potential victim sighted, the mission was postponed, and Fleming, who had joined the crew at their airbase before takeoff, was summoned back to the Admiralty in London to await a better opportunity, likely in the Portsmouth area. The surviving records show that Fleming remounted the operation just five days later, but it too suffered the same inglorious fate, leaving the pinch on hold.[7]

Even though Operation Ruthless did not reach its desired dramatic climax, the fact that Fleming's wild and cut-throat initial plan was ever authorized clearly shows the lengths to which NID would go in order to obtain what the cryptanalysts at Bletchley needed to press on with their vital work. More significant, Ruthless demonstrates that operations of a Machiavellian nature had found official acceptance with the heads of both the Royal Navy and the RAF, along with the Joint Intelligence Committee, all eager to foster pinch operations of varying brands at one of the most desperate and pivotal moments in British history.

⁓

'Far be it from me to paint a rosy picture of the future,' Winston Churchill told a worried House of Commons in the weeks following Operation Ruthless. 'Indeed, I do not think we should be justified in using any but the most sombre tones and colours while our people, our Empire and indeed the whole English-speaking world are passing through a dark and deadly valley.'[8] Britain, as the prime minister so eloquently expressed it, was 'alone.' The fate of the democratic world, not only of the British Empire, hung in the balance: an accumulation of recent events had fundamentally changed the complexion of the entire conflict, and in particular of the critical war at sea.

Just thirteen months before, in September 1939, Churchill had set out to 'contain' the German fleet. A similar policy had been successfully adopted during the Great War of 1914–18, when a blockade had hemmed German surface and U-boat fleets into their home waters and prevented them from breaking out into the Atlantic Ocean, or elsewhere, to wreak havoc on British merchant shipping. For Great Britain, a small island nation with a far-flung empire, control of the sea routes has always been essential for its prosperity and, in times of conflict, its survival. Without an unfettered flow of imports and exports, it cannot – then or now – feed its people or maintain its economy. But as the world once again veered towards the outbreak of war, the naval authorities did not seem particularly worried. The German navy, they said, with fewer than 30 serviceable U-boats and only a small number of modern and powerful surface raiding craft, presented a potential rather than an imminent threat.

This complacent view changed radically when, shortly after the start of hostilities, a handful of submarines skulked through the less than hermetically sealed blockade and made a harsh impression on both the Admiralty and the British psyche. On September 3, 1939, a lone U-boat managed to sink the liner SS *Athenia* on its way from Glasgow to Montreal, with some 1,420 on board. More than 100 passengers perished that day, including the first Canadian to die from enemy action in the Second World War, ten-year-old Margaret Hayworth.[9] The loss of the *Athenia* and the child's death deeply affected Canadians. Newspapers publicized the story widely, some calling it 'Canadians' rallying point.'

Two weeks later, submarine *U-29* sank the British aircraft carrier HMS *Courageous*, an event surpassed only by the actions of Günther Prien who, on October 14, slipped his *U-47* into the home of the British fleet at Scapa Flow in the Orkney Islands in Scotland and, under the nose of the Royal Navy, sank HMS *Royal Oak* while at anchor. Churchill, now in his second stint as First Lord of the Admiralty, was apoplectic. One way to avoid catastrophe at sea, he then astutely realized, was to revive the ability British intelligence had possessed in the First World War to read enciphered German naval messages that revealed U-boat locations and, with luck, their intended plans for attack well in advance of first contact.

Ultra – or, as it was initially known in naval circles, Special Intelligence – was initially dismissed by British naval commanders, who either misunderstood its vast potential or were ignorant of its past success. Relying on conventional and less profound sources of intelligence, such as aerial photographs, prisoner-of-war interrogations, naval attaché reports and traditional espionage informants, or forgoing it altogether, they blundered into a series of disasters in 1940 that thrust Special Intelligence back into the limelight. The first came in April, when decrypted traffic clearly showed the German interest in Norway; this intelligence went for naught, leading the British and French to engage in a series of costly and ultimately futile actions that paved the way for Hitler's conquest of that resource-rich country. The next disaster was the sinking of the lumbering aircraft carrier HMS *Glorious* and her two destroyer escorts at the hands of the German battlecruisers *Scharnhorst* and *Gneisenau*. Despite warnings from Bletchley Park's Naval Section that the two predators had left German ports and were now on the prowl, the *Glorious* was left to their mercy on her journey home from Norwegian waters.

But worse was still to come. By the autumn of 1940, after the rapid German advance through Norway, Denmark, Holland, Belgium and France, the Kriegsmarine was able to establish a presence along the entire coast of Western Europe, from the Arctic to the Bay of Biscay – a position never seriously considered by the Admiralty, and one that clearly threatened British survival. Luftwaffe aircraft and German U-boats could now reach the sea lanes around the British Isles, and their surface raiders could hide in French ports if they chose to break out of their North Sea or Norwegian ports past the now-crumbling British blockade. The French fleet, which the British had counted on to provide additional escort vessels for its merchant-ship traffic, surrendered to the Germans soon after the Italians declared war on France and England in June. Almost overnight, these events extended the Royal Navy's area of responsibility and stretched its resources to the limit, if not beyond. The Admiralty now had to contend in the Mediterranean with the Italian navy, which was endangering the Suez Canal and British holdings in Egypt and the oil fields in the Middle East. Moreover, on the other side of the world an increasingly belligerent Japan, taking advantage of France's demise, was making aggressive moves in South-east Asia that threatened to spill over into the Indian Ocean, cutting Britain's lifeline to its Far East resources. Even more worrying, back in the English Channel, reports indicated ongoing preparations for a German amphibious invasion of England under the code name *Seelöwe* (Operation Sea Lion).

By October 1940, when Commander Ian Fleming was waiting in vain for Operation Ruthless to produce results, Great Britain had reached the lowest point in its history. At night, bombs rained down on British cities; by day, what was left of the British army units that had escaped from Dunkirk in June attempted to re-form and rebuild their depleted ranks, augmented by the Home Guard units that, for lack of weapons, drilled with broomsticks while expecting a German invasion at any moment. In London, plans went into effect to evacuate children, treasure and the British government to safer locations in the countryside or in other parts of the Empire, and to continue the fight even after the first Nazi jackboot landed near Dover. On the high seas, during this 'Happy Time,' as the German U-boat crews ghoulishly called it, increasing numbers of German submarines armed with potent torpedoes sent hundreds of thousands of tons of merchant shipping and their precious cargoes to the bottom. Meanwhile, seemingly indestructible German super-battleships – *Bismarck* and soon *Tirpitz* along with other formidable surface raiders – sat poised to pounce from their lairs and join the feeding frenzy. The overstretched and beleaguered Royal Navy and RAF were the last lines of defence. With England's survival hanging in the balance, breaking the Enigma codes was seen as nothing short of essential.

The failure of Ruthless and the subsequent postponement of further attempts struck through the hearts of the cryptanalysts labouring in the huts at Bletchley Park. 'Turing and Twinn came to me like undertakers cheated of a nice corpse,' Frank Birch, who had served in both the Royal Navy and Naval Intelligence in the First World War and who now headed Bletchley's Naval Section in Huts 4 and 8, wrote to Fleming. 'The burden of their song,' he continued, was the 'importance of a pinch.' Did the authorities in the Naval Intelligence Division realize, he asked despairingly, that without a pinch 'there was very little hope of their deciphering current, or even approximately current, Enigma for months and months and months – if ever'?[10] With the backdrop of the war at sea ever-present in their minds, the cryptanalysts had toiled and struggled in vain to produce a breakthrough in decrypting the naval Enigma machine. Fleming reassured Birch that they 'needed to have no fear that the value of a *pinch* was underestimated.'[11]

༄

The magnitude of all these developments in Europe and the Mediterranean, as well as at home, caught the Admiralty off guard.

Nothing since the days of Napoleon Bonaparte had posed such a potent threat as the Axis air force, surface fleet and U-boat menace did now. For the British government, the ability to monitor an opponent's plans, intentions, capabilities and movements well before any action was under way was of prime concern, particularly for the Royal Navy. In naval warfare, the key feature that more often than not determines victory or defeat is surprise. With its resources stretched to breaking point, the Admiralty could not afford to keep watch in the physical sense on all parts of its empire, and it now needed to develop and maintain a highly accurate intelligence weapon to ensure a cost-effective approach to imperial defence.[12] Accurate insight into the enemy situation would allow the Royal Navy to effect an 'economy of force,' positioning its assets wisely around the globe and eliminating, or at least reducing, the odds of overspending in one area or being caught short in another.

To this end, the Admiralty spared little expense in developing the capability to monitor the Kriegsmarine's situation daily or even hourly, through cryptography and its 'poor relations' in the signals intelligence family – direction finding, or DFing (establishing the direction from which a received signal was transmitted); radio fingerprinting, or RFP (identifying a transmitter by photographing its waveform); and traffic analysis, or TINA (analysing the characteristics of the radio operator himself).[13] Intelligence defined the command structures and orders of battle among the Admiralty's enemies and could tap into the minds of their rivals – Kriegsmarine commander Erich Raeder and U-boat fleet commander Karl Dönitz, among others – gauging their strengths and weaknesses and the way they intended to play the game.

From various forms of SIGINT – signals intelligence – the staff at the Operational Intelligence Centre (OIC), located in the brown bombproof bunker connected to the Admiralty Citadel in London, could infer the number of enemy vessels in repair or under construction and project when and where they would make an appearance on the high seas. They could discover, often in advance, new technological developments that might swing the naval balance of power. Perhaps most important, in general terms they could locate and track surface raiders and U-boats from their bases right across the Atlantic Ocean, revealing where the giant surface raiders *Bismarck*, *Tirpitz* or others might suddenly appear or where U-boats were gathering in wolf packs to attack oncoming Allied convoys bringing vital supplies to wartime Britain. This same information, relayed by the OIC to the convoy's command with a simple 'change course to ...' message, allowed them either to scatter, in the case of raiders, or to sidestep the submarines lying in wait.

Within the mysterious world of naval intelligence, where signals intelligence reigned as the most vital of all intelligence sources, a pecking order developed. Ultra, a subset within SIGINT, dominated during the first half of the war. Reports from human sources – aerial photographs, traffic analysis and radio fingerprinting – which suggested that something was stirring with a particular vessel or group of vessels, were helpful and sometimes adequate, but Ultra went further because it could provide direct or indirect information about Nazi Germany's intentions and capabilities, sometimes in great detail. When it was available, Ultra provided the most accurate and consistent form of intelligence, and in this sense, it was priceless.

Fortunately, by the early months of 1941, Ultra did triumph – and it did so because of the changing nature of naval warfare. Unlike its army or air force counterparts, which restricted the use of the Enigma device to the upper echelons of high command, the Kriegsmarine relied on Enigma-encrypted communications for almost all classes of ships and its multitude of shore facilities. With the war at sea controlled for the most part by wireless communication since the turn of the century, the world's navies strove to develop codes and ciphers to protect their top-secret communications from enemy cryptographic efforts. The seemingly impregnable Enigma machine appeared to be the answer for the German navy. Almost every vessel in the fleet was outfitted with this device – from their super-battleships, pocket battleships, cruisers, destroyers, torpedo boats and U-boats right down to their minesweepers, E-boats, R-boats and flak ships, as well as their anti-submarine and weather trawlers. They all enjoyed the anonymity of Enigma-encrypted communications not only with each other but with shore-based facilities as well.

As Admiral Ludwig Stummel, the head of the Kriegsmarine naval intelligence (*Seekriegsleitung* or SKL) and the man most responsible for the security of Enigma ciphers admitted, the German navy fully understood the risk involved with outfitting the smaller ships with the machine. To Stummel, the spectre of their capture necessitated the best defence against compromise, which came in the form of the latest Enigma device with highest grade of ciphers.[14]

As such, this wide distribution formed the fertile playing ground for John Godfrey and Ian Fleming to pinch the materials so badly needed by the cryptanalysts at Bletchley Park.

༆

The Enigma machine came to obsess anyone involved with decryption, no matter how marginal the association. It was an intellectual Everest; enticing, taunting, and at times seeming to ridicule its opponents as no other technology in existence had done. It posed impossible riddles and engaged some of the finest minds in England. It led to nightmares, emotional and psychological breakdown, and universal frustration; yet, because of the secrecy surrounding it, for decades only muted glory came to those who eventually conquered it at Bletchley Park.

Initially designed in the closing months of the First World War by Arthur Scherbius, a German engineer, for commercial use to protect banking and industrial secrets, the aptly named Enigma encryption device was indeed a riddle, and it soon drew the interest of the German armed forces in the inter-war period. Physically, the machine resembled a portable typewriter with a keyboard, a plugboard, an illuminated lamp board, and a set of three (later four) rotors that protruded through the top, giving the appearance of a large combination lock. The machine could encipher each letter of the alphabet individually, unlike other machines and forms of encryption that encoded complete words, word for word. The Enigma machine was far more subtle and therefore more difficult to crack. It did not actually transmit messages itself, as a wireless or telegraphy set would do. Instead, it scrambled or enciphered each letter of each word of a message into unintelligible gibberish, before transmission to a recipient via wireless. The recipient then deciphered the received message letter for letter using an identical Enigma machine set to precisely the same specifications.

Early in the 1920s, the Enigma machine had made its commercial debut on a limited basis. It was sold domestically on the premise that its contrived internal set-up was so complicated that, should it fall into the wrong hands, it would remain impregnable unless that person also possessed the current setting sheets displaying the exact configurations of the rotor wheels and the plugboard settings that changed daily. The beauty of these code sheets was that, with these materials in hand, the machine was foolproof, allowing any secretary, clerk or, later, private or naval rating to encipher material quickly and accurately after a modicum of instruction. The staggering number of variations of ciphered text that could be produced was virtually unlimited and became the machine's main selling feature. As one account later claimed, it could encipher 'every book on earth ... differently without the machine settings having to be repeated.'[15] By 1926 the German navy, followed quickly by the army, saw Enigma's massive potential benefits and adopted it wholesale, with each service improving on the basic design, particularly once the Nazis came to power.

The version employed by the Kriegsmarine was more complex than the German army's version of Enigma. Housed in a square wooden-lidded box that resembled a silverware case stamped with the trademark *Enigma*, the machine required only three-rotor wheels but offered eight removable wheels in all, each of which had its own distinct electrical wiring.[16] These wheels formed the basis of the multi-layered or multi-step design that proved the hallmark of its security. When the signals operator wanted to begin transmission of a message, or to receive one, while at sea or on shore, he needed to consult a bigram table and a key sheet that contained what we would today call the daily 'password,' or 'pin number.'

In the first step, the bigram table produced a random letter set known as the indicator. This set was sent as the plain-text heading of the enciphered message to instruct the receiver how to set up the machine. The next step involved the daily key setting, which usually came every month in the form of a booklet, called a K-book, or in a set of sheets and tables printed in water-soluble ink. This information was issued to both the senders and the receivers of messages. To make sure they were on the same page, all the operators on a given network, after receiving the indicator, consulted these materials to establish the starting position of the machine – specifically, which three of the eight possible rotor wheels to insert into the naval version of the device, and in what order to place them in the slots at the top. Each rotor wheel was wrapped with a removable rubber ring with letters of the alphabet stamped on it, which was then clipped in a preordained position, also listed in the key sheets. The operator turned each rotor wheel separately until they all reached the given starting position for the day listed on the key sheet. With each wheel corresponding to a letter of the alphabet, the operator then lined up the letters, as if lining up the numbers of a combination lock, to produce the key setting itself.

At this point yet another security layer appeared: the operator inserted the plug cables – similar to patch cords on a TV or sound system – into the plugboard at the base of the machine in a particular configuration provided by the daily key sheet or sometimes, to strengthen security, by a completely separate key sheet. That done, the operator was ready to type the text message he wanted to send on the keyboard directly connected via electric cable to the rotor wheels, which in turn were connected to the lamp board. On the lampboard was another alphabet, as on the keyboard, but the difference was that each letter lit up once the machine was in operation. With every punch of a key, an electrical pulse would race into the individual wiring of each rotor and turn the right-hand rotor one position, to select at random another letter of the alphabet, which would appear in enciphered and illuminated form to replace the plain-text letter in the original message. With each keystroke, the rotor would turn, providing another unique encrypted letter for the operator to note and write down – by all these means eventually creating an encrypted version of the formerly plain-text message. The message was then transmitted via wireless using Morse code.

When the message arrived, or was intercepted, it seemed to be unintelligible nonsense – unless the receiver had the corresponding key or password to unlock the true meaning of the message. With the key sheet in hand, the receiver proceeded in reverse steps, using his Enigma machine to decrypt the message and reveal its meaning in plain German text.[17]

To pry into an Enigma-enciphered message, cryptanalysts had to establish the machine's configuration, then which three of the eight wheels were in use, the clip position of the rings, and the setting of the three-letter key. Once that was done, they had to figure out the configuration of the plugboard.[18] Complicating this task was the fact that each service possessed its own keys and constantly introduced more keys and networks after every victory in Europe or every security scare. In 1940, for instance, the Kriegsmarine employed one basic key for home waters traffic, which it called *Heimisch*, or later *Hydra*, and which the British code-named *Dolphin*. After the German invasion of Western Europe, the navy branched out into more keys. By mid-1941, it had separate keys to denote Norwegian, Baltic and Mediterranean traffic. Eventually the U-boat fleet had its own unique key, code-named *Triton* by the Germans and *Shark* by the British, along with two special derivative keys that officers and staff (*Offizier* and *Stab*) used for highly sensitive messages. To complicate matters still more, each key could have further security precautions attached: there might be special instructions for different internal settings for the staff, in contrast to an operational command, or even separate plugboard settings for individual commands or commanders.

Physically, the machine and its rotor wheels usually remained under the tightest security, with the operator given specific instructions to destroy the components if capture seemed imminent. The key sheets and codebooks, sometimes printed and stored for a month or even a year in advance, required special precautions. At sea, where capture and compromise could occur at any time, ships stored the requisite setting sheets for a limited period, such as 30 to 90 days. They were heavily guarded, either in the captain's safe or squirrelled away in his footlocker or the panelled wall of his cabin, or hidden in other parts of the vessel. On land, the shore-based facilities, depending on their function and position in the communications chain, could stock six or twelve months' worth of sheets and codebooks, likely in the commanding officer's safe. The German navy, like most of its counterparts, printed cipher materials in water-soluble ink so the writing would vanish if they were tossed into the sea by the crew.

On land or at sea, standard operating procedures called for the destruction of the machine and its parts in the event of imminent capture: first, remove and dispose of the rotors; then pull out the plugboard cables; finally, destroy the machine by physically smashing its components or by disposing of them (or the entire device) in a fashion that would render recovery impossible. In some German shore-based facilities, such as in the port of Dieppe, the Kriegsmarine employed specially trained units who would quickly gather all the machines and cipher materials, and destroy them.

Given all these precautions, it is not surprising that the German high command placed such great faith in Enigma. Even if the Allies got a break, it would be limited in time and scope and therefore temporary in nature, meaning the Germans could simply let the current material expire, without going to the enormous expense of overhauling their entire signals system. Because of the time and energy required to wade through the data and decipher messages, they believed that any captured materials would yield vastly outdated information. According to a pre-war estimate, one Enigma machine could produce 10.5 quadrillion possible keys for each message, meaning it would take 1,000 enemy cryptanalysts working with four captured or copied keys close to 1.8 billion years to test them all.[19]

However, the Nazi high command, despite some brilliant and maverick minds at work in their own code-breaking organization, *Beobachtungsdienst*, or *B-Dienst* for short, suffered from an institutionalized anti-intellectualism and arrogance that gave Britain the time and space needed to conquer Enigma. The British harnessed their greatest intellectual resources right from the outbreak of war in 1939 and put them to work at Bletchley Park. They challenged these people to overcome the staggering odds and take the science of cryptography to levels never before imagined. To make an analogy, they stood the same chance of defeating the three-rotor naval Enigma in 1939 as an individual would have of winning a national lottery once a day, every day, for nearly 100 years. Nevertheless, by mid-1941, the cryptographic team – led by the legendary Alan Turing, Peter Twinn and Dilly Knox, among many other stellar minds – had done just that. The journey to this great accomplishment was anything but smooth, however, and when Turing first took on the project with his team in Hut 8 – the

Bletchley hut devoted to cracking the naval Enigma ciphers – he did so under a cloud of pessimism.[20]

As Frank Birch summed up the situation:

At the outbreak of the war in September 1939, no German naval signals had been read for 20 years. Several of their minor codes were broken by the following spring, but every success reemphasised the conclusion that as far as wireless was concerned, 95% [of] all worthwhile German naval traffic was enciphered on the Enigma machine. By that time, the pessimism formerly prevailing concerning the chances of ever breaking into naval Enigma had been dispelled, and special machinery, designed for the purpose, was already in the making. Nevertheless, it was certain that, even with this machinery, continuous and up to date reading would be impossible without at least an initial capture of either the key sheets for a month or a set of the digraph tables. The possibilities of obtaining the necessary data by interrogation of prisoners of war or by capture of documents had been canvassed since the outbreak of war, and on the 10th of December 1939, the head of GC&CS informed the Director of Naval Intelligence that, without outside assistance from one or other of these 2 sources, we are far from hopeful of success.[21]

Fortunately, help for the Bletchley Park cryptanalysts came in several forms. First, they received tremendous aid from the work of exiled Polish cryptanalysts, who had pioneered the cryptographic assault on an earlier version of the German army Enigma in 1932 and who turned their work over to the British and French just before Germany invaded their country in 1939. The Poles invented the original 'Bombe,' a high-speed electromechanical device designed specifically to attack Enigma encryption. It in turn was improved upon by Turing, who created the first machine able to decipher the German encryption – something that Fleming would have appreciated, given his fascination with Charles Babbage's pioneering work in computers and cryptography.[22]

There were fundamental differences between the two designs. Unlike the Polish Bombe, which relied strictly on mathematical principles, Turing's Bombe was based on 'cribs,' or 'cheats' – a system similar to possessing answers to one or more questions on the *Times* crossword which also hint at the solutions to other questions. In essence, the Bombe sifted through all the possible configurations of the three Enigma wheels, searching for a pattern of keyboard-to-lampboard connections that would turn the encrypted letters into plain German.[23] Although the Bombe worked in mathematical terms at superhuman speed, reducing the man-hours needed to a mere fraction of what the human brain alone would have required, in real time during a war it simply wasn't fast enough. Each Bombe took days or even weeks to crack an out-of-date message from an Enigma key. Turing tried using one of his Polish-inspired inventions, 'Banburismus' – a cryptographic process that in theory could speed up the machines by enabling code-breakers to narrow down the number of wheels that could have been in place when a message was sent. Still, without any bigram tables to consult, he had no matching pieces of German and English text to help him reduce the odds. Hugh Alexander, who worked in Hut 8 (devoted to German Naval Cryptanalysis) noted that 'The only really satisfactory solution to the problem' was '1) a pinch either of the key sheets for a month (or rather less valuable) of the set of bigram tables, combined with 2) maximum bombe production to enable such a pinch to be exploited. Failing a pinch or a really large number of bombe there was little hope of any progress on up to date material.'[24]

✎

On April 26, 1940, when the German armed trawler *Schiff 26*, disguised to resemble the Norwegian vessel *Polaris*, which was taking mines and torpedoes to German forces in Narvik, crossed paths with the British destroyers HMS *Griffin* and HMS *Acheron*, a most fortuitous pinch of material in Norway provided just what Turing required. In one short, sharp action, the destroyers disabled the trawler and captured her crew before they could destroy their cryptographic documents. The haul, delivered promptly to Bletchley Park, was a godsend for Turing: it revealed the precise form of the indicating system, the plugboard connections, and the starting positions of the three rotors for a 24-hour period. In addition, the operators' log contained a significant stretch of plain text and enciphered material for the cryptanalysts to analyse.

These documents were the 'cheat' they needed. Feeding the results of the Banburismus into the nascent Bombe, the result demonstrated, despite the out-of-date and essentially useless immediate results, that their overall deciphering approach had merit. Banburismus in itself was not a stellar leap forward, but it was still significant. As one veteran of Hut 8 recalled, it was 'not easy enough to be trivial, but not difficult enough to cause a nervous breakdown.'[25] Soon, however, the joy and relief felt within the sparse confines of Hut 8 turned into despair when the Germans changed their bigram tables just weeks later, in June of that year.

Ideally, the solution lay in building more Bombes that could work together, harnessing their collective might to break into intercepted Enigma messages. But each Bombe was extremely expensive and difficult to produce, and the cryptanalysts in Hut 8 did not have time on their side. Additional Bombes would take months or years to arrive, leaving pinched material the only alternative to enable the British to attack German naval codes and ciphers.

Thus, with the stark reality of defeat facing them in 1940, the various sections that made up British intelligence, and specifically naval intelligence, knew they had to get what they needed by any means at their disposal – and as quickly as possible. For the great mathematicians at Bletchley, Alan Turing and Peter Twinn, even a small pinch would again meet their immediate requirements. However, 'if the whole bag of tricks was pinched,' Frank Birch informed Fleming, 'there'd be no delay at all.'[26] 'Ideally,' he said, 'those on board should not have been able to destroy anything,' or have time to get rid of 'papers on their persons, or to throw anything overboard.'[27] Birch, isolated at the Naval Section in Bletchley Park from the hub of the war effort in London, argued that alternative methods of capturing the essential materials should be examined and the concept of pinching continuously maintained. The Germans, he said, could 'muck their machine about' at any moment, which would right away require another pinch. He demanded to know if there was 'anything in the wind,' because 'there ought to be.'[28]

The superficial treatment of Operation Ruthless in most past accounts portrays it as a lone-wolf operation, lacking in context or a sound basis, conceived by the impetuous Fleming and launched in cavalier style without any regard for its consequences. Recently declassified files clearly show that this interpretation needs overhauling. Once the Germans changed their bigram tables in June 1940, the Naval Intelligence Division, with Fleming in the lead, began a methodical and well-reasoned search for pinch targets within arm's reach of English shores. Researchers began tapping into the wireless frequency and plain-language traffic of German salvage ships operating in the Channel, and before long they had established a 'hit list' of vessels that possessed Enigma machines and related material or other codes that could be used as temporary solutions to the problem. The list focused on four types of vessel: S-boats (patrol boats) or German motor torpedo boats known popularly as E-boats; German torpedo boats that resembled mini-destroyers; aircraft security boats specifically dedicated to the rescue of downed flyers and aircraft; and minesweeping craft such as R-boats and M-boats that carried out rescues at sea along with a wide array of other duties.

By early September, all this research was collected in a special report on the 'Activities of German Naval Units in the Channel.'[29] Without doubt, it made an impression on Fleming. The report analysed the strengths and weaknesses of each potential target. The habits of S-boats and E-boats were difficult to read because, generally, they were night predators, attacking British coastal convoys before returning to friendly ports by first light. They had no specific routine or patrol area, so the chances of intercepting them were slim. The larger torpedo boats had arrived in the Channel only recently, so little was known yet about how they would use Enigma. Aircraft security boats, which operated from the Dutch, Belgian and French coasts and engaged in daily rescues of Luftwaffe airmen, remained too close to the German-occupied coast unless they could be drawn out into mid-Channel and away from the view of potential witnesses to a pinch. In addition, evidence suggested they did not carry Enigma at all, but rather a minor salvage code known as *Seenot*, which was not yet readable by Bletchley. That left the minesweepers as the most promising prey. They generally hugged the coast and operated daily off Boulogne and Calais, carrying out their sweeping duties unless interrupted by a distress call from a downed plane in mid-Channel.[30] Again, because they had no regular positions, intercepting them depended on a surprise attack – if they could be lured further from the coast.

'Is it too fantastic to suggest,' wrote Frank Birch in response to the report, 'that efforts should be made to capture one of these in circumstances which would prevent the destruction of the Enigma Machine, attachments and papers?' He could not think how to attempt such a daring exploit himself, so turned it over to NID and the imaginative Ian Fleming. 'We are incompetent to suggest the means,' he admitted, 'but the elements would seem to be surprise, shrapnel and boarding.'[31] The result was Operation Ruthless, six weeks later.

In December, Birch, who was still wrestling with Enigma, put forward another proposal along similar lines. 'Though operation Ruthless has been postponed on practical grounds,' he wrote, 'the reason which caused it to be proposed has lost none of its force.'[32] That month new information obtained from traffic analysis surfaced to suggest that aircraft security vessels, once believed Enigma-free, now carried both naval and air force Enigma materials, along with lower-level material corresponding to the German naval air code and the *Seenot* code. Immediately they became prime targets for a pinch.[33]

Birch and his colleagues in the Naval Section at Bletchley Park suggested a plan that same month that was almost a carbon copy of Operation Ruthless, except that this time it would be carried out by ships instead of aircraft. In this case French *chasseurs*, or patrol boats, in the employ of the Free French would carry the commando strike force to its target. The first victim decided on was the *Bernhard von Tschirschky*, an 880-ton seaplane tender operated by the Luftwaffe. Travelling under cover of darkness or in the obscurity of last light, the *chasseur* would approach the *Von Tschirschky* using the appropriate signal to announce that it had wounded on board in need of immediate attention. Having learned the commander's name from an intercepted lower-level signal, the organizers in Naval Section suggested that the boarding party should shout out to him in perfect French or German as they approached, to gain the confidence of their intended victims.

Once close enough, the raiders would open fire with their sub-machine and deck guns in an effort to panic and scatter the crew, followed by a tear-gas attack to incapacitate all aboard and prevent 'destruction of the books and alteration of the settings of the Enigma machines.' The planners placed great emphasis on this aspect of the mission, directing that the plug settings, locked in position by the commander, be left in place.[34]

In the end, the suggested operation against the *Von Tschirschky* was shelved, just as Ruthless had been, leaving Birch apoplectic. In a series of terse letters, the head of Bletchley's Naval Section urged the head of Bletchley Park, Commander Alastair Denniston, to act aggressively towards the naval Enigma problem, telling him: 'The present position is a nightmare ... and it is wearing the life out of me ... Not enough is being done to break German naval ciphers.'[35]

Birch's frustration boiled over to include shots at the Admiralty too, which he accused of foot-dragging, even though Fleming and his section had provided clear evidence of the type of material to be pinched and where it could be found: 'The long and short of it is that the Navy is not getting a fair dose.'[36] Birch's solution went straight to the heart of the problem. 'At the present rate of advance,' he chided, his cryptanalysts would do little more than:

> trundle along, getting out odd days, but at ever increasing intervals from the present unless they are given either a pinch or a very large number of bombs [*sic*] ... Well, the issue is a simple one. Total up the cost and the difficulties and balance them against the value to the nation of being able to read current Enigma. The value of the latter has been put at 1,000,000 a day. Could the cost of any number of machines, plus the difficulties of making and running them, exceed that value? ... I have never been in favour of the very melodramatic Operation Ruthless, but there are many ways of trying to pinch a small craft intact – it was done in the last war, so why not in this? It certainly is not a forlorn hope, it only needs perseverance.[37]

Eventually, Birch's tone simmered down; he wrote later that 'Apart from the defects inherent in the schemes themselves, the narrow waters of the English Channel were unfavourable to cutting-out expeditions of any kind; men and craft were scarce and above all, the latter half of 1940, when German invasion was imminent, was not a favourable moment for such distractions.'[38]

Despite this bitter disappointment, the building up of the *Von Tschirschky* file provided them with a rich corpus of material to draw from for future pinch attempts. While tracking the movements of this seaplane tender, they came to realize that all ships at sea using Enigma needed to communicate with shore-based facilities strung along the Channel coast, which made these ports, with their naval headquarters and signals equipment, prime targets for a pinch as well. They also saw that vessels like the *Von Tschirschky*, as well as other types of hotly desired ships employed by the Kriegsmarine's 2nd Defence Division, maintained an operational course that ran from Brest east through Cherbourg and finally terminated in Dieppe where they would take on supplies, reverse course and embark on their return journey.[39]

CHAPTER 4

Annus Mirabilis

*The Atlantic is the vital area[,] as it is in that ocean and
that alone in which we can lose the war at sea.*
Admiral Dudley Pound, First Sea Lord, August 28, 1941

*A**nnus mirabilis* was the only phrase John Godfrey felt accurately described the flood of captured material that transformed the complexion of the cryptographic war in 1941. And not only Godfrey – many in the Naval Intelligence Division and at Bletchley Park rejoiced in this 'year of miracles,' especially as the year had got off to a very rocky start.[1] The frustration and impotence of the cryptanalysts in those early weeks had mirrored the miserable collective experience of the British people. Yet, in the vicissitudes of war, fortunes continuously change, and as we shall see, the so-called miracle of 1941 would, in turn, give way again to despair in 1942 – and the pressing need for ever more 'pinch' missions on Bletchley Park's behalf.

For several weeks following the late summer of 1940, while nightly bombings rocked London and other cities during the Blitz, the English had faced the even greater threat of a German invasion from across the Channel. Mounting attacks by German U-boats reinforced the sense of smothering claustrophobia, as the submarines tightened their grip around the British Isles with each passing day. Admiral Karl Dönitz, the brilliant 50-year-old commander of the submarine fleet, had convinced Hitler that his nimble submersible vessels, working together via radio communications in the 'wolf pack' tactic he had devised, could locate, stalk and destroy the convoys and thereby starve Britain and its war economy into defeat.[2] Before long, the successes scored by the U-boats in this 'Happy Time' transformed Germany's top-scoring aces – Otto Kretschmer, Fritz-Julius Lemp, Günther Prien and Joachim Schepke – into media darlings rivalling the famed German fighter aces of the First World War. In just six months between June and December 1940, U-boat attacks sank nearly 350 ships and claimed almost 3,000 lives in just 180 days, while only nine of these seemingly invincible submarines were lost. A distraught Churchill lamented: 'Without ships, we cannot live, and without them we cannot conquer.'[3]

It was staggering: in the first 28 months of the war, U-boats claimed some 5.3 million tons of British and neutral shipping, or 1,124 ships – a loss rate five times greater than the number of vessels currently under construction in British shipyards.[4] Planners projected there would be a 7-million-ton deficit in raw materials, including 2 million tons of food. But what really alarmed them was the 300,000-ton deficit in the crucial imports of oil that fuelled the British war machine. As imports fell to half their normal levels, strict rationing policies for food, petrol and other essential items in the United Kingdom had to be imposed, threatening to drain the already limited morale of the British people and restrict the nation's ability to maintain, never mind expand, its power. And more bad news was about to come.

Although Hitler had neglected the U-boat fleet in the run-up to the war – a curious oversight given that German submarines had almost crippled England during the First World War – these early successes soon translated into a concerted building programme that would see a fourfold increase in the number of U-boats threatening the vital Atlantic lifeline. By the end of 1941, 88 U-boats (up from 28 earlier in the war) were on patrol, even though twenty had already been sunk or captured. Beginning in July 1940, Hitler promised Admiral Dönitz 25 new submarines a month – meaning a grand total of 300 within the year. Although it was questionable that Hitler would reach this target, Churchill, the chiefs of staff, the Admiralty and the NID were nonetheless all deeply worried.

Submarines, however, were not the only problem. The Germans also possessed a small but potent surface raiding fleet that posed a major threat to Great Britain's Atlantic trading routes, even though it was not yet large enough to rival the Royal Navy ship for ship. Admiral Erich Raeder, the head of the Kriegsmarine, was no fool: he had nothing like the Kaiser's Grand Fleet of the earlier war, but he knew that merely maintaining a 'fleet in being' to make periodic convoy raids would do more to tie up British resources than actually engaging in a traditional *Götterdämmerung*-style showdown with the Royal Navy. In many ways, the war at sea was a war of innuendo and perception – not about what your opponent *will* do but what he *could* do. However, Hitler grew tired of this chess-like waiting game being played at sea and, in the spring of 1941, ordered his surface raiders, including the super-battleship *Bismarck*, to launch attacks on British convoys to supplement the deadly work of the U-boats. It appeared that Germany was about to attempt a knockout blow.

Then, seemingly in an instant, the course of the war at sea began to change.

✍

As the dismal winter gave way to spring in 1941, a series of momentous events started to unfold that would run the course of the year. In the last few days of March, having broken the Italian naval version of Enigma, a less complicated but still daunting version of the German machine, Bletchley Park provided Admiral Sir Andrew Browne Cunningham (nicknamed ABC), the Commander-in-Chief of the Royal Navy's Mediterranean fleet, with an early warning that an Italian naval 'task force' had sortied to intercept and destroy highly vulnerable British convoys bringing troops from the Egyptian city of Alexandria to Greece. Swiftly, Cunningham devised a plan to outfox and ambush his Italian adversary, Admiral Angelo Iachino.[5] First, he sent reconnaissance aircraft out to 'discover' the task force, so as not to betray the source of the intelligence – a requisite for any action based solely on Ultra. Second, he found a way to keep his own movements secret as he made a surprise attack – the key to victory at sea. Cunningham – again through the good graces of Ultra – knew that the Japanese consul general in Alexandria maintained a vigil on his whereabouts, figuring that if Cunningham remained in Alexandria, so too did the Mediterranean fleet. The cunning British admiral realized, therefore, that he must delude the consul general.[6]

On this occasion, while the fleet prepared for battle, Cunningham arranged for a false story to circulate in the local golf club about a grand ball aboard his flagship that night. When he arrived in the afternoon for his habitual round of golf, he had his dress uniform in his bag and made his presence felt. That evening, nothing appeared in Bletchley Park intercepts to suggest that the Japanese consul general suspected subterfuge, even though by then Cunningham had slipped out the back door of the club, jumped into a waiting car and sped to Alexandria harbour to catch up to his own fleet moments before it sailed for its historic confrontation with the Italian fleet. The only warning Iachino received of an approaching British strike force came from the roar of shot and shell crashing into the decks of his ships.

Two days of heavy fighting ensued, which left three Italian cruisers and two destroyers at the bottom of the sea, while the pride of the Italian navy, the battleship *Vittorio Veneto*, limped back into the port of Taranto heavily damaged; it would never see battle again. It was, as Churchill later claimed, the 'tearing up of the paper fleet of Italy.'[7] In 48 hours Cunningham had inflicted the greatest defeat in Italian naval history. It not only secured the sea lanes to North Africa for the British but restricted the Italian fleet to its ports. When the ships emerged two years later, en masse, it was to surrender to the Allies.

Great Britain had scored an outstanding victory at the bleakest of times, one that Churchill suggested rivalled Horatio Nelson's legendary triumph at the Battle of Trafalgar nearly a century and a half earlier. The victory certainly illustrated what Birch later wrote, that 'in providing material for such a background, Special Intelligence (ULTRA) may be said to fulfill its utmost purpose. The enemy, encompassed by his opponent's knowledge, is deprived of the power of surprise and maybe fought or outmaneuvered, no matter where or in what strength he may appear.'[8]

The decisive role Ultra played in the spectacular victory demonstrated to John Godfrey in Room 39 the full weight and power of what

Bletchley Park's Naval Section could deliver: not only had it defined the Italian fleet's intentions and location, but it had also ensured that the intelligence source and the subsequent ruse remained undiscovered. So impressed with the fruits of Ultra was Cunningham that, on his return to England, he made a priority visit to Bletchley Park to thank the cryptanalysts in person for providing the critical intelligence required for the victory in the Mediterranean – once again Churchill's 'golden eggs' had proved priceless.

In addition to the U-boat worries, the British also had to concern themselves with periodic breakouts into the Atlantic by the deadly German surface raiders, which presented a constant threat to the vital convoys. Between October 1940 and March 1941, the pocket battle-ship *Admiral Scheer* sank sixteen merchant ships, accounting for nearly 100,000 tons. In the first three months of 1941, the battlecruisers *Scharnhorst* and *Gneisenau* took down another 22 ships comprising over 115,000 tons, while the heavy cruiser *Admiral Hipper* sank more than 40,000 tons during its two raiding cruises.[9] However, just two months after the Ultra-inspired victory over the Italian fleet, the cryptanalysts at Bletchley would contribute in no small fashion to sinking the pride of Hitler's fleet, the super-battleship *Bismarck*, after she broke out of the Denmark Strait into the North Sea with the battlecruiser *Prinz Eugen*, intending to prey on the Allies' convoy traffic in the Atlantic.

The Royal Navy's legendary hunt for the *Bismarck* that followed revealed just how potent an intelligence weapon Godfrey's NID had become by the late spring of 1941, with signals intelligence (cryptography, direction finding, radio fingerprinting, traffic analysis), naval attachés' reports and aerial photography all combining to help the Admiralty carry out Churchill's instruction to 'Sink the *Bismarck*.' Together, they allowed the Admiralty to maintain an almost constant vigil over the movements of the behemoth battleship and gain insights into the intentions and decision making of Admiral Günther Lütjens, the German task force commander, who joined the *Bismarck*'s Captain Otto Ernst Lindemann on her bridge for the operation.

This remarkable story began on May 18, when Ultra reports indicated that German aerial reconnaissance had suddenly increased in the area between Jan Mayen, a Norwegian island in the Arctic Ocean, and Greenland. Although the intelligence did not reveal the exact nature of the German interest, it was clear that something was afoot.

That night, unknown to British intelligence, the *Bismarck* moved quietly from her anchorage in Gdynia, in German-occupied Poland, and the following afternoon entered Kiel, Germany's traditional home port for its navy, where she joined the *Prinz Eugen* and a group of destroyers. The next night, they quietly and secretly sailed out through the Great Belt, a strait that divides Denmark in two. It wasn't until late on May 20 that the Admiralty received a report through its naval attaché in Stockholm that neutral Swedish vessels had spotted 'two large warships escorted by three destroyers' making for the north-west.[10] The report did not immediately set off alarm bells in the Operational Intelligence Centre in London, though it raised suspicions requiring further investigation. Aerial reconnaissance flights eventually spotted the *Bismarck* and *Prinz Eugen* off Bergen, on the southern coast of Norway, but the NID viewed the ships' movements at this point as nothing more than an administrative reorganization or a training run. Just as the picture was building, bad weather prevented further reconnaissance flights, leaving the OIC in the dark for the next 29 hours – until Bletchley Park came to the rescue. The cryptanalysts had dug up a series of out-of-date decrypts from April, and although the first messages did not reveal anything overt, on May 21, Bletchley Park sent the following message to the OIC: '*Bismarck* embarked five prize crews with necessary charts at the end of April and been carrying out practices in the Baltic with *Prinz Eugen*.'[11]

The Operational Intelligence Centre responded immediately: 'prize crews' used for manning captured merchant ships plus requests for charts of the North Atlantic could mean only one thing. It informed Admiral John Tovey, the Commander-in-Chief of the Home Fleet, that 'it is evident that these ships intend to carry out a raid on trade routes.'[12] With the original message so far in the past, Tovey initially regarded the OIC's interpretation with some suspicion, thinking that the *Bismarck* might be sortieing for a 'winner takes all' showdown with the British ships. However, based on the accumulating evidence, Tovey accepted the OIC's breakout theory. Now he was faced with another decision that Ultra could not answer: what route would the beast take?

Intelligence is seldom complete or 100 per cent certain; it generally requires a highly educated weighing of the odds. Tovey knew that Lütjens had several routes to choose from: he could cruise through the English Channel, or between the Faroe Islands and either Scotland or Iceland, or through the Denmark Strait. Although the odds heavily favoured a dash through the Denmark Strait, Tovey took no chances and spread his force out to intercept the *Bismarck* no matter what course she chose. In the process, he spread his line too thin, leaving HMS *Hood* and the battleship HMS *Prince of Wales*, along with a collection of cruisers, at the mercy of the *Bismarck*'s long-range fifteen-inch guns in the Denmark Strait. In less than ten minutes, the first round was over: the *Hood* disappeared in a giant explosion following a salvo from the *Bismarck*, taking the lives of all but three members of her crew of 1,418. The *Prince of Wales*, severely mauled, pulled back outside the range of the big guns. Immediately the Royal Navy ordered all battleships in the area to join the pursuit – and the race to sink the *Bismarck* began.

For more than a week, the Royal Navy's Home Fleet chased the pride of Hitler's fleet from the North Sea to the Bay of Biscay and hounded her back again towards the coast of France, using direction-finding (DF) apparatus to pick up a constant stream of radio messages from the hunted ship. The British had a real-time picture of where she was, but not of what she intended to do. The DF apparatus was at the mercy of the fickle nature of the ionosphere, and for a whole day, the pursuing fleet floundered along amid complete radio silence. Fortunately, the *Bismarck* resumed regular transmissions, which eventually betrayed her position again to the Operational Intelligence Centre. To identify the transmissions, the OIC called on its radio fingerprinting and traffic analysis experts. The fingerprinting group used a 'photograph' of the intercepted radio transmission to distinguish a unique pattern in radio waves produced not only by each transmitter but also specifically by each radio operator – a pattern as recognizable and unique as a human fingerprint. The traffic analysis group examined the characteristics of the method by which the wireless messages appeared. When both concluded that the messages indeed came from the *Bismarck*, plans went ahead to attack the majestic German warship with torpedo bombers.

The strike damaged the *Bismarck* badly enough to force her to forgo her raiding mission and head to port for repairs. But the analysts in the Operational Intelligence Centre were not privy to the extent of her damage, so had no idea what she would do next. Three courses of action seemed possible: Admiral Lütjens could steam to the west, hoping to fix the problem at sea; turn tail and head back through the Denmark Strait, making for a German port; or move south-east towards the French port of Brest or, better yet, St Nazaire – the only dry dock big enough to properly repair the ship. Soon, new direction-finding bearings indicated that the *Bismarck* was making for Brest. However, the signals quickly died as Lütjens shut down the wireless sets, leaving Admiral Tovey working from well-reasoned guesses until Bletchley intercepted a series of messages on the *Bismarck*'s predicament from land and air sources. They revealed preparations for her arrival and repair at St Nazaire.[13] Within minutes the OIC informed Tovey: 'Information received graded A1 that intention of *Bismarck* is to make for west coast of France.'[14]

With his hunch confirmed, Tovey confidently proceeded, using a combination of direction-finding, traffic analysis, radio fingerprinting and Ultra intelligence to move in for the kill. After a small but inconclusive encounter that allowed the *Prinz Eugen* to slip away ahead of the *Bismarck* and make for Brest, it took almost two full days to catch up with the giant battleship. Finally, on May 27, with the *Prinz Eugen* already in Brest for repairs, the Royal Navy put more than 400 shells and several torpedoes into the *Bismarck*.[15] Only when the ship had become a burning hulk did the order to abandon ship sound, followed by orders to scuttle the vessel. Quickly the battleship slipped beneath the surface with Lütjens, Lindemann and more than 2,000 of her 2,200 crew.[16]

The victory over the supposedly invincible *Bismarck* was a great relief to the Admiralty – one that also provided a massive and desperately needed propaganda coup to inject life back into the sagging morale of the British people. In the space of the following two months, the war at sea took a drastic turn in the Allies' favour as the Royal Navy's Home Fleet turned its attention to the battleship's many support vessels. During May, Bletchley Park provided the OIC with accurate locations for the 21 tankers, trawlers and ships that had been tasked with providing fuel, supplies and weather reports to the *Bismarck* and *Prinz Eugen*. That information allowed the British to attack the vessels in piecemeal fashion into the second week of July – and by the 11th they had sunk or captured fifteen of them. Unfortunately, popular history has focused exclusively on the dramatic hunt for the *Bismarck* and ignored this important epilogue to the battle.[17]

✎

In the North Atlantic, the 'Happy Time' for the U-boats also came to an abrupt end that spring, with the four top U-boat aces captured or killed in action. Until June 1941, except for a slight lull in early winter, German submarines had continued the deadly pace set the previous year. In May alone, U-boats had claimed 66 ships or 324,000 tons of British shipping in just one month, followed by another 65 and over 300,000 tons in June. But then their success dropped dramatically, to 21 ships and 61,000 tons in July and 32 ships totalling 81,000 tons in August. By the end of June, despite the rising numbers of U-boats operating in the Atlantic sea lanes, the submarines' proficiency in locating convoys suddenly vanished, with ships slipping past their patrol lines to arrive unmolested in British ports. More alarming for Admiral Karl Dönitz was the fact that only 49 British ships fell victim to his crews during the lean summer months of July and August. Meanwhile, by the autumn, sinkings of his own craft had risen at an alarming rate, with 35 U-boats gone by the end of the year, ten in December alone.

The change in fortune was, in large part, directly attributable to the new-found ability of the Operational Intelligence Centre to locate U-boats at sea and redirect vulnerable convoys away from potentially disastrous collisions – a move that saved more than 300 merchant vessels from the clutches of these deadly underwater predators.[18] It also provided the Admiralty with the 'tremendous advantage' of knowing 'continuously and in minute detail' how German naval authorities were reacting to the various anti-submarine weapons and operational tactics that the British were trying out.[19] All these developments had a considerable impact on Dönitz, eventually forcing him to pull his U-boat fleet out of the Atlantic to regroup.[20] Although the inexperience of his new crews and the growing demands of other theatres of battle such as the Baltic and the highly charged Mediterranean played a role, his decision to withdraw stemmed mainly from his crews' inability to find and sink merchant vessels.

The turnaround in British fortunes was stunning. It was explained in part by the sheer guts, determination and skill of the commanders and crews of Royal Navy and Royal Canadian Navy ships and aircraft. In practical terms, the success was the cumulative result of emerging strategy and doctrine, sound convoy organization, increased air support, and a greater number of escort forces, including destroyers and corvettes. Added to this mix were the development and improvement of new and existing anti-submarine technologies such as ASDIC (sonar), radar, and high-frequency direction finding (HF/DF or 'Huff-Duff'), all of which were used to track U-boats at close range above or below the surface.

Most significant of all, Special Intelligence had now exploded onto the scene. The cryptographic abilities of Bletchley Park, buttressed by the other forms of signals intelligence and by the deft work of the staff of the Operational Intelligence Centre in translating all this information into focused activity, had led to unparalleled success on the high seas by the middle of 1941 – something that Ian Fleming and John Godfrey in NID, not to mention Alan Turing, Peter Twinn and Frank Birch at Bletchley Park, could only have dreamed of after the postponement of Operation Ruthless in October 1940.

The cryptanalysts at Bletchley Park recognized that the dramatic success they were enjoying did not result, at this point, from any major technological breakthrough. Instead, it stemmed directly from the concerted efforts by the NID and Bletchley's Naval Section, backed by the Admiralty, to implement a uniform and systematic approach to pinching.

⸙

By the end of 1940, the British had acknowledged the crucial importance of pinched material to cryptographic breakthroughs. Theoretically, there was no limit to the complexity possible in cryptography: with every alteration, tweak or fundamental change in the messaging sys-tems, the cryptanalysts' difficulties increased, and their chances of breaking into the codes by analytical means dropped further. The only way they could make progress was through a steady supply of pinched Enigma machines or parts and the supporting codebooks and setting sheets. Fortunately, because the German navy relied heavily on radio communications to coordinate its actions, equipment of all kinds was widely distributed onshore and to U-boats and ships of all classes at sea, making it vulnerable to seizure and exploitation so long as it could be stolen without the Germans catching on.[21]

For years after the war, the only information historians had about pinch raids came from anecdotal evidence or from the limited number of after-action reports written by a few participants in pinch operations. Documents related to the pinch policy and doctrine – the framework or 'playbook' for carrying out these operations – remained classified until 2014, and establish just how the British planned to carry out these operations. Following the 'tentative and crude' attempts in 1940, by early 1941 'the dire need of a pinch had been well and truly chimed into every authority responsible for operations' and a clear and distinct pinch policy had begun to emerge, which, as the year wore on, proved 'well-informed and practical.'[22] After that, the British spared no effort in developing their pinch doctrine whenever the opportunity arose.[23]

Pinch operations were divided into categories – by chance, by opportunity and by design – reflecting a more mature and systematic approach than previously suggested. The first type, 'pinch by chance,' involved the incidental capture of enemy intelligence material during the course of an unrelated action. As the Admiralty gained more experi-ence with these opportunities, it published a series of general advisories in the form of a Confidential Admiralty Fleet Order (CAFO), laying out the ground rules for British crews, whether boarding parties or raiders, to follow so they could exploit chance discoveries as they arose and cover their accomplishments with plausible excuses or security measures.

These advisories had two objectives: to create a general aware-ness among the crews of the importance of this material within the context of the overall war effort, and to make clear the vital need for crews not only to capture the materials but to bring them safely home, protecting them from overzealous boarding parties bent on looting or ransacking vessels (as had occurred on one ship, the *Polaris*, in early 1940). These orders included detailed photographs and diagrams to assist boarding parties in their tasks, with suggestions about possible locations where they might find what they were after on a particular vessel. The orders also gave strict instructions for the safe delivery of the Enigma machine, if one was captured, and its ancillary codebooks and setting sheets into British hands. The Enigma machine 'should be carefully packed and forwarded to the Director of Naval Intelligence [John Godfrey, in London] ... by the quickest possible route' under officer guard and 'should not be touched or disturbed in any way, except as necessary for its removal and packing.'[24] The second category, 'pinch by opportunity,' called for quick planning when a particularly attractive target or set of targets came into reach as the result of a planned operation on sea or land. Usually, that meant piggybacking the pinch onto an existing operation or one in the planning stages, allowing the size and scope of the operation to provide both the delivery vehicle and the security cover for the pinch.

In the third category, 'pinch by design,' the pinch itself formed the imperative or main driver for the entire mission. In other words, the pinch was not merely the passenger carriage hitched to the locomotive for the ride – it was either one of the locomotives or the only locomotive pulling the train. In this case, to ensure surprise and cover, a much larger operation was built up around the pinch to conceal the truth, which falls precisely into line with the proviso in the report operations of 30 AU that prompted this reinvestigation.[25]

The essential precursors to any successful pinch operation, whether by opportunity or by design, lay in surprise, shock and security. As soon as the first contact was made, the clock began to tick in a race against time between the force attempting to pinch the material and the defenders bent on destroying whatever sensitive equipment and paperwork they possessed. To reduce the German defenders' chances of success, the British plans instructed the raiders to appear suddenly, seemingly out of nowhere, to close in at top speed, and to employ heavy firepower either to kill the defenders or to create enough confusion so they could be overwhelmed before they destroyed anything of value. In this respect, the British hoped to exploit what they interpreted as the 'cultural characteristics' of their German enemy. As one pinch policy observer noted: 'Theirs is the normal occidental attitude, personal safety first. Hence, under surprise attack, only a certain amount of classified material is destroyed, only as much as can be accomplished without endangering the individual responsible.'[26]

For reasons of security, the raiders had to cover the true intent of the mission and any success they might achieve. The Germans must never be able to discern their genuine intention to capture vital cryptographic materials whether by design or opportunity. So John Godfrey's Naval Intelligence Division designed pinch operations that took advantage of Churchill's 'steam-hammer to crack a nut' approach, where the pinch would be cloaked with disproportionate efforts to shade the intent, passing it off as something much larger or more orthodox in nature.[27] In theory, this reasoning was sound: no enemy would ever suspect that the allocation of such large amounts of resources was merely a cover for a different purpose and most contact could be explained away as 'incidental.' And that disbelief was precisely what the British were counting on.

Because of the sensitive nature of all these pinch operations, responsibility remained firmly in the hands of Godfrey and his well-organized Naval Intelligence Division in London. But Bletchley Park's highly secret Naval Section, housed in both Huts 4 and 8, was designated to receive the captured enemy naval documents immediately after they arrived in England so the code-breakers there could put them to use. In some cases, Frank Birch, the director of the Naval Section, and members of his staff drafted and revised the Confidential Admiralty Fleet Orders or suggested possible targets for pinches.[28] One of the most gifted of the highly accomplished experts in the Naval Section was the young Cambridge history undergraduate Harry Hinsley, whose skills in interpreting decrypts and the other fruits of signals intelligence were unrivalled, as was his ability to sense that something was afoot from an accumulation of tiny clues.

In general, though, NID and the Admiralty held the reins for pinch operations as they controlled the resources needed to conceive, plan and execute a mission, with input from Bletchley's Naval Section secondary and responsive in nature. Other than noting what the experts in the Naval Section required, the NID was under no obligation to act on the methods suggested by Frank Birch to obtain the desired material. Together with Ian Fleming, who had a firm understanding of cryptography and a key role in Section 17 'to co-ordinate intelligence' and liaise between the NID and the other intelligence bodies, Godfrey could move ahead confidently to organize and launch pinch operations without the knowledge of the Naval Section.[29] To maintain that authority and channel Birch's increasing demands, Godfrey created an official liaison position with Bletchley Park to reinforce the direct link already handled by Fleming, who visited there regularly. Early in 1941, Godfrey posted several representatives from his NID to Bletchley; they were expected to find out precisely what the Naval Section and the cryptanalysts needed for their work, help plan the pinch operation, and physically go into action with the attacking forces and bring the critical stolen material home.

∽

Very few people have heard of, let alone ventured to, the Lofoten Islands – a tiny snow-swept archipelago just inside the Arctic Circle off the coast of northern Norway. On March 4, 1941, 500 of the newly formed British commandos, supported by 52 Norwegian Marines and a section of Royal Engineers, swept ashore from Royal Navy landing ships as part of Operation Claymore. In a matter of hours they had captured more than 200 German prisoners and destroyed fifteen fisheries-related factories as well as a bunker crude-storage facility. In the process, they also sank ten German trawlers and captured one, the *Krebs*. Not only were these results good for public relations, but they also provided the Naval Section with a landmark pinch – the first since it had put the Operation Ruthless and the *Bernhard Von Tschirschky* pinches on permanent hold.

As Birch noted, 'by the beginning of 1941 ... the dire need of a pinch had been well and truly dinned into every authority responsible for operations ... when the first Lofoten raid was planned ... it was realized that useful SIGINT material might be pinched under cover of such an operation ... special efforts were made to this end.'[30] Indeed, the Lofoten Islands presented a chance for Combined Operations Headquarters – another Churchill creation – to conduct its first sizeable amphibious raid of the war.

Established in the summer of 1940 during the final days of the war in France, Combined Operations had yet to make much of a splash, having engaged so far in only a few pinprick raids of little or no consequence on the French Channel coast. Exasperated with this lack of aggressiveness on the part of its original commander, General Alan Bourne, a career Royal Marine, Churchill pressed for larger and bolder attacks. He replaced the cynical Bourne with Admiral Sir Roger Keyes, the hero of the daring Zeebrugge Raid in 1918 during the First World War. Keyes appeared to be the man Churchill was looking for – someone who could establish a thoroughly aggressive raiding programme that would not only signal Britain's will to fight on alone but placate or channel what John Godfrey later called Churchill's appetite for 'wildcat' operations – such as the Gallipoli landings in the previous war.[31] The opportunistic Godfrey seized the chance to wed his pinch requirements to this enticing vehicle for raiding.

Under Keyes's command, Churchill ordered the creation of a 'band of brothers,' as he called them, a highly trained but lightly armed elite force designed for raiding enemy shore facilities in amphibious operations. They were known as commandos – a name he pilfered from the Boer raiders he had witnessed during his time in South Africa at the turn of the century. Drawn at this point from army volunteers, the commandos – forerunners of today's Special Operations and other elite units – planned to make their combat debut at Lofoten.

The squadron of five destroyers and two landing ships crowded with commandos managed to sail the roughly 800 miles from Scapa Flow in the Orkney Islands undetected by the Germans. Code-named 'Rebel,' this task force arrived at its destination at dawn on March 4 in a surprise attack. Quickly, both commando units were able to land and take their objectives with little or no enemy resistance, grabbing prisoners with ease. At sea, the *Krebs*, a German trawler outfitted for harbour defence, put up a short fight, but the Tribal-class destroyer HMS *Somali* knocked her out, running her aground and killing her captain in the process.

When the boarding party arrived, however, they discovered that the captain had tossed the Enigma machine overboard seconds before his death – but had left other 'valuable cypher material' in place, which was seized by the commandos.[32]

It was this haul of pinched material that allowed Bletchley Park, after almost a year in the dark, to read Enigma-enciphered messages on the *Dolphin* key (the primary Kriegsmarine naval key used by all vessels other than U-boats) for February and April. In addition, the information Turing gleaned from the material enabled him to reconstruct the current bigram tables – a breakthrough that eventually helped Bletchley Park unlock the naval Enigma code.[33] As Birch crowed: 'Nothing succeeds like success. For one thing, Hut 8, fortified with these data, managed to break cryptanalytically the whole of the April traffic and all May except for the first six days though none of it currently. For another, the flood of Special Intelligence released by this capture encouraged the Admiralty to make further attempts and provide detailed information as to how they could best be directed.'[34]

Right from the start, the planners of Operation Claymore made the capture of seemingly innocent German trawlers their prime objective, as the evidence obtained through traffic analysis and radio fingerprinting indicated that these vessels either used the Enigma machine in their work or maintained other material that Bletchley could use for cribs.[35] On that basis, Claymore was 'planned with this end in view,' with Churchill fully aware of the pinch imperative at the core of the operation, while other objectives found a seat on the Combined Operations train leaving for the Lofoten Islands that provided the necessary cover for the pinch.[36]

For instance, two of Churchill's other pet projects were both part of Ian Fleming's liaison portfolio in NID and made their debuts in Operation Claymore. The first project, the highly secretive Special Operations Executive (SOE), which was sometimes called Churchill's Secret Army or the Ministry of Ungentlemanly Warfare, had been formed in July 1940 by amalgamating various sections from the Foreign Office, the War Office and the Secret Intelligence Service. It was explicitly established to coordinate subversion and sabotage against the enemy in Europe and in countries occupied by Germany.

The express purpose of the second project, the clandestine Political Warfare Executive (PWE), established in August 1941 and reporting to the Foreign Office, was to attack the economic heart of Nazi Germany by direct means or by radio or print propaganda designed to lower morale. Because the Lofoten Islands had several small fisheries and large oil-storage tanks for fish oils and bunker crude, they naturally caught the interest of the PWE. As for the SOE, Lofoten also offered an opportunity to score propaganda points by demonstrating the organization's destructive capabilities in a grand fashion while rounding up quislings (Norwegian collaborators with the German occupiers), providing weapons to the local resistance and fulfilling Churchill's cry to 'set Europe ablaze.'

The NID also hoped to score a propaganda triumph from the Lofoten raid. Fleming was responsible for public relations too, and once again he had full support from Godfrey – perhaps the only high-ranking Royal Navy officer to grasp the need for a cooperative press. Godfrey, sometimes accompanied by Fleming, regularly called on editors from most of the London papers, just as he had from the time he was appointed Director of Naval Intelligence in early 1939. In addition, he held weekly conferences at the Admiralty for naval correspondents, designed to draw them in as unofficial members of the NID team.[37] According to Godfrey, the newspapers generally 'played the game,' led along with titbits of specially fed 'off the record' information that they used in formulating their background material. The journalists soon learned not to question too closely what they were told.[38]

With their ability to dictate when and where they would launch these raids, the NID had the luxury of constructing its public relations lines well in advance of any operation – a crucial element not only in striking a blow in the propaganda war but also in covering each pinch. With the ability to 'spin' events in their official communiqués following a victory, defeat or any other outcome, Godfrey, Fleming and their cohorts provided carefully crafted versions of events which satisfied the contemporary press and permeated post-war historical accounts as well, ensuring that the documents classified as Ultra Secret remained just that, even decades after the guns fell silent. In the case of Lofoten, the communiqués, reported almost verbatim, featured the military and other intelligence objectives, except for anything to do with the pinch. By offering explicit confirmation of the sinking of all the enemy ships the raiders encountered, they allayed, or at least reduced, German suspicions of the capture and compromise of their precious communications gear.[39]

Although the planners drew many valid conclusions from the Lofoten operation of March 1941, the main lesson was something that remained hidden to the public for 70 years. Emerging in the aftermath of Claymore was a nascent brand of special operations warfare – a template for properly organized pinch raids that whetted the appetites of both the Naval Intelligence Division and the Naval Section at Bletchley Park for a repeat performance. A series of operations materialized starting in May, just a few weeks before the *Bismarck* made her fateful breakout into the North Atlantic.

෴

As in the Lofoten raid, trawlers and minor ships became the focus of the next pinch operation, for several reasons. First, from what he could deduce from traffic analysis, the gifted Harry Hinsley noted that the small vessels, mainly weather-reporting ships, employed a series of codes and ciphers and, at times, the Enigma machine. The odds were therefore extremely high that these lightly armed and thoroughly vulnerable ships could deliver the materials that the experts at Bletchley Park required; moreover, isolated as they were, they would prove easier to capture. Second, the weather-reporting ships operated alone and in remote areas of the ocean, far from prying eyes onshore or above – a decided advantage compared with the Lofoten Islands and other harbours where small ships worked as part of a group of vessels or a flotilla.

Because these seemingly insignificant vessels did not present an obvious target, capturing them ran a distinctly lower risk, at least initially, of raising suspicion in Admiral Dönitz's headquarters than an intentional, or even unintentional, capture of one of his U-boats. In an impressive piece of signals intelligence sleuthing drawn from inferences in wireless transmissions and the material captured from the *Krebs*, Hinsley put together a detailed 'hit list' of target weather ships, providing both their potential hauls and their suspected operational locations.[40]

The first in this series of operations, the oddly named Operation EB, went into effect on May 7, with unprecedented support. To effect the pinch, the Admiralty allocated three cruisers (HMS *Edinburgh*, *Manchester* and *Birmingham*) and four destroyers (HMS *Somali*, *Eskimo*, *Bedouin* and *Nestor*) from Admiral John Tovey's Home Fleet, putting them on hold and ready to move at a week's notice. The scale of this preparation testifies to the utmost importance of the raid, given that these precious assets, particularly the destroyers, were in high demand for anti-submarine patrols with the U-boat war at its most intense. In addition, with Godfrey's formalization of the pipeline between his NID and Bletchley's Naval Section, Captain Jasper Haines, RN, became the first liaison officer to work at Bletchley Park specifically for pinch purposes. A striking figure with movie-star looks and silver hair, Haines stood out in the bleak surroundings of the huts and attracted attention from the many young women who worked there. His job was to cull information about specific needs and then go into action with the pinch forces to retrieve what was required and escort it back to London – a risky proposition should he be captured, given his intimate knowledge of Bletchley Park and the cryptographic effort.[41]

Before Operation EB began, Haines briefed the force commanders (cruiser squadron commander Vice Admiral Lancelot Holland and his destroyer captains) on the requirements of the mission – clear proof of the significance of the pinch and the increasing power and influence of Naval Intelligence in such matters. Holland, who would soon lose his life during the battle with the *Bismarck*, listened intently while Haines explained that he would accompany the raiding force and personally deliver any pinched material directly back to London. He emphasized that 'drastic action was important on first sighting to induce the enemy to abandon ship in a panic and ... fail to destroy as much as they otherwise might.'[42] Although the cruisers had floatplanes for reconnaissance, Haines had them grounded. He knew that the sight of a search plane would give away the presence of the strike force and lead the crew to dispose of the invaluable signals material. Surprise, followed by what we would now call 'shock and awe,' proved the key to success.

By 1500 hours on Wednesday, May 7, the ships were on station just inside the Arctic Circle, actively searching for the German weather-reporting ship *München*. At 1707 they sighted the tiny trawler between *Somali* and *Edinburgh*. Quickly, *Somali* opened fire at long distance to frighten the trawler crew and then proceeded at a full 36 knots towards its prey in 'sledgehammer' fashion, with *Edinburgh* carrying Haines on board, following. The tactic of rushing headlong with all guns blazing partially worked, but the trawler's crew still managed to dispose of the Enigma machine and most of its signals material and to fire off a message to their headquarters that they were under attack. By the time Haines arrived on the stricken vessel, the boarding party had seized and bagged what remained of the code and cipher material and had brought the surviving crew on board as prisoners. Later, in the privacy of a wardroom on the *Edinburgh*, he found 'interesting documents ... in the spoil' – the Enigma keys for June and the short-signal book (for messages of fewer than 22 characters) used by submarines, weather ships and other small vessels in certain circumstances.[43] Immediately he photographed the material and, once he returned to Scapa Flow, had the originals flown straight to Godfrey at the Admiralty, who then sent them on to Birch at Bletchley Park, fulfilling the DNI's promise that the cryptanalyst 'can literally not have too much.'[44]

To cover the pinch, particularly as the *München* had got off a signal before she was boarded, Haines sent a Hush Most Secret message to the Admiralty about his imminent return with an 'important' document.[45] He suggested that a press announcement be released mentioning that the *München*, now in tow, had actually been scuttled by her crew and not captured. Promptly, the story appeared, reporting in great detail the sinking of the ship and, to alleviate German suspicion, portraying the action as strictly incidental, which had the desired effect. 'These suspicions,' writes Birch, 'were forestalled by an Admiralty communiqué announcing the scuttling' of the ship '<u>before our forces were able to board</u>.'[46]* The Kriegsmarine seems not to have suspected any compromise of their cipher material, and the *München* remained hidden in Scapa Flow until the end of the war.[47] Before Haines reached British

---

* Underlining in the original.

shores, however, another pinch, this one a classic 'pinch by chance,' occurred in the North Atlantic – and it propelled the code-breakers' penetration of the German naval Enigma to unprecedented levels.

෧෨

For more than a year, not one scrap of paper bearing on the Enigma problem had fallen into British hands, yet within days of the seizure of the *München*, the British destroyers HMS *Bulldog* and HMS *Broadway*, along with the corvette HMS *Aubretia*, captured submarine *U-110* after it engaged a convoy off Iceland on May 9.[48] The U-boat, commanded by Captain-Lieutenant Fritz-Julius Lemp, the ace who had sunk the *Athenia* while captaining *U-30* in the opening hours of the war, gave up what Bletchley Park would come to consider the 'richest prize' so far. After three days of almost constant depth-charge attacks, Lemp ordered the submarine to surface and its crew to abandon ship.[49]

Fearing that the Germans had set scuttling charges on a timed fuse and racing against time to reach the submarine before it exploded, a boarding party led by Sub-Lieutenant David Balme from *Bulldog* paddled quickly in a launch under the watchful eye of cameras that caught the extraordinary events as they unfolded. Once on board, Balme entered the vessel through its conning tower and slipped into its control room, 'abandoned in great haste,' he recalled, 'as books and gear were strewn about the place.' The signals room, in contrast to the rest of the ship, was in 'perfect condition,' with no signs of destruction. Here he found signals books, logbooks and correspondence – and, sitting on the desk, the Enigma machine, still plugged in, as though it had been in use when abandoned. Quickly, Balme organized a human chain and took every book, chart and scrap of paper, along with the Enigma machine, from the vessel, moving it one armful at a time up the conning-tower ladder to the waiting launch. Only when the whole dangerous job was completed did Balme return triumphantly to *Bulldog*, where he reported the find while the destroyer took *U-110* in tow as a cherished prize.[50]

That night a delighted First Sea Lord Admiral Dudley Pound fired off a congratulatory signal to the Captain of *Bulldog*, offering his 'Hearty congratulations,' and noting that 'the petals of your flower are of rare beauty.'[51] To provide cover for this most impressive haul, Godfrey instructed the crew of *Bulldog* to maintain utmost secrecy and to refer to *U-110* hereafter by the code name 'Primrose' following public reports of its 'sinking.'[52] The next day, under circumstances that remain mysterious, reports claim that *Bulldog* cut loose the floundering submarine which subsequently sank 185 miles south-east of Greenland. The attributed cause came down to either a combination of heavy seas and the damage sustained in the earlier fight or a direct order from Godfrey to scuttle the vessel to avoid accidental detection by German reconnaissance aircraft.[53]

When *Bulldog* arrived in England, a Naval Intelligence officer met the ship and whisked the pinched machine and documents by air to the Naval Section at Bletchley Park.[54] The materials stolen from the *München* and the *U-110* only days apart provided the answer to Bletchley's prayers. As a result of this recent flurry of captures, the cryptanalysts could now read naval Enigma messages on the *Dolphin* key in real time for June and, even more critically, they possessed a copy of the special *Offizier* codebook – a key to the most secret information circulated to U-boat commanders, such as notifications of upcoming changes in key and encryption systems.

∽

The overwhelming joy and relief unleashed in the Naval Section by the twin pinches, and later the sinking of the *Bismarck*, proved short-lived: on June 15, the Germans issued new bigram tables. Foreseen as a distinct possibility, this development prompted the Naval Intelligence Division to launch a repetition of the *München* pinch.[55] Again Harry Hinsley's targeted trawlers played the starring role, with the *Lauenburg*, one of ten weather trawlers that ploughed the Atlantic in support of the *Bismarck*, the intended victim. In an almost carbon-copy replay of the earlier pinch, a task force of two cruisers and three destroyers was specifically laid on for this operation, briefed by Lieutenant Commander Allon Bacon, who worked with Fleming in Section 17. As handsome as Captain Jasper Haines, the 38-year-old Bacon, 'rangy, dark-haired, round-faced,' who before the war had worked in London's financial sector and for the Foreign Office on signals intelligence assignments, had been recruited into the NID for his intellect and resourcefulness, both of which would be called upon in the upcoming operation.[56]

Once aboard HMS *Jupiter* for the mission, Bacon inspected his boarding party, outfitted like privateers of old with cutlasses and axes, along with their modern sub-machine guns. The intermittent fog and rain presented perfect conditions, cloaking the progress of the raiding force towards the trawler and maximizing the chance of surprise. After a series of icebergs set off false alarms, the crew finally spotted their quarry in the distance.[57]

Jupiter immediately increased to flank speed and headed straight for the trawler. It opened fire with the main armament, intending to frighten rather than kill the crew.[58] The men quickly abandoned ship without destroying their communications material; the boarding party entered and grabbed what they were looking for, then sank the vessel to cover their tracks.[59]

The excitement of this pinch not only reverberated within the walls of the Naval Section, the OIC, Room 39 and the Admiralty but echoed right across the British intelligence landscape. Guy Liddell, the head of MI5 charged with counterintelligence operations, was ecstatic upon learning of the capture, confiding in his diary: 'A trawler has been intercepted somewhere in the vicinity of Iceland. It has been brought in with its crew, and it is reported that it has onboard an Enigma cipher. A notification has been made to the press that the trawler was sunk but that members of the crew were saved.'[60]

Once again, as Liddell recorded, the press played a role in covering the pinch, with a banner headline reading: 'Depression off Iceland for 22 Germans.' The news report stated that in the course of a 'periodical sweep' to the north of Iceland, 'our forces sank a German weather reporting trawler, capturing her crew of 22.'[61]

This pinch allowed the cryptanalysts at Bletchley Park to continue to read the naval Enigma traffic after the expiration of the key sheets captured for June and July. In terms of breaking the three-rotor Enigma code, the pinches provided Alan Turing with the 'cheats' necessary to mine for the current operational gold and with 'cribs' for the increasing number of Bombes being used in the Naval Section's investigations. By July 1941, Naval Section could boast that all first-class naval ciphers, short signals for U-boats and weather codes were 'readable' and that 'great progress' had been made on Gemini codes for raiders and the Reserve Hand Cipher used in emergencies and known as RHV.[62]

As the year went on, the experts employed anything that might give Bletchley a break, even through the back door, into Enigma: weather codes, short-signal codes, the restricted *Offizier* and *Stab* ciphers, the German dockyard cipher, RHV, and Long-E bars. In fact, the cumulative success of the pinches provided the basis for an almost daily penetration of the *Dolphin* key for the remainder of the war.

Frank Birch considered the *Lauenburg* pinch the 'masterpiece of cooperation between Naval Section and the Navy.'[63] Along with the other operations, it showed just how far the Naval Intelligence Division had progressed in the twelve months since Operation Ruthless – and how integral these operations had become to both the cryptographic war and the war at sea.

༜

The sudden change in British fortunes against the deadly U-boats in the summer and autumn of 1941 did not go unnoticed in higher quarters. In September, Winston Churchill paid his only visit to Bletchley Park to survey the inner workings of the 'intelligence factory' that provided his golden eggs. He was already thoroughly addicted to Bletchley's end products. Ultra was unique and offered him a direct line to something that nobody else had: a finger on the pulse of the enemy war effort. It was an intoxicating power that the micromanager in him could not resist.

As First Lord of the Admiralty, he had enjoyed access on-demand to all the naval Ultra. 'Shortly before he became Prime Minister,' Godfrey remembered, 'I had some piece of information to impart and was asked by his private office to go to Mr. Churchill's bedroom in Admiralty House. He was sitting up, freshly shaved, in an enormous double bed smoking a cigar and surrounded by his morning's correspondence, dispatch boxes, papers, breakfast, a bottle of white wine, coffee, cigars.'[64] By the time he became prime minister and the highest authority in the land, he received a daily delivery of all forms of Ultra (not just naval) direct from the head of the Secret Intelligence Service, Stewart Menzies

– the man called 'C' – who was responsible for the overall production of this rare commodity. Each morning a locked red security box, marked 'Only to be opened by the Prime Minister,' would arrive containing the Ultra that kept Churchill thoroughly engrossed for hours on end. It is not surprising, then, that on his congratulatory visit to Bletchley Park, when he was confronted by demands for additional funding for the projects there, he responded with a 'prayer,' or decree, stamped *Action This Day*. It ordered full and unending financial support for Bletchley and its parent organization, the Government Code and Cypher School (GC&CS).[65]

But with that came control and constraint on the users, producers and anyone involved with the process of decrypting naval Enigma. Following the overwhelming success of the pinches, Churchill took it upon himself to issue updated rules and regulations for Ultra. In what was now a field that was growing exponentially, he instructed Admiral Dudley Pound to take action. On June 13, 1941, Pound issued a Special Admiralty Memorandum, which reinforced the rules of the game and announced his 'in the know book' – a register used to log all members of the Royal Navy indoctrinated into Ultra. As the First Sea Lord wrote:

The Prime Minister and Minister of Defence* are confident that you will appreciate the supreme importance of preserving our most secret sources of information. This might well determine the result of the war.

If full use is to be made of information of an operational character received through these sources, it must often be passed to a fairly large number of officers. But the most stringent orders are necessary to secure that the smallest number of officers, compatible with efficiency, are made aware of the secret source of this information.

It is, therefore, essential to impress upon all personnel who deal with information derived from secret sources, the personal responsibilities of each one of them in this matter. It must be brought home to each officer concerned that he must never discuss the origin of

---

* Winston Churchill held both posts simultaneously during the war.

most secret information and that it is incumbent upon him to assist in preventing any possible leakage in regard to vital channels.

Special attention is called to the provisions of the Official Secrets Act 1911 and 1920. Among other things, it is an offence under these acts for any person to disclose, otherwise than to an authorized person or in the course of his duty, any matter of information which is obtained or to which he has access going to his official position. This covers disclosures in any form, whether verbally or in writing or by publication in the press or in book form, and applies to all persons employed in the service of the Crown, not only during the period of service but also after that employment has ceased.

For purposes of security and record, it is necessary to request officers to whom the above is shown to sign this book in acknowledgement that they have read and understood the implications and instructions contained in the foregoing and of their intention to carry out its provisions.[66]

In stark contrast to Churchill, Admiral Dönitz had no idea of the depth, size and scope of the British cryptanalytic effort; still, he remained alive to the fact that successful cryptographic penetration would occur periodically.

In late April of 1941, in the wake of the first Lofoten pinch, the head of Hitler's U-boat fleet began to fear the compromise of his communication security when it appeared that Allied convoys had begun to sidestep his submarines 'according to plan.'[67] As he noted in his war diary on April 18, 'our attack areas are known to the enemy in some way or other.'[68]

When the 'First Happy Time' for his U-boats came to an abrupt end and a series of curious events at sea began in the late spring and early summer, Dönitz's anxiety began to heighten. Although the sinking of the *Bismarck* in late May did not immediately raise concerns about cipher security, the sudden disappearance or sinking of fifteen of her support vessels between May 7 and July 11 did. During this period, *B-Dienst* (*Beobachtungsdienst*) – the Kriegsmarine's SIGINT service – took note of the emerging pattern caused by the 'feeding frenzy' of pinch operations that came at the behest of Godfrey and was underscored by the detailed intelligence supplied by Harry Hinsley and Frank Birch at Bletchley.

Indeed, as with their German counterparts, the overzealous nature of these operations did not go unnoticed in the Admiralty either. Sensing that John Godfrey, who had quickly gained a reputation for 'bold' action, had planned to push the envelope even further, First Sea Lord Dudley Pound felt compelled to intervene personally.[69] Worried that the bloated hit list would constitute a 'grave risk' to security, Pound ordered two of the remaining eight targeted vessels (*Gedania* and *Genzenheim*) to be struck from the list to lessen the odds of drawing German attention. As it turned out, no amount of precaution could offset a stroke of bad luck, and as Birch noted, Naval Section quickly learned 'the lesson that chance might play ... in wrecking any scheme of security.'[70]

On June 4, HMS *Marsdale* and HMS *Nelson*, moving independently, stumbled across the *Gedania* and *Genzenheim* in the course of normal operations, which resulted in the capture of the former and the scuttling of the latter.[71] Three days later, on June 7, two more supply ships from Hinsley's list fell victim to the Royal Navy in preordained pinch operations. The cumulative effect of these events set off alarm bells within the Kriegsmarine as well as NID and Bletchley. Although NID attempted to deflect lingering suspicion by passing off each encounter at sea as 'incidental,' *B-Dienst* reported to Dönitz's headquarters that something seemed amiss. Later that day, the Kriegsmarine's communications service (*Seekriegleitung* or SKL) launched the first major investigation into the security of the three-rotor naval Enigma and its high-grade cipher.[72]

The Kriegsmarine inquiry, which lasted throughout the summer, considered a wide range of possibilities, including insecurity of the naval ciphers against cryptanalysis, loss, betrayal, treason, espionage, loss of operational orders and similar papers, and the failure to observe proper wireless security procedures as part of the mix.[73]

Likewise, they tested the theory that cipher documents from one of the ships had fallen into enemy hands but rejected this notion almost immediately. In their estimation, a boarding party could hardly surprise a German ship so completely that its crew would not have time to douse at least some cipher documents in water.[74]

According to the report, the investigators reached this conclusion after 'very extensive tests' which showed that penetration of three-rotor naval Enigma ciphers without access to a complete set of cipher documents was 'unanimously regarded as impossible by all (German) cryptanalysts.'[75] In this case, betrayal of documents, although 'improbable,' was a more likely candidate than a successful cryptographic attack. Although the investigators firmly discounted a cipher break, they could not explain the repeated Allied successes that unfolded in such a short time frame (and in three different areas of the North Atlantic) without the aid of some sort of 'special circumstances.'[76] Nevertheless, the report offered 'no tangible positive explanation' and suggested that Allied success stemmed from a marked improvement in Allied direction finding and radar, coupled with improper signalling procedures employed by U-boat crews.[77] Reading the document following its capture at war's end, Frank Birch could only shake his head at the 'air of postponement' that guided 'the entire memorandum.'[78]

Part of this foot-dragging stemmed from the reality of bureaucratic limitations. The relatively uncomplicated use of the naval Enigma machine, coupled with its wide distribution, meant that any attempt to replace it would constitute a massive undertaking with enormous financial outlay, delays and the headaches associated with large-scale retooling.[79]

Another reason was the pride and rivalry within the various Kriegsmarine communication departments. As Birch recalled, 'Personal prejudice was against the acceptance of the possibility of successful cryptanalysis, and the reputation of German intelligence seems to have been staked on providing the inviolability of German cyphers.'[80] Fuelled by German cryptographers and communications specialists who wed their reputations to the success or failure of their ciphers and cryptographic devices, a cult-like dogma developed that created an impenetrable blind spot surrounding the invulnerability of the naval Enigma system.[81] When alarms sounded, the search for the causes of any lack of security bypassed this cryptographic clique, as the notion of systematic cryptanalytical success was simply 'out of the question.'[82] Nothing, it appeared, could shake the '*idée fixe*' that underwrote the entire intellectual approach to the problem. At no time did the

Germans fathom (let alone articulate) that their British counterparts were capable of converting pinched material into a consistent cryptanalytic attack; still less did they consider the conception and creation of a device like the Bombe to speed up and maintain the process.[83] As such, Dönitz's suspicion, entirely justified by the circumstantial evidence, smacked headlong into an internal 'wall of fixed opinions' within German naval communications that 'protected against the thrusts of suspicion from without.'[84]

No doubt frustrated, Dönitz reluctantly accepted the report's expedient conclusions, attributing recent Allied successes to the 'far-reaching location apparatus of some unknown design.'[85] Far from assured, the U-boat Admiral unilaterally embarked on a series of incremental measures designed to tighten security in the summer months. First, he severely restricted access to information regarding U-boat situation reports, denying them to Gruppe West, responsible for operations in France, as well as Luftwaffe units operating in the Atlantic and the Italian naval liaison officer stationed at Bordeaux. Then he introduced the '*Stichwort*' system, an additive to the daily key to be used by U-boat commanders (or their senior communications officers) when they feared cipher compromise; and finally, on June 16 (the day after the new bigram tables came into effect), he introduced a new system of reference points for disguising U-boat position assignments.[86]

Nevertheless, by late August, Dönitz's fortunes had failed to change. His U-boat patrol lines had continued to come up empty, which obliged their relocation to the Greenland Operational Area. Here, he thickened up his force, expecting that 'more eyes' would increase results, but alas, they did not. Then on August 27, when *U-570* disappeared off Iceland after reporting that she was under attack by British aircraft and surface vessels, his disquiet returned full bore.[87]

Although Dönitz had no clue that a Royal Navy boarding party had entered the submarine and pinched the remains of a destroyed cipher table and the lid of a smashed Enigma machine as part of its haul, the submarine's disappearance (coupled with the general trend of futility) led him to note by mid-September that 'the enemy has obtained information concerning the areas of these lines through sources or methods not yet known to us.'[88] Yet again, circumstance demanded another inquiry. Once again, his security advisers assured him that even if the British had managed to break into the *Dolphin* cipher using captured material, their success would only be temporary; citing that the odds against permanently subverting the machine were astronomical.[89] Unconvinced and frustrated, Dönitz managed to wrestle one concession – the creation of a separate key, apart from *Dolphin*, for his U-boats. *Triton*, as he called it – the British code-named it *Shark* – came into effect on October 3, 1941, following yet another alarming incident.

On the night of September 27 and 28, *U-67* and *U-68* arrived in Tarrafal Bay in the Cape Verde islands for a replenishment rendezvous with *U-111*, only to find His Majesty's Submarine *Clyde* (directed there by Godfrey after Bletchley intercepted the rendezvous orders) lying in wait. Following a wild melee, the U-boats escaped, but the incident left Dönitz convinced that this encounter had not come by chance, noting: 'Either our cypher data have been compromised, or ... there is treason at work.'[90] Once again, the investigation toed the party line, with Admiral Eberhard Maertens, the head of the Naval Communications Service, concluding that there remained no reason for concern. After all, if the British did manage to breach the cipher, his U-boats now had the *Stichwort* system to fall back on. As the GC&CS history makes clear, with a tone of astonishment: 'the Communications Service did not apparently appreciate that a hypothetical temporary cryptographic success resulting from the capture of cipher material might set off a hypothetical continuous cryptanalytical success, which required something more than a "Stichwort" to counter.'[91]

In the first week of December, Dönitz's frustration came to a head with two more suspicious ambushes on the high seas and the continuing impotence of his U-boat patrol lines that now stretched into its eighth month.[92] 'Accident does not fall on the same side every time,' he wrote, adding: 'the British receive knowledge of our concentrated dispositions from some source or other and evade them, and in so doing they occasionally pass before the periscopes of single U-boats which are proceeding independently.'[93] Still, the question remained how?

Frustrated with the lack of progress, Dönitz refused to wait any longer and moved forward with a plan to launch a new weapon, long in preparation, into the cryptographic war. As Naval Section had discovered with the capture of *U-570* at the end of August, this change was well in train by the end of summer and picking up steam as 1942 loomed. What appeared at first nothing more than a large mound of debris retrieved from the bowels of the sub turned out to contain part of the smashed lid of the U-boat's Enigma, its brown-washed label still affixed to the inside denoting manufacturer and type. Unlike the conventional three-rotor specimen that bore the stamp '*Schlüssel* M3,' this one possessed a sinister difference: '*Schlüssel* M4' and the serial number '3172.'[94] Immediately, NID and the cryptanalysts understood its watershed implications: an improved naval Enigma machine that employed four rotors and correspondingly four-rotor keys, had made its way aboard Dönitz's U-boats plying the Atlantic. This dramatic development now threatened to swing the balance of the war at sea back in favour of Hitler's fleet – an event that came as a profound shock to the British, but not at all as a surprise.

CHAPTER 5

Swimming With Sharks

Of course, as far as we are concerned here,
pinching is the best form of cryptography.
Nigel de Grey, Room 40 veteran
and deputy director of Bletchley Park

News that a four-rotor version of the Enigma machine existed did not catch the British by surprise.[1] Ten months earlier, in January 1941, John Godfrey had learned from a set of captured instructions for adapting the new machine to the M3 cipher that such a version existed, and had been distributed in small numbers as early as 1940 and perhaps even before the war. However, as the Bletchley Park history of Hut 8 notes, 'forewarned in this case was not forearmed.'[2]

The four-rotor's appeal was precisely that – an extra rotor that took the already astounding odds against decryption to an otherworldly 92 septillion to one without pinched material or the help of a then non-existent four-wheeled Bombe.[3] These astronomical odds made the four-rotor nearly 300 times more daunting than its predecessor, which rendered it impervious to penetration and led one cryptographic scholar to suggest that the scale of the challenge it posed to the Allies was greater than the number of atoms in the universe.[4]

To tackle this enormous task, the cryptanalysts at Bletchley attempted to harness the three-rotor Bombes to the problem but, as Hugh Alexander noted with dismay: 'The 3 wheel bombe was not adequate to deal with the 4 wheel Enigma' and would have 'taken 6 hours to run (one) Wheel Order' and to get through all 336, '24 hours' with '80 to 90 machines' all chugging away.[5] The cryptanalysts had pleaded in vain for the rapid development of specially engineered Bombes that could tackle the four-rotor, but failing to move swiftly on this threat when its existence was confirmed in early 1941 meant that delivery would only come in April 1943 – at the earliest – and even then the machine would require a steady diet of cribs and pinched material to operate in a timely and efficient manner.[6]

In the interim, pinching provided the only way to mitigate the issue, and recent declassifications indicate that this conundrum lay at the heart of the bold series of operations against *Bismarck*'s supply and refuelling vessels. At first blush, sweeping up 'fifteen enemy supply, weather reporting and merchant ships ... in just two months' appeared greedy and ill-informed, bordering on the reckless.[7] However, when additional evidence from early May suggested that the Germans were ramping up distribution of the new machine for use by their U-boat fleet and eventually their surface raiders too, the aggressive approach to pinch operations became easier to understand. Given the growing spectre of a return to an intelligence blackout and the threatened loss of this most precious intelligence weapon system, it made perfect sense to target vessels known to stockpile machines and material set for future distribution to an ocean-going fleet.

Of course the response to this came with Dönitz's incremental strengthening of his U-boat ciphers that eventually led to the abandonment of the *Dolphin* key for his submarines operating in the Atlantic in lieu of the *Triton*, which the cryptanalysts at Bletchley referred to simply as *Shark*. At first, the switch had Turing and the cryptographic team in Hut 8 baffled and fearing the worst, and they struggled frantically with the problem for several days until they discovered that this U-boat key worked on the three-rotor and not the new four-rotor machine. In the meantime, this primordial scare rocketed up the chain of command straight to Churchill, who was by now accustomed to his daily delivery of naval Ultra in the 'small red box' direct from Stewart Menzies at the Secret Intelligence Service.

Suddenly deprived of all U-boat message traffic from the Atlantic theatre, the centre of gravity for the western Allied war effort, Menzies wrote to Churchill immediately to explain the unfolding situation and to assure him that everything was indeed in hand. 'From the beginning of October, our difficulties have been increased by the Germans separating the U-boat ciphers from the Main Fleet traffic,' he told the prime minister. 'The latter should present no increased difficulties, but the U-boats present a separate problem which will have to be solved by our machines.'[8] When Menzies reported several days later that Turing had made inroads on the problem, Churchill responded with a measured and encouraging note: 'Give my compliments to those concerned.'[9] When confirmation of Turing's success using the dockyard cipher (*Werftschlüssel* or *Werft*) as the 'cheat' came a few hours later, the prime minister responded with a curt, one-word dispatch: 'Good.'[10]

By this time, Bletchley Park had mastered the use of cribs and existing Bombes to break into the three-rotor Enigma traffic – an approach Turing hoped would mitigate the four-rotor challenge should it appear.[11] First, however, his team would require the materials from which to crib. For months the cryptanalysts relied on the lower-level codes and ciphers to provide what they needed. RHV (short for *Reservehandverfahren*), for example, was an emergency hand cipher used by vessels as a back-up for the Enigma when it broke down, or by ships not yet outfitted with the machine.[12] E-bars, B-bars and WW (or *Wetterkurzschlüssel*), the weather code, were all 'short-signal' ciphers (specially formatted, re-enciphered messages) that gave German U-boats and ships a quick way to send brief but standard messages without staying on the air for too long, which would risk betraying their position to British direction finding, radio fingerprinting or traffic analysis.[13]

Other ciphers, such as the *Werft* dockyard cipher, touched on the activities of all vessels from the lowliest harbour dredger to U-boats, right up to the *Tirpitz* (the *Bismarck*'s sister ship) while operating in port, providing cribs and rounding out messages sent via the Enigma machines.[14] Used by all vessels of every class in the Kriegsmarine, these messages, seemingly of 'lesser' importance, contained information about damage to ships, building progress, and special orders for radio silence on certain occasions, making these ciphers a crucial band-aid solution during Enigma blackout periods.[15] During the blackouts, these formed the leading sources for the cryptanalysts when it came to U-boats, as mentions of them were a 'common occurrence' in this increasingly valuable cipher, particularly when it came to keeping tabs on the numbers of newly commissioned boats.[16]

Unfortunately for the cryptanalysts, every so often these codes and ciphers changed too, requiring further pinches. Using the latest *Werft* cipher to produce a steady flow of cribs, Naval Section was able to break into Enigma without a hiccup until the end of November 1941, when the Kriegsmarine introduced another new set of bigram tables for the Enigma. A month later, on December 17, they introduced a new version of the *Werft* cipher, leaving the cryptanalysts to play catch-up yet again.[17]

The great worry for Godfrey was the double-edged nature of pinch operations: they helped to solve the problem, but they also piqued German interest in their own security, making it progressively more challenging to maintain that success. As a result, NID had to approach the situation in a more guarded way. When Combined Operations Headquarters (now under the command of Lord Louis Mountbatten) approached both Section 1, the 'country section' of the NID that covered Scandinavia, and the Inter-Services Topographical Department to draw up targeting work-ups for a return raid to Norway, Godfrey pounced. At this juncture, COHQ provided the only vehicle capable of taking the fight to the enemy which could bring targets most desired for pinch purposes into view. As NID had demonstrated earlier that year in the Lofoten Islands, the guise of a larger raid provided near iron-clad cover compared with the isolated pinch operations at sea; operations they now feared had twigged the Germans to cipher compromise.

〜

In late October 1941, Churchill lost patience with Sir Roger Keyes, his Director of Combined Operations, and appointed the youthful Captain Lord Louis Mountbatten, a great-grandson of Queen Victoria, to replace him. By this time a growing pessimism had engulfed the indomitable old First World War veteran, who told Mountbatten as he passed the torch that 'Britain had lost the will to fight.'[18] Keyes was utterly frustrated by the lack of cooperation between the land, sea and air service branches. Without any real power, he had been forced to struggle constantly with the chiefs of staff and with Churchill himself to get the precious assets he needed to conduct even pinprick raids along the European coast.

'Dickie' Mountbatten, as he'd been known since childhood, represented the new war. He was bold, vain, diplomatic and highly ambitious, ready to engage with the enemy. Churchill ordered him to go on the offensive and develop a programme of commando raids along the Norwegian and Atlantic coastlines that would tie up German resources and help prepare for the Allies' eventual return to Europe. Before long Churchill promoted him to commodore, and in the spring of 1942, he changed his title from Director of Combined Operations to Chief of Combined Operations (CCO) – the same position Keyes had argued for in vain. That distinction allowed Mountbatten to serve as a member of the Chiefs of Staff Committee, despite palpable resentment from the other service chiefs, who viewed his organization as a bastard stepchild and resented his rapid rise in rank. In due time Churchill promoted him to vice admiral in the Royal Navy, bestowing on him simultaneously the honorary ranks of air marshal in the Royal Air Force and lieutenant general in the army, making him the only individual besides the King to hold rank in all three services. It was an extraordinary rise to power, despite his reckless 'palace playboy' image.[19]

Mountbatten had entered the Royal Navy as a cadet at thirteen, and at 41, after a quarter-century of service aboard battleships, submarines and destroyers, he exhibited a flair for signals and the nascent wireless technology they employed.[20] By 1941 he was commanding destroyers in combat in the English Channel and the Mediterranean – though with dubious results. Six months before his appointment to Combined Operations, his destroyer HMS *Kelly* was lost while evacuating British troops from Crete, following a direct hit from Stuka dive-bombers – a scene played out heroically in the film *In Which We Serve*, starring his friend and rumoured lover Noël Coward.[21] At the time of his appointment, he was preparing to take his rising star to the bridge of the aircraft carrier HMS *Illustrious*. As far as Churchill was concerned, however, Mountbatten was the perfect candidate to handle the new raiding operations he intended to expand in size and scope.

Like Godfrey, Fleming and Churchill, Mountbatten possessed a maverick personality and displayed little fear of doing things in unconventional ways. Later, he would skilfully manoeuvre his way through the treacherous waters of Whitehall by relying on his well-oiled personal 'force enhancers' – matinee-idol looks, royal bloodline and innate charm. As Elizabeth Nel, Churchill's secretary, recalled years later: 'His was quite the most glamorous personality among our circles; not only was he tall and extremely good-looking, with gold braid flashing on his uniform, but he seemed to exude a special kind of charm which had us all falling over backward.'[22] Critics claim, however, that much of Mountbatten's meteoric rise stemmed from a mix of Churchill's guilt and his notorious penchant for patronage appointments. Churchill had sacked Dickie's father, Prince Louis of Battenberg, as First Sea Lord at the outbreak of the First World War because of the political optics of his German heritage and name. Now he was ready to make amends and repay the son – with his newly anglicized name, Mountbatten – for his unwavering support during Churchill's own years in the political wilderness when his repeated warnings about Mussolini and Hitler had met with scorn and ridicule.

What has never been appreciated in the standard biographies of Mountbatten is that this upstart royal possessed something vitally essential both to Churchill and to Britain's pressing needs: an understanding of the fundamental nature and significance of intelligence, along with an intimate knowledge of signals intelligence and cryptography that appealed to the prime minister in an instinctive way. 'I was born and bred in an atmosphere of Naval Intelligence,' Mountbatten wrote. His father, who had held the posts of Assistant Director and then Director of Naval Intelligence at the turn of the century, 'continued to talk of the fascination and importance of Intelligence even after he had moved on.'[23]

Furthermore, like Ian Fleming, Mountbatten exhibited technocratic zeal and embraced modernity. He developed the signals intelligence capabilities for his station while working as a fleet wireless officer in the Mediterranean, where he raised the standard of signalling to new heights. During a brief stint at the signals school in Portsmouth, he earned a reputation for energy, efficiency and inventiveness, and was well respected for his cryptographic foresight. He urged the Royal Navy to adopt the Typex encryption machine as the British equivalent of the German Enigma at a time when few of his colleagues had any faith in this device. Later it was readily adopted.[24]

'I realized I could not expect to achieve any successes without really good Intelligence and a knowledge of how to use it,' Mountbatten wrote, attributing many of his achievements as Combined Operations chief and later as supreme Allied commander in South-east Asia to the fruits of this work.[25] His interest in and devotion to naval intelligence, and in particular to signals intelligence, reveals a long-ignored cornerstone of the Mountbatten–Churchill relationship. Despite his daring and aggressive spirit that bordered at times on the reckless, he recognized the need to foster the intellectual and technological work at Bletchley Park – a process and a product that was increasingly viewed as a new-found natural resource.

The injection of a charismatic and influential character like Mountbatten into the intelligence-gathering world reinvigorated the potential the raiding scene offered to the war effort. For Godfrey, Mountbatten's ascendancy to the crown of Combined Operations not only ensured continued cooperation on pinch matters but amplified the possibilities. The coming twin raids on the Lofoten and Vaagso Islands in the final days of 1941 were proof of that – especially as they turned out to be the most successful pinch raids of all.

⸻

Until this point in the war, attacks carried out by Combined Operations had been limited to small hit-and-run raids along the coast or to unopposed landings – as in Lofoten the previous March. The plan to return to the Lofoten area had been on the books since June, when the Ministry of Economic Warfare (MEW), which was responsible for attacking German economic interests, approached the Special Operations Executive (SOE) about conducting a fierce campaign of industrial sabotage throughout Norway. At this point, however, the means for such action was lacking. SOE needed a catalyst, a vehicle and a 'coalition of the willing' to put any raid into effect. As things turned out, very rarely was a mission or operation carried out for just one reason. Rather, to attract cooperation from the other services, even in a minor way, targets had to offer something that appealed to them all. Initially, under Sir Roger Keyes's direction, Combined Operations had shown little zest for spearheading such raids but had started to work on them following the first Lofoten raid. When Mountbatten took over, it dovetailed with the increasing pinch needs of Godfrey's NID, who happily took a seat aboard the only delivery vehicle capable of accomplishing his goals under the most urgent and delicate of circumstances.

After Hitler's invasion of Stalin's Soviet Russia on June 22, 1941, the British had entered into a tenuous alliance with their former enemy. Despite his intense hatred of Communism, Churchill had no hesitation in joining forces with the Soviet Union at this time. 'If Hitler invaded Hell,' he declared, 'I would at least make a favourable reference to the Devil in the House of Commons.'[26] Simply put, the British and the Western world, in general, needed the Soviet Union and its most precious natural resource – manpower – to have any hope of defeating Hitler's armies. Yet they remained fearful that the Russians might give up more quickly than the Tsarist armies had done in the First World War. To encourage Stalin to sustain the struggle, Churchill needed to demonstrate the value of his alliance in any way possible short of opening a second front by invading Western Europe – an impossible proposition at the time.

So Churchill decided to extend the hand of friendship, arranging for British-made weapons and materials vital to the Soviet war machine to reach the Soviet Union via massive Arctic convoys that would skirt German-occupied Norway and bring the goods to northern Russian ports. In addition, using a series of amphibious raids along the Norwegian coast, he hoped to fix Hitler's attention on that region. If he could convince the Nazi leader that Norway had become the 'zone of destiny' where the war in the west would be won or lost, he would draw German air and land forces away from the Russian front.

A return to Norway would not only satisfy these desires but offer a further opportunity to restock the bare shelves at Bletchley Park.

If Mountbatten could deliver the crucial pinched material, he would prove the value of Combined Operations under his command.[27] With all these objectives in mind, Churchill and the Chiefs of Staff Committee approved a twin operation – Operation Anklet and Operation Archery – that Combined Operations would carry out close to the Norwegian coast. Together, these two operations could deliver a one-two punch in the Lofoten Islands (Operation Anklet) and on the island of Vaagso, 300 miles to the south, between Trondheim and Bergen (Operation Archery). The ostensible purpose of Operation Anklet was to seize and hold the harbour at Reine as an advanced naval base from which the British could prevent German interference with the Arctic convoys, but in fact, it would allow the SOE and the MEW the chance to wreak havoc on the local fisheries industry and provide a fertile environment to dig for further Enigma-related material.[28] A strike at Lofoten would also serve as a diversion to draw German attention away from the main raid – Operation Archery – which was explicitly designed to fulfill the intelligence-gathering requirements of the NID. In other words, it would be a pinch raid.

With Operation Archery, the age of combined operations truly began. All three services – the British Army, the Royal Navy, and the RAF – worked together to plan and execute it. Right from the beginning, each service provided a force commander and staff to integrate its particular contribution into the overall or combined plan to achieve the common goal – a process that is normal now in planning military operations but was startlingly new at the time. Moreover, Archery laid the groundwork for the coming raids at Bruneval and St Nazaire – and, in August 1942, for Operation Jubilee at Dieppe.

Publicly, the aim of Operation Archery was the destruction of the fisheries on South Vaagso and the tiny island of Maaloy, which guarded the waterway known as the Ulvesund – the sound that separates these beautiful but isolated islands from the Norwegian coast.[29] These fisheries provided minerals that were used to manufacture two essential products for the German navy: vitamin supplements for U-boat crews long deprived of sunlight, and glycerine for the explosive charges in submarine torpedoes. Unlike Operation Anklet further north in Lofoten, where little resistance was expected, the Germans had garrisoned the

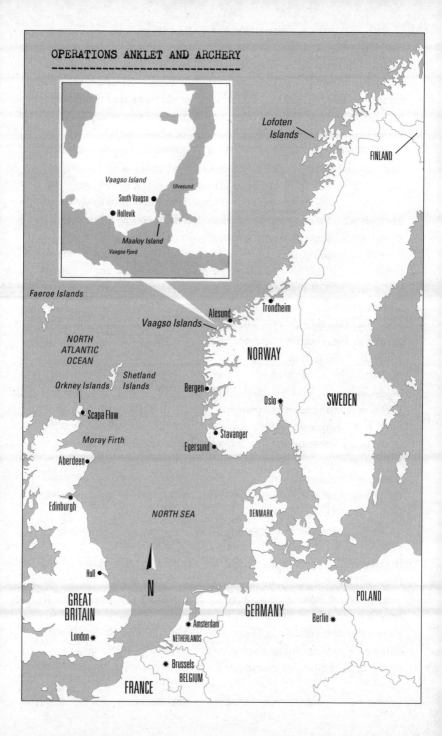

OPERATIONS ANKLET AND ARCHERY

Lofoten Islands

FINLAND

Vaagso Island

South Vaagso

Ulvesund

Hollevik

Maaloy Island

Vaagso Fjord

Faeroe Islands

Alesund

Trondheim

Vaagso Islands

NORTH
ATLANTIC
OCEAN

Shetland Islands

NORWAY

Orkney Islands

Scapa Flow

Bergen

Moray Firth

Oslo

SWEDEN

Aberdeen

Stavanger

Edinburgh

Egersund

NORTH SEA

DENMARK

Hull

N

GREAT
BRITAIN

London

Amsterdam

NETHERLANDS

GERMANY

Berlin

POLAND

Brussels

BELGIUM

FRANCE

village of Vaagso in respectable numbers, so Mountbatten prepared for a fight – an engagement welcomed by the men of Lieutenant Colonel John Durnford-Slater's veteran No. 3 Commando unit who had participated in the first Lofoten raid and would later be called upon again for Dieppe. According to the plan, the commandos would launch an amphibious raid on four areas to knock out the German gun positions and defences as well as the built-up area in South Vaagso. To support the attack, the Royal Navy sent a cruiser squadron with destroyers, troopships and a submarine. The RAF supplied several squadrons of Blenheim and Beaufighter aircraft, marking the first time it contributed significantly to a Combined Operations plan.

However, the imperative for the operation was the pinch – either during the capture or sinking of German patrol boats, trawlers and merchant vessels or on land, with the commandos targeting a wireless station and the local Kriegsmarine headquarters, each housed in a hotel, in an attempt to scrounge the critical codebooks and other materials Bletchley Park urgently needed.[30] The operational instructions prepared for Operation Archery included this carefully crafted advisory:

> It is very important that ships, particularly escort ships, armed trawlers, etc., be prevented from destroying or throwing overboard any papers, etc. On boarding, a thorough search is to be made for papers, especially those found in the charthouse, wheelhouse or captain's cabin. All papers are to be brought off and great care is to be taken to avoid damaging such documents or moving the keys of typewriters or similar machines as the value of their capture may be reduced thereby. The discovery of any of the above must be reported at once to the rear admiral commanding 10th Cruiser Squadron. It is of the greatest importance that this signal should NOT be made in plain language.[31]

With the pinch net spread, John Godfrey attached a liaison officer from the Naval Section to the raid to home in on desired cryptographic targets. On December 18, just days before the twin raids, Lieutenant Commander Allon Bacon, the veteran of the *Lauenburg* pinch and the officer sent by Godfrey to retrieve the material from *U-110*, evaluated the potential pinch targets offered by both operations.[32] The resourceful Bacon based his assessment on the intelligence provided by a Norwegian fisherman whose brother worked for the Special Operations Executive. He concluded that both operations offered good pinch opportunities.[33] 'In view of this report which provides 4 possible Z targets and greater speed than the Northern Anklet party,' he decided that 'this party i.e. Archery offers best chances.'[34] Most significant, Operation Archery appears to be the first time that military forces took an active part in a pinch alongside their naval counterparts.

Another conspicuous 'first' was Mountbatten's decision to attach one of his own staff officers, Royal Navy Lieutenant Commander Ackroyd Norman Palliser de Costobadie, to the raid. Better known as 'Dick' to his colleagues, De Costobadie had earned the Distinguished Service Cross for 'good judgement and initiative' while he commanded the flat-bottomed Royal Navy river gunboat HMS *Locust* during the Dunkirk evacuation in 1940.[35] After his investiture by the King at Buckingham Palace at the height of the Battle of Britain, he joined Combined Operations, where he worked on the staff of the naval adviser responsible for the selection of targets and the creation of outline plans for all Mountbatten's operations.[36] His attachment to Operation Archery did not seem curious at the time because the staff at Combined Operations were still learning their trade, and observers were commonplace.

When the day for the mission arrived, Mountbatten tasked De Costobadie with commanding the boarding party slated to protect Bacon while he sought out and pinched the vital material. This move clearly reflected Mountbatten's personal interest in the raid, and its crucial importance to Combined Operations – spurred by the potential 'political' gain for his organization should the pinched materials provide another triumph.

It was not until he was on board HMS *Onslow* that De Costobadie found that the ad hoc collection of officers and ratings provided from the destroyer's crew seemed to have no training at all as a boarding party.[37] 'I was more than worried. I was in fact, horrified. They consisted to the best of my recollection of one Sub-Lieutenant, one Midshipman, one Petty Officer, one Leading Seaman, three seamen and two stokers.

None of these men appeared trained. They turned up when paraded in any sort of rig, so I roared them up and sent them off to get into proper rig.'[38] He was in an invidious situation: he was a guest on the ship, with no knowledge of the men now under his command. He would have much preferred to go into battle with a specially organized and trained pinch unit, but at this eleventh hour, he had no choice but to make the best of the situation.[39]

The raid kicked off after a short delay caused by foul winter weather over Scapa Flow and following a brief address from Mountbatten, who reputedly told the troops in his closing remarks: 'One last thing. When my ship, the destroyer *Kelly*, went down off Crete earlier this year, the Germans machine-gunned the survivors in the water. There's absolutely no need to treat them gently on my account. Good luck to you all!'[40]

The *Onslow* headed into Vaagso Fjord. It did not have to wait long for a victim. Directly in front of the oncoming destroyer was the German trawler *Fohn*, which on first sighting turned and fled, accompanied by two other vessels, steaming up the inlet and firing at the British aircraft overhead while its crew desperately jettisoned documents over the sides. When the collection of fleeing ships reached a bend in the waterway, they turned hard to port and beached themselves, with *Onslow* closing fast. Within minutes, the order 'Away All Boarding Parties' bellowed, and both De Costobadie and Bacon stood amidships on the destroyer's motor launch, steaming for shore.[41] They quickly crossed the 300 yards to the *Fohn* with rifles, pistols and bayonets at the ready. By the time they reached the stranded trawler, most of her German crew had leapt ashore, positioning themselves across a road from where they began to snipe at the boarding party. Without a properly trained commando unit schooled in infantry fieldcraft and close-quarter fighting, capturing the *Fohn* proved too much of a near-run thing. After a delay that could have spelled the difference between success and failure, the boarding party managed to evict the remnants of the German crew, leaving De Costobadie and his band to press on to the next vessel while Bacon commenced his search of the *Fohn*.

Stepping over the body of the German captain, Bacon entered *Fohn*'s wireless room, which yielded nothing. He proceeded to the captain's cabin, where 'the application of a jemmy to the Master's desk produced the highly-prized list of Enigma daily settings.'[42] A more detailed search of his wardrobe revealed 'the current bigram tables encased in a celluloid container and stowed away amongst his well-laundered shirts.'[43] Bacon immediately placed the documents, printed in water soluble ink, inside a double-skinned, watertight rubber bag specially made for this purpose and moved on to the other ships.[44]

Not as lucky on these vessels, the commando party quickly made their way back to *Onslow* in time to witness the destroyer's four-inch guns obliterate all the German craft – part of the pre-arranged plan to cover their tracks. On shore, explosions and fires raged in the wake of the successful simultaneous operations by Durnford-Slater's No. 3 Commandos who displayed 'utter ruthlessness and complete professional competence' and 'stopped at nothing' to reach their objectives.[45] As Durnford-Slater reported later: 'We carried out demolitions ashore ... before any German-occupied building was blown up. A member of our intelligence section searched through it for documents. These precautions paid off beautifully when we found the master code for the whole of the German navy.'[46]

The scale of the destruction wrought by the commandos shocked the German commander when he arrived days later to the smouldering ruins in South Vaagso. Everywhere he looked, German barracks, telephone exchanges, gun positions, the wireless station, fish canneries and oil-storage tanks all lay in smashed and burned-out ruins, as did the Hotel Ulvesand, which had housed the German headquarters. But the level of the devastation hid the truly vital thing that had taken place; it gave no indication that a pinch had occurred – or that a 'precious haul' had returned to England.[47]

The prized materials – some of them seized from another patrol boat, the *Donner*, and by another boarding party from HMS *Offa*, coupled with material from the patrol vessel *Geier* – made these two operations the most successful pinch raid of the war thus far.[48] At least two complete three-rotor Enigma machines, parts of a third, extra rotors, and a variety of tables, key sheets, RHV emergency and WW weather codebooks, short signals, and the long-sought-after bigram tables ended up in Alan Turing's hands by New Year's Day 1942.[49] This material paid huge dividends, enabling the cryptanalysts at

Bletchley Park to break the keys for the Kriegsmarine home waters, the Mediterranean, and the Norwegian and Baltic waters, and the cryptanalysts to gain invaluable insights into German encryption methods and technology. The only black spot was the failure to uncover anything substantial connected to the four-rotor Enigma machine. With fingers still firmly crossed, the British moved on into a new year and a new war.

૭

On December 7, 1941, the Japanese launched their surprise attack on the American Pacific fleet based at Pearl Harbor, Hawaii, and ushered in a new era that took the European conflict worldwide. In the House of Commons that night, Winston Churchill seemed relieved, proclaiming with almost boyish glee what he saw as the course of the eventual Allied victory. 'In the past, we have had a light which flickered,' he said; 'in the present, we have a light which flames, and in the future, there will be a light which shines over all the land and sea.'[50]

Indeed, the prime minister had reason to be ecstatic. For close to two years he had desperately courted the United States, using every means at his disposal to bring the sleeping giant into a formal, overt alliance. Churchill's campaign of covert subversion, propaganda and diplomatic cajoling had already brought the two nations closer, with President Franklin Roosevelt extending what help he could during the isolationist period by trading much-needed 'Destroyers for Bases' and entering into the all-encompassing Lend-Lease agreement. Meanwhile, Godfrey and the Admiralty cosied up to the 'neutral' US fleet on convoy and intelligence matters. The sum total of this relationship saw the Americans adopt an increasingly belligerent stance towards Germany and Japan as 1941 wore on. With luck, one of those enemy countries would react with an incident that would sway the isolationist American public opinion to favour a declaration of war. The devastating bombing of Pearl Harbor by Japan was perhaps more than Britain and Roosevelt had bargained for, but it had a galvanizing effect on the Americans. They were now set on war – an attitude reinforced two days later when Hitler joined Japan and declared war on the United States.

But the entry of the Americans proved a double-edged sword, for although their economic and potential military and naval might appeared to be 'manna from heaven,' it also ushered in a whole new theatre of war with grave implications for the British. For the Admiralty, the widening war immediately brought with it increased responsibilities, which in some cases were impossible to meet. Life was dire in the weeks and months following Pearl Harbor: the garrison of Hong Kong quickly fell to the surging Japanese army, as did the Dutch East Indies with their vital oil and rubber resources. The pride of the Royal Navy, the battleships HMS *Prince of Wales* and Godfrey's former flagship HMS *Repulse,* succumbed to Japanese air attacks off Malaysia, leaving little doubt of the vulnerability of surface ships to Japan's air power. Meanwhile, the Japanese fleet launched carrier raids from Hawaii to Australia and into the Indian Ocean at Ceylon (now Sri Lanka). In February, the British bastion at Singapore fell to the Japanese in the most humiliating capitulation in British history.

As a result of all this sudden activity on the other side of the world, the Royal Navy found itself in an exceedingly precarious situation, overtaxed in all aspects and with ever-increasing demands on it worldwide.

When Admiral Dudley Pound met with his American counterpart – Commander-in-Chief of the United States Navy Admiral Ernest J. King – in the weeks following the attack on Pearl Harbor to lay out priorities for joint Allied strategy in the war at sea, protection of sea communications in the Atlantic was the top priority, followed by those in the Indian and Pacific Oceans.[51] Assuring those priorities, however, proved a daunting task given the current predicament of the Royal Navy and it came down to a judicious positioning of overstretched assets where 'the maximum force is stationed where it can be used offensively, and the minimum necessary forces stationed where required for defensive employment.'[52] Rear Admiral James Dorling, Pound's 'supply representative' for the discussions, chimed in that warship production and the current supply situation in Great Britain showed great strain, as did the 'magnitude of deficiencies in the British Fleet' now that the Japanese had entered the war, including a dangerous dearth in convoy escort shipping that paled in comparison to the climbing rate of German U-boat production. As Dorling calculated, the war at sea, which underpinned the entire Allied war effort, required 470 new convoy escort vessels to maintain communications between the United States, the

United Kingdom, and the various widespread vital theatres of active operations. 'Without these vessels,' he warned, 'the United Kingdom cannot be supplied with either the minimum foodstuffs necessary to sustain her population, or the raw materials required to keep her war industries in constant production.'[53]

Indeed, as Pound continued, 'as there are insufficient forces, either surface or air, to provide adequate strength in every area, the forces in all areas should be reduced proportionately' as 'the shortage of fleet destroyers is acute' and 'British responsibility for the escort of trade [is] very extensive' over the entire area, as well as 'requirements in the Northwestern approaches, to Iceland, and to Russia, besides the long routes between the United Kingdom and Gibraltar and between the United Kingdom and South Africa. The safety of troop convoys is an additional heavy commitment.'[54]

The British faced a long, precarious year ahead, during which they would be, for the most part, on their own. The massive US industrial potential was not yet organized for the war effort and could have no immediate impact on the war situation. The British would have to survive on their own all through 1942 until the retooling of the American economy shifted into high gear and the much-anticipated American troops, aircraft and naval vessels reached the United Kingdom. Once there, they would help build up the forces for the eventual liberation of Europe.

First and foremost, Britain had to maintain the vital North Atlantic convoy routes, deliver convoys through the treacherous Arctic Ocean to Russia, and keep lines of communication open and supplies flowing to its armies in the field in Gibraltar, Persia, Iraq and India, and in West Africa, East Africa and North Africa. With the fall of the Dutch East Indies to the Japanese, the vital Middle East and the Persian Gulf oil reserves became more vulnerable to submarine attacks. An already overburdened anti-submarine force now had to reinforce the Arabian Sea and the Persian Gulf area, where any blows against tankers and their precious supplies were likely to produce a paralysing effect on the Allies. The answer, in part, came with Dorling's call for an increase in the number of escort vessels in addition to the employment of long-range heavy bombers to both cover the convoys' routes and keep up pressure on the U-boats. Neither one, however, would come to fruition in the short term.

Unlike modern submarines that operate fully submerged, the Second World War version was, in fact, a submersible vessel. When not involved in direct combat, it sailed on the surface, powered by its diesel engines that also recharged the batteries that controlled the vessel once it dived beneath the waves. Once underwater and operating on her batteries, a U-boat's speed declined by half or two-thirds, meaning that the ships in the convoy the U-boat was stalking could escape as the U-boat used up its precious fresh-air supply and battery power. Eventually it would have to surface, where it would be at the mercy of any aircraft or surface ships in the area.

Until the increased use of long-range aircraft to hunt submarines in the second half of the war, the convoys' escort vessels, including destroyers and corvettes, formed the protection against U-boats, featuring depth charges, rudimentary short-range shipboard radar and high-frequency direction finding or 'Huff-Duff' instruments. But the critical shortage of these vital craft left merchant vessels hopelessly exposed to organized groups of U-boat wolf packs in the first years of the war. Unfortunately, the growing demand for long-range aircraft brought the Admiralty into direct conflict with the RAF, which required the same type of long-range, heavy-payload planes for the nascent bombing campaign over Germany. As such, the Admiralty searched for a weapons system that would serve as a force enhancer to make the most of an already overstretched arm of service. As Frank Birch wrote:

In U boat warfare, German and allies alike were faced throughout with the same tactical problem – location of the enemy for attack or evasion. Now, the problem of locating enemy surface craft in harbours or in coastal waters is difficult enough, but it has certain obvious limitations, and some guidance, at least, may be expected from a number of opened sources. Consider, in comparison, the chances of sighting, in the vast open spaces of the Atlantic, on the one hand, a U-boat, and on the other a convoy at the height of a U-boat's periscope. It was the business of the opposing intelligence services to narrow the field of search, and, in the battle of the Atlantic, location of the enemy depended, to a far greater extent than in surface craft warfare, on one particular source of intelligence – SIGINT.[55]

Part of Churchill's relief over the recent pinches stemmed from the fact that, thanks to the resumed flow of Ultra, he no longer had to divert his attention and scarce resources away from his most recent panacea – the strategic bombing of Germany. Ultra offered him a tool he could wield to manage his strategic assets more effectively and to engage in operations and policies based on calculated rather than blind risks.

∽

The tremendous intelligence and pinch successes of 1941, capped off by the Lofoten and Vaagso raids, ushered in a new era the following year for both the Naval Intelligence Division and Bletchley Park. Not only had the Bletchley boffins broken into all of Germany's major naval keys enciphered on the three-rotor Enigma via the crib-fed Bombes, but lesser codes, the ones used initially to get in the back door, began to contribute intelligence dividends themselves. This payoff forced Godfrey to revamp his pinch priorities. Over the year, his NID, working in conjunction with Frank Birch at the Naval Section, had created a simple rubric to denote their vital needs. Using a letter-and-number method, the letters A to G represented the level of importance of the particular code and cipher, while the number marked the reliability of the actual information obtained. In this scheme, *A* represented the most secret codes and ciphers; *B*, small-ship ciphers; *C*, naval air codes; *D*, merchant navy codes; *E*, meteorological codes; *F*, miscellaneous; and *G*, Armistice Commission codes.[56] Intelligence derived from naval Enigma remained, as it had been since the beginning of the war, *A1*, but now, with the ascendancy of the 'lower-level' codes in the cryptographic realm, RHV – the emergency hand cipher used when Enigma broke down, and which changed very rarely – appeared as *A2*; short-signal codes (E-bars, B-bars and the WW weather codes) as *A3*; Kriegsmarine general cipher as *A4*; and the *Werftschlüssel* dockyard cipher as *B1*.[57] Each one of these codes and ciphers could now be tapped to provide cribs for the Bombes or for their own intrinsic value.

The cumulative results of all this pinching and decoding during the previous twelve months proved staggering: by year's end in 1941, almost every area of the Kriegsmarine's operations was under British surveillance to one degree or another. Godfrey refused to push his luck any further. On January 20, 1942, he convened a meeting with his senior staff and with Frank Birch, where he laid out a pivotal change in pinch policy.[58] It was an extremely challenging time, despite the recent success at Lofoten and Vaagso, because ominous warnings about the imminent introduction of the four-rotor Enigma machine continued to surface. A new series of 'four-rotor duds' – setting mistakes by German operators using the new machine as though it were a three-rotor – confirmed the suspicion that some U-boats stationed in the Atlantic already carried the device.[59] Then, just a week before the meeting, an intercepted message indicated that some surface vessels too were using the four-rotor.[60]

Godfrey refused to be discouraged. Currently, penetration of German message traffic enciphered on the three-rotor naval Enigma was both fruitful and free-flowing, and the last thing he desired was to alert the Germans and accelerate the introduction of the four-rotor machine.[61] Part of this change in approach sprang from the discovery in January of 1941 that a four-rotor device existed (probably created before the war) and concern only increased when the device's expected distribution to U-boats was confirmed following the capture of the M4 lid from *U-570*, mentioned earlier.[62]

Cross-checking the serial number with existing three-rotor machines, Naval Section had calculated that too few four-rotor machines existed to outfit the entire Kriegsmarine immediately, and thus they still had some breathing room before a wide-scale replacement would be introduced.[63] They rationalized that as long as the Germans continued to cling to their delusion that the three-rotor was impenetrable, the Kriegsmarine had no immediate reason to incur the considerable cost and effort of introducing the new machines en masse. With all that in mind, Godfrey decided to suspend pinch raids for the time being but to set out explicit provisions for renewing them when Dönitz changed the bigram tables as he did periodically. Birch added: 'If the U-Boats were put on basically different keys to surface craft or began to use a fourth wheel, a pinch would be the only hope.'[64]

In his new policy, Godfrey tried to balance current and potential needs with security. The recent operations in Norway had demonstrated the potential for cloaking the pinch within the framework of a larger raid on a port or other shore-based facility.[65] Given that surprise and speed were paramount in any effort to obtain the desired material before the Germans could destroy it, it seemed more promising to attack ships in a confined area to overwhelm them quickly and prevent a chase or even their escape. Inland waterways or ports offered enticing possibilities, particularly with the ships berthed in tight groups along the docks and quays, either lightly guarded by skeleton crews or even unguarded in some cases, rendering them relatively easy targets for pillage.

Besides, ports offered other tantalizing features – signals facilities, such as wireless stations, and communications equipment storage depots – which, along with the local naval headquarters, made up a target-rich environment for pinches.[66] At Vaagso the Germans had proved adept at moving their signals stations at short notice, but a naval headquarters, fixed in a particular location, would remain in operation almost to the bitter end of the fight, giving the raiders a better chance of capturing vital material.[67] There, stockpiles of signals-related material for the current period and, even more critical, for months into the future would be found tucked into files and desks or in the safe, most likely in the commandant's office or quarters but also in the local supply depot. It was the job of the German harbour headquarters to maintain wireless contact with all types of vessels at sea, as well as with other headquarters in the wireless chain. Regardless of size or location, these headquarters would have to possess various forms of the Enigma machine, along with the associated codebooks, tables and setting sheets, not to mention copies of RHV, short-signal codebooks, weather codes and dockyard ciphers – all of critical importance to Bletchley Park.[68] As an added bonus, other materials – such as plans, charts, technical documents, lists of commanders and the order of battle, and the key for the nomenclature of German naval operations and procedures – were generally held in the naval headquarters. It was one thing to read the enemy's mail, but quite another to understand the technical terminology that resisted standard linguistic translation.[69]

From the perspective of security, pinch raids on headquarters under the cloak of larger operations were also ideal for several salient reasons. First, because most of the desired target locations were housed close to the shoreline, they could be overrun quickly and effectively during amphibious operations. Second, the ransacked facility could then be destroyed, leaving the Germans unaware of what, if any, material had been pilfered.[70] And third, as earlier operations had established, a veil of secrecy could quickly be drawn by cloaking the pinch mission under cover of a larger raid offering up other legitimate, but nonetheless secondary, objectives, thereby deflecting any suspicion from the prime target. In short, from the pinch perspective, taking these raids to shore offered the British a form of 'one-stop shopping.'

With the new shore-based policy accepted, Frank Birch created a card index of probable targets, with a description of all the German communications and headquarters establishments likely to contain the desired material. The index was based on information from all possible sources – Ultra, captured documents, photographic reconnaissance, agent reports, and prisoner-of-war interrogations.[71] Eventually, he built up a network of all enemy communications facilities, the type of traffic they handled and the codes that might be pinched from them.[72] This information was posted on a large wall chart in the Naval Section at Bletchley, with pins of various colours and shapes indicating the different codes and ciphers held at each location. One glance at the chart showed what a raiding force could expect to capture at any given shore establishment, 'and a careful study was made of code and cipher distribution with particular reference to the location of Book Administration Centres and other branches.'[73] Quickly, this became the 'chief source of information' used in the planning of operations undertaken for pinch purposes.[74]

But the discussions between Godfrey and Birch over this issue also marked the beginning of a dramatic change in their relationship. In the weeks and months following the January 1942 meeting, Frank Birch's Naval Section would play an ever-decreasing role in the planning and execution of pinch raids. As before, it could offer up potential targets, relay needs and even suggest methods to obtain the material, but it no longer had any representative attached to the Section who actively participated in the raids. Instead, by the spring of 1942, Godfrey preferred to keep this role 'in-house,' joining forces with the delivery vehicle provided by Mountbatten's Combined Operations Headquarters – a budding collaboration cemented during the wildly successful raids at Vaagso, and later at Bruneval and St Nazaire. 'You will be interested to know,' Godfrey told Mountbatten, 'that you are the first person, occupying any position of importance, who has given the NID such unstinted and unsolicited praise.'[75] Ever quick to seize a chance to charm, Mountbatten replied: 'I am amazed at your statement ... because I thought it was commonly accepted that NID was far and away the best Intelligence department and running better now than at any time since the famous Blinker Hall days.'[76]

With the courtship between the two organizations growing in intensity, Naval Section was left to play the role of a jilted lover. Birch complained loudly about their exclusion from the pinch-raid process, claiming that, if they had possessed advance knowledge of a raid or its specific objectives, he and his staff could have enhanced its overall success.[77] But no argument from Bletchley Park penetrated the thick walls of Godfrey's and Fleming's Room 39 in the Old Admiralty Building. Birch was fobbed off with practical reasons for his exclusion: first, to meet security concerns, the number of those in the know about upcoming raids had to be limited; second, because most raids never moved past the planning stage, it would be a waste of time and effort to generate unnecessary interest; third, there was little that Frank Birch and his Naval Section could bring to the table that Godfrey's NID did not already know about naval cryptography.[78] The cryptographic knowledge that Ian Fleming and others possessed, the expertise with pinch raids gained by Allon Bacon and by Jasper Haines as the liaison officer between the NID and Bletchley Park, and the close association that the NID was developing with Combined Operations had all made Godfrey more comfortable in proceeding without the need for consultations with Birch and Bletchley.

⁓

On January 21, 1942, Combined Operations' target search committee, led by Captain John 'Jock' Hughes-Hallett (who would eventually become the naval force commander for the Dieppe Raid), began to make plans to fulfil Churchill's wish for a raiding programme along the German-held coast of France. Mountbatten's selection of Hughes-Hallett to pilot this committee, to recommend potential targets, and to oversee the creation of outline plans for future operations was indicative of a new direction for his Combined Operations organization. A career Royal Navy officer who had gained brief combat experience at the end of the First World War, Hughes-Hallett had been educated at Dartmouth Naval College and at Cambridge before serving as a torpedo officer in 1918. In the inter-war period, he became a torpedo specialist on the aircraft carrier HMS *Courageous* and gained praise for his ingenuity with torpedoes, mines and shipboard electronics. During the Norwegian campaign in 1940, he was mentioned in dispatches for his role in whisking the Norwegian royal family to safety amid the full-blown Nazi invasion of the country.

Following his short stint at sea, which never included a command appointment, Jock Hughes-Hallett had spent the next year and a half as the navy's lead planner for various schemes to defend British ports and beaches against German invasion. He had developed an intimate knowledge of and expertise in this field. His course and career progression reports were outstanding, marking him as 'an officer with a brilliant and original mind.' He had 'intellectual capacity of a very high order and is full of ideas. He has great energy and drive and pushes through schemes to their conclusions, undeterred and unperturbed by practical difficulties. A strong personality with great confidence in himself, he expresses himself clearly and decisively both in speech and in writing.'[79]

Although he had talent and possessed a 'clear brain,' Hughes-Hallett was tagged as the 'ambitious type,' and was not 'the money of a very large number of naval officers.'[80] As Rear Admiral Baillie-Grohman, the man who preceded him as naval force commander at Dieppe, told Mountbatten, Hughes-Hallett was 'insufferable' and 'is considered, and I think with reason, as too loud-voiced, overbearing, and too cocksure of himself without adequate reason.'[81] Mountbatten concurred, but chalked any criticism up to nothing more than professional jealousy. 'It is just because he is right 99% of the time that he does annoy so many people,' he replied. To the Combined Operations chief, Hughes-Hallett was 'one of the most brilliant and outstanding officers in the service' who had 'more than fulfilled expectations,' but he did acknowledge that his new naval force commander 'is perhaps a little fond of laying down the law,' to the point where 'his friends call him Hughes-Hitler.'[82]

In December 1941, after Jock Hughes-Hallett had caught Winston Churchill's eye for his work preparing to repel the expected German invasion of England, Mountbatten recruited him to Combined Operations to act as his naval adviser. Given Churchill's increasing desire to take the fight to the enemy, coupled with the new policy of launching pinch raids at enemy ports and naval facilities, who better to call upon than the man responsible for defending British ports from attacks by the Germans? Hughes-Hallett's intimate knowledge of port defences and the tactics used to breach or subvert them was likely to be priceless. Having joined Mountbatten's headquarters just before the last round of Norwegian pinches, where his subordinate Dick de Costobadie would play a key role, Hughes-Hallett set about creating a raiding programme for the following six months.[83] 'Our urgent task,' he recalled on his arrival at Combined Operations Headquarters on Richmond Terrace in Whitehall, 'was to select targets for raids on France and Norway,' something 'everyone agreed ... must fall to the Navy ... [because] it was no use suggesting places which could not be reached by appropriate landing craft or other vessels.'[84]

Despite the 'combined' nature of Mountbatten's headquarters, the Royal Navy's interests were often front and centre. The air adviser was little more than a liaison officer who sought cooperation from the RAF squadrons in covering and supporting a raid, while the military adviser provided the land force elements, such as the army commandos, and helped to create the detailed military portion of the combined plan. This division of responsibilities left the genesis of any raid – the creation of the vital outline plan, including the original objectives and intent – firmly in the hands of the naval adviser. He, in turn, kept both the Admiralty and the Joint Planning Committee informed of what was going on at Combined Operations Headquarters.[85]

The sudden appearance of Dieppe as a proposed target could not be a coincidence, particularly given the men who assisted Jock Hughes-Hallett in making the decision and the timing, just one day after the change in pinch policy in the last week of January 1942. Along with Lieutenant Commander Dick de Costobadie came Commander David Luce, fresh from a year as the head of the Admiralty's Plans Division and now recruited by Mountbatten to be Hughes-Hallett's main adviser on raid planning.[86] Hughes-Hallett would recall in his memoirs: 'David Luce, Costabadie [*sic*] and I sat down to make tentative proposals for one raid every month up to and including August,' but were not 'concerned at this stage with the intrinsic value of objectives on a particular raid, but rather with the feasibility of reaching the place undetected.'[87]

With his hands often tied by logistical concerns – such as a limited amount of specialized landing craft at his disposal – Hughes-Hallett planned to start small, with an attack on the coastal radar station at Bruneval in late February, followed by another on a Luftwaffe hospital in the Ostend area in early March.[88] As their logistical capabilities increased, he envisioned proportionately larger and bolder raids, including a daring and almost suicidal attack on the large dry dock situated at the German U-boat base at St Nazaire for March, followed days later by another Vaagso-style attack on the port of Bayonne in south-western France.[89] For May, he suggested the seizure of Alderney, to cut the supply route for U-boats, and in June and July back-to-back raids on the same target – the port of Dieppe. He offered no particular purpose for these two raids in his carefully measured memoirs written in veiled tones, long before the declassification of any information about Ultra.[90]

In the background, larger schemes such as the opening of a limited second front on the Cherbourg peninsula (Operation Sledgehammer), the invasion of Madagascar (Operation Ironclad), and the potential seizure of the Canary Islands (Operation Puma) were all in the works. But they were quite different operations, with strategic implications involving other elements outside the direct control of Mountbatten's COHQ.

Each one of Hughes-Hallett's proposed operations had to meet two objectives: it had to offer an overt strategic purpose, as the earlier raids in Norway had demonstrated; but it also had to contain provisions for a 'pinch' – either by opportunity or by design. Because these requirements were not mutually exclusive, this symbiotic relationship offered the perfect natural cover: on the one hand, the operation could legitimately satisfy strategic demands, while on the other, it could capture vital material to inject into the intelligence infrastructure in a way that no other arm of service could deliver at that time. On paper, these proposals seemed the perfect plan to serve as the blueprint for a unique 'brand' of warfare that both Godfrey and Mountbatten were anxious to parlay into political currency. Churchill was Ultra's greatest devotee, and the ambitious Mountbatten, in particular, wanted to position his organization to deliver the precious goods and justify its existence to both the all-powerful prime minister and the sceptical chiefs of staff.[91]

According to Hughes-Hallett, on January 23, just days after Godfrey announced the change in pinch policy, Mountbatten gave him permission to draw up a rough plan for what they eventually named Operation Rutter – the first incarnation of the raid on Dieppe.[92]

—————

CHAPTER 6

Fade to Black

The first of all our dangers is the U-Boat peril. That is a very great danger. Our food, our means of making war, our life, all depend upon the passage of ships across the sea. The whole power of the United States to manifest itself in this war depends upon the power to move ships across the sea ... what a terrible waste it is to think of all these great ships that are sunk.

Winston Churchill, October 31, 1942

February 1, 1942, 0330 hours, 250 miles off the New Jersey shoreline

From the bridge of the surfaced *U-109*, Captain-Lieutenant Heinrich Bleichrodt peered through the targeting binoculars at the silhouette of an 8,000-ton British merchant steamer cutting across his bow less than 2,000 yards in the distance. The 32-year-old Bleichrodt, nicknamed 'Ajax' after the Greek hero from the Trojan War, was one of Germany's leading U-boat aces, sinking 25 ships and 150,000 tons of shipping in just eight war patrols – a feat that warranted the highest award for valour in Nazi Germany, the Knight's Cross with Oak Leaves. Following a brusque series of commands, three torpedoes in quick succession lurched out from the submarine's bow tubes and streamed towards the unsuspecting *Tacoma Star*, which was zigzagging unescorted through the darkness.

On the same day that Combined Operations had raided Lofoten and Vaagso, *U-109* slipped out of her berth in the giant concrete U-boat pen at Lorient, France, for the month-long journey to reach the eastern seaboard of North America and participate in Admiral Karl Dönitz's new submarine offensive, Operation *Paukenschlag* (Operation Drumbeat). Suspecting that North American waters might provide a fertile killing ground, Dönitz had shifted his U-boats from the mid-Atlantic and unleashed them on merchant vessels carrying troops, passengers, and essential food and war supplies. The submarines had a wide swath of ocean to cover, as the ships travelled from the Caribbean and the Gulf of Mexico to critical points along the eastern seaboard of the United States and Canada, penetrating at times the Gulf of St Lawrence.

In the last two years of the Great War, the British had learned that the most efficient way of moving vast quantities of supplies and manpower through U-boat-infested waters was to form their merchant vessels into protective convoys, numbering anywhere between 30 and 70 vessels, and then sail them across the ocean at almost a snail's pace, zigzagging or rerouting as needed to avoid enemy submarines. The upside was increased security for these vessels: packed together and sailing with a naval escort of destroyers and corvettes (later joined by aircraft and aircraft carriers), there was safety in numbers. If warned in advance, the entire complement of ships could avoid a single U-boat (or a group of submarines working together as a wolf pack) or, in some cases, prepare for a fight. The downside was lost time – not only the slow passage but the wait to form the convoy, unload all the ships once they reached their destination, and regroup them for the return voyage. The convoy system indeed reduced the number of trips each ship could make in a year, but the British were willing to pay that price.

The Americans, however, stubbornly chose to send ships individually and without escort, leaving them at the mercy of roving U-boats and with little means of defence. Stifled by their own antiquated strategy, the United States Navy had initially rejected the convoy system, opting for speed rather than safety. Compounding this vulnerability, the Americans lacked sufficient air cover along the US coast and were still lax about implementing the basic precaution of blacking out bright lights in cities and seaside communities along the Atlantic coast, making it easy for seasoned hunters like Bleichrodt to pick out their victims as they steamed past the shore, perfectly silhouetted. As Dönitz would later boast:

> The U-boats found that conditions there were almost exactly those of normal peacetime. The coast was not blacked-out, and the towns were a blaze of bright lights ... The lights, both in lighthouses and on buoys, shone forth, though perhaps a little less brightly than usual. Shipping followed the normal peacetime routes and carried the normal lights. Although five weeks had passed since the declaration of war, very few anti-submarine measures appeared to have been introduced. There were, admittedly, anti-submarine patrols, but they were wholly lacking in experience. Single destroyers, for example, sailed up and down the traffic lanes with such regularity that the U-boats were quickly able to work out the time-table being followed.[1]

It was a painful beginning to the war at sea for the Americans, while the German U-boat crews called it their 'Second Happy Time.' But even harder times lay ahead after the Allies experienced that new kind of blackout they had been dreading: the silence that followed the introduction of the four-rotor naval Enigma to the Atlantic U-boat fleet on February 1, 1942.

Blissfully unaware of the submarine only 1,300 yards to starboard, Master Robert George, the captain of the *Tacoma Star*, believed that his ship led a semi-charmed life.[2] Already sunk once in Liverpool harbour by a German bomb during the Blitz in 1940, she had lived to fight another day after being raised, repaired and relaunched.[3] Now, as she steamed towards Liverpool on her way home from Buenos Aires with her cargo holds full and 93 souls on board, her legendary luck ran out. In just under three minutes, two of *U-109*'s three torpedoes fired from essentially point-blank range struck the forward hold and the engine room amidships, engulfing her in a giant detonation cloud. When she finally emerged, the mortally wounded cargo ship turned hard to starboard and settled fast by the bow.[4] Sinking in less than four minutes, the steamer had the dubious honour of becoming the first of nearly 1,000 Allied merchant vessels, totalling an unprecedented 7.1 million tons of vital shipping, sunk during the four-rotor blackout that lasted from February to December 1942.[5]

According to the report from *U-109*, the captain and his crew made it to their lifeboats, but in the panic, before they abandoned ship, they sent the wrong coordinates in their frantic distress call. Never seen again, the 93 souls on board the *Tacoma Star* joined close to 10,000 others whose names appear in the sombre lists of the missing and dead from the Battle of the Atlantic.

To boast of his success and arrange a rendezvous to restock dwindling fuel supplies, Bleichrodt sent a triumphant message to Ernst Kals, the captain of the nearby *U-130*, which, if Bletchley Park had been able to decipher it, would have provided near-perfect intelligence. 'Just sank *Tacoma Star*,' he reported. 'Please meet me earlier in CB 4965 at 0900 hours.' Kals quickly replied: 'Can't reach rendezvous point before 1500 hours.'[6]

Only 24 hours earlier, when the three-rotor Enigma was still in use on Dönitz's submarines operating in the Atlantic, the contents of these messages would have been gold for the Submarine Tracking Room. Located in the basement of the Citadel, the brown fortress-style bunker attached to the Old Admiralty Building in London, the tracking room formed one annexe of the Operational Intelligence Centre. There, women from the Royal Naval Service, the Wrens, placed coloured markers tracking the location of each German U-boat and every Allied ship or convoy at sea on giant wall-mounted map boards showing the world's sea lanes. If they had been privy to the positions of *U-109* and *U-130*, these U-boats would have appeared on the wall as well. Immediately, the analysts there would have sent messages to Western Approaches Command in Liverpool, and the alarm would have been repeated to tracking rooms in Canada and the United States. Other vessels could be rerouted, or an 'incidental' ambush by anti-submarine forces orchestrated, turning the hunters into the hunted.[7] But without the intelligence, nothing happened.

∽

In hindsight, the failure to take immediate and direct action against the potential threat posed by the four-rotor naval Enigma is likely the greatest miscalculation made by both John Godfrey's NID and Frank Birch's Naval Section at Bletchley Park during the entire war. The combined effects of wishful thinking and a 'wait and see' approach – something Godfrey railed against in others – led to a near catastrophe on the seas and stirred up the ghosts of the First World War when U-boats threatened to bring the UK to her knees in the latter half of that conflict.

Looking back on the current struggle after the Second World War, Winston Churchill noted: 'I am sure that no one knows so much about dealing with U-Boats ... as the British Admiralty, not because we are cleverer or braver than others but because, in two wars, our existence has depended upon overcoming these perils [and] when you live for years on end with mortal danger at your throat, you learn in a hard school.'[8]

The learning curve was steep. One week after the changeover from the three- to the four-rotor Enigma, few if any of the colourful submarine-shaped markers used to denote the position of individual U-boats on the map board in the Submarine Tracking Room remained. One by one, the Wrens returned them to their cabinet drawers alongside the Ultra docket marked *Shark*, which was no longer stuffed and sagging. Dönitz's submarines had begun to fade from sight in the most vital of all theatres – the Atlantic Ocean.

Godfrey would later write: 'The tracking of U-Boats is perhaps the most important of NID's functions.' The demanding job of the talented analysts toiling in the dungeon-like atmosphere of the tracking room was to stay on top of current events and predict the future. Their ability to 'foresee, day, week, month or even longer ahead' was their sole purpose.[9] Also, they had to know what was happening with their own warships, convoys, aircraft and enemy U-boats. Their work relied on piecing together countless clues and scraps of information to create a background of knowledge against which to judge and weigh probabilities. When available, Ultra served them well, and indeed it had quickly formed the backbone of their work. Now, with the four-rotor naval Enigma in place, the analysts had little current intelligence to draw from, which left them gravely disheartened, particularly when the sombre distress signal from a stricken Allied tanker, troopship or merchant ship, such as the *Tacoma Star*, became their only source material.[10]

The four-rotor was not the only enormous challenge facing Alan Turing and the cryptanalysts at Bletchley Park. The Germans had also introduced a new weather codebook just days before the four-rotor appeared, and they followed that up all through February with new editions of other codes and ciphers as well. Cumulatively, these new versions of the lesser codes blocked Bletchley's 'backdoor approach' and, for the time being, effectively shut them out of cribs. From this point onwards, there was a steady fade to black. It began with a sudden 'grey-out' in early February, darkened quickly, and spread like a cancer, leaving the Submarine Tracking Room, the Operational Intelligence Centre and the Naval Intelligence Division to rely on an 'estimate and guess' approach – or, in the term Godfrey coined, a 'working fiction' – rather than the solid base provided by Ultra that had served the English so well up until then.[11]

This left the cryptanalysts and the intelligence officers in OIC crestfallen as 'the quality and quantity of naval [Ultra] was such that it altered the whole view of naval intelligence, and so an entirely unexpected standard in the product created an equally unexpected standard in the demand for it.'[12]

During this 'depressing period,' as the future head of Hut 8, A.P. Mahon, wrote, any message enciphered by the Germans on the new four-rotor device withstood the intellectual and electromechanical probes from the cryptanalysts at Bletchley Park.[13] Nothing, at least in the immediate future it seemed, could fix the problem. Lamenting the situation, Mahon recorded: 'Clearly, we had lost the most valuable part of the traffic, and no form of cryptographic attack was available to us.'[14] Shaun Wylie, who worked with Alan Turing in the hut as a crib specialist, recalled:

> We knew it was coming. But it was a grim time. We were very much
> frustrated; the things that we'd hoped to use went bad on us. We real-
> ized that our work meant lives, and it ceased to be fun. We did what
> we could, of course, and we got on with what there was, but we kept

an eye out for any possibility on Shark [the new key introduced for the U-boat fleet] that might present itself. There was a lot of pressure and we were trying all we could, but we didn't have many opportunities. We had to get Dolphin [the principal key used by naval Enigma] out, but Shark was the prime target, the focus of our interest.[15]

When Rolf Noskwith, a German Jew who had escaped from Germany a decade earlier and a fellow crib specialist, was asked years later if the relative impotence and the resulting loss of life created a sense of guilt among the cryptanalysts, he soberly recalled:

While we knew the seriousness of the situation, I cannot say that we felt guilty. First, we genuinely felt that, without more captured material, there was no short-term solution. Secondly, we knew that there was a long-term solution because of plans, in collaboration with the Americans, to build more powerful Bombes capable of breaking the four-wheel machines. Thirdly, we were still regularly breaking Dolphin.[16]

Except for a few odd days in March, when Bletchley took advantage of cribs supplied by an operator's mistake to decrypt already stale traffic (ironically, a message announcing Dönitz's promotion to full admiral), *Shark* would remain impenetrable until a heroic chance pinch of material from the *U-559* in the last days of October 1942.

Through that warm and unusually dry summer, the Bletchley Park cryptanalysts worked literally round the clock to attack the four-rotor naval Enigma in the same way that had led to breakthroughs with earlier versions of the machine, but with no success. Although they attempted to solve their dilemma with the less sophisticated three-wheeled Bombes they had in their arsenal, these proved much too slow to outwit the improved device. Even when an occasional operator's transmission mistake provided Bletchley with a few cribs, it took six of the three-wheeled Bombes working together for seventeen straight days to decrypt the settings for just one day of traffic, providing messages that were more than a month out of date. This usage was a nonsensical waste of valuable resources; the few precious three-wheeled machines were desperately needed to decipher message traffic encrypted on three-rotor Enigma machines from other theatres of war (at this point, the German high command had put the four-rotor machine into operation only in the Atlantic), so it made no sense to devote their precious time to a task that offered little chance of success.[17]

The reaction in the short term from Godfrey at the Admiralty, from Bletchley Park and from the Operational Intelligence Centre in London was to fall back on the still-breakable German home waters key (*Dolphin*) and on lower-level codes and ciphers. As the history of the OIC records, [Ultra] may have been 'by far the most important information received,' but at least for now experts there maintained the ability 'to read German local signals relating to local moves or tugs, escorts, minesweepers, repair and supply facilities ... [and] had knowledge of new construction, completions and exercises in the Baltic.'[18] However, they knew that as the use of the four-rotor Enigma machine spread more widely throughout the German navy, these lower-level codes and ciphers would likely disappear incrementally in the intelligence equation. To meet that possibility, the OIC attempted to rely on other sources to fill in the blanks – aerial reconnaissance, for example, and other signals intelligence technologies and techniques that the English were fast developing.

∽

The most promising sources in lieu of cryptography for the Operational Intelligence Centre were high-frequency direction finding (HF/DF or Huff-Duff) and very high-frequency direction finding (VHF/DF) technologies, in either their shore- or ship-based forms that played, as Frank Birch recorded, the 'humbler role of handmaid to the production and interception of [Ultra].'[19]

These technologies could detect the general location of a vessel by intercepting its radio signals, but they could not pinpoint the specific location.[20] Unfortunately, because the Germans suspected that the Allies employed such measures, they drastically restricted their radio time on-air to the absolute minimum to limit the chances of being found. Even if they were located, the information would quickly grow stale unless Allied ships or aircraft were in the immediate area to take action, and after a few hours, it likely became useless.[21] In addition, the radio intercepts could not establish the direction in which the vessel was travelling; only if the Allies picked up subsequent transmissions could they confirm that they came from the same vessel and thereby know the direction of travel. All this sleuthing was more art than science – and to round out and properly interpret the findings, the cryptanalysts required a consistent corpus of evidence to draw on as needed.[22]

Bletchley Park also dabbled with the techniques of radio fingerprinting (RFP, where they identified specific transmitters by photographing the particular waveform) and TINA (where they analysed the characteristics of the radio operator himself). On their own, as Godfrey noted, these techniques were 'without operational value as far as the U-Boat war was concerned,' but they paid dividends with regard to large surface vessels such as cruisers and battleships.[23] Combining these two sources of SIGINT – signals intelligence – offered a much better chance of identifying a particular boat and inferring from its movements its possible intentions, though again, Godfrey complained, 'neither RFP or TINA was precise.'[24] Moreover, all these methods lay at the mercy of ionospheric conditions and were further crippled by the fact that U-boats generally maintained radio silence. They used their radios only when they were near Allied ships or convoys, meaning that by the time the British picked up a signal, it was far too late for the hunted vessels to implement the avoidance strategies that had been so successful in the latter half of 1941.[25]

The other promising cryptographic weapon was something the British called 'Tunny' – a dual code name given to the deciphered message traffic passed by non-Morse teleprinters called *Hellschreiber* and *Geheimschreiber* and to the first analogue device developed in an attempt to decipher these encryption machines. Unlike the Enigma, which was widely distributed throughout to all services and handled day-to-day operational traffic, these teleprinters were extremely rare and provided a direct and 'secure' link for only the most sensitive strategic material passed between Hitler's headquarters and his diplomats abroad and high-level headquarters in the field.[26] Eventually, Bletchley Park, much to Ian Fleming's delight no doubt, would take the analogue machine light years ahead and develop the world's first programmable computer, a monstrosity code-named Colossus that produced what Bletchley called 'Fish' traffic, which played a pivotal role in the Allied successes from 1943 onwards. However, in the late spring of 1942, when the blackout was hitting its peak, Tunny was still in the developmental stage, leaving Godfrey, who was at the cutting edge of naval SIGINT development, to lament in early June that 'the bulk of the traffic is non-naval.'[27]

Potent as all these alternative sources would become later in the war, in the spring and summer of 1942 they had yet to reach maturity as consistent intelligence weapons. Meanwhile, the three-rotor *Dolphin* key, combined with the lower-level dockyard cipher, continued to produce a limited amount of intelligence. Reports of ship movements in home waters, the Baltic training grounds and Norway, along with details of the inner workings of U-boat bases on the west coast of France, allowed the Operational Intelligence Centre to track the comings and goings of U-boats from their ports. Using a combination of methods, it could glean intelligence regarding the commissioning of new craft and their trial runs, the names of their commanders, their new armaments, and even their departure from and return to port through the Bay of Biscay. Crucially, however, the OIC remained in the dark as to the location of submarines while in the vast expanse of the vital Atlantic Ocean. As the Submarine Tracking Room reported, 'Little can be said with any confidence in estimating the present and future movement of the U-boats.'[28]

$\backsim$

By the end of February 1942, the direct effects of the blackout on shipping were already setting off alarm bells within the Admiralty. The worry snowballed rapidly and became a full-blown crisis by the summer and autumn. In January, an 'acceptable' 440,000 tons of merchant shipping had been lost in the opening of the new U-boat offensive off the American coast – a regrettable number, but not too serious as long as the rate of sinkings did not rise and continue unabated.[29] In February, these dramatically increased, claiming 615,000 tons and leaving the Admiralty worried about future possibilities. Its concerns were recorded in a policy draft prepared for Admiral Sir Dudley Pound, the First Sea Lord and, in 1917, the officer who had been appointed to lead the first Plans Division in the Admiralty after it was established: 'So far our naval operations ... have been successful in maintaining our essential imports and war supplies, and bringing safely to this country large Dominion military forces. But the losses have been severe, and during January and February ... have again risen to dangerous figures.'[30]

If losses in the first two months of the year, which averaged 500,000 tons, could be classified as 'dangerous' and 'severe,' the peak months of March and April, respectively, whose average rose to 750,000 tons, brought near panic.[31] At least half the shipping losses were British or Dominion vessels. Although help from the American merchant fleet was able to offset this haemorrhage to some degree, the losses placed an enormous strain on all aspects of an already overtaxed British war economy. Told to expect replacements for the lost vessels in 1943 through either the British or the American shipbuilding programmes now gearing up, the Admiralty's Trade Division, headed by the son of the renowned Blinker Hall, viewed the overall 'acceptable' loss rate for the entire year at 4.5 million tons of shipping.[32] By July, losses had eclipsed that level, and by year's end, they were almost double.[33]

The trend continued throughout the summer and into the autumn as well, with the enormous monthly average of 685,000 tons lost in the remainder of the year.[34] This figure was almost twice the crisis level identified in 1941, forcing Pound's staff to warn:

> We are now approaching a crisis in the war and we must face the facts. We have lost control of the sea communications over a very wide area, and wherever we have lost this control, we have also lost all that depends upon it. Every day the enemy is extending his challenge to new areas and is increasing in strength ... our merchant losses are immense; the tanker situation is grave, and the supplies reaching this country are less than we require.[35]

In the interim, 'economizing efforts' across all fronts were stepped up as Great Britain faced an 8.4-million-ton deficit in non-tanker imports. Running down existing stocks cut this by half and another million was saved by economizing efforts in steel and steel-making, while the drop in wheat and bulk imports resulted in the dilution of bread with oats and potato flour to compensate for wheat shortages and a corresponding drop in morale on the home front.[36] More important than the broad drop in imports was the loss of specific items that formed choke points in industrial production. The shortage of phosphates, for example, sparked grave concern as imports from the United States dropped to dangerous lows. As R.S. Hudson, the Minister for Agriculture, summed it up in July: 'If we have sinkings, then we shan't be able to keep factories going after June (1943),' as there 'isn't enough in the country to last beyond Christmas.'[37]

Even more alarming were the types of ships suffering at the hands of the U-boats. In the first two months of Operation Drumbeat, the Admiralty calculated that it could absorb a 20 per cent loss rate for merchant vessels and a 13 per cent loss rate for the tankers that brought oil – the very lifeblood of the modern war machine – across the seas to British ports.[38] By March, the rate of merchant ship sinkings held, but the tanker toll skyrocketed to a staggering 24 per cent – meaning that one quarter of the vital oil heading to Great Britain was lost and, even more important, so were these specialized vessels and their crews.[39] In one short period in May, six U-boats alone took down more than 30 tankers in the Gulf of Mexico. That led to extraordinary temporary measures such as the suspension of oil shipments and the wide-scale rerouting of convoys.[40] By the end of the year, tanker losses would amount to over 1.5 million tons, with only a little over 200,000 tons set to be replaced by the current shipbuilding programme – indicators that pointed to a near-crippling choke point for the Allied war machine if the situation was not dealt with quickly and effectively.

Highly concerned with the declining state of affairs, the United States Navy stepped forward in an attempt to put these losses into a clearly relatable context:

If a submarine sinks two 6,000 ton ships and one 3,000 ton tanker, here is a typical account of what we totally lost: 42 tanks, 8 six-inch Howitzers, 88 twenty-five pound guns, 40 two-pound guns, 24 armored cars, 50 Bren Gun Carriers, 5,210 tons of ammunition, 600 rifles, 428 tons of tank supplies, 2,000 tons of stores and

1,000 tanks of gasoline ... To knock out the same amount of equipment by bombing ... the enemy would have to make three thousand
successful bombing sorties.[41]

As if all these material losses weren't discouraging enough, the need to
adopt blind and evasive rerouting of convoys from 'suspected' rather
than 'known' U-boat positions and hunting grounds exacerbated the
problem. Such defensive manoeuvres began to extend trips by thousands of miles. They also elongated the convoy cycle – the time at sea
– meaning that without the Germans even firing a shot, the mere threat
of running into a wolf pack without warning during this period contributed to a dangerous slowdown and corresponding drop in Britain's oil
quotas, which averaged 30,000 tons a month. By June, only 75 per cent
of required petroleum products were reaching the United Kingdom
because of actual and threatened U-boat attacks, compared with more
than 85 per cent the year before.[42] The United States may have been
able to out-produce the world's oil supply twenty times over, but that
potential was useless if the oil could not leave home shores or wound
up floating in one of the many slicks that now dotted the oceans. It
became clear, on a global scale, that without oil entire war economies
faltered – factories ceased production, trucks and ships did not move,
tanks could not fight, and aircraft could not fly – and that meant severe
restrictions on the power Great Britain could wield on the world stage.
Power, position and prestige were at stake.

In both parliament and the press, Churchill faced increasing attacks
from his political rivals who had already forced one parliamentary no-
confidence vote in January and now began to circle for another in late
spring. In a hurriedly called secret session of parliament that convened
on April 22, the prime minister addressed what he termed 'the gravest
matter' facing the Allies – 'namely, the enormous losses and destruction
of shipping by German U-boats' off the east coast of the United States.[43]
'In a period of less than thirty days,' he divulged, 'more tonnage was
sunk in this one stretch than we had lost all over the world during the
last five months of the Battle of the Atlantic before America entered the
war.'[44] He went on to admit that 'tonnage sinkings and the multiplica-
tion of U-boats constitutes [his] greatest anxiety.' In typical Churchillian

fashion, he couched the dismal news concerning the critical shortage of tankers in the best possible light, admitting on the one hand that severe losses had forced the suspension of shipments, while on the other lauding Great Britain's 'very large' (but albeit dwindling), oil reserves. No amount of positive spin, however, could quiet the escalating dissent.[45]

A month later, on May 19, Clement Attlee continued to rail in the House of Commons that sea transport remained a national 'tender spot' that provoked 'constant anxiety.'[46] Sir Stafford Cripps responded with a less than satisfactory retort that His Majesty's government was 'aware of the critical need of doing their utmost to cope with the situation.'[47] His reply set off an uproar that only increased with each ship lost over the next weeks. By the second day of July, Lord Maurice Hankey (who had dealt with the U-boat threat in the Great War as part of the Lloyd George Cabinet) had gone on the offensive in the House of Lords with Attlee's remarks, chastising Churchill for his lack of action, suggesting that the government was downplaying the crisis by stating that U-boats continued to 'take a heavy toll of cargo ships.'[48] In Hankey's estimation, that 'seem[ed] to be a rather modest description compared with President Roosevelt's ... recent statement that 'the battle of distribution is at a critical stage,' and he challenged the government's emphasis on increased shipbuilding as their strategy to offset the losses.[49] 'Well, it's obvious,' he told his fellow lordships, 'that protection is much more important even than replacement. Every ship saved is a built ship.'[50] From there, he invoked Lloyd George's memoirs concerning the menace faced 25 years earlier: 'It is a horrifying thought that it very nearly achieved the destruction of British sea-power, with all that such a disaster would have meant to the fortunes of the Alliance and humanity. It seems to me that this is really the vital issue of today.'[51]

The issue was coming to a head not only in the political realm, but also, more importantly, on the high seas with the Kriegsmarine. When the war began, the situation for the British was relatively straightforward and manageable in naval terms: the German navy was small in comparison with the Royal Navy and, though it possessed a handful of U-boats and a small surface fleet, it was bottled up in home waters that were vulnerable to blockade. Two and a half years later, close to 300 U-boats streamed unharmed out of bases on the western coast of France, in Germany and in Norway to raid shipping at will in the Atlantic, the Arctic and, as of the new year, the Mediterranean as well. Most of the key German surface vessels, including their battleships and cruisers, now called the Norwegian fjords home, standing ready to pounce on the vital Arctic convoys to Russia at any moment. The Italian fleet, despite its mauling at Cape Matapan a year earlier, remained a potential regional threat in the Mediterranean, while the French fleet, under the control of the collaborationist Vichy regime, formed a wild card that needed constant monitoring. In the Pacific, the Japanese navy proved more than a match for the American fleet in the opening rounds of their fight. That left the United States no longer capable, at least in the short term, of honouring in full its pre-war naval commitments for the Atlantic theatre; for the time being, the British had to shoulder the major responsibility there as well.

The great worry permeating the Admiralty, given the mounting success of the U-boats against Allied shipping, along with the active German naval building programme, was that Germany was slowly winning the war at sea through attrition, reducing British naval and merchant capacity while their own side remained untouched or, at least, did not suffer proportional losses.[52] As early as February, based on the estimates supplied by Godfrey's NID, the Admiralty's incisive Plans Division raised the alert:

> All this points to the expectation[,] and intelligence tends to confirm this, that in the Atlantic, the German navy will during the spring and summer of this year [1942] make an all-out effort to break down our sea power and bring the war to an end. For us, it is vital to win this battle by providing an adequate counter to the anticipated German naval and air measures.[53]

The proposed remedy was 'early intelligence,' coupled with 'persistent attack on enemy submarines' and 'adequate air cover.'[54]

And what of the future? It looked grim. The estimates Ian Fleming brought to Godfrey's attention at their weekly meetings in Room 39 concluded that Dönitz's fleet now had 90 of its nearly 300 submarines working in the Atlantic, with that overall number, based on current projections of German construction, set to increase by 60 per cent the following year.[55] In June, Sir Dudley Pound reflected the growing alarm. He warned his political master, Albert Victor 'A.V.' Alexander, the First Lord of the Admiralty: 'If we do not do something to stop the sinkings, we should, as an alternative, immediately introduce most drastic steps in civilian consumption and the use of raw materials.'[56] Attempts to placate Pound with assurances that the new shipbuilding programme would make good the losses did nothing to convince the wily old sailor. There were just too many 'ifs' in the equation – *if* the shipbuilding programmes lived up to expectations and *if* the sinkings did not increase. 'We cannot be certain of either of these things,' Pound told Alexander. 'For instance, we do not know what toll will be taken on our shipping when the German U-Boats number 500 as they will in July 1943.'[57]

The rate of U-boat construction far outpaced the Allies' ability to destroy the submarines – a feat exponentially harder now that the British had lost their ability to hunt them down effectively. In fact, in early 1942, only 20 per cent of the fleet had been sunk, leaving 160 of them in operation, with 115 training for battle in the Baltic. Every month, an additional 22 submarines were delivered fresh from German factories, far outpacing the measly five to seven U-boats sunk or lost to other causes each month.[58]

Without a doubt, all indicators pointed to an imminent crisis, and Pound had to confront both the enemy on the high seas and the Air Ministry at home. In part to make up for the void left by the loss of Ultra in the Atlantic, the Admiralty had demanded a portion of the heavy bombers that the RAF was presently using to bomb German cities – the only practical support, apart from the Arctic convoys, being tendered to the hard-pressed Soviets on the eastern front. The Admiralty wanted a chunk of this precious air commodity to maintain a constant vigil over stretches of the Atlantic and the Bay of Biscay, where the bombers would attack U-boats departing for or arriving from their bases in western France. In addition, Pound argued that Bomber Command should target assembly plants – or U-boat 'hatching' areas, as Churchill called them – or even take a shot at U-boats inside their impregnable pens. On this last point, the Admiralty now had strong support from President Franklin Roosevelt.[59]

There is no doubt that Churchill was fully alive to the situation. In the annexe close to his flat, he kept his own map room – as he had during his time as First Lord. The room was run by a tall Irishman, Captain Richard Pim – a civilian, like Ian Fleming, commissioned into the RNVR – who marked the maps with pins showing the positions of British (now Allied) forces and, where known, of enemy forces. There he also recorded naval engagements, air attacks, ships, convoys, shipping losses and, now infrequently, U-boat locations. The pins' positions were constantly updated, so the prime minister was never out of touch. As Elizabeth Nel, Churchill's personal secretary, recalled:

> Each morning while we were in London, a Map Room officer would present himself soon after Mr. Churchill waked to give the latest news, and at all hours of the day or night, somebody was on duty to report anything new or to investigate any inquiry we might wish to make. From the time of Casablanca onwards, Mr. Churchill never travelled without a detachment from his Map Room, which always included Captain Pim, complete with maps, dividers and other trappings, so that wherever the Prime Minister was, even aboard ship, a Map Room could immediately be set up.[60]

Knowing Churchill's keen interest in the navy and that his steady diet of U-boat Ultra had ceased, Dudley Pound suggested a course of action that shrewdly took account of the Admiralty's needs and of the prime minister's very demanding idiosyncrasies. With Churchill doubling as minister of defence, his influence within the War Cabinet was decisive when it came to the allocation of resources. Pound, therefore, made sure, in his bid to gain the aircraft he needed to solve the pressing crisis at sea, to include a prioritized list of the glaring issues that he felt coincided with Churchill's personal interests – intelligence, the *Tirpitz* (the *Bismarck*'s sister ship) and the defeat of the U-boats all topped the list.[61] This list was the opening shot in what Pound later dubbed the Battle of the Air – the fight over allocation of air resources for the Admiralty and the Air Ministry and, ultimately, over the direction of British grand strategy.[62]

But Pound's tactic with Churchill backfired: he had miscalculated the prime minister's approach to the issue. Although Churchill in no way dismissed the urgent and pressing needs faced by the Royal Navy and the British merchant fleet, he viewed the war at sea and the Battle of the Atlantic as purely defensive in nature. Strategic bombing, in contrast, gave him an immediate *force de frappe* – the only offensive weapon capable of bringing the war directly to the German people while hammering away at their morale and their crucial industrial infrastructure. With mounting air raids, sometimes in excess of 1,000 bombers over a given city on one night, strategic bombing was for Churchill 'better than doing nothing and a formidable method of injuring the enemy.'[63] Also important, it provided substantial propaganda value in lieu of a second front for Stalin's Soviet Union. Unfortunately for John Godfrey and Dudley Pound, the increased focus on strategic bombing denied the allocation of resources that the Royal Navy desperately needed to offset the results of the intelligence blackout.

So far as the Admiralty was concerned, this refusal of its request appeared to show that Churchill, in his quest to bring maximum pressure to bear on Germany, was willing to trade heavy shipping losses at sea for his own priority – strategic bombing. Indeed, in July 1942, Churchill wrote a memo that included these telling words: 'It might be true to say that the issue of the war depends on whether Hitler's U-boat attack on Allied tonnage or the increase and application of Allied Airpower, reach their full fruition first.'[64]

Although Pound brokered a limited agreement for the transfer of four squadrons of long-range aircraft in mid-April, they were still not enough to fill the void left by the loss of Ultra. By June, frustration within the Admiralty had reached a crisis point. Admiral John Tovey, the Commander-in-Chief of Home Fleet and the officer who not only had led the final charge against the *Bismarck* but was responsible for protecting the Arctic convoys to Russia, told Pound:

> It was difficult to believe that the population of Cologne [Germany] would notice much difference between a raid of 1,000 bombers and one by 750.
>
> I informed Their Lordships that, in my opinion, the situation at sea was now so grave that the time had come for a stand to be made, even

if this led to Their Lordships taking the extreme step of resignation. I was supported in my contentions by Admiral of the Fleet Sir Charles Forbes and Admiral Sir Andrew Cunningham.[65]

To these men, it clearly appeared that Churchill had abandoned the Royal Navy at its darkest moment. However, the likely scenario is that, wisely or unwisely, he maintained faith in the eventual resumption of the flow of Ultra. Certainly, John Godfrey did, and why not? After all, the bold and increasingly systematic approach to pinch raids the previous year had paid handsomely when the problem with the three-rotor Enigma was equally dark and daunting. With Mountbatten's Combined Operations in place – an exciting and virile delivery vehicle – optimism made sense. Already it was basking in the results of its Norwegian escapades and a set of spectacular raids on the French coast in February and March 1942 (exploits which are explored in more detail in chapter 7).

Mountbatten's nascent brand of Combined Operations offered a relatively cost-effective approach to accomplish several essential goals simultaneously: in the wake of recent defeats in Asia and North Africa, to demonstrate Britain's continued will to fight and raise morale; to assist the hard-pressed Soviet Union; to develop the amphibious capabilities for an eventual second front; and to work covertly to maintain, or in this case re-establish, cryptographic success and break the black-out with a major pinch.

၅

Britain had yet another reason to fear the four-rotor Enigma and *Shark*, the key used by Dönitz's U-boats in the Atlantic. Cryptanalysis, and in particular Ultra, was not only a remarkable British breakthrough but, arguably, one of the last indigenous natural resources that Great Britain possessed. The technology and processes developed in Bletchley Park's code-breaking huts to exploit both the Enigma machine and, a year later, to build Colossus, the world's first programmable computer, to break Tunny, were undeclared national treasures that remained wrapped in a cloak of secrecy for decades following the war. The fruits of the collective intellectual labour at Bletchley Park were expected, first, to help defeat the Allies' enemies on the field of battle and, later, to give Great Britain a rare commodity for the future.

With the sun setting on the Empire, monopolization of cryptographic technology gave the British the ability to stand toe to toe with the rising Americans, who would soon eclipse them as a superpower on the world stage. Right from the beginning of the war, the British jealously guarded their cryptographic abilities. They went to great lengths to control and protect this source, not only from their enemies but in certain respects from their allies as well – unless circumstances dictated otherwise.

In the summer of 1940, while Ian Fleming was devising Operation Ruthless, Churchill, spurred on by his country's dire predicament and the need to protect vital interests in the Atlantic, had approached President Roosevelt with an offer to establish a limited signals intelligence partnership built around the basic premise of 'spheres of influence.'[66] By this time, the Americans were already engaged in their own cryptographic pursuits, primarily centred on message traffic from Asia and the Pacific. Churchill's proposal called for a division of labour in which the Americans maintained their Far Eastern focus while Great Britain dominated the production of signals intelligence in Europe.[67] Part of this approach stemmed from the sober realization that the aggressive rise of Japan in Asia and Nazi Germany in Europe would likely draw the United States into the war sooner rather than later. However, as Churchill knew full well, the entry of the Americans was a double-edged sword. On the one hand, this new ally brought unprecedented economic and industrial might that would likely guarantee ultimate victory. On the other hand, if left unchecked, this power threatened to bleed proportionately into the realm of cryptography, leaving Britain as a bystander rather than the lead actor in both a new world order and the dawning of the information age.

Several additional factors cast shadows over the proposed special relationship between Britain and the United States. The British harboured a justified fear of the cavalier, indiscreet way in which the Americans tended to treat the fragile nature of cryptographic security. For example, at the height of the Great Depression and in desperate need of money, Herbert Yardley, the former head of the American cryptographic bureau who had worked with the British and the French during the last years of the First World War and into the inter-war period, published *The American Black Chamber*.[68] The book was based on his personal experiences and exposed the work not only of the US bureau but also of his allies, particularly the reading of Japanese envoy messages during the Washington Naval Conference in 1920–21. As expected, the book was an instant bestseller on three continents. It succeeded in pulling the bon vivant and rumoured serial womanizer out of his financial bind but left him a pariah. Immediately, it set off a firestorm of controversy and bitterness, with the British in particular feeling betrayed.

In British eyes, Yardley exemplified a careless American brashness that should be avoided at all costs in an industry where discretion and security were paramount. Eventually, he resurrected his career, offering his talents in mercenary fashion first to Chiang Kai-shek's Nationalist Party in China in the late 1930s and then to the Canadian government, which in 1940 seemed bent on joining the exclusive signals intelligence club. His tenure was short-lived: once the British got wind of his employment, the Government Code and Cypher School refused to continue its support for the novice Canadian signals intelligence community as long as Yardley remained on staff. And so he was fired – the day before the Japanese attack on Pearl Harbor – and replaced by Oliver Strachey, a legendary Bletchley Park cryptanalyst, whose work on breaking German agent traffic led to the ISOS process being named after him: Intelligence Service Oliver Strachey.

This British fear was entirely genuine and legitimate. The Americans had not experienced the same level of cryptographic success that the British had already enjoyed for decades – first during the Blinker Hall days in the Great War and later in the early years of the new war. As such, cryptography, at least at first, did not occupy the same pedestal position as it did with the British, who viewed the Americans as essentially loose cannons when it came to security. The British knew that American codes and ciphers were notoriously porous and that even the State Department cipher had been penetrated by friend and foe alike. In England, Bletchley Park and cryptographic work, in general, came under the control of the Foreign Office and the Secret Intelligence Service, while in the United States the navy, the army, the FBI and the

State Department all delved into signals intelligence and cryptography independently for their own, at times competing, purposes. Protecting their fiefdoms became their main focus, and the lack of a central coordinating body left the British fearful that one jealous, ignorant or even malicious dispute could jeopardize their whole mission.

Despite this mistrust, when events in the Atlantic heated up, the British were forced to approach the Americans about becoming active participants and intelligence partners in the war at sea – even if, ideally, they would keep them as limited intelligence partners. That meant that the issues surrounding Germany's Enigma machine became the major points for discussion in most of their intelligence dealings.

ꝏ

Neither side at first rushed into the other's arms, but despite British promises of full disclosure, it was the Americans who extended the first hand in late 1940, when they gave Bletchley Park a reproduction of the 'Purple' machine that the Japanese used to encipher diplomatic messages. That allowed Britain's Far East Combined Bureau in Singapore to attack Japanese ciphers.[69] Hot on the heels of this historic exchange, Churchill permitted representatives from the Government Code and Cypher School to discuss Bletchley's breakthroughs into all forms of the Enigma, but then, despite earlier promises, he pulled up short of authorizing a full exchange of technologies. Although the Americans demanded a physical specimen of a captured Enigma for their cryptanalysts to work with, the mission team they sent to Bletchley Park for two months late in 1940 came away with only a paper copy of the inner workings of the machine. Citing security concerns and potential redundancy of work, the British guarded their precious commodity tightly. Also, the Americans were not permitted to take notes about anything related to the Enigma, nor could they view documents or other material about its solution.[70]

The sudden change in the British approach to sharing intelligence with the Americans was a curious development that warrants clarification. On February 13, 1996, a little over two years before he passed away, I met with the recently knighted Sir Harry Hinsley, who, fresh from his valuable analytical work in Hut 8 in the early years of the war, had gone on to be the GC&CS representative for naval cryptographic negotiations with the Americans for the remainder of the war and for some time after. He then returned to St John's College, Cambridge, where he enjoyed a stellar academic career as an international relations historian and, in particular, as the author of the voluminous official history of British intelligence in the Second World War.

And so it happened that, five decades later, when I arrived in Cambridge after an overnight flight from Montreal for our scheduled meeting, I was told at the college that both Sir Harry and Lady Hinsley were at home ill, but that I should phone him at once. In his legendary enthusiastic way, Hinsley refused my offer to come back on another day. 'My dear boy,' he said, 'you have come a long way across the ocean to see me – and you shall.' For Sir Harry, 'all the way across the ocean' conjured up a two-week journey on an ocean liner that had to ply U-boat-infested waters. He insisted that I come to his flat near the university. By this time in his late seventies and rather gnomish in stature, he greeted me with a broad smile and an outstretched hand, which was withered and malformed by rheumatoid arthritis. For the next few hours, we sat and discussed signals intelligence, Ultra and intelligence-sharing with the Americans. On that point, he confided, 'control of the technological know-how was the overriding theory in guiding GC&CS relations with the US.'[71]

Harry Hinsley made it clear to me that, from the start, the British were adamant about agreeing to a partnership only after 'it became obvious that another power was on its way to create the technology necessary to discontinue reliance on GC&CS.'[72] If confronted with this scenario, they would 'provide ... any information they required from this type of technology, partially to protect the source, but primarily to protect their monopoly.'[73] In other words, it was one thing to open the taps to the pipeline and allow the Americans as much of the product as they required, but under no circumstances should they help the Americans find and develop their own deposits, let alone gain the knowledge to create their own refinery and pipeline system. They were adamant that control must remain in British hands, and only if met with an inevitable takeover or duplication would they move quickly to establish a full working partnership.

When the British achieved the first breaks into the three-rotor naval Enigma in early 1941, they were more than happy to offer the products of their findings to OP-20-G, the acronym used to denote the 'Office of Chief of Naval Operations (OPNAV), 20th Division of the Office of Naval Communications, G Section / Communications Security' – the Washington-based version of the Operational Intelligence Centre. The British needed material cooperation from the US Navy to protect their shipping in American waters, and the provision of Ultra seemed a small price to pay for American assistance during this period of neutrality.

By June 1941, a regular delivery of Ultra passed from England to the United States, via cable and diplomatic pouch direct to the offices of the British Security Coordination in the Rockefeller Center in New York.[74] In August, the Government Code and Cypher School posted a liaison officer to OP-20-G to handle Ultra. By the time Pearl Harbor was bombed on December 7, the United States and Great Britain had been limited signals intelligence partners for almost a year.

But the relationship was tense and, according to Godfrey, quickly developed into a 'very prickly subject' by December of 1941.[75] Less than a week before Pearl Harbor, complaints from the United States Navy put a strain on the special relationship. Having waited for more than a year for a reciprocal delivery of the naval Enigma machine they had requested earlier, the US Navy now accused the British of foot-dragging on Enigma-related material. It threatened to withhold further information on the Pacific unless it received full reciprocal information on European work. In response, the GC&CS representative in Washington warned: 'There is a grave unrest and dissatisfaction in free exchange of [Ultra] ... You will appreciate the importance of this matter as United States are developing rapidly. The question should be faced and settled with the least delay or our relations will deteriorate, and lost ground will be hard to recover.'[76]

Up to this point, the Operational Intelligence Centre had been providing the Americans with daily reports listing U-boat dispositions as known through Ultra. However, when the wolf packs shifted to American shores and, soon after, the four-rotor Enigma appeared, that service was quickly snuffed out; an already tense relationship approached a breaking point.[77]

Faced with legitimate demands from the Americans for help in curbing the German U-boat feeding frenzy off the American coast inflamed by the blackout, the British found themselves in an awkward situation. At first, not realizing that the Americans were planning to embark on their own design for a Bombe, they explained that they had neither the time nor the machines to solve the issue – an honest response but, nonetheless, a grave miscalculation. The Americans, who had been content at first to take a back seat and play a supporting role in the signals intelligence effort in the Atlantic, were no longer prepared to sit idly by, given their own skyrocketing shipping losses and the failure of the British to produce the cryptographic goods promised. The United States had genuine operational concerns. By June 1942 the head of the US Army, General George C. Marshall, told Admiral Ernest King, the head of the United States Navy, that 'losses by submarines off our Atlantic seaboard and in the Caribbean now threaten our entire war effort ... I am fearful that another month or two of this will so cripple our means of transport that we will be unable to bring sufficient men and planes to bear against the enemy.'[78]

If the losses continued, operational issues would turn into political criticism as well. Soon enough, the press would begin to ask even more difficult questions about the mounting number of sinkings and the loss of life, and the lack of offensive action would lead to public demands for answers. The congressional or Senate investigation that would inevitably follow would force President Roosevelt to pressure the navy to adopt corrective measures. And those measures, in turn, could well mean that the Americans, with their deep coffers, would press ahead on the naval Enigma issue, leaving the British behind if necessary.[79]

In the early spring of 1942, the British learned that the Americans were indeed taking the first of several huge steps in that direction. Tucked away in an obscure structure innocuously named Building 26 on the grounds of the National Cash Register Company in Dayton, Ohio, the Americans had assembled an impressive array of intellectual talent and embarked on their own Bombe-building scheme, which was given equal priority and funding with the Manhattan Project – the attempt to build the world's first atomic bomb.[80] How long it would take to achieve results was anyone's guess, but it was clear that the

Americans were embarking on a parallel approach to the problem. This overt industrialization of the American cryptographic mission, backed by millions of dollars (trillions by today's standards), meant that the clock was indeed ticking on British efforts at Bletchley Park.

In response, the Government Code and Cypher School sent a team of cryptographic liaison officers across the Atlantic to exercise damage control. It was led by Lieutenant Colonel John Tiltman, or 'the Brig' as he was later affectionately known in intelligence circles (he became a brigadier in 1944), one of Bletchley Park's finest cryptanalysts on non-machine systems.[81] Tiltman had been an early and eager advocate for British cooperation with the Americans in cryptography, and his task now was to buy time for the British to solve the four-rotor riddle by direct or indirect methods. His précis on Enigma policy, written in 1942, confirms what Hinsley referred to during my interview with him. Operating under explicit instructions from both Stewart Menzies, the head of the Secret Intelligence Service, and the 'gruff, rough and burly' Edward Travis, the loved and respected successor to Alastair Denniston as head of GC&CS, Tiltman was asked to 'point out that we did not wish to hide from the services in Washington the details of our successes, but that we wished to discourage them from attempting any exploitation until it became essential.'[82] Failing that, he was to channel or quarantine American anxiety and determination in order to minimize any damage to Britain's own programme either through competition or security leaks.

When Tiltman arrived in the United States, the tension was running high, and tempers among American cryptanalysts rapidly growing thin. Greeted at his first meeting with open derision by some American cryptanalysts, the thoroughly professional Tiltman kept his equilibrium, recording only that it was 'clear that the [US] Navy Department were extremely disturbed over the German U-Boats situation.'[83]

Despite the rough beginning, the British mission produced encouraging results. First, Tiltman smoothed ruffled feathers by candidly revealing the problems Bletchley Park faced with the Germans' recent introduction of a four-rotor machine – a move that apparently thawed the tense atmosphere after the Americans, who had received no previous confirmation of the existence of this new machine, realized that the value of their initial work on the three-rotor Enigma was now moot.[84] Even in the current critical situation, he downplayed the need for the United States to develop its own Bombe, attempting to assure the Americans with false promises that the British had one in the works that would crack the machine shortly. Finally, Tiltman agreed to open up the stingy lines of communication and share more information on naval Enigma. He even invited the US Navy to send a team of experts to Bletchley Park to see everything they were doing to solve the crisis.[85] The Americans now realized that 'thefts, German errors, and cryptanalytic craftsmanship had been, and would be, the only ways into naval Enigma.'[86]

Before long, Tiltman managed to win his American counterparts over, principally through his disarming nature, which they viewed as the embodiment of eccentric British brilliance and quite unlike the intellectual and cultural condescension they had expected. They warmed to his relaxed style, devoid of deference to uniform or tradition, along with his paternalistic but never patronizing use of 'old boy' with everyone he encountered.[87]

Reporting back to Commander Travis, Tiltman explained that he had reached an agreement with the United States Navy that the solution and exploitation of Enigma could best be carried out by Bletchley Park.[88] He warned, however, that certain considerations must be taken into account. 'In view of the fact that they [the Americans] are now at War and have a vital interest in Submarine traffic,' he wrote, 'they are entitled to results or a detailed statement as to why this traffic cannot be read at present and what are the prospects for the future.' This compromise formed only a band-aid solution, and he went on to warn Travis that 'unless a rapid and satisfactory solution is found[,] the High Command will insist on their naval Cryptanalysts attempting to duplicate our work on E[nigma].'[89]

It was clear that Tiltman's visit had achieved the desired effect of calming the fires, at least in the short term, but it was equally certain that American patience on the matter was running out. In June, the spectacular success afforded the US Navy by their deft cryptanalysts, who had pierced the Japanese navy's main fleet cipher in the pivotal battle of Midway, once again inflamed their appetite for Ultra.[90] Fuelled by unresolved losses to their merchant shipping that reached an all-time high that month, American angst grew exponentially, leaving one GC&CS liaison to warn Travis at Bletchley that 'sooner or later, the United States Navy is going to tackle the U boat traffic whether we like it or not.'[91]

Indeed, the writing was on the wall, and the US Navy was bound to become an undeniable force with an insatiable hunger in the British-dominated world of cryptography. In *realpolitik* terms, this realization meant that the British could either attempt to solve the issue immediately or, in the face of futility, admit as much to the American Navy and bring them on board as full rather than limited partners. Full cooperation with the Americans on the four-rotor Bombe could be viewed as an 'acceptable' loss and the cost of retaining the remainder of their evaporating cryptographic monopoly.[92]

With all these complexities in mind, the best course of action for the British was to hedge their bets by acting on both fronts simultaneously: they would move ahead full throttle on their own development but, when necessary, cooperate with the United States. Either way, even if both sides could develop an operational four-rotor Bombe in 1942, they would still require pinched material for it to work efficiently. Another successful pinch was, therefore, of the utmost urgency.

CHAPTER 7

Kick at the Darkness

We must not lose our faculty to dare,
particularly in dark days.
Winston Churchill, March 24, 1942

With the Allies in full-blown retreat or on the defensive on almost every front at the dawning of 1942, Mountbatten's Combined Operations stood out as the lone delivery vehicle capable of offensive action and thus feeding Bletchley Park's voracious appetite for German code and cipher materials. Having built his reputation in part on his work in signals intelligence, Mountbatten understood what was at stake when he tasked Jock Hughes-Hallett and his planning syndicate to create a raiding programme for a series of targets along the French coast.

With outline plans rapidly taking shape for raids on Bruneval, St Nazaire, Bayonne, and the upcoming invasion of Madagascar, the relationship between COHQ and NID began to congeal. During that period Mountbatten began to lean heavily on Godfrey's brainchild – the Inter-Services Topographical Department (ISTD) – to lay down the basic framework for each amphibious operation. In the wake of the fall of France, Godfrey had recognized that a highly detailed knowledge of the terrain ashore would prove crucial to the success of any amphibious operation and created the ISTD specifically to support that purpose.[1] Responsible to the chiefs of staff through the Joint Intelligence Committee (which he sat on as the naval representative), the ISTD as Godfrey envisioned it was a 'top secret department' that dealt with 'the fruits of covert intelligence, much of which was obtained by clandestine methods' to create intelligence work-ups on selected target areas for projected raids.[2]

According to Godfrey, 'one of the most important subjects of ISTD Work was naval – viz Ports,' and the reports his department produced were considered first-class for its time, containing impressively thick planning dossiers and maps, aerial photos and diagrams, local post-cards, and even family holiday snapshots submitted by the general public of both the natural and urban environments. The ISTD quickly became his pet project, his crowning glory and the centre of gravity for his burgeoning intelligence empire.[3]

Like clockwork on Wednesday mornings, John Godfrey climbed into his chauffeured staff car with briefcase in hand and headed north to Bletchley. The trip that began in the rubble-strewn and, at times, smoke-filled streets of London ended roughly 90 minutes later in the splendour of the Buckinghamshire countryside. The journey provided the Director of Naval Intelligence with a rare opportunity to engage in uninterrupted study and peaceful reflection as well as a short visit with his wife, Margaret, and their eldest daughter, Katherine.

In the best nepotistic traditions of the intelligence world, Godfrey had placed first his wife and then his daughter in support positions at Bletchley Park, as had his RAF counterpart on the Joint Intelligence Committee, Air Marshal Charles Medhurst, whose daughter Rozanne worked alongside Kate and the 'boffins' in the huts. In his other roles as a member of the Joint Intelligence Committee and of the Y Committee, which set policy for signals intelligence, Godfrey found that these regular visits to Bletchley allowed him to keep abreast of the latest developments in both the Naval Section and Hut 8, where he liaised with Frank Birch, Alan Turing and others involved in cryptanalysis. Just days before he announced his January 1942 change in pinch policy, Godfrey could rightly boast to Bletchley's overlord, Stewart Menzies: 'I have seen more of the workings of B.P. than any other Director of Intelligence and probably more than any outside authority.'[4]

The secret home of British cryptography was just the first stop on his Wednesday route. Later in the day, Godfrey would drive the 40 miles into Oxford to visit the Inter-Services Topographical Department, where he kept an office with a direct link to Room 39 in the Old Admiralty Building in London. Godfrey transferred Margaret, after her brief tenure at Bletchley Park, to the ISTD, and there she very ably played much the same role for her husband as Ian Fleming did in the Naval Intelligence Division.[5]

The purpose of ISTD was to act as a central collecting, collating and compilation department for all the topographical knowledge bearing on a proposed site for amphibious assault.[6] The concept stemmed from yet another of Blinker Hall's First World War ideas, where he recruited civilians from the universities to create a series of geographical handbooks. Godfrey's Second World War version occupied several buildings in the Schools of Geography in Manchester and Mansfield colleges and in the Bodleian Library. For Godfrey, the location was vital: first, he needed to tap into the brightest minds that Oxford and Cambridge had to offer, much in the same way that the Government Code and Cypher School had stocked Bletchley Park's cryptographic endeavours; and second, it gave him full access to the machinery of Oxford University Press, which printed, among other highly sensitive documents, the Most Secret Royal Navy signals codebooks. By 1942, the ISTD accounted for more than two-thirds of all the material published by the university press, including a series of pamphlets known as the Inter-Services Information Series (ISIS) and special topographical intelligence work-ups on potential landing areas, which were used in the planning for amphibious operations.[7]

Ironically, it was Winston Churchill's return to the Admiralty as First Lord on the opening day of the war that had set the wheels in motion for the creation of Godfrey's Topographical Department. The signal sent by the Admiralty board announcing emphatically and defiantly that 'Winston is back!' came as both a blessing and a curse. Not all members of the Royal Navy interpreted the magisterial pronouncement as a 'second coming.' Churchill's return put the Royal Navy on its toes and drove some members, such as Dudley Pound, the First Sea Lord, and John Godfrey, to strive to harness or at least channel Churchill's notorious proclivity for incessant meddling and 'wildcat operations' of the type that had led to the disastrous landings at Gallipoli in the Dardanelles during the First World War.[8] They could only redouble their efforts when, in May of the following year, he was also appointed prime minister.

Godfrey had initially created the Inter-Services Topographical Department – with ample backing from the chiefs of staff – to prevent another Gallipoli, in which Allied troops suffered heavily in large part due to their profound ignorance of the Turkish terrain, defences and enemy forces.[9] As he would later write:

> Every year between 1919 and 1939, the staff college spent a month or six weeks examining every aspect of combined operations and opposed landings. We knew in 1939 how to conduct an amphibious operation, what preparations were needed, and what to avoid, but at Gallipoli we were ignorant of [the] nature of the country over which we were to fight, of the condition of the defences we were called upon to assault, and of the morale, equipment and order of battle of the Turkish Army.[10]

He records in his unpublished memoir that the chiefs of staff, the Joint Planning Staff, the Joint Intelligence Committee and the Joint Intelligence Staff all 'carefully curbed ... Churchill's appetite for diversionary operations ... but not until the ISTD ... had put in a great deal of hard preparatory work.'[11] Ironically – and happily for Godfrey – it was precisely Churchill's interest in these 'diversionary operations and landings on hostile shores' that accelerated the growth of his new organization.[12]

Godfrey's vision for the ISTD was for it to act as a combined intelligence body, or as a clearing house that would cut across the partisan rivalries that had plagued operational planning and execution during the First World War, and provide the essential intelligence needed to carry out successful amphibious combined operations.[13] He hoped that, when the chiefs of staff and the joint planners could not effectively dissuade or contain Churchill in one of his ill-conceived schemes, they could at least satisfy his orders and filter the idea through a proper planning process – one founded on reliable intelligence provided by all three services and coordinated under one roof. 'Total War deserved Total Intelligence,' Godfrey believed, and the Topographical Department gave him the machine for serving up information on unusual topics at very short notice – a valuable commodity with Churchill at the helm.[14] At the same time, Godfrey knew he was crossing a Rubicon of sorts by delving into this domain: the work, while decidedly military in character, came under naval direction and could quickly 'ricochet on the DNI and Admiralty if anything [went] wrong.'[15]

From its inception, the beaches, the landing areas and, above all, the ports along the Channel coast were the 'cardinal interest' for the Topographical Department.[16] Yet when Dudley Pound requested a full work-up on the French coastline to prepare for the Dunkirk evacuation in late May 1940, Godfrey discovered that his Naval Intelligence Division had no information to share; nothing in advance of this historic moment had required intelligence on an area they expected would remain in Allied hands. Immediately, he called on several captains from a British shipping firm that regularly plied the Channel for their expertise and dispatched two reconnaissance teams to scour the coastline for the much-needed intelligence.[17] With the German armies advancing towards them, one team covered the area from Le Havre to Dieppe while the other raced from Dieppe to Cherbourg.[18] Given the circumstances, both reports were crude, hasty endeavours, with photographs of the terrain pasted onto folio-sized brown paper and linked by a simple text. 'It was I think inadequate and shabbily dressed compared with the elaborate productions used later,' Godfrey recalled, 'but at least it was a start.'

Meanwhile, Godfrey sent Ian Fleming to France as well, though not to do scouting along the coast. Even as the German invaders advanced towards Paris, Fleming was in the capital trying to maintain links with the French navy and to ascertain Admiral François Darlan's intentions concerning the disposition of his fleet if France fell to the enemy. Arriving to find that Darlan had moved his headquarters to Tours, on the west coast of France, Fleming removed the Royal Navy's Top Secret teleprinter from the British embassy and the cash contents from the Secret Intelligence Service safe in the city and beat a hasty retreat towards Bordeaux, keeping Godfrey informed on the rapidly unfolding events via wireless. The man who travelled with him and helped him signal Godfrey was Patrick Beesly, Godfrey's future biographer.[19]

Initially, the Inter-Services Topographical Department had been greeted with apathy in wartime Britain. But with Churchill's increasing demands for operations of all sorts and the creation of Combined Operations to carry them out, the unit swelled from its first seventeen members after it was set up on June 12, 1940, to 72 by the end of 1941 and eventually to 541 by 1944. It became, as Godfrey remembered, 'an inter-service monster' that, as his biographer notes, signalled a bid for 'empire-building on a grand scale.'[20] From June 1940 onwards, 'no single Commando, hardly an agent of SOE and certainly no major Allied force set foot on German or Italian held territory without the benefit of detailed information about the terrain and its natural and man-made features and characteristics supplied by ISTD.'[21]

By the time 1942 rolled around, the monster had taken on several heads and was 'continually bombarded with requests for topographical data about possible landings and enterprises, many of them filtering down from the Prime Minister's fertile mind.'[22] Churchill was not the only suitor: all three services, along with the SIS, the Special Operations Executive and the Joint Planning Staff, made regular use of the information it provided, as did its greatest client, Mountbatten's Combined Operations Headquarters.

The association with Combined Operations predated Mountbatten's tenure; it had started immediately after the organization was established. At first, Combined Operations had been inclined to produce its own topographical data, but Godfrey soon persuaded Admiral Sir Roger Keyes, the first director, to attach one of his staff to work in Oxford – a move that paid immediate dividends.[23] Very quickly, close cooperation developed between the two organizations as they worked in conjunction to gather intelligence for a large number of raids and an even larger number of plans – some of which never went into effect.[24] Initially, the requests were small, supporting pinprick raids along the French coast in 1940. Within a year, however, the ISTD had produced the report that would be the basis for the very successful raids on the Lofoten Islands and Vaagso.[25] By May 1942, Mountbatten had come to rely so heavily on the work of the Topographical Department that Godfrey felt compelled to issue a memo, circulated inside the Combined Operations intelligence section, to stop sending requests for a short period 'as the ISTD staff are working 24 hours a day and it is feared some may collapse.'[26]

Godfrey's caution was not without foundation: during a 90-day period between October 1941 and January 1942, the ISTD created more than 30 'special reports' in response to urgent requests from both Mountbatten's staff and the Joint Planning Staff. Among the demands that topped the lists were work-ups on the areas of St Nazaire, Bayonne and Dieppe.

∽

The raid on St Nazaire has been dubbed the 'Greatest Raid of All,' with scores of articles, books, a feature film and a recent BBC documentary canonizing the bravado, courage and sheer audacity that brought about spectacular results.[27] It was not by any means as large an operation as Dieppe – but it was successful. And it still remains a showcase for what Lord Louis Mountbatten's Combined Operations could accomplish. The bold idea of attacking Hitler's heavily defended *Festung* (Fortress) St Nazaire at the mouth of the river Loire on the Biscay coast first arose in the weeks following the successful hunt for the *Bismarck* in 1941. In the summer, the Admiralty had learned through Ultra that her sister ship, the *Tirpitz*, an equally daunting and powerful adversary, had just finished sea trials in the Baltic before heading into position to blockade the Soviet fleet near Leningrad. So far, there were no indications that she would venture out to wreak havoc on the Atlantic trade, but preparations had to be made for that eventuality.

Within the NID, the French part of Section 1 was responsible for intelligence concerning the Channel coastline and the rest of France. It was headed by retired Royal Navy commander George Edmund Gonin, a British businessman who lived in Antwerp and had a particular interest in ports. With Godfrey's blessing, Gonin, who represented NID at the first meeting following the formation of Combined Operations in 1940, approached Keyes's staff in the hope of gaining their support for a cunning plan. The approach did not come out of left field given the close association that had already developed between the NID and

Combined Operations Headquarters, with the former providing intelligence and advice in the selection of raiding targets.

The idea Gonin proposed was straightforward: because Ultra had clearly revealed that the *Bismarck*, when she was attacked and sunk, was making for the Normandie dry dock in St Nazaire – the only facility in western France with a dry dock capable of housing the 42,000-ton vessel for repairs – why not launch a commando raid on that port itself, which also housed one of the largest U-boat bases?[28] With one bold move, the British could achieve two major goals. Destroying the lock gates or disabling the pumping mechanisms used to control the flow of water into and out of the dry dock would render the port 'tidal,' flooding the dry dock and denying the *Tirpitz* a repair facility. That act alone would dramatically reduce, if not eliminate, the chances of the giant battleship venturing into the Atlantic. At the same time, the attack offered an opportunity to destroy or disable a few of Dönitz's deadly submarines while at anchor and, although this was not stated, pinch vital material in the process.

Unsure of whether their current operational capabilities would permit such a daring raid, Keyes initially baulked at the idea, leaving it in limbo for months, until the Admiralty's Plans Division, thoroughly prompted and backed by Godfrey, decided to push ahead with the scheme, generating a planning docket that included intelligence gathered by both his ISTD and the wily Gonin.[29]

Having discovered through his myriad contacts that the engineering firm which helped construct the locks was based in London, Gonin had obtained a model of the lock gates along with detailed reports and air photographs, and then consulted the Special Operations Executive on where best to place the explosive charges. The resulting plan was desperate, bold – and close to suicidal. It involved taking a group of highly trained commandos and placing them on board a collection of motor torpedo boats (MTBs) and an obsolete and therefore expendable destroyer, HMS *Campbeltown*, which would be disguised as a German vessel. With the destroyer's bow lower decks primed with a timed explosive charge, the entire force would then sail into St Nazaire harbour at night, the *Campbeltown* would ram headlong into the lock gates, and the commandos would storm ashore to knock out the pumping stations and other targets while waiting for the destroyer to explode. Once the mission was accomplished, the commandos would essentially be on their own. The lucky ones would make it back to the MTBs for departure or, more probably, would try to find their own way through south-western France and across the Pyrenees into neutral Spain before setting out to return to England.[30]

On September 14, Gonin met with the Plans Division, which had initially hoped to deliver the attack on Trafalgar Day, October 21, as a public relations nod to the great victory of the British fleet over Napoleon's navy in 1805. Unfortunately, environmental conditions reduced the likelihood of surprise, and the plan was shelved for the time being.

And so it remained until January 1942, when Ultra from Bletchley revealed that the *Tirpitz* was on the move: she had left the Leningrad blockade and sailed first to the port of Wilhelmshaven in northern Germany and then on to Norway, suggesting she might break out into the Atlantic and follow in the *Bismarck*'s path. The Operational Intelligence Centre, tracking her every move through the German home waters key and then the Norwegian key, was relieved at first to report to Churchill and the Admiralty that her immediate objective was the fjords rather than the Atlantic sea lanes. But once she had made the move to Norway, the battleship was clearly positioned within easy striking distance of both the North Atlantic and the vital convoys bound for Russia. Churchill feared it was only a matter of time before she made her move for open water. As he related melodramatically in his memoir *Hinge of Fate*, he informed Major General Hastings 'Pug' Ismay, his shrewd and loyal personal liaison with the chiefs of staff, just days before the four-rotor Enigma machine went into action on February 1 on Dönitz's U-boats in the Atlantic, that 'the destruction or even the crippling' of the *Tirpitz* was, in his estimation, 'the greatest event at sea at the present time. No other target is comparable to it.'[31]

Previously, in November, when Mountbatten had first taken over the reins of Combined Operations, his headquarters had begun, as Godfrey relates, 'a keen search for targets' that revived Gonin's 'hope for his neglected child.'[32] After Churchill sounded the alarm in late January, Gonin's daring but relatively low-cost strategy to cripple the *Tirpitz* before she could position herself in the Atlantic became an imperative. Suddenly, the raid was back on the table. When Gonin approached Combined Operations with the idea, the result, according to Godfrey, 'was magical.' Instantly, Dickie Mountbatten latched on to the scheme, and he put his naval advisory team onto detailed planning for the mission. In late February, Operation Chariot was born – a commando raid that would prove to be one of the greatest acts of heroism and self-sacrifice of the entire Second World War.

What is not commonly known is that the St Nazaire Raid also doubled as an elaborate pinch operation. Restricted by the Official Secrets Act, which for years prevented any whisper of Ultra or the four-rotor crisis, Churchill properly made no direct mention of this side of the story in his carefully crafted memoirs, although there are vague and veiled references to 'other sources.' Nor did he dare touch upon the second half of the St Nazaire saga: its long-forgotten twin operation called Myrmidon, which took place in April 1942 some 260 miles to the south at Bayonne, France.

As with Vaagso and Lofoten, the plan was to launch twin attacks – Operations Chariot and Myrmidon – within 24 hours of each other to deliver on the two imperatives of the day, the *Tirpitz* and the four-rotor-derived intelligence blackout. On February 25, Mountbatten presented both outline plans, drawn up by Jock Hughes-Hallett, David Luce and Vaagso pinch veteran Dick de Costobadie, to the chiefs of staff and the prime minister for approval, admitting that both operations were 'somewhat hazardous' but 'the prize was considerable.'[33] While the primary goal of Chariot was the destruction of the Normandie dry dock, the secondary target was the destruction of all the U-boats and shipping gathered there for repairs. The plan made no particular mention of pinch provisions, but the operation obviously did offer the potential for 'opportunity' pinches.

With pinch doctrine in mind, the stated objective of Operation Myrmidon at Bayonne – 'to clear the French Coast of the enemy troops in the areas between the river Adour and the Spanish Frontier' by landing 3,000 soldiers to disrupt rail and road transport in that area – appears so vague as to be suspect.[34] In fact, the details of the planning papers reveal that Myrmidon, unlike Chariot, was a pinch by design.

In this case, a naval task force with No. 1 and No. 6 Commando units, carried in Assault Landing Craft (ALC) and destroyers, would sail up the Bayonne estuary to the harbour, where it would strike shore-based strategic facilities, including explosives and petrochemical plants, an unspecified headquarters (likely naval) and a Luftwaffe airfield. Meanwhile, specially raised boarding parties would capture shipping in the tight confines of the estuary and the harbour specifically in search of 'code and cipher material.'[35]

After examining the outline plans, the chiefs of staff and Churchill 'fully approved' both proposals, with the prime minister stating for the record that in his opinion, the 'risks were justified.'[36] He followed this with a request to 'hear further details of Op Myrmidon in due course,' but it is not recorded whether or to what degree Churchill made himself intimately aware of the details of Operation Myrmidon. But if he did flip through the detailed orders, he would certainly have seen that the driving imperative of the operation was clear: 'Boats may proceed as far up as the junction of the rivers Nive and Adour if no opposition is encountered, but are not to press on in face of opposition, as casualties in the boarding parties will compromise the successful obtainment of the object.'[37]

Once in range of the trawlers, however, the attacking force was instructed to attack 'with the utmost ruthlessness at short range with pom pom and small arms weapons, the object being to kill or panic the crew but to leave the ship relatively undamaged in order that search may be made for codes, cyphers etc. If this search is successful, it is essential that there should be no survivors other than prisoners, and that the ship should be sunk as soon as possible.'[38]

Later, the plan reiterated this imperative; crews from any ship, enemy or neutral, should be overpowered and any resistance should be dealt with ruthlessly. 'If German,' the instruction warned, 'they are better dead, though a Naval Officer would be of value as a prisoner for interrogation.'[39]

Operation Myrmidon was scheduled to take place within 24 hours of the St Nazaire Raid, but it was dogged by problems. Weather conditions delayed it, and the records are unclear whether it was then pushed back or the St Nazaire Raid was pushed forward. In the end, the raids were separated by one week, with Myrmidon following Chariot. Even then, although the raiding force reached the mouth of the river Adour, leading to the Bayonne estuary, a shifting sandbar – of which the ISTD had made Combined Operations Headquarters fully aware – prevented it from entering. Although the landing craft could not get through, the naval force commander, Captain A.H. Maxwell-Hyslop, considered taking his warships into the estuary to carry out the pinch but refrained due to security concerns.[*40] The raid was aborted without the Germans catching on to what had been planned. Given the spectacular success at St Nazaire on March 28, 1942, the failure at Bayonne proved easy to gloss over, but it nevertheless came as a great disappointment.

൸

Although it is now clear from the declassified records that a pinch was the driving force behind Myrmidon, the main idea in Operation Chariot was primarily preventative in nature: to destroy St Nazaire's giant dry dock and prevent the Kriegsmarine from unleashing the *Tirpitz* on the already beleaguered merchant fleet in the Atlantic. The word 'daring' does not sufficiently describe the plan.

The strategy drew heavily on the legendary Zeebrugge Raid, which had garnered much-needed positive propaganda in the dark days of the spring of 1918. Like it, Operation Chariot required complete surprise: the raiding force, led by the disguised *Campbeltown*, would have to sail unobserved past the coast of Brittany and down the French west coast through U-boat-infested waters dotted with French and Spanish fishing trawlers. Mountbatten issued strict instructions that, if the element of surprise was lost, the raid should be aborted, the ships returned to English ports, and the mission remounted on the same target once the frenzy had abated. However, if the surprise held, the raiding force would capitalize on the detailed report the Inter-Services Topographical Department had issued, which revealed that an unusually high spring tide would permit a 'one time only' chance for a light

---

* Maxwell-Hyslop had earned the rare Albert Medal (later the George Cross) for saving lives on HMS *Devonshire* following an accidental explosion in X turret in 1929. Following the Bayonne Raid he took command of HMS *Nelson* and later became the aide-de-camp for King George VI in 1944.

ship to pass over the shallow water close to shore and avoid the big German guns dominating the approaches to the port. Once the convoy had got past the guns, the *Campbeltown*, disguised as a German destroyer, would create heavy diversionary fire designed to suppress or otherwise occupy the gunners, just as the raiding force closed on the port entrance at the mouth of the Loire.

The final plan followed Gonin's original scheme quite closely. To take full advantage of the confusion, Robert Edward Dudley 'Red' Ryder, the naval force commander, riding in a motor torpedo boat (MTB), would use a captured low-level German codebook to send a series of deceptive messages to the port to hold fire, passing the force off as a German coastal convoy in need of emergency shelter. Once they breached the harbour defences, one of the MTBs would blast the gates leading to the U-boat pens, the commandos on the other boats would land on the harbourfront and destroy the four lock gates leading to the old dock, and *Campbeltown* would deliver the *coup de grâce*. With its bow packed with high explosives rigged up by the experts at the Special Operations Executive and set on a timed fuse, the old destroyer would ram headlong into the main lock gate of the Normandie dry dock. Once lodged, the commandos riding her 'back,' or main deck, would jump off and attack the pumping stations and lock mechanisms that controlled the dry dock. In that way, there was an inherent redundancy built into the planning to achieve the primary objective: even if the *Campbeltown* failed to explode on time, three hours after it struck, the commandos would at least disable the dock temporarily.

In the end, the raid turned out to be as effective as it was daring and deadly. It began badly: the plan was nearly scuttled when the convoy encountered a German submarine, which was chased off, and then two French trawlers, which Ryder boarded and sank. Nothing in the available documents indicates whether he did so for pinch purposes or strictly for security reasons, but his unpublished memoir shows that in the process he did seize lower-level French and Spanish material. This bold and courageous commander then pushed on with the mission because none of the Germans on shore had yet raised the alarm. When the diversionary bombers arrived, however, surprise was no longer possible, and at that moment the commandos hoped the German gunners would be more interested in taking on the bombers than their quickly approaching raiding force. At that time in the war, a Cabinet order forbade the blind bombing of French towns, and with the skies overcast, the airmen's view of the target below was obscured. All the bombers managed to do was fly around above St Nazaire, putting the gunners on full alert rather than drawing their fire or making them run for cover. As a result, although the raiding force succeeded in reaching the mouth of the Loire and the harbour in good shape, the captured-code ruse worked for only a short time before the Germans responded with full force.[41]

Immediately, searchlight beams and heavy fire bathed the raiding force, hitting a few of the torpedo boats while the others made a dash for their targets on shore. As planned, the *Campbeltown* rammed into the target lock gate at full speed, crumpling her hull in the process. Her commandos leapt off the decks and hit the majority of their targets on the shore. The others following in their MTBs were not as successful, but the 37-year-old commander of No. 2 Commando, Lieutenant Colonel Augustus Charles Newman, or 'Colonel Charles' to his men, managed to seize and establish his headquarters in the German harbour commandant's office.[42] From there, he organized the attack on shore. They met heavy and increasing German resistance from the start, including from an armed trawler he tried unsuccessfully to subdue.

Initially, it appeared that the main objective of the raid had failed: the explosive charge, carefully welded shut into the bow of the *Campbeltown*, did not blow up on schedule. But the next day, when the ship was crowded with German soldiers, sailors and a few captured commandos and surrounded by French bystanders, it suddenly exploded, knocking out the gate, flooding the dry dock and leaving a grisly scene strewn with the body parts of those on board and nearby.

Only 228 of the original 622 commandos and Royal Navy personnel were able to return to Britain over the next few days, with the total casualty lists recording 169 dead and 215 in German hands. This list included 'Colonel Charles' and his small band, who heroically attempted to fight their way out of the port. Newman was awarded the Victoria Cross for his conspicuous bravery and valour, but because he was captured, whatever code and cipher material he may have been able to seize – and it is possible he jettisoned it in advance of being taken – went for naught.

Not surprisingly, given the long-classified Ultra Secret nature of such information and of these kinds of materials, nothing has surfaced in the years since in any in-house histories of the Government Code and Cypher School or in other files relating to pinches that failed outright or missed their mark.

Despite the hefty cost, the St Nazaire Raid can be considered a success because it achieved several of its intended objectives – and some that were unintended too. On the tactical and operational levels, the destruction of the lock gates rendered the dry dock tidal and successfully denied the *Tirpitz* a maintenance or repair facility with direct access to an Atlantic coast. Although the raiders did not succeed in knocking out the other three lock gates and flooding the inner port where the U-boats berthed, the brief capture of the port commandant's office forced Hitler to issue orders to relocate all naval headquarters from shorelines to less accessible locations slightly within ports.

On the strategic level, the raid – which Churchill called a 'brilliant and heroic exploit' and 'a deed of glory intimately involved in high strategy' – demonstrated that Great Britain could strike offensively and remain steadfast during this very bleak period in the war. The success also impressed the Americans, who were looking for signs of life from a war-weary Britain.[43] Glowing headlines spoke of the tremendous daring and supreme sacrifice of the raiders – a feat that instantly captured imaginations not only in Britain but around the Allied world. The *New York Times* ran the banner headline: 'British raid St. Nazaire U-boat base, Ram dock with Exploding destroyer,' and the *Boston Globe* likened the event to the celebrated Zeebrugge Raid. For the first time in the dismal opening months of 1942, positive news of daring offensive action greeted readers who were becoming stoically accustomed to stories of Allied reverses.

More importantly, the hefty cost (83 per cent of the 611 men on the raid were killed, wounded or taken prisoner), coupled with its ruthless and daring nature, clearly demonstrated that the British were more than willing to expend casualties on any objective deemed worthy; one which at that time paled dramatically when compared to the scope of the problem dogging the cryptanalysts at Bletchley and strategic underpinning of the entire Allied war effort.

On the German side, the raid forced the adoption of a defensive mindset in the west. Hitler slackened his intense focus eastward towards the Soviet Union somewhat and allocated extra *matériel* and personnel to the French coast, mostly slave labour, to speed up and improve defences all along his Atlantic wall.

For Godfrey, St Nazaire clearly demonstrated that the targeting information provided by Gonin's French sub-section of NID and by his own ISTD had proven its worth. The triumph also further solidified his working relationship with Mountbatten's rapidly rising Combined Operations Headquarters.[44]

The grand success of St Nazaire invigorated Mountbatten and his staff at Combined Operations and led to a major escalation in operational planning there. The mission seemed to vindicate Mountbatten's sudden and dramatic rise to prominence under Churchill's patronage. Just weeks before the raid, the prime minister had promoted Mountbatten three levels to vice admiral and widened his official powers, elevating him from 'adviser' to 'Chief' of Combined Operations. Initially, the now-ailing Dudley Pound interpreted this unprecedented rise as Churchill's bid to put Mountbatten in Pound's own seat as First Lord of the Admiralty; but it was more likely a recognition of the growing importance of Combined Operations Headquarters within the framework of the armed services, as well as evidence of the prime minister's desire to inject younger blood into the British leadership. At 42, the charismatic Lord Louis Mountbatten was the youngest vice admiral in the long history of the Royal Navy, surpassing even the hero of the Battle of Trafalgar, Lord Horatio Nelson.

But within Mountbatten's own headquarters, this meteoric ascent had a sharp trickle-down effect on the staff that led quickly to a dangerous overconfidence. In the afterglow of St Nazaire, Jock Hughes-Hallett could not contain his excitement over 'Dickie's' promotion and its promise for the future. 'My own reaction,' he recalled, 'was one of exhilaration, almost exultation. At one stride, our organization had penetrated to the very centre and citadel of power. We were now to work for a man with access to all the secrets, and for one who could, and would, be an advocate at top level for any plan.'[45] Indeed, along with this sense of validation and vindication came a new-found arrogance and hubris. Yet St Nazaire, followed by the aborted Myrmidon, had done nothing to alleviate the most pressing issue of all: the four-rotor blackout.

Immediately after the abandoned Operation Myrmidon pinch raid at Bayonne, Mountbatten had dismissed charges from an army interrogator with experience in several raids (including Vaagso) of poor and hasty operational planning as well as almost criminal neglect of intelligence. In a confidential report penned for Combined Operations Headquarters (COHQ), this officer noted serious oversights, including incomplete briefings and operational orders devoid of basic information about the enemy. He had been shocked to find essential items – such as the location of the enemy in relation to key targets, and an assessment of the enemy's air and naval situation – absent from both the operational orders and the commander's briefing. He also noted other potentially critical mistakes: the wrong set of aerial photos had been issued for Myrmidon, along with a suspect demolition programme that, if carried out as planned, was bound to inflict more harm to friend than foe.[46] Even the commander of the Special Service Brigade (Charles Haydon) whose commandos carried out both Lofoten operations, expressed his alarm during the planning for the operation: 'I don't want to be depressing and unnecessarily gloomy but there is no doubt at all that this operation is being unduly rushed' and cited problems with lack of training time, proper assessment of landing areas, and 'no direct evidence as to the strength of the enemy garrison' all compounded by the lack of any dress rehearsals. 'The above are the gloomy aspects,' Haydon reported, but 'it is right that they should be pointed out because if in spite of every effort, they cannot be overcome, I shall have to tell you so and recommend that the operation be postponed.'

These mistakes were indicative of what Admiral Bertram Ramsay, the man in charge of the Dover area of operations, including the protection of cross-Channel military traffic, called the spirit of 'inexperienced enthusiasts' lurking in COHQ.[47] In response to Haydon's report, a thoroughly irate Mountbatten complained to Major General F.H.N. Davidson, the Director of Military Intelligence, but to no avail as the head of the Special Service Brigade remained unrepentant. In Mountbatten's words, Haydon painted the impression that if 'Combined

Operations had been a public company, the shareholders would have been within their rights to call a meeting to investigate the way in which the show was being run.'[48]

These complaints were serious and valid, but they went unheeded in any practical sense within the walls of Richmond Terrace where a mounting 'victory disease' had taken hold. In short order following the second Lofoten raid, corners were cut, and attention to inconvenient details waned; unsettling intelligence was downplayed, dismissed or ignored as nothing would be allowed to dampen spirits or potentially lead to postponement or cancellation. As Arthur Marshall, the British raconteur who worked as a security officer for Mountbatten quipped years later, the motto for COHQ should have been 'Regardless' – meaning 'regardless of effort, regardless of risk, and regardless of cost.'[49] But nothing at this moment, save an inglorious and costly defeat, could have shaken the headquarters out of its dangerously triumphant mindset.

The excitement over the St Nazaire Raid was particularly intense because it came at a very dark moment, following the fall of Singapore and amid General Erwin Rommel's mounting victories for Germany in the North African desert. To ramp up the public relations machine into overdrive, maximum press coverage was given when 38 decorations were awarded for merit and bravery, including four additional Victoria Crosses (besides Newman's), to members of the raiding force. Red Ryder, who would later play a pivotal role in the Dieppe operation, was one of this select group.[50]

⌇

Robert Ryder was a rare character in the annals of military and naval history, the almost perfect classic hero. He was as resolute, determined and courageous in battle as he was reserved, humble and self-effacing in its afterglow. Uncomfortable with small talk and ceremony, he remained, as his biographer put it, 'a reluctant hero.' On the occasion of his investiture at Buckingham Palace to receive his Victoria Cross, he chose to sneak out afterwards through a side door rather than deal with the throngs of reporters who waited to shower him with adoration and praise.[51]

Born in 1908 in Dehra Dun, India, where his father, Colonel Charles Henry Ryder, held the prestigious post of surveyor-general for that sub-continent, Robert, or 'Bob' as he was known to family and close friends, was the youngest of six children. Unlike his father and older brothers Lisle and Ernle, who held commissions in the army, he chose to buck family tradition and join the Royal Navy, driven by his love of sailing and his penchant for adventure. After he won the King's Dirk as the out-standing cadet in his final year, he went on to a spectacular career that led eventually to his command of the raiding force for St Nazaire – as well as the 'Cutting Out Force' for Dieppe and, ultimately, Ian Fleming's creation, 30 Assault Unit, his Intelligence Assault Unit.

First Sea Lord Sir Dudley Pound was one of Ryder's biggest fans, though Ryder initially was unaware of the old admiral's regard. Pound appears to have marvelled at the exploits of his young subordinate as far back as 1934, when 'Red' Ryder successfully piloted a Royal Navy yacht on a wild, year-long journey from Kowloon harbour in Hong Kong to Dartmouth, England. Ryder then signed on for a twelve-month stint with the famous British Graham Land Expedition, which explored Antarctica for three years, before finally crossing paths with Pound on HMS *Warspite* just before the outbreak of the war. Among his many hobbies were painting, writing and intelligence work – and this last interest was about to become very useful indeed.

During the First World War, the Germans had developed the con-cept of the Q-ship, which the British readily adopted, where a tramp steamer outfitted to carry concealed weapons and disguised to resem-ble a merchant vessel was used to lure submarines and their crews to their fate. Early in 1940, Ryder was given command of his own ves-sel, the Special Services ship HMS *Edgehill* (X-39), and he personally designed its camouflage to include two pigs roaming the decks for full effect. In February, he set out on the high seas in search of prey. To succeed, he first had to put his ship in harm's way, even absorbing a torpedo hit if necessary, to bring the U-boat to the surface. Once the submarine was above the waterline, Ryder intended to unleash his nine concealed four-inch guns on his enemy in a torrent of fire designed to sink the vessel. Nothing, however, went according to plan when the *Edgehill* met its first U-boat off the coast of Ireland in June 1940. Instead,

Ernst-Günter Heinicke, the wily captain of *U-51*, sent Ryder's ship to the bottom, leaving the captain alone in the water for four harrowing days until a passing ship rescued him from certain death.

From there, Ryder was given command of HMS *Prince Philippe*, a large landing craft of the type later employed at Dieppe. She too was lost, in 1941 off Scotland when, in the dead of night and thick fog, another vessel rammed her amidships and nearly cut her in half, despite Ryder's best attempts to avoid a collision. Much to his dismay, Ryder ended up in a shore posting, until he was offered the opportunity to command the seemingly impossible St Nazaire Raid. Notwithstanding his string of bad luck, nothing had tarnished his reputation with the First Sea Lord, who seems personally to have chosen him to command the naval force for St Nazaire. By all accounts, Pound was not disappointed by the results.

The success of this raid made Ryder a reluctant media star, but it also established him within the Combined Operations framework as a heavy hitter – the 'go-to guy' for tough raids of extreme importance. If a raid required the utmost in leadership, skill and intrepid courage amid the risk of heavy cost, Ryder was the man. As such, his inclusion in any operation warrants close scrutiny.

The St Nazaire Raid firmly planted a series of lessons learned – and perhaps mislearned – in the minds of the Combined Operations planners, which directly shaped the developing concept for Dieppe, and in particular Ryder's role in the raid. The very success of St Nazaire validated the brand that Mountbatten brought to the table, leaving the Chief of Combined Operations glowing in his assessment:

> I know of no other case in naval or military annals of such effective damage being inflicted so swiftly with such economy of force ... This brilliant attack was carried out at night, under vicious enemy fire, by a mere handful of men, who achieved, with certainty and precision, what the heaviest bombing raid or naval bombardment might well have failed to do.[52]

With raiding and pinching concepts still emerging, however, this was the critical time for Mountbatten and his planners to draw the right lessons from Operations Chariot and Myrmidon. Unfortunately, with Myrmidon aborted at the eleventh hour, Combined Operations learned precious little that challenged or qualified the concept of storming into an enemy port with commandos and boarding parties ready to strike targets and pinch vital material. At St Nazaire, David slew Goliath, but instead of recognizing it for what it was – an outlier – the Combined Operations planners adopted it as the norm, embracing a daring and adventurous attitude without reservation or qualification. And at this crucial point, this opinion was supported by both Prime Minister Winston Churchill and the chiefs of staff.

Unfortunately, with Mountbatten's Combined Operations relying increasingly on daring 'mission impossible' operations of a 'Boy's Own' nature to offset their limited assets, they were neglecting the very basics of strategy – the balance between firepower and manoeuvre – as they tried to reach their goals. From this point forward, deception, boldness and fighting spirit underpinned by surprise *supplanted* rather than *enhanced* the basics. The earlier operations in Norway and more recently at St Nazaire had shown how much could be achieved with few resources when, and if, all elements came together like clockwork. Now they were poised to rely far too much on the elusive element of luck and the overwhelming need for surprise, particularly in pinch raids. If these elements worked at St Nazaire, they reasoned, and would presumably have worked at Bayonne, why would they not be effective for other, larger operations?

CHAPTER 8

'Authorized Looters'

*Speaking on behalf of the Admiralty, Commander Fleming stated
that there was an urgent requirement for personnel who could be
intensively trained to carry out special naval intelligence duties ...
Commander Fleming went on to say that the Admiralty had pointed
out the urgency of this requirement as long ago as March, and he
emphasised the now increasingly urgent need for a permanent body
to which this type of naval intelligence work could be entrusted.*

Minutes of a meeting at COHQ to discuss the formation
of Special Intelligence Units, July 22, 1942[1]

In the daring and costly raid at St Nazaire, the army commandos
had once again proven their worth in spades, as they had during
several small amphibious assaults stretching from Norway to the
Mediterranean. At this darkest point of the war, they were highly
sought after, and it was difficult for any commander to get them
without friction and corresponding delay that risked cancellation of
future operations. For Mountbatten, it was frustrating not to have
them directly under his control; like many of the forces employed by
Combined Operations Headquarters, the commandos had been sec-
onded from the army's Special Service Brigade.[2] The confident Dickie
Mountbatten refused to be dependent on other branches of the armed

services, and he determined to create his own force to carry out his objectives.

Already, at the end of 1941, he had tasked Jock Hughes-Hallett with planning a series of raids along the north-western coast of France for strategic and intelligence purposes. But with raiding a specialized field and the subset 'pinching ... by its very nature, haphazard and unpredictable,' the call went out for the Admiralty to create a well-trained and cohesive group of 'naval' commandos to carry out these operations in a more efficient and secure way than previously attempted.[3] By January 1942, Mountbatten had made progress and turned to his beloved Royal Marine Division – and their newly designated A Commando – to be the permanent land force strike arm of Combined Operations.[4]

The Royal Marines had grown slowly but surely in stature over three centuries, acting as the assault force for the Royal Navy. They were legendary. Tracing their origins back to the Second Anglo-Dutch War in 1685–87, they had played a dual role on His Majesty's ships: ensuring discipline among the crew and leading boarding attacks on enemy ships or raiding shore facilities. Fighting in all major Royal Navy engagements, their long and stellar history included chapters in the Seven Years' War, the American War of Independence, the War of 1812 (where they carried out raids along the Virginia and Maryland coasts) and the Crimean War. As sail power passed to steam and oil, the Marines added another duty to their list: manning the aft (rear) turrets on Royal Navy cruisers.

During the First World War, they were transformed into the Royal Naval Division – which Winston Churchill observed in action as they defended Antwerp from German attack in 1914 – and later played vital roles in both the Gallipoli campaign and the Zeebrugge Raid; all told, five of their men earned the Victoria Cross. Not long after, however, scandal hit, when one battalion mutinied in Murmansk while serving in the tumultuous Russian Civil War, until finally, during the inter-war retrenchment years, the Marines succumbed to the budgetary axe, which left them with fewer than 10,000 men – down from nearly 60,000 during the Great War. In 1939 they reformed into the Royal Marine Division but had no real role in the Royal Navy's order of battle, and instead of keeping together as a unit, their battalions spread around the globe in 'penny packets' fighting independently in Asia, North Africa, Norway and on the island of Crete. Despite proving themselves on the field of battle, this once-proud division seemed destined to be broken up and used only to reinforce other units.

Hoping to stave off their dissolution, Roger Keyes, Lord Louis Mountbatten's predecessor at Combined Operations, had already suggested converting the Royal Marines into a series of battalion-sized commando units, each roughly 500 strong, for use in raiding operations. Mountbatten now took up the torch, arguing that the Royal Marines were Britain's natural amphibious commando force, one that could and should be equal to the army commandos.[5]

Right from the formation of this new force, the 'commando concept' transformed the face of the Royal Marines into the elite unit they are today. Initially there was tension within the unit itself: some of the officers refused to lower themselves to undergoing the same gruelling regimen as their men in the 'rough fun and games' of commando-style training.[6] Other officers pushed convention aside and saw merit in combining the commando role with the ethos of the Royal Marines. 'The commandos are tough,' their own journal, the *Globe and Laurel*, proclaimed. 'Vaagso is proof of that. The Marines are tough. Crete and Norway – where they fought two hopeless Thermopylaes* – are the proof of that. Wait till they mill together.'[7] For Mountbatten, however, a commando unit from a naval bloodline not only provided a tangible role for the Royal Marines – a goal he had championed for months – but also gave Combined Operations and the Admiralty their own private army of sorts, to be used as they saw fit.**

Training for the 300 men of the first Royal Marine Commando started in early February in Deal, on the Channel coast near Dover.

---

* Thermopylae refers to the ancient battle for the small mountain-pass town in Greece in 480 BC, when a vastly outnumbered force of soldiers (mostly Spartans) held off, with self-sacrificing courage, an advancing Persian juggernaut.

** There is nothing in the Admiralty's intelligence files to suggest that the creation of the Royal Marine Commando in February 1942 stemmed either from the change in pinch policy in January towards operations on shore rather than at sea or from the need to solve the looming four-rotor crisis. The reason seems to have been the need to save the division from the bureaucratic chopping block. The timing, however, could not have been more fortunate for all concerned.

To pay tribute to their naval heritage, the commando unit was divided into three fighting companies entitled A, B and X – corresponding to the turrets on His Majesty's cruisers – and one 'headquarters company' (comprising the commander, his staff, communications and heavy weapons). Each of the fighting companies was further broken down into three platoons of 30 officers and men, numbered 1 to 3 for A, 7 to 9 for B, and 10 to 12 for X.[8]

These platoons became the homes – the surrogate families – for the fresh-faced recruits, mostly aged between eighteen and 21 (some weren't even shaving yet), who flowed in from commands throughout England. They volunteered to come, attracted by the adventure, the challenge of hazardous duty and a modest raise in pay. Greeted by an officer review board, the tone was set immediately with one sobering question: 'What makes a young lad like you tired of living?'[9]

Once through the initial interview, the men paraded before the commanding officer, the diminutive 32-year-old Lieutenant Colonel Joseph Picton Phillipps, rumoured to be a descendant of Wellington's General Picton, who had been shot through the temple by a musket ball at the Battle of Waterloo in 1815.[10] A career Royal Marine officer with a high-pitched voice, pencil-thin moustache and fiery temperament, he was always immaculately dressed. When he arrived on the back of a white stallion to inspect the men, he only reinforced the new recruits' belief that he suffered from a 'small man's complex.' He was a 'sight to behold and his mannerisms, to many of us they were hilarious,' recalled one Marine. 'We knew then that we had someone *very* different.'[11]

In one of his many attempts to inculcate his version of Spartan-like discipline and initiative among the men, Picton Phillipps forbade the use of the main gate, forcing them to scale an eight-foot wall every time they entered or exited the barracks. Later he dispatched them into the wilderness for a three-day survival exercise, simply stating, 'Fend for yourselves.'[12] Soon his antics became the stuff of comic legend, forever ensconced in Royal Marine 'dits' – those cautionary tales told to while away the off-hours.* Within the first few months, recruits who survived

---

* 'Dits' were Royal Marine tales, repeated in the barracks or the mess, that conveyed essential lessons learned in a less than formal manner.

their initial training without being returned to unit, or RTU'd – the ultimate disgrace – became accustomed to maintaining an almost 24-hour vigil for their tightly wound commander, 'Tiger' as they called him, who habitually prowled the grounds at night, hoping to catch an unwary sentry off guard. At one point the overzealous Picton Phillipps's bizarre actions nearly got the better of him when a startled sentry unloaded the full weight of his rifle butt on the colonel's collarbone, leaving him to cry out in pain, 'It's your commanding officer. Carry on!' The next day, when summoned to Picton Phillipps's office, the young Marine expected revenge but emerged minutes later with a promotion to lance corporal – the reward for his ruthless vigilance.[13] Picton Phillipps may have appeared 'daft as a half-penny,' but at least there was some method to his legendary madness.[14]

Idiosyncratic or not, 'a general hardening up' started immediately, designed to weed out those considered physically, spiritually or psychologically unfit. 'It rained all the time, so we were never dry, and then there were the speed marches, six or seven miles in an hour for hour after hour, in full kit with platoon weapons,' recalled one recruit; 'many would have fallen out, but were helped on by their mates.'[15] Another hallmark of commando training, in addition to the near-death forced marches with 65-pound packs, called for the use of live ammunition in exercises to simulate conditions on the battlefield – a policy that sometimes claimed 'friendly fire' casualties but reinforced most effectively the violent nature of the business at hand. 'Climbing cliffs, crawling through bogs, under barbed wire, while the staff shot over us with Brens, or chucked grenades about' was all part of the daily routine for the prospective commandos.[16] Today, 'precise application of will' rather than mere violence defines the ethos of a Royal Marine Commando, but this modification developed during the peacekeeping era. For the Marine commandos in 1942, the violent application of will was front and centre.

By the end of the first week of training, nearly 20 per cent of the recruits voluntarily returned to unit – a rate of attrition that held throughout the formation period. One did not merely *join* the Royal Marine Commando; one *became* a Royal Marine Commando. The extremely hazardous nature of the job, particularly with men so young, required full immersion in the new elite ethos that demanded high standards, unity, fortitude, humility, adaptability, and the wry and at times irreverent sense of humour essential for psychological survival in this stressful environment.[17] As the training regime increased in intensity and realism, the basic instruction in the handling of small arms, mortars and hand grenades evolved into advanced subjects such as the recognition and disarmament of enemy land mines and booby traps, and then to the use of Hawkins grenades or 'sticky bombs' designed to disable enemy tanks. The recruits also took courses in demolition and counter-demolition, learning how to use timed and untimed explosive charges to destroy a multitude of targets.[18]

In the end, the result was a tight-knit cohort at the platoon level ready to take on all comers. The very nature of commando-style special operations called for the platoon to be prepared to operate independently during a raid. Of necessity, they had to work together like a well-oiled machine, the senior commanders continually warning that 'there will come a day when you will depend on each other.'[19] The Royal Marine commandos wisely permitted the platoon commander and his sergeant to have the final say on whether a man made it as a commando or not. If they, or the group, lacked full confidence in an individual or felt that his attitude was not right, they immediately cut him loose with no reason offered besides one simple comment: 'Unsuitable.'[20]

By Easter Sunday, the same day that Operation Myrmidon was planned for Bayonne, the first cadre of Royal Marine A Commandos, who had survived six weeks of indoctrination at Deal, moved on for further gruelling training to the Combined Operations training centre at Acharacle in Argyll, Scotland, known as HMS *Dorlin*. This isolated former naval base now became the elaborate training ground for Mountbatten's Combined Operations Headquarters. Despite its name, it was not a ship; the *Dorlin* estate included six luxurious houses and offered the commandos a half-dozen demanding assault courses over a seventeen-mile radius, pitting them against natural and artificial obstructions and challenging them to hone their tactical skills, particularly in street-fighting, which was expected to be a crucial part of their deadly raiding repertoire on shore. In addition, the landing craft, cutters and drifters, as well as a former French fishery protection vessel at the base, gave ample opportunity for the commandos to practise assault landings, boarding of enemy ships and simulated pinch operations.

Once this portion of the training was complete, the recruits moved on to the primary intelligence-training phase, where they learned to recognize enemy vehicles, uniforms, documents and equipment; to conduct searches of premises to recover sensitive material; and to interrogate prisoners – and endure interrogation themselves should they fall into enemy hands. They then went on to advanced intelligence work – in chemical warfare and the interpretation of aerial photos. They received demonstrations of enemy electronics, wireless sets and radar, and learned how to photograph documents on the spot. Some of them specialized in map reading, topography and hydrography, and a few allegedly went off to Scotland Yard for an 'intensive three-day crash course in safe blowing and other such arts.'[21]

In late May, the Marines moved to the Isle of Wight, where, unknown to them at the time, the training regimen was shaped specially to prepare them for their first significant role – in the small French coastal town of Dieppe. During this stage of training, one of the platoons, No. 10, would be tapped on the shoulder to become the prototype for Ian Fleming's latest brainchild – a naval intelligence commando unit for pinch purposes, or, as he would call it, his Intelligence Assault Unit (IAU).

ↂ

On March 20, 1942, Fleming approached Godfrey with an intriguing proposition in response to an urgent development in the four-rotor crisis.* His memo, entitled 'Proposal for Naval Intelligence Commando Unit' and signed with his famous 'F' scrawled at the bottom, went straight to the heart of the matter.[22] He conceded that he had poached the concept directly from the Germans, and that he intended to draw the original cadre for his IAU from the No. 10 Platoon of the Royal Marine Commando's X Company. (After Dieppe, the platoon would evolve into the nucleus of the illustrious 30 Assault Unit, whose motto would be 'Attain by Surprise.')[23]

---

* See page 201 below.

'These "commandos,"' he wrote in his proposal, would 'accompany the forward troops when a port or naval installation is being attacked and, if the attack is successful, their duty is to capture documents, cyphers etc., before these can be destroyed by the defenders.'[24] Their first duty, before any operation, would be to assemble a list of the types of materials required by all sections in the Naval Intelligence Division and then to ferret out every scrap of information they could about possible locations where these pieces might be found in a given port. Once the target had been established, the unit would be inserted into a combined operation to train with the assaulting force. It would 'proceed with 2nd or 3rd wave of attack into the port, and make straight for the various buildings, etc., where the booty is expected to be found, capture it, and return.'[25] Undoubtedly incorporating the lessons from the pinch raids on Lofoten and Vaagso, Fleming's proposal for the NID to create its own intelligence-gathering commando unit stemmed straight from the four-rotor crisis and the desperate need to pull in German intelligence materials. At first, Fleming envisioned that his small elite group would comprise a platoon's worth of hand-picked men, specially trained to conduct pinch raids ashore under cover of larger, more 'orthodox' operations.

Fleming's proposal did not come at Godfrey out of left field. In early December, a month before the pinch policy shift that abandoned targeting lone ships at sea in favour of pinching material onshore, the Secret Intelligence Service, headed by Stewart Menzies – known to all as 'C' – had warned the NID that German naval intelligence had successfully employed a commando unit of its own – the *Marine Einsatzkommando*, or MARES* for short.[26] Members of this unit would accompany the assault waves of advancing forces and seize 'documents, charts and naval stores,' perform 'counter-demolition missions in captured harbours,' provide 'operational intelligence concerning the harbour,' and interrogate 'POWs [and] civilians' while conducting 'counter-espionage

---

* Although the report did not mention it, Fleming had escaped the clutches of MARES in 1940 when he was cleaning out the SIS safe in Paris ahead of the advancing Germans. In 1943 MARES carried out the highly successful raid on Gran Sasso, where the rescued Mussolini failed miserably later that year in trying to capture Marshal Tito, the Communist partisan leader in Yugoslavia.

work' – even going so far as to work in plain clothes during the invasion of Russia so their capture of documents would not be traced back to Germany.[27] The report highlighted the great successes of the German commandos in Greece, Crete and Yugoslavia, where they had captured not only Top Secret British material but the entire staff of the Yugoslav army's North West Command, along with a complete set of their papers.[28]

For Godfrey, the notion of 'a force of armed and expert authorized looters' made a great deal of sense, for several reasons.[29] First, instead of relying on ad hoc boarding parties as had happened in the Norway raids (and later at St Nazaire and Bayonne), his Naval Intelligence Division would be able to select and rigorously train its own 'private army' with intimate knowledge of its unique requirements – and, by extension, of Bletchley Park's too. Armed with the appropriate firepower, the commandos would be able to overtake the local defences, prevent the last-minute destruction of the Enigma machines and their supporting code and cipher books, and get out undetected.[30]

Second, having a trained commando unit at the ready would give the Admiralty a consistent and dedicated tool for pinching. In a sense, such a development was a natural extension of the process Godfrey had been building up over the previous year, and it offered, if successful, a chance not only to solve the four-rotor problem but to re-establish and maintain a constant flow of the vital materials needed to feed the Bletchley beast.

Third, the NID would no longer have to risk sending Ultra-indoctrinated officers, as it had done in Norway with Captain Jasper Haines and Lieutenant Commander Allon Bacon, to execute the pinch, which had created the possibility of precious secrets being compromised should these officers be captured and interrogated. The employment of a fully armed commando unit explicitly trained for this hit-and-run work would greatly limit that unwanted prospect. Their knowledge would be confined to these particular missions and specific target requirements; and although the commando unit's officers and senior non-commissioned officers would know what to look for and where, they would remain ignorant of why it was needed, and even of the very existence of Bletchley Park and its secret work.

Fourth, now that the NID was working closely with Combined Operations, it had the vehicle with which to deliver a commando unit effectively to an onshore target and to cover the commandos' existence by either blending them seamlessly into existing operations or building up a raid around them to fulfil their imperative.

That was the young Commander Ian Fleming's ostensibly simple, yet game-changing suggestion. He also proposed that the unit should come directly under the command of the new Director of Combined Operations, Louis Mountbatten, about one month before it took part in any raid, so it could train with the general assault forces.[31]

The whole idea had a swashbuckling flair to it, well in line with the prevailing tone that Mountbatten sought for Combined Operations and that Churchill adored. Sweeping down on the target in lightning-quick fashion, overcoming the enemy, and scooping up Ultra Secret material that could help win the war or re-inject life into a now sagging empire had a romantic allure for officers who were hopelessly desk-bound in Room 39. After the war, Fleming reflected flippantly on his various plots to outfox the enemy, calling them 'nonsense' and chalking them up to 'those romantic Red Indian daydreams so many of us indulged in at the beginning of the war.'[32] In truth, however, many were deadly serious – a matter of life and death for those involved, with enormous potential in their results – and more calculated than he was willing or able to admit publicly given the restrictions of the Official Secrets Act, even in the post-war period.

Stripped of their swagger, these schemes reflected a sober reality that was consistent with Fleming's Machiavellian nature. Essentially, he and Godfrey deemed the unit expendable in those operations designed to pinch what they listed as 'A1 targets' – the code and cipher material. The history of 30 Assault Unit lays out the lethal intent underlining this target grading with cold aplomb, defining it as 'material and documents of the highest operational priority, the importance of which is sufficient to justify the mounting of special operations and the incurring of heavy casualties on the part of 30 Assault Unit.'[33] Taken in isolation, this passage is remarkable, but given the context of the times and what was at stake, it is not surprising.

With the raid at St Nazaire and the pinch attempt at Bayonne less than two weeks away, Fleming suspected that a new operation currently in development, and loosely scheduled to take place in August or September 1942, would provide the earliest opportunity to get his assault unit into action. Operation Sledgehammer was essentially a strategic operation with political overtones, designed to postpone demands from the Soviet Union for the Allies to open a second front in Western Europe. It called for the landing of British and American (mostly British) divisions to capture either Brest in Brittany or the Cherbourg peninsula in Normandy. The plan, pushed by the Americans to aid the Soviets by seizing the Cherbourg peninsula to lure German land and air forces into a giant battle of attrition, had generated little enthusiasm among the British chiefs of staff. For Fleming, the idea of slipping his newly minted Intelligence Assault Unit into the larger operation made perfect sense and Godfrey concurred:

> The larger the operation, the more important, indeed indispensable, such a party becomes. One can imagine a case where the Germans have demolitions, or blocking operations laid on and where timely action might prevent them. A direct contact between the Commando and NID might be invaluable in such a case. In any event, nothing but good could come of an organization that would enable our intimate knowledge of the port to be constantly at the disposal of the attacking force.[34]

In late March, and with Godfrey's blessing, Fleming sent the proposal to Louis Mountbatten's flamboyant Combined Operations intelligence officer, Wing Commander Marquis de Casa Maury. 'Bobby' de Casa Maury, a Cuban-born playboy, was a controversial figure who attracted open scorn and ridicule from the established set in Whitehall. Although he had flown for the Royal Flying Corps in the First World War and, during the inter-war period, had held a commission in the air force reserves, he was rumoured to have been promoted far above his ceiling. With no apparent background for the job – his main claims to fame were revitalizing Bentley Motors and establishing the Curzon and Paris cinemas in London as arthouse theatres – his personal connection as a former admirer of Mountbatten's wife, Edwina, appeared to be his primary qualification for the job.[35] On April 1, De Casa Maury returned Fleming's docket with an encouraging note attached: 'CCO [Mountbatten] likes the idea and suggests a conference should be called at this Headquarters under his chairmanship to discuss the matter fully.'[36]

But the covetous tone of Mountbatten's request made John Godfrey baulk. Realizing the immense potential of Fleming's concept, he ordered that the IAU remain firmly in the hands of the Admiralty – or, more particularly, of his own NID:

> On further consideration, I think it would be a mistake to turn over the working out of an 'advanced Intelligence unit' to the CCO. CCO's main function is chiefly of an operational nature, and an Intelligence set-up similar to what has been proposed is bound to get low priority. Moreover, to turn it over to him is an admission that he and his Intelligence staff are better able to work out such an arrangement than DNI, DDNI and Section 17. I should, therefore, like the matter to be tackled by Cdr Drake and Cdr Fleming under the supervision of the DDNI, who is requested to treat the matter as one of primary importance.[37]

Part of Godfrey's opposition stemmed from his genuine desire to ensure the commando unit's proper organization, training and development and its potential for solving the crisis. At the same time, his memo clearly demonstrates an increasing tendency within the Naval Intelligence Division to go it alone – and especially for Godfrey to add yet another resource to his ever-widening empire.[38]

Operation Sledgehammer would soon be pushed to the back burner and eventually shelved permanently, much to the relief of the British chiefs of staff. Instead, they decided to embark that autumn on Operation Torch – the invasion of North Africa. The cancellation did not deter Godfrey and Fleming from pressing ahead: with the failure of Operation Chariot at St Nazaire to produce any German intelligence materials, and with the abortion of Operation Myrmidon at Bayonne before it had even begun, Dieppe suddenly loomed large on their radar screens.

CHAPTER 9

Darkness to Daylight

Dieppe was a small seaport, and it would be interesting to capture
it for a time and then withdraw. It had no particular military
significance but was about the right size for a divisional attack.
Captain John Hughes-Hallett, unpublished memoir

August 19, 1942, did not mark the first enemy attack on the seaside resort of Dieppe and its inhabitants, *les Dieppois*. Over its thousand-year existence, its geographic location, less than 70 miles from England and not far from the Dover Straits, the narrowest part of the English Channel, had led to both fortune and suffering. Vikings, foreign navies, marauders, pirates and privateers had all paid the old settlement costly visits, the most recent being just two years before when the Germans invaded France and unceremoniously evicted the British Expeditionary Force from the continent at Dunkirk. The British had held on to Dieppe, the closest port to Paris and one of the six principal deep-water ports in France, until the last possible moment, then quickly tried to destroy its facilities to deny their use to the Germans. The combination of German attack and British sabotage inflicted some damage, but the port remained operational even though several 'block ships' had deliberately been sunk just outside the harbour mole or breakwater. Although the submerged wrecks did not cut off access completely, they prevented large ships from accessing the port and made navigation treacherous for smaller inbound vessels as well.

Located at the mouth of the river Arques in a break in the cliff-lined coast, Dieppe sits squarely between two formidable 300-foot headlands that stretch a mile and a half in opposite directions to the tiny seaside villages of Puys and Pourville. In between the two headlands lies the chert-rock beachfront, 'the poor man's Monte Carlo,' beloved of British summertime visitors. For more than half a century, British tourists had arrived in Dieppe's sheltered port on ferries from Dover, Newhaven and Portsmouth, anxious to walk along its beaches, picnic in its fields, paint its stellar vistas or lounge in its seaside or port-side cafés before a stroll on the grassy promenade or a game of chance in its famous beachfront casino. Dieppe was a convenient draw for military and naval officers, writers, painters and socialites – *la colonie* of temporary émigrés who leased or purchased property by the sea. Among them was the beautiful Clementine Hozier, Churchill's future wife, who called Dieppe her home for a year at the turn of the century.

Tucked away just a few hundred yards behind the line of vacated hotels on the beachfront lay the town proper, including the port, its entrance guarded by the eastern headland known in English as Pollet Cliff (the Dieppois call it *le Pollet*). Crowned by a large church, Notre Dame de Bonsecours, this vantage point provided a spectacular view out to sea for visitors – and for defenders too. Anyone standing atop the cliff could see halfway across the Channel, glance over the beach to the 14th-century castle on the western headland, or gaze straight down into the inner channel that led to the port behind this promontory – to the interlocking basins of its outer and inner harbours.

At the base of the same eastern headland lay the harbour mole, a massive stone breakwater protected by two jetties that protruded like giant, welcoming arms for scores of holidaymakers arriving by ferry as well as the small fleet of cargo and fishing vessels returning from a day's work along the coast. But getting into the port, particularly after the events of 1940, was a complicated affair. Before a ship could reach either of the harbours, it had first to slip past the blockships and squeeze through a slim 330-foot gap in the mole, with the chalk bluff of Pollet Cliff rising above on its east, or left, side and some of Dieppe's buildings and shops on the right, to the west. Then it entered the inner channel, a claustrophobic funnel that, depending on the tide and the frequency of dredging, forced any vessel to remain arrow-straight for nearly 500 yards or risk running aground. Once the ship got through this narrow passage, the outer harbour appeared to the right while, directly in front, another channel opened up that led to the inner harbour, which connected to the Bassin Duquesne and the Bassin du Canada, named before the war to honour a group of colonists who sailed to New France from Dieppe in 1632.

The outer harbour was the centre of action in Dieppe. Much smaller than Le Havre, Cherbourg or Boulogne, it housed fishing boats, pleasure craft, ferries, steamers, dredgers and barges that all jockeyed for berths alongside one of the three quays that ringed its sides. On the right, as ships entered the tight confines of the inner channel that led to the 'outer harbour,' stood the small port railway station, the Gare Maritime on Quai Henri IV, which catered for people travelling by train to or from Paris.[1] Directly across the outer harbour to the left was 'the island,' an artificial construct roughly 500 by 300 yards in size that housed a small dry dock, a ship-repair facility, and a fish-curing factory on the Quai du Carénage where the fishing fleet offloaded the daily catch for sorting. Connected to each side of the port by a series of swing bridges, the island controlled all the traffic in the port for pedestrians and vehicles, along with the shipping accessing the 'inner harbour' and the two large basins that connected to the customs house, rail yards and several warehouses stocked with coal and timber. Straight ahead lay the Quai Duquesne, where the fish market once drew crowds that congregated in front of the hotels and cafés that 'arcaded' the outer harbour. There the port control office guarded a small drawbridge that connected to the island and the Quai de Carénage. Quai Duquesne was also the main route linking the port to the beachfront, running past an oddly placed tobacco factory that sat sandwiched between the hotels, schools and cafés lining the boulevard de Verdun. From there, pedestrians could stroll across the grassy promenade to the boulevard Maréchal Foch, which connected to Dieppe's main beach. Traditionally, Dieppe was a lively, thriving place, save for the dark years of German occupation.[2]

The German army's 302nd Infantry Division was responsible for defending the area surrounding Dieppe, with units from the Kriegsmarine in control of the port defences, coast guard stations and coastal artillery batteries positioned roughly five miles off to each flank. As part of their defensive doctrine for foiling raids, the Germans focused on firepower, making the most of fixed fortifications and obstacles such as bunkers and pillboxes, roadblocks and barbed wire to maximize their manpower. Given the natural defensive topography at Dieppe, they did not need to man every inch of the beachfront with infantry. As long as they had machine guns, artillery, anti-aircraft guns and mortars that could cover the area and dominate the ground, they could bring down punishing fire on any invader at short notice, buying time to bring in reinforcements to drive the enemy back into the sea.

In the eighteen months leading up to the Dieppe Raid in August 1942, the Germans progressively laid out a series of fortified zones along the coast, including one that covered the sea approaches to Dieppe and potential landing beaches in the area. The defences included concrete pillboxes and bunkers, weapons pits, abandoned seafront buildings turned into fortified positions, and the numerous natural caves clawed deep into the chalk headlands that now housed machine guns, anti-tank guns and artillery pieces. Together, these carefully crafted killing zones would expose any raiding force to a torrent of bullets and shellfire. The Germans marked each zone on a special gridded battle map as an easily recognizable two-digit location reference, rather than the six- or eight-digit indicators traditionally used on military maps, to provide the defenders with a rapid way of communicating and calling in additional firepower during the heat of battle. Having been in the area for two years by 1942, the Germans also enjoyed the home advantage of knowing every crack and crevice, every bottleneck, and they pre-sighted their weapons accordingly and held regular drills to rehearse their reaction to every situation that might suddenly appear.

Five potent artillery batteries ringed Dieppe; later, Jock Hughes-Hallett, the lead planner and naval force commander for the Dieppe Raid, would code-name them Hitler, Rommel, Goering, Goebbels and Hess. In theory, these batteries were designed to work together to destroy a raiding fleet as soon as it approached any beach in the area – particularly the main beach. Two of the bigger batteries, Hess and Goebbels, were of the larger coastal type that belonged to the navy and straddled Dieppe on its extreme flanks about five miles out on either side of the town. To the east, around the hamlet of Berneval, stood the six 150-millimetre guns of Goebbels battery, which could sling a salvo of six 113-pound shells a distance of thirteen miles once every minute. On the opposite flank, just outside the little town of Varengeville, lay Hess battery, with seven guns, three of the 170-millimetre type that could deliver a walloping punch to any exposed ships preparing for or supporting a landing. The other batteries held smaller guns but were located closer to the city – Rommel behind Puys, Hitler south of Dieppe on the high ground next to the river Arques, and Goering to the south-west.

Closer to Dieppe, in and around the flanking towns of Puys and Pourville, German defensive works sprouted up on the hills and cliffs overlooking both of their respective beachfronts. At Puys, situated in a narrow bowl with two great bluffs on either side, three concrete bunkers stood poised on the eastern heights carefully sighted to pour down heavy enfilade fire on the left flank of any invader rushing up from the waterline. A fourth, further down on the bluff overlooking the seawall, covered one of only two obvious ways to get off the beach and head inland – a narrow staircase built into the seawall – while a fifth stood guard high atop the cliff that led to the eastern headland. But dense barbed wire entanglements clogged the stairs and lined the base of the bluffs, protecting the bunkers and slit trenches manned by the German defenders.

To the west, the seaside village of Pourville sat in the valley of the tiny river Scie. The surrounding terrain was more open than in Puys, and the Germans, considering it the natural landing spot for any raiding force attempting to capture Dieppe, went to considerable lengths to defend the area. They placed bunkers and pillboxes in the town overlooking the beach, and others along the valley walls further inland. These defences were to catch raiders in fully exposed enfiladed fire as they attempted to work up the river valley towards the Luftwaffe airfield on the south-western outskirts of Dieppe a few miles in the distance, or along the rolling hills that led to the western headland overlooking Dieppe's main beach.

On this commanding point, in the shadow of the old castle, the Germans used the cliff caves that ran just under the bluff's crown to place artillery that could cover the far end of the main beach and hit invading boats a few thousand yards out into the Channel. On the beach lay the decrepit hulk of the formerly whitewashed casino that had siphoned many a fortune from a British tourist over many decades. Now, it sat near empty, camouflaged with swaths of greenish-brown and yellow paint. Inside, instead of games of chance, the Germans maintained a modest barrack and the odd machine gun. Outside, small-calibre anti-tank guns flanked the structure while snipers perched themselves on the roof or its tall twin towers, joining others scattered and carefully concealed on the floors of the vacated hotels and other buildings that faced the water, lining Dieppe's main beach.

Looking ahead over to Pollet Cliff, the defenders could see the hotels, the grassy promenade and the beach, the tobacco factory, the left arm of the jetty and the harbour mole. The long, narrow beach, devoid of sand but covered with pieces of chert rock the size of a person's fist, is one and a half miles long but stretches only about 100 yards deep from the waterline to the seawall. At this point in the war, the Germans had yet to sow the beach with land mines, but they had erected underwater obstacles designed to rip the hull out of any vessel attempting to land troops onshore during high tide. The beach itself changes with every tide, with parts of it left in either a steep or a gentle rise, creating small rolling valleys whose dips provide the only cover, or 'dead ground,' a man might find between the sea and the seawall. And from that barrier wall, the Germans erected a sizeable barbed wire entanglement stretching out for fifteen feet towards the beach. It was designed to slow or stop any invaders, allowing the defenders to subject them to murderous fire.

On the other side of the seawall lay the 300-yard-wide grassy promenade between the boulevard Maréchal Foch on the town side and the now-vacated hotels, schools and cafés on the waterfront boulevard de Verdun. Here the Germans dug a series of slit trenches, and strategically placed machine-gun pits and pillboxes, protected by a labyrinth of barbed wire and backed up by machine-gun and sniper positions in reinforced rooms in the hotels behind. On the tiny streets that ran perpendicular to the boulevard de Verdun and led to the port, they erected ten-foot-high concrete barricades to prevent raiding tanks or vehicles from penetrating the town and the port beyond. If these defences withstood destruction, enemy vehicles would remain trapped on the main beach, open to fire from the town and from the headlands on either side.

In the port, however, the Germans placed few fixed defences – only a pillbox and a long string of barbed wire that ran along the western bank of the inner channel, through the Quai Henry IV and then down the Quai Duquesne. They did, however, keep a Kriegsmarine security force in the town, which in the event of a raid was tasked with destroying the pumping stations, swing bridges, and any classified material that was housed in the port commandant's headquarters and other facilities. Otherwise, they placed their faith in the defences along the eastern headland.

Pollet Cliff formed the other arm in the horseshoe that overlooked the main beach. Like the west headland, the caves on the sides and at its base provided excellent natural positions in which to place weapons designed to hit the main beach or control access to the port. On top of the cliff, the Germans built an observation bunker and set up a battery of anti-aircraft guns near the port's signals station. In the cliff itself, they positioned artillery pieces that faced the harbour mole and the beach. In the caves at the base overlooking the inner channel, they fixed anti-tank and machine guns to shoot up any vessel daring enough to attempt to breach the harbour and run the deadly gauntlet of fire.

By the summer of 1942, the once-peaceful seaside resort of Dieppe had become a fortified area designed to stop raiders dead in their tracks with all the will the defenders could muster. And in the spring and early summer of that year, Lord Louis Mountbatten's Combined Operations Headquarters was intent on making bold plans that would test that resolve.

〜

There is not one single piece of credible evidence that explicitly states when the original idea for the Dieppe Raid materialized. Although Jock Hughes-Hallett revealed in his memoirs (penned before the declassification of Ultra) that he laid down the concept for Dieppe during his January 1942 meeting with Luce and De Costobadie (and the day after Godfrey changed his pinch policy), there is no record of any serious planning or intelligence collection at that time to support his claim.

In fact, Dieppe does not register in anything but a cursory way throughout 1941 and into the first two months of 1942, save for the odd mention as part of routine intelligence collection by NID and General Sir Bernard Paget's GHQ Home Forces – the British army headquarters that held jurisdictional responsibility for military operations in the Channel. All, it appears, remained quiet on the Dieppe front as the COHQ planning syndicate moved ahead with Operation Chariot at St Nazaire, Operation Myrmidon at Bayonne, Operation Sledgehammer at Cherbourg and Operation Biting, a small raid designed to snatch the latest in radar technology from Bruneval on the French Channel coast. Then, in late March and into the first week of April – the intervening period between the St Nazaire and Bayonne raids and a week after Fleming's pitch to create the IAU – a flurry of reports for what would become Operation Rutter – the code name for the first incarnation of the Dieppe Raid – suddenly appeared.

By April 3, the previous trickle of intelligence had turned into a flood, with GHQ Home Forces offering information on military defences in the Dieppe area while the Ministry of Economic Warfare provided a list of potential industrial targets in the town. Two days later, on Easter Sunday – the same day that the commando forces involved in Operation Myrmidon failed to pinch material – Godfrey's ISTD delivered a special report on 'Dieppe and the Beaches Five Miles to Each Side.' This impressive and highly detailed report came in response to a direct request marked a 'matter of urgency' from Hughes-Hallett's planning syndicate and was facilitated through Fleming's Section 17 in Room 39.[3]

According to Godfrey, the creation of reports such as this, which appeared not long after NID had become 'acquainted with the idea,' stood as 'a first-class indication that the operation had got really hot.' This, then, pins the origin of any serious planning for a raid on Dieppe to the last weeks of March and the first week of April.[4]

At close to 80 pages, this extensive and intricate document displayed the best that the ISTD had to offer. Everything from terrain and targeting information was laid out, which not only provided a conceptual framework for the operation but clearly shows that NID was working hand in glove with Mountbatten's headquarters to shape and design the Dieppe Raid before the outline or detailed planning commenced. Given the necessary run-up time to produce such a detailed report, it affixes the origins of serious work for a raid on Dieppe to some time within the last ten days of March, which corresponds to the process for target selection outlined by Godfrey:

> When a target is suggested, it is examined by an examination com-mittee to decide whether it is worth proceeding with. For this, a brief intelligence summary is prepared – about [a] half-page of fools-cap. If the committee decides the plans are to be prepared, then detailed intelligence is collected and planning proceeded with. CCO [Mountbatten] also goes ahead with the work of collecting the craft, men etc. and bringing them in good time to the point of departure. When a detailed plan has been produced, it is submitted to COS, and the naval, military and Air Force Commanders are appointed who prepare at Combined Operations Headquarters all detailed plans, on intelligence provided by CCO's intelligence staff.[5]

In the two weeks that followed the delivery of the report, the planners weighed various outline plans for a raid on Dieppe for submission to the chiefs of staff (COS). The first scheme called for an indirect three-prong pincer attack: the infantry or commandos would land on both sides of Dieppe at the little towns of Puys and Pourville while tanks and infantry landed further west, down the coast at Quiberville, before rushing overland to envelop the town and port as rapidly as possible. On paper, this plan seemed the less risky option because it avoided a direct frontal assault on the town; this was the one to adopt if the objective was simply to test the ability of the various service arms to work together in an amphibious raid, score a quick propaganda victory, or attempt to draw the Luftwaffe into a battle of attrition.

The second option was a much riskier and more complicated proposition – a 1942 version of 'shock and awe.' In addition to the flanking attacks, it called for a direct assault in a crab-like fashion over the main beach. Under cover of darkness, infantry would land from the sea at Puys and Pourville, then push on towards the port while airborne units would drop from the skies to attack the coastal gun batteries at Varengeville and Berneval. That would be followed 60 minutes later by the frontal assault, led by tanks, infantry and engineers, which would storm the main beach in Dieppe after a bomber strike and naval bombardment had obliterated the hotels and other structures that lined the waterfront, separating it from the port tucked a few hundred yards behind. Using a carefully synchronized formula in which surprise was paramount, the assaulting forces would employ speed and a dual thunderclap of aerial bombing and naval bombardment to bewilder the defenders, allowing the raiders to close quickly on their positions, seize the dominating headlands and penetrate over the main beach into the town to capture the port.

While the main landing unfolded, an additional infantry battalion would land at Pourville and, with help from some of the tanks that had landed on the main beach, push south-west to capture the Luftwaffe airfield on the outskirts of Dieppe and the German army headquarters located in Arques-la-Bataille. A curious feature of this plan, one worthy of Horatio Hornblower, called for a Cutting Out Force of Royal Navy vessels, with a detachment of Royal Marine commandos riding on their decks, to storm into the port in the best 'privateering' tradition and snatch as many German barges as they could tow back to England as 'prizes.' This imperative featured in both outline plans and predated the inclusion of other land force elements. Unsure of the ostensible reason given for this measure, one critic summed up these elements as 'a classic example of a planning officer dreaming up a task for the lack of finding anything better since there was no possibility of these craft being of any use to the British.'[6] Or so it seemed.

Operation Rutter would be a race against time. Unlike an invasion attempt, where assaulting forces storm ashore to capture and hold ground, build up their strength and expand the bridgehead, then break out into enemy-held territory – as happened in Normandy in 1944 – the Dieppe Raid from the start was planned as a one-day 'return ticket' or 'butcher and bolt' raid designed to last no more than two tides – roughly seventeen hours. That meant the raiders had to cross the English Channel undetected to maintain the element of surprise, get ashore and quickly overwhelm the defenders, seize their objectives, wreak havoc in the port area, and withdraw under cover of darkness before substantial German reinforcements could arrive to obliterate them.

At this point, although the planning process clearly laid down the two options available when it came to the method, nothing revealed the specific goal or purpose for the raid. Obviously, the objective involved the capture of the port, even by frontal assault, if necessary. But what was so crucial about gaining the port in the first place, let alone in such a direct, risky and perhaps costly way?

∽

Technically, Jock Hughes-Hallett was correct when he wrote after the war that Dieppe had 'no particular military significance.' Bound by the provisions of the Official Secrets Act, he chose his words carefully while penning his unpublished memoirs, *Before I Forget*, long before the secret of Ultra was released to the public. Much of the truth behind his account of Dieppe has been left in the shadows, replaced by convenient excuses, omissions or redirections of sensitive issues that make no mention of any pinch, captured documents, or special operations that were planned to obtain these materials. When he employed the term 'military' in this context, the shrewd naval officer was using it in its proper sense. For most laymen, the word is synonymous with all branches of the armed services. Within the confines of the defence establishment, however, it was, and still is, applied only to issues involving the army or air force, and never the navy, which always used the term 'naval.' In this case, although Dieppe may not have offered Hughes-Hallett and his planning team a tantalizing 'military' target, it certainly loomed large for 'naval' concerns.

By the first week of February 1942, the NID and the Naval Section at Bletchley knew that Admiral Karl Dönitz's U-boats operating in the

Atlantic had begun to use the four-rotor Enigma machine to encrypt their top-secret messages. As frightening and potentially cataclysmic as this development certainly was, a more disturbing prospect had appeared just weeks before when Bletchley learned that a small number of German destroyers had received orders to pick up several four-rotor machines for distribution to ships that operated mainly in Norwegian waters. So far as the NID could tell, these vessels had yet to employ the new device, but the potential implication was clear: replacement of the three-rotor was in the offing. Godfrey went into overdrive to monitor the situation and actively pursue remedies, one of which included Fleming's proposed Intelligence Assault Unit.

First, however, Godfrey had to locate the right target – one that would house the desired material for the pinch but not be so evident as a heavily defended submarine base or an isolated U-boat or trawler at sea. As Godfrey had already laid out in January in his new pinch policy, port headquarters, naval wireless stations and other shore-based facilities were prime targets; the fluid nature of naval warfare meant that all these sites, regardless of location, had to possess the latest cipher machines and related materials to maintain the elaborate Kriegsmarine radio net. In the course of their investigation, Naval Section had surmised that as of July 1941, there were 'at least 910 Four-Rotors in existence,' although none at the moment had become operational with a four-rotor setting. With 187 Kriegsmarine shore stations in existence 'using the Enigma of all types,' they estimated that each would 'house three machines' per station.[7] Targeting these made perfect sense as the American Navy learned from studying British doctrine: 'Naval shore stations have always been a potentially rich source both of communications intelligence material and of the technological equipment and information,' for 'these shore stations are relatively accessible. Since the greater number are near the seaboard, they are soon overrun by invading armies. Being tied to fixed port installations, their mobility is limited, and it has not proved difficult to discover in advance at least their general location.'[8]

Three weeks earlier, during a meeting with SOE called to discuss their future work on the St Nazaire and Bayonne raids, Mountbatten announced that his long-term policy was 'to enable the British Army to land anywhere for offensive operations,' while in the short term he planned to 'pursue a vigorous raiding policy' and that his Royal Marine section would 'welcome all such ideas from anyone, provided they are backed by the necessary minimum of intelligence (both senses of the word).'[9]

On March 13, one week before Fleming put his bid to raise the IAU on paper, Naval Section intercepted a garbled message accidentally encrypted on the four-rotor Enigma in traffic enciphered by the Kriegsmarine's 2nd Defence Division, headquartered in Boulogne, responsible for operations that spanned the English Channel between Cherbourg in Normandy and Ostend on the Belgian coast. What drew the attention of the cryptanalysts was the unintelligible nature of the message, which revealed that it had been mistakenly encrypted using four-rotor settings from the new naval Enigma machine rather than the usual three-rotor settings employed for the home waters key. Immediately, Bletchley and NID realized the ominous nature of the development and Birch recorded with dread: 'Some ships in the [English] channel were provided with the new machine.'[10] Indeed, this confirmed Godfrey's worst fears – the new four-rotor device had spread to minor surface vessels plying the Channel. How many at this moment was anyone's guess, and there was no clear indication when they would spring into action in full force. These developments, however, could not be ignored, for this was first-class evidence that a switch to four-rotor settings was coming much faster than the DNI expected. Immediately, alarm bells sounded, and although hopes ran high that the raids at St Nazaire and Bayonne on the French west coast would deliver the desired material, NID and its delivery vehicle – Mountbatten's Combined Operations – now set their sights squarely on the Channel for prime pinch targets.

The revelation of the distribution of the four-rotor to minor surface vessels in the Channel, along with earlier reports of its dispatch to ships in Norwegian waters in January, confirmed that the malignancy had spread and that Godfrey's decision to hedge his bets had backfired. Nevertheless, at the same time, this news transformed the string of German-occupied ports along the Channel into potentially lucrative pinch environments. Given the current context, Dieppe appeared quite appealing from a tactical and operational perspective. The port lay well within easy reach of RAF air cover, yet it was small enough for a force limited in size by available amphibious resources to tackle, unlike the massive and heavily defended ports of Le Havre, Boulogne, Cherbourg, Dunkirk and Calais. Also, just 70 miles from British shores, it could, in theory, be taken by surprise given the right circumstances.

From a pinch perspective, Dieppe offered the potential gold mine. By late March of 1942, when the outline planning for Operation Rutter began, NID, through the combined efforts of the Operational Intelligence Centre in London and the Naval Section at Bletchley, had firmly established through codebreaking, traffic analysis, aerial photographs and agent reports that the port of Dieppe regularly handled a collection of vessels suspected of carrying the four-rotor material so desperately needed.[11] Although NID had sighted a sizeable U-boat flotilla in the harbour on several occasions a year earlier, this was not the usual fare that frequented the port.[12] In painstaking detail from 1940 onwards, the OIC had tracked all vessels that used Dieppe (and the other ports) and had assembled a veritable compendium (unparalleled for its time) for the planners. Every type of craft from the long-desired *Bernhard Von Tschirschky* and other salvage ships of this class (*Arc*, *Barfleur*, *Marshal Maurice* and *Avre*) to S-boats (or E-boats to the Allies), Siebel ferries, barges, drifters, trawlers and sizeable 1,000-ton torpedo boats that frequented the port all made it onto the list.[13] More importantly, their deft intelligence work established that the 18th Vorpostenboot (V-boat) Flotilla with ten flak ships that doubled as patrol craft, the 46th Minensuchboot (M-boat) Flotilla with six large minesweepers, and the 1st Raumboot (R-boat) Flotilla of fast minesweepers used for patrol and escort work all called Dieppe home on a permanent basis.

Among this collection of vessels could be found material directly involved with the naval Enigma device or other codes and ciphers that would provide the crucial cribs for the ideal backdoor cheats: RHV, short signals, E-bars, Z-bars, weather (*Wetterkurtzschlüssel*) and a dockyard cipher (*Werftschlüssel*), a Kriegsmarine general cipher, and books containing naval nomenclature. Although there was no guarantee that these vessels would be portside on the morning of an attack, the constant reading of their message traffic through Ultra gave Bletchley a good sense of the rhythm and routine of German channel traffic which increased the odds that a few would be berthed in the outer harbour with only skeleton crews to defend them. If not, Godfrey had another – fail-safe – plan.

Since the summer of 1940, Naval Section had cobbled together a card file on German communications establishments in the Channel (and elsewhere) based on information from all possible sources – Ultra, captured documents, photo-reconnaissance, agent reports and prisoners of war. As the US Navy's report on British pinch policy revealed: 'Gradually, the locations of all these establishments became known, at least approximately, and precisely what codes and ciphers they all held.'[14] All of this targeting information was 'posted on a large chart, pins of different colours and shapes being used to indicate the different codes and ciphers held at the various locations. A glance at this chart laid out what the Commandos might expect to capture at any given shore establishment.'[15]

As per standard procedure, the Kriegsmarine outfitted each naval shore station (regardless of size or shipping traffic) with at least three Enigma machines, usually located in the local naval headquarters.[16] Also, as Dieppe served as a naval supply base for this part of the Channel, it housed a specialized depot under the command of the navy's Communications Equipment Division. Here, they maintained stockpiles of code and cipher materials and new devices set for distribution months down the line, making Dieppe, from a cryptanalyst's perspective, more than qualified as a 'target-rich environment.'[17]

On April 6, just 24 hours after the abandonment of Operation Myrmidon and its failure to pinch material at Bayonne, German naval headquarters in Dieppe appeared as a central feature of the operation even before the ink on the outline plan had dried. This came in the form of an urgent addendum to the Godfrey ISTD report and it established the suspected location for the much-sought-after naval headquarters in the port, followed in short order by a request from the NID for the capture of vessels in the harbour housing the desired cryptographic material. Therefore, as the evidence clearly shows, the pinch was front and centre from the very inception of the raid, before the detailed operational planning began – and before Mountbatten's headquarters officially sanctioned Dieppe as its next raiding target.[18]

Not everything in the targeting process proceeded smoothly, however. Two days later, in a move that reflected the great urgency of the matter, Godfrey (or Fleming working on his behalf) challenged the initial intelligence report that a small hotel called the Moderne, apparently located at 21 rue Vauquelin on the corner with the Quai Duquesne, overlooking the inner harbour, housed German naval headquarters. Traditionally, discussions concerning specific targets were left to lower-ranking officers to work out the details, so the personal interest of these top men in NID is telling and indicates its essential nature. For Godfrey and Fleming, the detailed description of the hotel cast doubt on whether such a small structure as the Moderne would be used by the Kriegsmarine, who traditionally preferred seaside villas and other grandiose buildings:

> This hotel is situated on the RUE VAUQUELIN on the corner of the street nearest the harbour. The hotel is almost certainly on the north side of the street, but a possibility exists that it is on the south side. The full address is 21, RUE VAUQUELIN.
>
> The hotel is a small one consisting of a restaurant with a few rooms upstairs. The main entrance is on the quay and is in the centre of the building. This leads into the Restaurant. To the north of this is a second entrance leading upstairs. It is believed that there is a third entrance on the RUE VAUQUELIN. The quay at this point is arcaded so that the entrances open onto the Arcade.
>
> Since this hotel is so small, it does not seem likely that it is being used as Headquarters, and considerable doubt is therefore thrown on the original report. Special enquiries are being made, and it is hoped to give further information shortly.[19]

There are no indications in the documents as to what inquiries were made, and there is no paper trail in the public domain to establish precisely what changed their minds. However, six weeks later, in the second week of June, neither Fleming nor Godfrey had further concerns. Without any explanation, there is a simple note in the file to say that the Hôtel Moderne 'is now considered by NID to be Naval Headquarters.'[20]

From a historical perspective, whether the hotel housed a German naval headquarters or some other naval facility is still open to debate, but the point is quite secondary in importance; what is crucial is what the planners thought at the time. Although they did not know it, the first location at 21 rue Vauquelin was incorrect: it housed the Hôtel Les Arcades, which had been there from the turn of the century and, in 1942, still hosted German soldiers and sailors and the occasional civilian to lunch or dinner in its lobby restaurant. That ruled it out as a functioning naval headquarters.*

The secondary target, located across the street, was, in fact, the Hôtel Moderne; it fitted the physical description that the NID initially baulked at, but no record has surfaced to show what was happening there during the occupation. Some photographs from the wartime period clearly show one naval headquarters facility on the boulevard de Verdun located in an old school not far from the casino. At the same time, others show a similar facility near the end of Quai Henri IV, where it meets the inner channel. Although existing German documents do not reveal a specific location in the port, a preliminary

---

* While on location filming *Dieppe Uncovered* for UKTV in Great Britain and History Television in Canada, my filmmaking partner, producer/director Wayne Abbott, and I spent a day talking to some of the local inhabitants, including Karine and Mathieu Leducq, the present owners of Les Arcades hotel, which is still there. As Mathieu pointed out to us, with photographic evidence in hand, his hotel had been in the same location for over 50 years before the raid. He confirmed that there used to be a hotel/restaurant called Le Moderne across the street in the alternative target location, until approximately 1973. Wayne and I then checked in a phone book from 1939 in the local Dieppe archives, and it confirmed Mathieu's story, although we could not discover what became of the hotel during the occupation. We did, however, have with us an account from the diary of Georges Guibon, a Dieppe resident, who chronicled his experiences wandering through the town on the morning of the raid. Quite incidentally, he mentions the death of the owner of Les Arcades – a man by the name of Verel – who, after being hit by a stray bullet from Pollet Cliff, crawled into the tiny elevator and died. This account was confirmed by Mathieu, who then called the archives and had them produce a copy of Verel's death certificate. It was witnessed by one of his waitresses, meaning that his hotel and restaurant were in operation on the day of the raid. Obviously, then, the Hôtel Les Arcades did not host a German headquarters.

report drawn up by the German naval commander in the Channel area provides a list of the German naval formations on duty in the town. During the battle, while the commander worked from an army observation post high up on the bluffs overlooking the port, his naval headquarters and its ancillary facilities remained in the port, staffed by close to 360 men in total. Just over half (152) worked out of the harbour commandant's headquarters, while 44 toiled with an 'Army signals transmission station' and eleven with a 'naval signals station.' Four worked with a teletype detachment, while another four operated a 'wireless deception sender,' leaving 44 with the '6th Flotilla Base unit,' and roughly another 100 with the 'port protection flotilla.'[21] In the same file, another report makes mention of a special security unit comprised of two seven-man teams, tasked with destroying not only vital objectives such as pumping stations and lock gates, but also, even more critical, classified signals material located in the port should they be faced with capture.[22]

Although this information does not confirm that the Hôtel Moderne was the correct target, it clearly demonstrates that NID was in the ball-park and that at least one site containing the desired material did, in fact, exist somewhere in the tiny confines of the outer harbour. It also shows how well within reach these targets were for any raider storming in over the eastern half of the main beach on a direct path or barrelling down the inner channel straight into the outer port to berth dockside along one of the quays just yards from their prime target.[23]

Exact location aside, the significance resides in the personal involvement of Godfrey and Fleming, whose nitpicking leaves little doubt as to the critical importance and nature of the target. No other objective received so much attention. It also shows that the NID took an over-riding interest in locating a rich source of pinch material – a factor that was in play right from the beginning of the planning process for the raid, even before Mountbatten, the chiefs of staff and Churchill approved the mission.[24]

On April 14, just over a week after the aborted Operation Myrmidon failed as a pinch mission, Jock Hughes-Hallett, the head of Mountbatten's target search committee, convened the first recorded meeting to discuss a raid under the code name Rutter at Dieppe.

Brigadier Charles Haydon, the Vice Chief of Combined Operations (VCCO) and the man who had not only commanded the military force but organized the army commandos during the Lofoten pinch raids, presided that day. Hughes-Hallett opened the meeting with a brief pitch about Dieppe as a prospective target, and the group readily agreed that it seemed 'attractive and worthwhile,' an idea definitely worth pursuing.[25] Over the next five days, the planning syndicate laid out a set of objectives, which listed a series of German headquarters in and around the town, along with the role of a 'cutting out party' comprising a detachment of Royal Marines riding on a river gunboat (HMS *Locust*), tasked with capturing barges in the port. Conspicuous by its absence was any detailed mention of the Hôtel Moderne by name – probably because of its unconfirmed status as a German naval headquarters at that time. However, one of the earliest maps used during the outline planning stage clearly marks the hotel's location and singles it out as the only headquarters worth noting during this phase of planning, confirming its primacy as a target from the raid's inception.[26] The dicey frontal-assault option was also agreed upon, with the proviso that the raid be preceded by a heavy air bombardment and that the two batteries east and west of Dieppe be taken out before the landing by airborne troops. On hearing that condition, Hughes-Hallett remarked: 'Though ... hazardous, it was perfectly feasible so far as the Navy was concerned.'[27]

On April 25, Lord Louis Mountbatten chaired his first meeting on Operation Rutter, at Combined Operations Headquarters on Richmond Terrace in Whitehall. There the planning group adopted the outline plan and confirmed the method of direct assault.[28] At first, Mountbatten was taken aback by the prospect of this daring frontal raid, but he quickly came on side once the arguments were laid out before him. With surprise and shock essential for success, the planners argued, it made no sense to land tanks far out on the flanks where, even under good conditions, they would need considerable time to reach the port. Each group would first have to cross a small river, and if the Germans reacted quickly and destroyed the bridges, the tanks would be delayed even more.

Moreover, the latest intelligence assessment of Dieppe's defences indicated that only 1,400 low-category troops held the town and that reinforcements would be slow to arrive, bringing the total at most to 2,500 men in the first four hours after the attack.[29] Mountbatten was assured that the bombing would be of 'maximum intensity,' delivered in a combination of high- and low-altitude attacks to confuse and disorient the defenders – first by heavy bombers hitting the general area, followed quickly by low-level runs with fighter bombers that would strike specific beach targets during the landings. Suitably impressed, Mountbatten signed off on the outline plan for Operation Rutter, allowing it to proceed to the Chiefs of Staff Committee for their approval.

By the time the outline plan reached the chiefs of staff for their consideration on May 10, the target and the objective list had grown substantially. Now, in addition to the earlier goals, German E-boats and motor launches had joined the list, along with food stores, the town hall, the post office, the railway marshalling yards, the beach-front casino, and the coastguard station on the cliff at Puys, as well as the capture of prisoners and of secret documents from the divisional headquarters. The stakes were growing.

When the chiefs of staff met to discuss the operation on May 13, Mountbatten sought permission to move ahead with the outline plan so he could provide the force commanders, who had yet to be officially appointed although they had already been named, with guidelines to shape their detailed planning. At this point, the outline plan for Rutter envisioned it taking place over two tidal periods lasting roughly seventeen hours, giving the raiding force the maximum time on target before it had to withdraw. The date was set for the night of June 20–21 or any day after that up to June 26. In terms of shipping, it would be the largest raiding force yet put to sea. From the naval perspective alone, Jock Hughes-Hallett's plan called for a 250-ship armada that included six Royal Navy destroyers, seven infantry assault ships, 24 tank landing craft, 50 R-craft for transporting troops to shore, and a collection of motor gunboats, torpedo boats and motor launches, including HMS *Locust* – a flat-bottomed river gunboat formerly captained by Dick de Costobadie. This ship would carry the newly formed Royal Marine Commando, including Ian Fleming's Intelligence Assault Unit, into battle.[30]

If the proposed naval force was indeed impressive, the turnout in the skies in support of the operation was stellar. With more than 800 aircraft taking part, including 150 heavy bombers, eight squadrons of low-level attack aircraft, and more than 500 fighters providing an air umbrella above, it promised to be the most magnificent display of airpower since the Battle of Britain.

As for the military contribution, the plan required almost a full infantry division – roughly 4,000 men. There was also a battalion of tanks containing three squadrons of the latest Churchill tanks, supported by a battalion of about 500 airborne troops that included paratroop and glider forces.

The executive responsibility for launching, postponing or cancelling the raid came under the Commander-in-Chief, Portsmouth, Admiral Sir William James, one of Blinker Hall's veterans from Room 40 in the Admiralty. He would be responsible for giving the order to commence the operation. But once the forces left the harbours in southern England, they would be in the hands of the naval force commander, who would shepherd them across the Channel to their landing sites and deliver them to shore. From there, the military commander would take over once they landed and until they re-embarked for their return to England at the raid's end. The air force commander would conduct the air battle throughout from his base at home.

Although Lord Louis Mountbatten and Jock Hughes-Hallett would later cry foul after the actual Dieppe Raid, they, like Churchill and the chiefs of staff, expressed no hesitation about the outline or detailed plans laid down for the raid in the spring of 1942. At any point during the planning process, they had the opportunity and the obligation to shut the whole project down or to force a fundamental change if they felt they should. Yet they saw merits in the bold and risky nature of the operation even though, without inside knowledge, it seemed to make no sense at all. Even the obdurate Alan Brooke – the newly promoted Chief of the Imperial General Staff who strove hard to keep Churchill's penchant for wildcat operations in check and was equally dismissive of Mountbatten's martial ability – voiced nothing but support throughout the planning process. Brooke had in pre-war days spent his summers in Dieppe and, after hearing about the proposed raid for the first time,

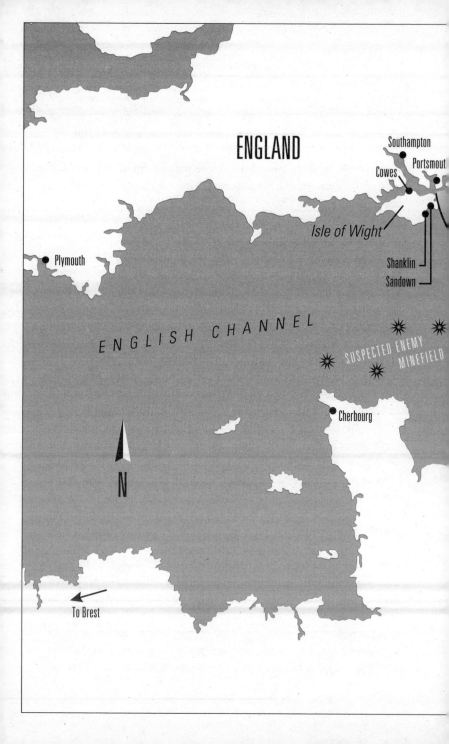

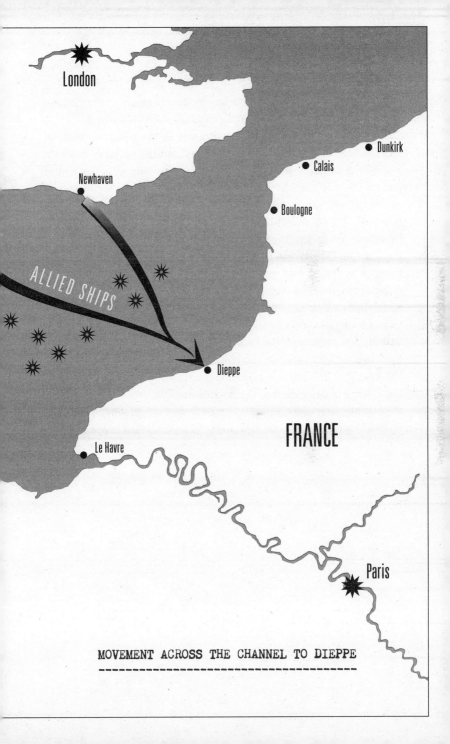

MOVEMENT ACROSS THE CHANNEL TO DIEPPE

eagerly recorded in his diary: 'Main interest of morning's COS was examination of proposed large scale raid in the vicinity of Dieppe. Little did I ever think in the old days of my regular journeys of Newhaven–Dieppe that I should have been planning as I was this morning!'[31]

Unlike the other operations currently in the planning stage at COHQ, Operation Rutter steamed ahead, at least officially, without a clearly articulated goal. The approval of the outline of the Rutter plan by the chiefs of staff, despite its many controversial elements, was unhesitatingly quick. Overzealous reliance on surprise and shock, the novel use of tanks, a 'cutting out' operation tasked to capture essentially useless shipping, and the frontal assault designed to capture the port and a suspected German naval headquarters as essential features right from its inception – all went seemingly unchecked, according to the minutes that reached the public domain. Given the fact that Churchill had issued orders for all mentions of Ultra or Ultra-related operations to be expunged from the official records, it is not surprising perhaps that these aspects appeared incongruous within the normal context of operational procedure.[32] In fact, they were not. But given what is now known about the vital role of intelligence in the war effort, the critical importance of pinch raids to the cryptographic efforts, the urgent need to solve the four-rotor Enigma blackout, and the preferred form for pinching at targets ashore – the Dieppe Raid does start to make sense.

CHAPTER 10

All the King's Men

'We just wanted to get at them.'
Private Ron Beal, Toronto's Royal Regiment of Canada

Since the fall of France in 1940, units from the Canadian Army had been stationed in camps along England's Sussex coast tasked with the vital role of standing guard against the threat of a German invasion. With Hitler's focus firmly on the eastern front and fears of an invasion supplanted by the increasing U-boat menace in the first months of 1942, the Canadian Army had become restless in their now immaterial defensive role. Monotonous schemes and training exercises did little to alleviate the situation, and officers and men longed for action, not only to break this dismal cycle but to add to the stellar legacy earned by their fathers in the trenches of the western front during the Great War.[1]*

To alleviate the growing tension among the men, the Canadian units had for over half a year been engaged in commando-like training for small-scale amphibious operations, and had hoped to participate in a series of hit-and-run raids along the French and Norwegian coasts. Up

---

* Indeed, by 1918, the Canadian Corps had become known as the 'Shock Army of the British Empire,' ready, willing and able to take on the toughest, dirtiest jobs such as the stunning victories at Vimy, Hill 70, Amiens and the Hindenburg Line, to name but a few.

to this point, the Spitsbergen Raid in Norway in August 1941, which had included some 500 Canadian soldiers, had been the only highlight, along with limited involvement in a few other pinprick attacks.

By February 1942, with no signs of substantial action on the horizon, the crusty and uncompromising technocrat General Andrew McNaughton, the senior Canadian Army commander in England, began to agitate for action.

At home, the Canadian public was getting equally restless for real action, fearing somewhat naively that the war would be over before the Canadians could take part in the fighting. Canadian prime minister William Lyon Mackenzie King added his voice to give weight to his generals' complaints, and from early 1942 onwards, the pressure from Canadian authorities to engage in active operations increased dramatically.

McNaughton's highly ambitious subordinate, 1st Canadian Corps commander Lieutenant General Harry Crerar, took the lead on the issue, calling upon his personal relationship with his old Great War compatriot General Sir Alan Brooke, the chairman of the Chiefs of Staff Committee, and approaching General Sir Bernard Paget at GHQ Home Forces for his support as well. In a move that one historian has called a clear case of 'misplaced nationalism,' the crafty and determined Crerar managed to obtain their backing, which left Canadian high command unknowingly muscling in on the embryonic Dieppe Raid.

For his part, Mountbatten, who had hoped to showcase the Royal Marine Division in Rutter and save it from the chopping block, seemed completely caught off guard by this development and was not happy: 'I remember going on and on at Brookie [Alan Brooke],' he wrote years later, 'and asking not to have to take the Canadians. However, he said that Crerar was absolutely adamant that they should be used and that the PM was prepared to accept them. I was thus overridden.'[2]

His reluctance, no doubt, stemmed in part from the starring role he had in mind for his Royal Marines tasked with the Ultra Secret pinch imperative. In a carefully crafted recollection of events penned years before the public revelation of Ultra, Mountbatten stated:

Brookie spoke to me personally about the desire of the Canadians to be brought into a raiding operation as soon as possible. My recollection is that I protested strongly because Dieppe was such a large scale and uncertain operation. We were still trying to find out things and even if successful in all our aims, there would be nothing much to show for it to the outside world, and we were bound to have heavy casualties.[3]

Certainly, Mountbatten's professed regard for Canadian casualties, or any casualties in this context, is strictly designed to distance himself from the disastrous results long after the fact, just as the vague mention of 'trying to find out things' is a euphemistic cover for the Ultra Secret nature of the assault.

Despite his protests, the political reality of the moment won the day with Mountbatten forced to accept the Canadians and the drastic paring down of the Royal Marines into commando-sized units to save them from the chopping block.[4] Undaunted, the Chief of Combined Operations begrudgingly welcomed the 2nd Canadian Infantry Division into the fold but withheld the starring role in Rutter for the newly formed Royal Marine Commando.[5]

Although members of the Canadian high command in England were not yet fully 'indoctrinated' into or apprised of Ultra (with the exception of Lieutenant General Kenneth Stuart, the Chief of the Canadian General Staff), there was nothing to prevent them from being partially let in on the secret.* But in the carefully stovepiped

---

* It is unclear whether Mountbatten knew at the time that Canada was an emerging, albeit limited, SIGINT partner. A handful of Canadians, including Prime Minister Mackenzie King, the Canadian Chief of the Naval Staff, Vice Admiral Percy Nelles, and his Director of Naval Intelligence, Commander Herbert Little, were aware of Ultra, with the latter two actively using the intelligence supplied by the Naval Section at Bletchley Park to help fight the convoy battle in the Atlantic. Both were all too aware of the terrible problems being caused by the current blackout, but most likely knew nothing about the pinch. Besides, the Canadians had made inroads of their own into cryptography with the establishment of the Examination Unit in Ottawa and a network of intercept stations across the country, which were providing intelligence to assist in both the European and Pacific theatres of the war. Perhaps more critical, Churchill's British Security Co-ordination, a covert organization established in May 1940 by the British Secret Intelligence Service (or MI6, as it was coming to be called at the time) for intelligence and propaganda purposes in the Americas, was run from its Rockefeller Center offices in New York City by William Stephenson, a

world of intelligence and the military, which operated on a 'need to know' basis, all they were told was the main objective for the raid, its general significance to the war effort and the fact that it was worth risking everything to obtain. In other words, they generally had the same limited information as did the men in Ian Fleming's Intelligence Assault Unit.*

On April 27, just two days after Mountbatten had signed off on the outline plan for Operation Rutter, Lieutenant General Bernard Law Montgomery, who under Paget commanded the South-Eastern Army, called Harry Crerar to a meeting at his headquarters. Monty, as he was fondly called, was about to head off to North Africa – and legendary fame as the hero of El Alamein. Never one to suffer fools gladly or deviate from his precise approach to military professionalism, he told the eager Canadian commander that a raid on an unidentified port was in the offing and asked whether the Canadians wanted to be part of the operation. 'You bet,' came the reply.

And with this quick, simple utterance, the Canadian Army, which had waited patiently for nearly three years for action, climbed aboard the operational train readying to depart for Dieppe.[6]

⤸

Now began the internal battle for command. The mixture of military and naval minds, talents and temperaments was, in theory, what Combined Operations was all about, with all three services putting aside their partisan differences for the common good under the

---

Canadian multi-millionaire industrialist who, by the end of the war, would be a close friend of Ian Fleming.

* At that time, cultural and nationalist lines between Canada and Great Britain were much more blurred than they are today, so it is not surprising that the British high command viewed Canada's contribution to the war as part of the Empire or Commonwealth effort. In their thinking, Canadian troops were to play their role as part of the imperial team, not as a stand-alone national force like the United States Army. The Canadian servicemen stationed in Sussex were thus under the Home Forces command of the British general Sir Bernard Paget, who was responsible for all military contributions to operations in the Channel area. Once persuaded by Crerar, Paget acquiesced to Canadian demands for action, even in an operation with an Ultra Secret core like Rutter.

overall leadership of Dickie Mountbatten – or so the theory went. Through late April, the three armed services had been selecting the men they wanted to nominate as force commanders for Operation Rutter. However, the appointments would not be made official until after the chiefs of staff had met on May 13. The raid, like other combined operations, would come under joint command, meaning that, on the day, each of the force commanders from the land, sea and air elements would have his own job to do, but there was no single head responsible for overall planning or execution. The RAF put forward Air Vice-Marshal Trafford Leigh-Mallory, who, as commander of No. 11 Group from Fighter Command, was responsible for the air defence of southern England, including London. The Royal Navy chose Rear Admiral Tom Baillie-Grohman, who was currently on active duty in the Mediterranean and would join the triumvirate after their first meeting in June. For the land force commander, General Paget's headquarters selected Major General Hamilton 'Ham' Roberts, the commander of the Second Canadian Infantry Division.

The 50-year-old Trafford Leigh-Mallory came from the Cheshire countryside and had studied history at Magdalene College, Cambridge, before becoming a barrister in the years leading up to the First World War. He had survived two gruelling years of front-line fighting in the trenches as an infantryman, including the first poison-gas attack in history at the second battle of Ypres, before transferring to the Royal Flying Corps, where he won the Distinguished Service Order for commanding aerial reconnaissance squadrons. In the inter-war years it was his older brother, the celebrated mountaineer George Mallory, who stole the headlines as he attempted to become the first man to reach the summit of Mount Everest, only to disappear on her slopes in 1924 not far from the peak.[7] By the time the Battle of Britain began in the skies over England in the summer of 1940, Trafford Leigh-Mallory had risen to command No. 12 Group, which defended central England, with fifteen squadrons containing nearly 200 Spitfire and Hurricane fighters under his command. He then moved on to No. 11 Group, which had already borne the brunt of the fighting on the south coast of England. Leigh-Mallory was as aggressive as he was ambitious, pioneering the 'Big Wing' theory of air warfare in the RAF: he advocated decisive battles with the Germans, using large groups of fighters in a pack, rather than the piecemeal, hit-and-run attacks currently employed. He wanted to try out this strategy in the skies over Dieppe.

Harold 'Tom' Baillie-Grohman is a minor figure in the Dieppe saga. Born in British Columbia to a British father and a Canadian mother, the 54-year-old rear admiral had, like John Godfrey, made the Royal Navy his home for nearly 40 years. Having served extensively in the Mediterranean and the Far East, he had then been captain of minesweepers in the Channel before taking command of the battle-ship HMS *Ramillies*. At one point he had even been Mountbatten's commanding officer. First Sea Lord Dudley Pound and Admiral Cunningham both thought highly of him as a consummate naval professional with valuable experience in combined operations in the Mediterranean. He had participated in the fight to save the besieged island of Malta and, earlier in 1941, had commanded the naval end of the brilliant raid on Rhodes, where he earned the Distinguished Service Order for his part in evacuating nearly 55,000 British troops from Greece – the same action that claimed Mountbatten's HMS *Kelly*. However, both Mountbatten and Jock Hughes-Hallett, his lead planner for Operation Rutter, regarded Baillie-Grohman with deep suspicion – and Baillie-Grohman was no fan of Mountbatten's mounting hubris or his style of combined operations. The prevailing feeling around Mountbatten's headquarters was that Pound had attached Baillie-Grohman, a stickler for tradition and procedure, onto the operation to act as the Admiralty's inside man, keeping watch on his one-time subordinate, who displayed a penchant for operating outside normal channels. More likely, it was Baillie-Grohman's strong personality and forceful character, coupled with his highly influential voice and excellent leadership, that Pound wanted to counterbalance the maverick tendencies displayed by Mountbatten and his hand-picked staff of 'inexperienced enthusiasts.' Whatever Pound's intentions, the Chief and his naval commander were ill-matched. Baillie-Grohman, as his personnel file reveals, was 'obstinate, tenacious of his own opinions and inclined to be intolerant of the opinions of others. A good man to have behind you in a tight corner, provided he agrees with your reasons for getting into it.'[8] Mountbatten never succeeded in drawing him fully into the spirit of the operation, nor was he ever likely to be, as Mountbatten later said, 'one of us.'[9]

When Baillie-Grohman arrived in England from the Mediterranean in early June, after the chiefs of staff had accepted the outline plan, and Mountbatten's staff had begun the detailed work-up for Rutter, he was immediately sceptical. Concerned about the unbridled enthusiasm surrounding the planning process, he pointed out significant problems with Jock Hughes-Hallett and his syndicate, informing Mountbatten that he did not 'trust the ambitious type.'[10] He complained about the general lack of experience of Mountbatten's staff – pointing out that half of them, for instance, had no idea of the capabilities of the naval craft they were about to employ.

Baillie-Grohman also questioned the role of a mysterious Royal Naval Reserve lieutenant commander who worked as a special liaison to Mountbatten's headquarters and 'was allowed to go on leave on several occasions and visit exercises,' meaning he was not available to handle the constant stream of requests.[11] Given that Section 17 in the Naval Intelligence Division handled that portfolio, it is highly likely that the man he was referring to was Ian Fleming – who did hold a Rutter card, giving him the essential security clearance to take part in the planning for the operation.

Baillie-Grohman's most serious complaint, however, was about the absence of a 'joint appreciation' – something that is standard procedure in any operational plan. A joint appreciation shows how all the service arms are to work together, ensures that commanders are indeed on the same page, and serves as a litmus test, reaffirming strengths, exposing potential weaknesses and allowing for amendments – or, in some cases, even the cancellation of the mission. Although Baillie-Grohman admitted that each service might have an appreciation of its own specific role in the mission, there was nothing to test the operational soundness of Rutter as a whole.

In contrast to the dour Baillie-Grohman, the third man, the military force commander, 52-year-old Canadian Major General Hamilton 'Ham' Roberts, was precisely the type Mountbatten wanted: eager and ambitious, just like Jock Hughes-Hallett and Trafford Leigh-Mallory. Responsible for providing the detailed military portion of the outline plan for Rutter under the watchful eye of General Montgomery, Roberts, from Pipestone in southern Manitoba, would ultimately become the officer who carried the blame for the Dieppe fiasco, forever vilified for his actions on that one fateful day in August. A 'gunner' or artillery officer by training, like most of the Canadian high command, Roberts had graduated from the Royal Military College in Kingston in 1914 and had gone straight into action in the trenches during the First World War. There he displayed conspicuous gallantry and determination, winning the Military Cross during the horrific slaughter at the Somme in 1916 and finishing the war in a training establishment after being wounded in 1918.

Between the wars, Ham Roberts continued his career in the tiny Canadian Army Permanent Force, and by 1940 he was in command of the 1st Field Regiment of the Royal Canadian Horse Artillery, briefly committed to the fighting in France. During the hurried evacuation at Dunkirk, his enthusiastic 'can-do' attitude and iron will to see a task through to the end caught the attention of his Canadian and British superiors alike. Imperilled by the quick German advance, he managed to extricate his two dozen guns to a waiting ship while under fire and, with that done, carried on and loaded several more precious British artillery pieces from the beach.

Within two years, he had risen to the rank of major general and, in April 1942, to the command of the Second Canadian Infantry Division – not long before it was selected to make its combat debut at Dieppe. In the interim, he eliminated what he considered weak links in the division by implementing a series of rigorous physical training schemes and intensified commando-style training. Apparently, this attention to detail and training is what initially caught Montgomery's attention. Ruthlessly efficient like Roberts himself, mainly when it came to his commanders, Monty considered Roberts the 'best divisional commander in the Canadian Corps' – an appraisal that might appear glowing but was actually faint praise.[12] In Montgomery's sober opinion, Roberts was 'very sound, but ... not in any way brilliant.'[13] Still, the Second Canadian Division commander seemed impressive in person, particularly to Admiral Sir William James, the Room 40 veteran who was now Commander-in-Chief, Portsmouth: in one of his letters from the time, he noted that Roberts was 'powerfully built' and 'looks like a real thruster.'[14]

Years after the raid, Jock Hughes-Hallett attempted to distance himself from Roberts, now the pariah. In his memoirs, he recorded that the division commander's enthusiasm had bordered on the 'over confident' leading up to the raid, that he was 'eager for action at all costs' and giving 'the impression of being prepared to take anything on.'[15] At the time, however, that was exactly what Hughes-Hallett and Mountbatten had wanted and expected from their military force commander. In an earlier proposed raid on Alderney in the Channel Islands, Hughes-Hallett had criticized the military commander for his reluctance to 'chance his arm' or to subject his troops to the hazards that are inevitable in raiding operations – the very same exploits he and Mountbatten expected Roberts to undertake at Dieppe.[16]

By the time the three force commanders came on board for Operation Rutter, its overall form, tone and objectives had been set by Jock Hughes-Hallett's planning syndicate and approved by the chiefs of staff, leaving little room for any fundamental changes to the scheme. The job now facing the commanders was not to reason why, but to flesh out the plan and put it into effect. Although responsible for the detailed planning and conduct of the raid, their hands were, in fact, already firmly tied.

∽

Before the Dieppe Raid, Lord Louis Mountbatten's Combined Operations Headquarters had suffered no serious setbacks on the battlefield and certainly no disaster to check the mounting enthusiasm and hubris that would plague the planning of Operation Rutter. The year before, the successful raids at the Lofoten and Vaagso islands had generated significant results for the cryptanalysts at Bletchley Park and clearly positioned Combined Operations as the principal vehicle for signals intelligence pinch raids. Although criticism had flared up over the planning of the aborted Operation Myrmidon, especially from General Charles Haydon, Mountbatten's chief of staff, the publicity surrounding the simultaneous brilliant raid at St Nazaire had produced an intoxicating and irresistible confidence within the COHQ on Richmond Terrace.

Even smaller raids, such as the one at Bruneval, outside Le Havre, had elevated the profile of Mountbatten's headquarters still further among the British and American publics, with headline stories about surreptitiously snatching a top-secret radar set from the German defenders. The United States, now a major Allied partner, sought cooperation and guidance from Britain on intelligence and combined operations techniques – and Mountbatten was ready to oblige.

On June 5, Montgomery called the three Dieppe force commanders – Trafford Leigh-Mallory, Tom Baillie-Grohman and Ham Roberts – together for a planning session in his headquarters building. General Charles Haydon represented Mountbatten, who was away in the United States showcasing his wares for President Roosevelt and the American Navy. The commanders reached a set of decisions that reinforced the frontal-assault option augmented by air support. Mountbatten would later claim that the disastrous frontal assault was strictly Monty's brainchild and that it appeared for the first time during this session. However, the reference to the formulation of two plans in the special report on Dieppe that Mountbatten requested from Admiral John Godfrey's Inter-Services Topographical Department at the end of March, along with the later outline plan, makes it clear that the frontal-assault plan was already a fait accompli by the time of the meeting at COHQ.

At first, the planners had considered launching the flanking and main beach assaults simultaneously, but Jock Hughes-Hallett dismissed that idea for logistical reasons: there was simply not enough sea room off Dieppe to accommodate 250 ships simultaneously delivering troops ashore and providing covering fire. Likewise, if they chose to start with the main beach assault it would leave the raiding force at the mercy of the large coastal batteries off each flank. More importantly, he decided, given the differing speeds of the ships in the assault force, it would be impossible to coordinate them all, from the moment they left various ports in southern England and the Isle of Wight, and deliver them all together off Dieppe in one fell swoop under the cover of darkness to achieve surprise.[17]

The one significant negative of the direct assault option was already apparent: by attacking the enemy frontally, the strategy courted disaster if the carefully crafted plan and all its elements did not come off like clockwork. Mountbatten's planners knew that, but intentionally disregarded it. They believed that, with the novel use of tanks rolling ashore in the first wave alongside the infantry (something that the British had tried during a raid on Bardia in North Africa the year before), the chances of pulling off such an audacious raid looked promising. That idea initially left Brigadier Churchill Mann, Ham Roberts's efficient chief of staff and deputy military force commander, shaking his head in disbelief and then with a sense of wonderment. 'Such a plan, on the face of it,' he wrote, 'is almost a fantastic conception.'[18] But in the gung-ho spirit of the times, he remained open-minded and receptive, finally viewing it as the 'outstanding feature of the plan.'[19]

Mann saw many positives in the direct assault, particularly given the force provided by 60 Churchill tanks from the 14th Canadian Tank Regiment – the Calgary Tanks. First, surprise and shock: the sight of successive waves of 38-ton tanks pouring out of landing craft and rolling towards them would no doubt have a 'terrific morale effect' on the enemy. Second, the plan seemed feasible logistically: recent training exercises on chert rock beaches in England had proven most encouraging; the fist-sized boulders occasionally clogged sprocket wheels and immobilized some of the giant machines, but they did not impede their ability to roll off the beaches in sizeable numbers. Third, the tanks were not alone. Aided by specially trained teams of Canadian combat engineers who would clear paths over the seawall, the tanks would proceed across the grassy promenade, where the engineers would destroy the anti-tank barriers in the tiny streets leading to the port. With that accomplished, the tanks would then rumble past the tobacco factory, down the short span of the Quai Duquesne and into the port with all guns blazing. Fourth, and most important of all, the tanks, if successful, would be 'in easy striking distance of the most appropriate objectives for their employment' – delivering their massed firepower to subdue the trawlers and any other German resistance in the outer port in the vicinity of the Hôtel Moderne.[20]

Air support was the other area of controversy. Initially, the planners had agreed to the frontal assault when they understood that the buildings overlooking the main beach would be pulverized by an attack from the heavy bombers of the RAF's Bomber Command two and a half hours before the raid began. Although Churchill and the Cabinet had agreed to lift the restriction on the blind bombing of French towns – a rule that had nearly led to disaster at St Nazaire – Leigh-Mallory now proposed that they should cancel the heavy bombardment and replace it with concentric bombing and strafing attacks by his fighters immediately before the commencement of the raid. He argued that the time lag between the heavy bombing attack and the landings was just too long and would allow the German defenders, by then fully alert, to mount a spirited defence. Ham Roberts agreed.

Leigh-Mallory further argued that the lack of precision in heavy bombing raids – with 150 planes dropping their bombs from 7,000 feet at night – would likely result in the bombs being scattered about rather than hitting their intended targets: the headlands and the beachfront hotels. All told, he feared the result would be uncontrollable fires and rubble-choked streets. Ham Roberts, in turn, foresaw the debris creating anti-tank obstacles that the engineers would not be able to handle in time. So instead, Leigh-Mallory proposed a series of timed attacks on the headlands and the beachfront by attack aircraft and cannon-firing Hurricane fighters from his command, just as the first assault boats approached the beaches.[21] The surprise and shock would then be reserved to the last possible moment, and the synchronized attack would overwhelm any defender with its intense ferocity.

If the raid itself was to achieve surprise, the force commanders would have to move the largest armada so far assembled by the Allies across the English Channel in the middle of the night without the Germans catching on – or at least without them figuring out its final destination until it was too late. To confuse the German radar, Leigh-Mallory arranged to bomb the nearby airfields at Abbeville-Drucat and Crécy and to strike both sides of the city of Boulogne.* At the same time,

---

* By June 29, Leigh-Mallory was worrying that his pilots, locked into the intricate Combined Operations plan for Dieppe, lacked the operational freedom they needed. He wrote to Air Vice-Marshal Sir William Sholto Douglas, his superior, that his No. 11 Group could expect to lose '60 to 70 pilots, and 120 aircraft.' The next day Douglas shot back: 'Thank you for your letter of 29th June, about the casualties you anticipate you may suffer during Operation "Rutter." I do not know however quite what you expect me to do about it. I certainly do not propose to

Baillie-Grohman would put on a naval operation designed to simulate an impending raid on the giant port at Boulogne, even as the raiding forces were creeping unannounced towards Dieppe, further down the coast.[22]

⸎

In the days following the June 5 meeting, the planning staff and the force commanders rushed to complete a highly detailed 200-page plan for Operation Rutter (which would later become the bible for Operation Jubilee), which was set to go in less than a fortnight. The plan demonstrated in great detail how everything should come together *if* all went according to plan. In many ways, Rutter was the amphibious version of a First World War-style 'trench raid': the English coast formed one line, the German-occupied coast the other, with the Channel as the 'no man's land.' Stealth, surprise, speed and split-second synchronization were critical to success.

In theory, everything was contained within the pages of this bloated and highly complex document, from the composition of the raiding forces and their objectives to the sequence of events laid out in a scripted and timed play-by-play account – with numerous graphs, tables, matrices and maps to show the dispositions of troops from the approach across the Channel to the landings and re-embarkation. Tacked on at the end, more than a dozen appendices covered in great detail the tasks of the infantry and airborne battalions, the tanks, the engineers, the naval and air bombardments, the 'cutting out force' and the search and demolitions programmes followed by the re-embarkation schedules for the ride back home to friendly shores.

---

call the operation off. If I may say so, I think that you are worrying too much about these possible casualties. Unfortunately, one cannot often win a battle without considerable casualties, however much one would like to do so.' Leigh-Mallory proved to be remarkably prescient: in the final tally for Dieppe, 70 pilots were killed or missing, and 106 aircraft were shot down. (Sholto Douglas to Leigh-Mallory, 30 June 1942, TNA AIR 16/760; Trafford Leigh-Mallory, 'Air Operations at Dieppe: An After-Action Report,' *Canadian Military History* 12, no. 4 (2003): app. C.)

In the initial plan, Rutter was to begin on the night of June 20–21 – or on any of the six nights following should adverse weather or any other event prevent its launch. Late in the afternoon on June 20, close to 5,000 Canadian infantrymen, including six battalions of Ham Roberts's 2nd Canadian Division, accompanied by 60 tanks from the Calgary Tank Regiment and teams of Canadian combat engineers, would board more than 250 ships and boats for the journey to Dieppe. It was to be one of the largest task forces yet seen in the Second World War, and it would comprise a vast assortment of vessels, including destroyers, troop transports, torpedo boats, converted Channel steamers, rescue craft, tugs, anti-aircraft vessels (Eagle ships), anti-submarine trawlers, minesweepers, gunboats, and a collection of new tank landing craft each hauling three Churchill tanks. Two specially refitted Hunt-class destroyer escorts – HMS *Calpe* and HMS *Fernie* – would serve as headquarters ships for the operation.

On board the *Calpe*, Ham Roberts, Tom Baillie-Grohman and Air Commodore Adrian Cole, the air liaison officer (who came from the Royal Australian Air Force), would work from the bridge and from the wardroom to ensure the safe arrival, landing and then re-embarkation of the raiding force. Meanwhile, Trafford Leigh-Mallory would monitor the air battle from his headquarters in Uxbridge, a specially constructed bunker on the Hillingdon estate west of London, with Dickie Mountbatten and Harry Crerar as his special guests for the show. On the coast, deep inside his Fort Southwick command bunker, Admiral Sir William James, the Commander-in-Chief, Portsmouth, would give the order to go (or scrub the mission if necessary), and relay current intelligence to the raiding forces once it was under way.

In any high-risk operation, redundancy and contingency planning are critical, so Mountbatten arranged for an alternative set of 'back-up' commanders under the control of Brigadier Churchill Mann, Ham Roberts's chief of staff, to be on board and work from *Fernie* in case *Calpe* succumbed to enemy fire or any other unforeseen event. Mountbatten, with full technocratic zeal, equipped both command ships, bristling with antennae, with nearly four times the usual allotment of transmitters and receivers, thereby linking the force commanders with the aircraft above, the vessels at sea and the troops ashore.

Once at the mid-Channel rendezvous point, the ships would form up into at least a dozen smaller assault groups. Together, they would follow British minesweepers on a predetermined course through a German minefield and head towards the four landing beaches in and around Dieppe – code-named Blue, Green, White and Red.

In the skies above, the air plan called for the largest and most sophisticated display of aerial warfare seen on the western front since the desperate days of the Battle of Britain two years earlier, when a vastly outnumbered RAF fought Hitler's Luftwaffe to a standstill. More than 800 aircraft, mostly fighters drawn from 74 squadrons, would maintain revolving air patrols over the landing zones throughout the morning. Most of them would come from British squadrons, with a smattering of Canadian, American, Czech, Polish, Belgian and Free French as well. Their job on the day was complex: to provide close air support for the troops on the ground, to locate German reinforcements and prevent them from reaching the port area by land or sea, to lay smokescreens to obscure the view of the German defenders, and to compose an impenetrable 'air umbrella' above Dieppe to fend off Luftwaffe aircraft attempting to strike the vulnerable ships below.

According to the air plan, just after midnight on the day of the raid, ground crews that had been working all day and evening would rush to top up fuel tanks, conduct weapons checks and load cannon shells for the Hurricane, Typhoon and Spitfire fighters or rack sticks of 250- and 500-pound high-explosive bombs and smoke shells onto Blenheim and Boston bombers. Soon after, the firing of engines would shake the dew from cowlings as pilots adjusted flaps, goggles and throat microphones, making a quick check of the maps taped to their upper thighs while throttling up for takeoff. Once aloft, the planes would form up for about 30 minutes before setting course for their targets along the French coast and above Dieppe, less than half an hour away. Meanwhile, a battalion of the British 1st Airborne Brigade, including some veterans of the Bruneval Raid, would squeeze into Wellington bombers or pack tightly into towed gliders for their journey to the landing zones on either side of Dieppe, carefully skirting the raiding force below to maintain surprise.

At precisely 0415 hours, all the various preparations would come together. As long as weather conditions cooperated, the paratroopers and glider-borne infantry would float to earth onto predetermined landing zones and launch their assaults on both the Hess and Goebbels coastal batteries at the same moment that two Canadian infantry battalions exploded onto the beaches of Puys and Pourville – Blue Beach and Green Beach.

The battalion landing on Green Beach would come from the South Saskatchewan Regiment, under the command of Lieutenant Colonel Cecil Merritt – who would go on to earn the Victoria Cross for his heroic actions on August 19. His 'prairie men,' drawn mostly from the Estevan, Weyburn, Regina and Moose Jaw areas, would land near the eight-foot-wide river Scie that snaked through Pourville into the English Channel. Here, Merritt's force would move fast to create a semi-circular bridgehead stretching from the hills on both sides of the river valley to the western headland at Dieppe, and as deep inland as 'la ferme des Quatre Vents' (Four Winds Farm) – a German stronghold. According to the plan, part of the battalion would move up the slope leading from the beach and take the western headland, knocking out German bunkers and a lone radar station en route, while the remaining men held the bridgehead.[23] Once there, they would ferret out defenders on the clifftop positions and neutralize any fire from the Norman castle perched atop the Dieppe skyline, while the others mopped up in Pourville and the hills west of the town, and captured the fortified farm.

One hour later – at the same time as the frontal assault was beginning on the main beach – the Queen's Own Cameron Highlanders of Canada, a Winnipeg regiment, would land and push through this bridgehead to a rendezvous point with one squadron of the Calgary Tanks, which would by then have climbed up from the main beach. In unison, the infantry and the tanks would move roughly three miles inland to capture St Aubin airfield and provide a shield to fend off any German counterattacks trying to reach Dieppe proper. With this protection in place, the raiding forces in the harbour area would enjoy the maximum opportunity to wreak havoc in the port and other targeted areas before retiring into the harbour area themselves to re-embark.

On Blue Beach in the tiny seaside town of Puys, nearly 500 men of the Royal Regiment of Canada would land in pre-dawn darkness under the command of Lieutenant Colonel Doug Catto, followed by a company of the Black Watch (Royal Highland Regiment) from Montreal. Their job was crucial to the success of the entire plan, for they had to overrun the entrenched German defenders, seize the clifftops above, and then move fast on foot over nearly a mile of German-occupied territory to their objective – a German gun battery, code-named Bismarck, on Pollet Cliff, able to shell the harbour mole.

The raid was essentially a race against time. Once the first shot had been fired, the clock would start ticking for both the airborne and infantry units: they had only 60 minutes to reach their targets and achieve their objectives before the frontal assault over the main beach began. Should they fail outright or suffer delay, the troops and tanks bound for the main beach would face murderous fire as soon as the ramp doors dropped and the first boot hit the beach. With little or no cover, they would advance into a horseshoe-shaped cauldron of withering German fire.

For the main-beach landings, the Rutter planners divided the zone into two interconnecting sectors, code-named Red Beach and White Beach – with the tobacco factory at the intersection of the Quai Duquesne and the boulevard de Verdun as the dividing line. There, more than 1,000 Canadian infantrymen from two battalions, the Royal Hamilton Light Infantry and the Essex Scottish, supported by teams of Canadian combat engineers and two squadrons from the Calgary Tanks (36 tanks from B and C squadrons), would storm ashore, race up the beach, scale the seawall, cross the promenade, and penetrate the town and port before the bewildered Germans could recover from the shock and awe of the initial attacks.

For the exposed men of the infantry and engineers, once they had touched down on the rocky beach, there was little tangible cover until they reached the boulevard de Verdun and the shadow of its hotels and restaurants and the towering smokestacks of the tobacco factory. To cross this deadly 300-yard expanse, they had to work in close concert with their tanks, moving in leapfrog fashion. First, the tanks would lay down covering fire from their main guns and hull machine guns while the engineers and infantry scrambled to cut gaps in the barbed wire at the seawall with wire cutters or blow through them with long snakelike sticks of TNT known as Bangalore torpedoes.

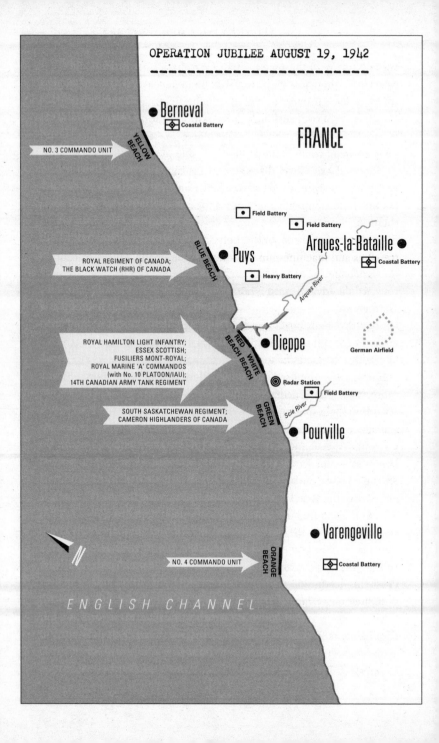

Depending on the course of the tide, the seawall could form a barrier standing anywhere from two to ten feet in height. But the engineers were prepared for whatever conditions they encountered: they would lay belts of chestnut palings across a low-rise tide or use timber crib ramps as needed to allow the tanks to get up and over the wall to the promenade beyond.

Once over this formidable obstacle, the tanks would creep forward with guns blazing in an attempt to kill or suppress any German defenders on the beach or in the buildings or pillboxes ahead. Following them in close order, the surviving infantry and engineers would dash through any remaining belts of wire protecting German slit trenches and machine-gun pits on the promenade, killing or capturing the defenders before they reached the buildings on the boulevard de Verdun.

In the White Beach sector, where the Royal Hamilton Light Infantry (RHLI) and B Squadron from the Calgary Tanks would land, there was one additional hurdle to overcome before they reached the old gates leading to their objectives in the town and the fields beyond: the once-crowded Dieppe casino (the centrepiece, some allege, for Fleming's *Casino Royale*). It was quite possible that the RHLI would have to clear the structure in a bloodcurdling hand-to-hand fight. Once the casino was either cleared or bypassed, however, the four rifle companies would infiltrate the town and fan out, linking up with the South Saskatchewan Regiment on the west headland and at Quatre Vents farm, as well as the Essex Scottish coming in off Red Beach.

In the Red Beach sector, which ran from the tobacco factory to the quay lining the west side of the harbour mole, there was no such obstacle or cover for either the Essex Scottish or the engineers once they landed. Their job was to advance into the town and port accompanied by eighteen Churchill tanks from the Calgary Tank Regiment's C Squadron. Should everything come together, they would quickly breach the seawall, cross the promenade and make it to the boulevard de Verdun in relatively good order. Then the four Essex Scottish companies would penetrate the town on foot via a series of tiny streets and approach the outer harbour, while the engineers cleared a route for the tanks by destroying the concrete anti-tank obstacles near the tobacco factory or, if that route remained blocked, on the streets further to the east.

With the assault wave ashore, the brigade headquarters of the 4th and the 6th Canadian Infantry Brigade – led respectively by Brigadier Sherwood Lett, a Rhodes Scholar lawyer from Vancouver, and Brigadier William Southam, president and CEO of Southam Press, working directly under Ham Roberts and monitoring the battle from wireless sets aboard their landing craft offshore – would move in and establish their headquarters near the tobacco factory. Their job was to control the general flow of the battle on land and to oversee the search and demolition plans as well. Given the intricate nature of the operation, Mountbatten issued explicit written orders for each brigade headquarters to bring a set of the detailed operational instructions ashore, into what he expected would be a relatively secure area by the time they landed.

If everything unfolded according to plan, the force commanders had two cards left to play once the bridgehead was secured. The first was the 'floating reserve,' containing a battalion of infantry from the Fusiliers Mont-Royal (FMR) from Montreal under Lieutenant Colonel Dollard Ménard and roughly 30 Churchill tanks from the remaining squadron of the Calgary Tanks waiting offshore for their cue to join the fray. The FMR and the tanks would land over the main beach at Ham Roberts's discretion and create an inner defensive shield within the town, forming a buffer for the assault troops to fall back on during re-embarkation at the end of the raid. If anything had gone awry in the previous phases of the plan, this floating reserve could be used anywhere in support, whether that meant reinforcing a breakthrough or bolstering a wavering part of the line.

The second card – and the one critical to the raid's 'pinch' object-ive – was Red Ryder's Cutting Out Force, whose stated mission seems ripped from the pages of a C.S. Forester novel.

The role of the Cutting Out Force has been the most misunder-stood aspect of the entire Dieppe operation, and it is also the most revealing. In some historical accounts, Ryder's force is just another part of the floating reserve – ignored by Dieppe chroniclers who have understandably, given what was known until recently, focused on the dramatic events of the raid itself rather than on what was supposed to have happened if all went according to plan. As things turned out, the commitment of Ryder's group to reinforce the Canadian infantry on the main beach has obscured the Cutting Out Force's real purpose, just as do the carefully crafted portions of Ryder's unpublished memoirs. But as his biographer would later point out, Ryder was a 'model of self-censorship.'[24]

According to what Ryder recorded for posterity, his job was 'to train a special body of artificers, stokers and mechanics etc. as well as a marine detachment to act as a covering force' that would swoop into Dieppe harbour, once it was safely in Allied hands, and snatch German barges to tow them back to England as 'prize' captures.[25] Although the mission 'opened up exciting possibilities,' he did not have faith in their ability to operate the 'complicated bridges and locks' while 'possibly under fire' and preferred to sink the barges instead. Given the spirit of the times, Ryder felt strongly that the job was 'worth trying' and that 'the Royal Navy should be ready to take on anything.'[26] This explanation makes no sense at all: wasting the talents of one of the few Royal Navy commanders with significant operational experience – and a recently minted VC winner as well – in an attack on an enemy-held port for a mere 'publicity stunt' was by any measure a gross misallocation of preciously scarce resources.[27]

But for the very few in the know, the Cutting Out Force led by Captain Red Ryder had, in fact, a very different duty to perform that day.

CHAPTER 11

Dieppe by Design

Thanks to their geographical position, it is the British who were responsible for the capture of most of the German material which has been important for communications intelligence in the German War. They, in the Mediterranean and off the coasts of France and Norway, have been fighting close to shore ... It is actions of this character ... which produces the richest hauls. Knowing this, the British have spared no effort in developing techniques that will enable them to make the most of their chances for pinching.

United States Navy, Ultra Secret report on
British procedures for capturing and exploiting
enemy naval documents, 1944

As planning for Operation Rutter unfolded, Ian Fleming was totally engaged in establishing the naval Intelligence Assault Unit he had proposed to his boss, Admiral John Godfrey – the new group, dedicated explicitly to pinching the critical naval intelligence materials that Bletchley Park urgently needed. It was a daunting task to create an unusual unit of this kind, and the major challenge at this stage was to get around the numerous administrative obstacles that blocked its way in Whitehall. Working in the best traditions of Blinker Hall, Fleming and Godfrey pushed hard to obtain official sanction for their Assault Unit, even as Combined Operations Headquarters feverishly embarked on the detailed planning for Rutter. Putting Fleming 'on point' for the job, Godfrey gave high praise to his talents: 'For such a novel enterprise,' he said, 'it is essential to have an officer with drive and imagination of the highest order.' It needed 'rapid transit,' and Fleming was just the man to steer the new unit through government departments, dodging the red tape to ensure it got into action – fast.[1]

Fleming's initial idea had been to have his IAU make its debut in Operation Sledgehammer, set for that autumn, with the German naval headquarters in Cherbourg as its first target. There, Godfrey explained, 'naval cyphers held by the authorities of the port concerned' would top the list of materials to be pinched by the new unit, whose job would then be to ensure 'that it reached the reception committee at a specified rendezvous with the least possible delay.'[2] By mid-May, however, with Operation Sledgehammer on the verge of cancellation and the four-rotor crisis gaining momentum day by day, Fleming suggested moving the Assault Unit's debut forward by four months so it could take part in the embryonic Operation Rutter.[3]

At the coastal town of Dieppe, the Hôtel Moderne and the trawlers in the port offered a plethora of targets that would suit Bletchley's needs. With a detachment of Royal Marines already tasked with a pinch *in utero*, this unit became the perfect nucleus for Fleming to employ as his experimental naval commando.[4] With that in mind, Godfrey approached the Joint Intelligence Committee, hoping to quickly gain official authorization to raise a larger inter-service intelligence commando using the Royal Marines as the nucleus. Perhaps not surprisingly in the partisan world of Whitehall, where the three forces – army, navy and air force – jockeyed for position and power, the response was initially lukewarm at best: the RAF already had its own shadowy pinch units, and the army viewed incursions into what it considered its domain – fighting ashore – with suspicion and jealousy.[5] In addition, intelligence collection on land traditionally fell to the army's field security forces, in conjunction with other duties such as interrogating prisoners and the prevention of looting. These security forces were quite prickly about their domain, particularly after they had been assigned this task for Operation Rutter.

The prevailing attitude in Whitehall at this time eschewed 'private armies.' Fleming and Godfrey realized that official authorization for a unit like the one they proposed would take time and a good deal of bureaucratic manoeuvring, cajoling and arm-twisting to achieve. To speed up the process, they chose to adopt Blinker Hall's long-standing advice to act first and seek sanction later. In the past (as in the adventures of Dick de Costobadie and Allon Bacon in Vaagso), boarding parties drawn from ships' crews had provided ad hoc protection forces for the pinch personnel – a quick and easy solution, but not a viable alternative to a standing unit devoted to pinching. The new naval Intelligence Assault Unit, in contrast, would require cutting-edge training year-round. The obvious place for Fleming to turn was the newly created Royal Marine Commando, the amphibious fighting arm of the Royal Navy that Mountbatten had tried to protect.[6] This idea instantly met with the approval of Godfrey and, not surprisingly, Mountbatten. They agreed to start small, carving out one platoon, or 30 men, from the almost 300 commanded by Lieutenant Colonel Joseph Picton Phillipps.

In late May, the Royal Marine commandos had moved to the Isle of Wight to begin training for their intended role in Operation Rutter as part of Red Ryder's Cutting Out Force. There, the IAU conducted a series of exercises in Portsmouth harbour 'in conjunction with special Naval Parties'; their 'main object' was to remove 'important cargo vessels' and 'carry out certain other special tasks' – a euphemistic reference to the role played by Fleming's fledgling Assault Unit.[7] Tucked away in the Royal Marine Commando War Diary is a copy of a training scheme performed in this harbour in the last week of June. Its significance has never been considered in the Dieppe story before, yet it indicates what Jock Hughes-Hallett had in mind for Ryder's Cutting Out Force in Rutter.[8]

This scenario called for the Royal Marine commandos to leave their billets near Cowes on the Isle of Wight and load onto HMS *Locust* (a flat-bottomed river gunboat designed for colonial policing on the Yangtze river) for a 45-minute journey to Portsmouth harbour.[9] Once at the harbour mouth, the 'main task' in the training scheme involved the *Locust* rushing into the dockyard area to berth at a specified quay, followed by the Royal Marine commandos swooping down from her decks onto the quayside to surprise the startled dockyard workers and sailors. While the majority of the platoons would spread out to destroy swing bridges and lock gates and capture vessels in the port, one platoon, known as No. 10 Platoon, would take advantage of the confusion in the dockyard area to carry out its own 'special task to be detailed later.'[10]

It was this one platoon – No. 10 – that became Fleming's Intelligence Assault Unit. And that 'special task,' according to the recently declassified Ultra Secret history of 30 Assault Unit, involved 'a special section of No. 40 Royal Marine Commando, led by Lieutenant Huntington-Whiteley, R.M. ... specially briefed on behalf of DNI [Godfrey, the Director of Naval Intelligence] to attempt the capture of a certain German headquarters in Dieppe.'[11] The history does not shed any more light on why Fleming chose this particular unit or why he tapped the 22-year-old Huntington-Whiteley to command the first naval IAU.

∽

Throughout the hundreds of thousands of documents currently in the public domain and the scores of books and articles written about the Dieppe Raid, the name of Peter Huntington-Whiteley rarely appears. Any mention of the young man from Fareham, Hampshire usually focuses on his later exploits leading the Royal Marine detachment of 30 Assault Unit in North Africa, Sicily and later Normandy and concludes, in a sad irony, with his death at the age of 24 outside Le Havre, just over a week after the Allied liberation of Dieppe in 1944.[12]

With little more to go on than the mention of his name as the leader of the IAU, I reached out to the Royal Navy's Historical Branch in Portsmouth for help. After searching through their files, to little avail, I laid out my research for the historians there – subjecting it to the ultimate litmus test. Within a few minutes, the Royal Marine historian, a former lieutenant colonel who had served on active operations during the Falklands, said, 'I think you may be on to something,' and disappeared into another room. He reappeared minutes later with a sheet of paper on which he had written a name and phone number. 'Here, you might want to give this man a call,' he said with a big smile. 'He's the last living member of Fleming's IAU who fought at Dieppe.'

A few days later, I was on a plane bound for Edinburgh to meet Paul McGrath, a former corporal with No. 10 Platoon who had gone on to fight with 30 Assault Unit for the remainder of the war. In a small seaside town outside the Scottish capital, McGrath's flat overlooked two of his many passions – the Firth of Forth and a wild golf course on which, in his late eighties, he still played. On the mantel were pictures of his elegantly beautiful wife, now passed on.

Conducting historical interviews is extremely difficult. Even at the best of times, not to mention nearly eight decades later, memory is notoriously unreliable and must be cross-referenced with textual documents or other evidence. Still, oral history gives something documents cannot provide: impressions of tone, feeling and atmosphere that can bring historical research to life. And that is precisely what my interview with McGrath offered. No sooner had I knocked on his door than the famous wry, dry wit of the Royal Marines came through. As I squeezed my six-foot-five, 250-pound frame through his doorway, the six-foot, wiry octogenarian looked up and said, 'Oh my! You are a big one. Okay, I'll come quietly!'* When we sat down to talk, McGrath apologized that his memory was not what it used to be. With that, I asked him to describe what his role had been within the newly founded IAU. Immediately his jovial demeanour turned sombre and flat, and his ice-blue eyes took on a fixed gaze that revealed the resolute, professional intensity of nearly three-quarters of a century earlier: 'Well, old boy, I was nineteen – and I was there to kill Germans.' When I pressed for

---

* McGrath's sense of humour was again on display during the seventieth anniversary of the raid, when Wayne Abbott and I, with the generous help of History Television and Veterans Affairs Canada, hosted the world premiere of *Dieppe Uncovered* in a local theatre in Dieppe, less than 100 yards from the Hôtel Moderne. After the showing, the group, which included two young executives from History Television, went for dinner at Les Arcades across from what used to be the Moderne. Not having met either of these young men before, McGrath was on top form, drawing one of the star-struck executives close to him as he sat down at the dinner table. He broke the ice with a question: 'You know what the trouble with humans is?' Suitably intrigued by the man who had not only worked behind enemy lines on Ultra intelligence missions but possessed a wealth of worldly experience, my colleague listened intently, expecting the very secret of life to be revealed. 'There are too many of them,' came the quick reply. 'Now,' he continued with a sly smile, 'what's on the menu?'

an explanation, he explained that he was 'simply' a 'minder' or 'body-guard' for those making the pinch, with orders to breach the harbour on the deck of HMS *Locust* and hit the Hôtel Moderne, leaving nothing and nobody standing in their wake to tip off the Germans to what had been removed.

McGrath's reply all those years later was both chilling and revealing, for it fell directly in line with the cold-blooded tone Fleming struck in Ruthless in 1940 and that he would adopt again, as revealed when he briefed his commandos before the Normandy invasion in 1944:

> Should any first priority material be discovered, an officer or NCO must be detailed to immediately break off operations and ensure its safe arrival in the Admiralty. The necessity for avoiding or eliminating witnesses to the successful action and for the demolition of any building or ship's cabin which has yielded results, and which is likely to be re-occupied by the enemy, is emphasized. It is important to insure that every scrap of paper, including ashes, used blotting pads, carbon paper, the contents of waste paper baskets and odd pieces of paper which may be found concealed under furniture, behind maps or mirrors, etc. should be collected and forwarded into the Admiralty. It is also necessary to ensure that all codes, books and ciphers should be kept dry, as water causes the text to disappear. Care should be taken to see the troops do not meddle or play with any Enigma machines which may be captured. It is easy to break the settings of the machine by playing on the keys or altering the plugs or junction boxes. It is essential when searching intercept stations to secure all papers, especially the operators' record books, in order to establish the priorities attached by the enemy to the various types of allied signals.[13]

McGrath confirmed that Fleming delivered the same refrain before the Dieppe Raid and then turned to the question of his platoon commander, Peter Huntington-Whiteley. 'Red' as the men called him (but never to his face) had a 'softly spoken ... languid air, his spare frame reaching a little over six feet high.'[14] He was 'well-liked and popular with the men,' a good officer, whom the men trusted and respected.[15] Like his teenage charges, he too was young – yet in command of a platoon of highly trained killers whose average age was just nineteen.

To gain more insight about his platoon commander, McGrath suggested that I speak to Huntington-Whiteley's brother, Miles, who knew little of their exploits but could fill me in on the family background.*

∽

At the time of our meeting, the Ministry of Defence in England had yet to authorize the full release of personnel records of individuals who served in the Second World War, so Miles was able to provide me with information that was otherwise unavailable. He told me that Peter, as the family and close friends called his brother (whose given names were Herbert Oliver), was commissioned into the Royal Marines in 1938 after he failed to attain the required results on his naval entrance exam. Never genuinely interested in a military or naval career as such, Peter joined out of a sense of duty, as the eldest son in a family with a long tradition of naval, military and public service. Eventually, he was attracted by the daring and unique nature of the Royal Marine Commando.[16] With his father and one of his younger brothers away at

---

* When I sat down to interview Miles Huntington-Whiteley in his living room, I noticed the paintings and pictures on the walls and end tables which revealed the family's remarkable history, including a rare portrait above the fireplace of a very young Queen Victoria. After examining the photos from his side of the family, I inquired about the portrait. Miles simply shrugged and said, 'My wife's relations.' Soon after, his stunningly attractive wife appeared and introduced herself. Graciously responding to my question about the origins of the painting, she proudly explained that she was the great-great-granddaughter of Queen Victoria, the great-granddaughter of Kaiser Wilhelm of Germany, and the great-niece of both King George V of England and Tsar Nicholas of Russia. Her full name, Viktoria Adelheid Clementine Luise Gräfin zu Castell-Rüdenhausen, evokes her aristocratic lineage, but disarmingly she quipped, 'You can call me Vicky.' At that point, I realized I was chatting with perhaps the only living person with a direct family connection to the three men who played a central role in bringing the world to war in 1914. She went on to explain that, as a small child during the Second World War in Germany, she used to bounce on Heinrich Himmler's knee when he paid a visit to her grandfather Charles Edward, who served in the Nazi Party. At the end of the war she moved to England, where she met and married Miles Huntington-Whiteley in 1960.

sea, his failure to pass the naval exam was a blessing because his posting kept him in England, where he maintained a watchful eye on his mother and youngest brother Miles who, nine years his junior, idolized the dashing and daring commando.[17]

Like Ian Fleming, Huntington-Whiteley was very much a product of his privileged background and family tradition of Eton and Trinity College, Cambridge, though he never attended the university. Known as a 'fine athlete and musician,' he mastered both the piano and the trumpet and excelled on the cricket pitch, playing at Lord's for Eton against Harrow. Ever the stickler for formality and social etiquette, he, like many others of his station in the class-conscious Britain of 1942, kept a healthy distance from his men, despite their intense training regimen and the intimate and potentially lethal conditions in which they worked together. Always formal, he addressed the men by their full names or rank and maintained strict standards. On one occasion, he threatened to discipline a man for uttering an expletive in the heat of battle.[18]

The central reason for the creation of Fleming's IAU was the need to reduce the security risk associated with sending fully indoctrinated intelligence officers who possessed intimate knowledge of the British cryptographic landscape into pinch operations. The danger was too great that if they were captured, they might be broken under intense interrogation. But to do their jobs effectively, the commander of the unit and his senior non-commissioned officer would have to know what types of textual material and equipment or technologies the NID needed from the pinch. Even this partial indoctrination and familiarization with the target material produced a mammoth potential security risk, and Fleming naturally sought assurance that they had an individual to command the IAU who was both trustworthy and accountable. By the standards of the time, he found the ideal candidate in Huntington-Whiteley.

The incestuous nature of British intelligence and the closed world of Great Britain's social and political elite probably played a large part in the young officer's selection, as did the tight-knit world of personal connections inside the Royal Navy. Peter Huntington-Whiteley's paternal grandfather, Herbert James Huntington-Whiteley, had served alongside Fleming's father as a Conservative member of Parliament during the First World War. His father, Commander Maurice Huntington-Whiteley, a career Royal Navy officer, succeeded in obtaining a rare baronetcy – a hereditary rank just above that of a knight that established the family's status as part of the aristocracy. He crossed paths on numerous occasions before and during the war with Jock Hughes-Hallett. The men held the rare position of torpedo officer on different aircraft carriers in the early 1930s, meaning they would have attended the same courses, conferences and training schemes. Later, during the war, both worked under the same roof at HMS *President*, the 'stone frigate' or shore establishment on the banks of the river Thames near Tower Bridge, though in different departments – Huntington-Whiteley in the Admiralty's Trade Division, led by Blinker Hall's son, while Hughes-Hallett toiled in the Local Defence Division before going off to COHQ.

But the greatest endorsement for young Huntington-Whiteley came from his mother's side of the family, which defined the very notion of Establishment in imperial Britain. His maternal grandfather was Stanley Baldwin, the former head of the Conservative Party and three-time prime minister of Great Britain; and his grandmother, Anne Baldwin, was related to the famous painters Sir Edward Burne-Jones and Sir Edward Poynter, both of whom had headed the Royal Academy of Arts, and counted Rudyard Kipling as part of her clan – a legendary writer who expounded the glory of the Empire. Peter was as capable as any Royal Marine Commando platoon officer of taking on the responsibility of an Ultra Secret role, but being the former prime minister's grandson gave him that extra edge: his pedigree communicated a level of trust and accountability of the highest order.

As Huntington-Whiteley and his men prepared for Rutter, they 'received a careful and detailed briefing from [the] Naval Intelligence Division in particular requirements which were of extreme urgency at the time,' but their indoctrination was only partial, based on a 'need to know' principle: the significance of the material they had to pinch or any information related to Bletchley Park remained above their pay grade.[19] They needed only to recognize what was required: the remains of a smashed Enigma machine, samples of its wheels and wooden case, along with specimens of its codebooks, including damaged publications printed with soluble ink.[20]

⁓

In early June, long after the outline and detailed plans had been finalized, Mountbatten's headquarters sent out a call to the other intelligence agencies, aside from the NID, that might want to benefit from the Combined Operations train leaving for Dieppe in the coming weeks.[21] The Special Operations Executive, which was already helping to locate targets in Dieppe, attached its agents to the raid, as did the Ministry of Economic Warfare and the Secret Intelligence Service.[22] Their objectives are listed in Appendix L of the Rutter plan, the 'Search Plan,' which details the work to be carried out by General Ham Roberts's 2nd Canadian Field Security Section. In conjunction with these intelligence agencies, the field security teams would follow the assault troops ashore to search the various hotels that housed barracks and headquarters, as well as other targets such as the town hall, the post office and, as Mountbatten suggested, possibly 'raiding the local banks for cash for the Treasury.'[23] The only caveat put on any target in Dieppe was attached to the building that Godfrey and Fleming had set their sights on more than two months earlier: the Hôtel Moderne, located at the junction of the rue Vauquelin and the Quai Duquesne on the direct route running from the main beach to the port, and just 100 yards from the shadow of the beachfront tobacco factory. This proviso forbade the field security teams from entering the building, with strict orders to 'contact Lieut. Huntington-Whiteley, Royal Marines, and follow his instructions before searching Hotel Moderne.'[24]

This crucial piece of evidence ties Fleming's IAU to the NID's most desired targets and confirms that a pinch component designed to solve the spreading four-rotor crisis was indeed part of Operation Rutter. Once the raid at St Nazaire and the aborted raid at Bayonne had failed to produce gold for the cryptanalysts at Bletchley Park, it became essential for the next sizeable raid to hit a channel port where they could grab material related to the new device. So the question is straightforward: was the plan for Dieppe a pinch by opportunity or a pinch by design?

As far back as the opening days of 1942, when Jock Hughes-Hallett pointed to the meeting on January 21 as the conception date for the raid – immediately after John Godfrey announced the change in pinch policy and just weeks after the most successful haul of captured material to date at Lofoten and Vaagso – the odour of a pinch operation for Dieppe was evident. Although Godfrey had imposed a temporary moratorium in late January for fear of provoking or speeding up the employment of the four-rotor, its introduction with U-boats on station in the Atlantic Ocean on February 1 forced his hand. To make matters worse, a month earlier, a new Short Signal Book had come into play which compounded the general misery, as did fresh sets of bigram tables, weather and dockyard ciphers that appeared periodically. Within weeks of the introduction of the four-rotor to Dönitz's Atlantic U-boat fleet, the effects had hit home in no uncertain fashion. Losses of both American and British merchant shipping rose to dangerously high levels – a trend that continued with each passing month and increased pressure in both a material and a political sense in all corners of Allied leadership. To make matters worse, the distribution of the new device to destroyers plying Norwegian waters, which Naval Section and NID learned about in mid-January, now endangered the vital Arctic convoys heading to Russia, as did its adoption by U-boats in the Mediterranean which threatened the lifelines to Malta and Egypt, and the Allied invasion of North Africa, now in its embryonic stage. This gloomy spectre became even more threatening with the revelation on March 13 that vessels operating in the English Channel had also been outfitted with the new machine which made it quite clear that the blackout would soon expand beyond the U-boats in the Atlantic and encompass the entire Kriegsmarine, cutting off Bletchley, NID, the Admiralty, Allied high command and Churchill from their precious naval 'golden eggs.'

In the interim, the sudden jolt of planning frenzy for a Dieppe operation in the weeks following the Channel discovery (crowned by the publication of the Inter-Services Topographical Department report on Dieppe at the behest of Hughes-Hallett) and the sudden bid by Fleming to create a naval intelligence commando dedicated to pinching, all give weight to the idea that this would be a pinch by design. Indeed, the fact that a detachment of Royal Marines (the only land element in the outline plan) had orders to seize material from German naval headquarters that would solve the emerging crisis, no doubt played a crucial role in selling the signals intelligence-savvy and empire-building Mountbatten on Dieppe as an 'attractive and worthwhile' location for the next Combined Operations raid.

With the contextual case in hand, the key to determining the 70-year-old question of the intent behind the Dieppe Raid comes down to weighing the relative merits of opportunity and design. In this case, that involves the examination of three particular realms: the detailed military plan for Operation Rutter in June, which, with but a few refinements, was remounted as Operation Jubilee in August; the allocation of resources to carry out the plan, and the inherent redundancy or contingencies built into the plan to get into the trawlers and the Hôtel Moderne.

෴

Initially, Operation Rutter was planned for June 20, or any of the six days following. However, a dress rehearsal for the raid, known as Yukon I, carried out at the behest of Rear Admiral Tom Baillie-Grohman while Lord Louis Mountbatten was touring the United States just ten days before, revealed critical defects with the Royal Navy's performance – and forced a two-week postponement. 'The first rehearsal from the naval point of view was a shocker,' wrote Baillie-Grohman. 'In a short run in of 6 to 8 miles from a known position, most landing craft failed to land a large number of troops where required, some indeed several miles from their proper beaches.' With close synchronization, shock and surprise the crucial factors for success, the rear admiral realized that even a fifteen-minute delay 'could mean a disaster.' He persuaded Mountbatten to postpone the operation to rectify the problems. Rutter would now go in on July 4 at the earliest.

In the original concept for what Churchill called the 'butcher and bolt' raid, Hughes-Hallett afforded a maximum of fifteen hours on shore to accomplish all the many objectives. Even that length of time seemed short, given the enormous challenges facing the raiders: dropping airborne forces to silence the coastal gun batteries on the wings and landing two infantry battalions on each side of Dieppe to race and capture the headlands overlooking the harbour and the main beach – all in an hour flat. Following that came the daring frontal attack, with two more infantry battalions landing side by side on the main beach, backed by teams of Canadian combat engineers and two squadrons of Churchill tanks that would storm ashore to capture objectives in the port and beyond, then link up with yet another Canadian infantry battalion driving south from Green Beach to capture the airfield and division headquarters at Arques-la-Bataille, where finally they would form an outer shield to protect the bridgehead from the inevitable German counterattack.

Just after the landings on the main beach came Ryder's Cutting Out Force, which, with nearly half the new Royal Marine Commando aboard the *Locust*, would run the gauntlet into the outer harbour, by then in Canadian hands, and hit the various targets ashore. Twenty minutes later, the rest of the Royal Marines, riding on French *chasseurs* and a collection of tugs, drifters and anti-aircraft barges known as Eagle ships, would enter the harbour and tow out German barges as 'prize' captures – in what Red Ryder later dismissed as a mere 'publicity stunt,' and Hughes-Hallett refused to elaborate on, calling it simply a failed attempt to take the enemy defences from behind. Needless to say, because both men penned their memoirs before the release of Ultra, these passages were deliberate attempts at obfuscation, primarily for security purposes. In truth, the role of the Cutting Out Force was as dramatic as any Hollywood representation or, perhaps more to the point, any James Bond novel.

The delay from the latter part of June to early July forced changes to Operation Rutter because environmental conditions no longer permitted amphibious landings over a two-tide period. Limited now to only one tide, where the landings would take place at the low-water mark and re-embarkation at high water, the raiding force had only six, rather than fifteen, hours to accomplish its objectives, meaning that raid imperatives had to be compressed to only the most urgent and fundamental of all. In this sense, the new time frame spawned a bastardized version of Rutter that few, if any, have heard of – one the planners called Rutter II. In essence, the new plan was a shortened version of the original, with the inland objectives either scrapped or downgraded from 'definite' to 'contingent.' The 'aerodrome and division headquarters will be visited and the local game destroyed, but there is only enough time for a cursory search and quick demolitions.'[25] Major General Ham Roberts welcomed the change: he had feared that the original time frame gave the Germans ample opportunity to call in reinforcements and launch a coordinated counterattack designed to hit the raiders when they were most vulnerable – during re-embarkation. 'The concentration of all effort over a shorter period ought to produce good chances of a success,' he said.[26] That left the units landing on the flanks with only 30 minutes to accomplish their objectives before the frontal assault began.

Faced with a number of changes, the commanders convened a meeting of the forces involved with the pinch component of the plan – a meeting that has never entered the Dieppe debate until now, yet one that reveals there was much more to the pinch than simply hitching Fleming's IAU as a caboose to the Dieppe train. On June 28, representatives from the Royal Navy and the Royal Marines, as well as the Calgary Tanks, the Essex Scottish and the Royal Canadian Engineers, met at Roberts's headquarters. In short order, the cast of characters involved with the pinch had grown to a significant portion of the entire raiding force and, perhaps more shockingly, it now directly involved the Canadians on a par with the Royal Marines. For decades, the explosive record lay tucked away in a Rutter file in Library and Archives Canada marked 'General'; it was likely read by other historians over the years but, lacking the contextual knowledge of what was at stake, they would have discarded it as ancillary or even unnecessary.[27] Similarly, across the Atlantic in the British National Archives, another Dieppe file labelled 'Miscellaneous' contained a rare set of operational orders for the Royal Marine Commando that detailed their part both in Rutter and later in Jubilee.

Now, for the first time in close to eight decades, the role of Ryder's Cutting Out Force and the Royal Marine Commando is crystal clear. Their mission, if it had succeeded, would have rivalled St Nazaire as the stuff of legend.

~

TARGETS IN DIEPPE HARBOUR

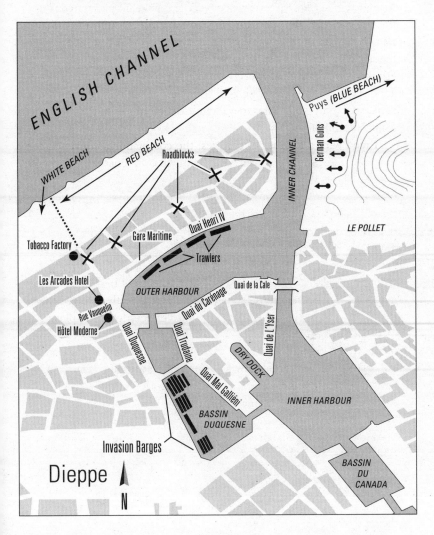

ENGLISH CHANNEL

WHITE BEACH

RED BEACH

Roadblocks

Puys (BLUE BEACH)

German Guns

INNER CHANNEL

LE POLLET

Tobacco Factory

Gare Maritime

Quai Henri IV

Trawlers

Les Arcades Hotel

Rue Vauquelin

Hôtel Moderne

OUTER HARBOUR

Quai du Carénage

Quai de la Cale

Quai de L'Yser

Quai Duquesne

Quai Trudaine

DRY DOCK

Quai Mal Gallieni

INNER HARBOUR

Invasion Barges

BASSIN DUQUESNE

BASSIN DU CANADA

Dieppe

N

05:20. INFANTRY AND TANKS LAND ON BEACHES AND DESTROY ROAD BLOCKS

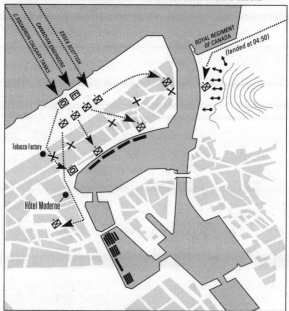

APPROX. 06:00. HMS *LOCUST* ENTERS THE INNER CHANNEL (THE 'GAUNTLET')

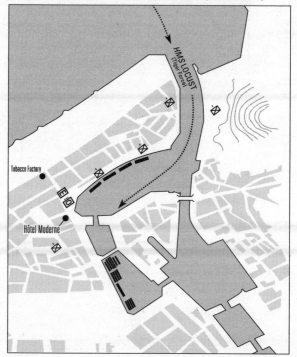

06:10–06:40. ROYAL MARINE COMMANDOS AND IAU OBTAIN INTELLIGENCE BOOTY

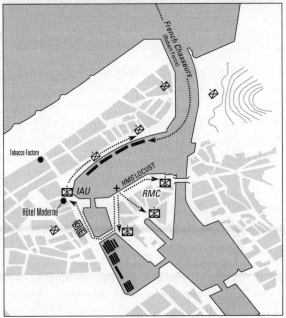

06:30–07:00. IAU DEPART DIEPPE WITH INTELLIGENCE BOOTY

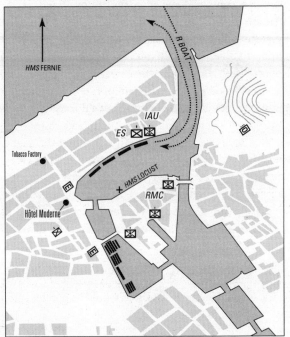

For all these intervening years, veterans have wondered why the Dieppe Raid was planned the way it was. Why was so much emphasis placed on the elusive element of surprise that underpinned the entire operation? Why were tanks used in the raid and, moreover, landed on the main beach as part of a highly controversial and seemingly suicidal frontal assault? Why was the heavy bomber raid on the town cancelled and replaced by carefully synchronized air attacks to hit just as the landing force arrived at the beach? And why was neither a battleship nor a cruiser positioned offshore to support the operation? The answers to all these questions can be found in understanding how Hughes-Hallett and his staff designed the pinch and how, with the help of the force commanders, they built up the detailed plans to accomplish this vital mission.

By stitching together the outline and detailed plans, along with the record of the June 28 coordinating meeting and the operational orders for the Royal Marine Commando, the concept for the Dieppe Raid unfolds in dramatic form. Broken down into two battle groups, the first, code-named 'Tiger Force' after Lieutenant Colonel Joseph Picton Phillipps, contained one company of Royal Marines, including No. 10 Platoon under Lieutenant Peter Huntington-Whiteley, and a demolition team riding on the decks of HMS *Locust*. The second, code-named 'Robert Force,' under Picton Phillipps's second-in-command, Major Robert 'Titch' Houghton, the career Royal Marine who at the age of 30 was considered 'the old man' of the Commando, held the remainder of the men, parcelled out in half a dozen French *chasseurs* grouped with a pack of tugboats, drifters and Eagle ships.

After embarkation from various points on the Isle of Wight, where the commandos had completed their advanced training, they would rendezvous with the rest of the raiding force off Portsmouth before proceeding across the English Channel through one of two mine-swept lanes. The *Locust* would arrive off Dieppe in time to take part in the bombardment scheduled for 0515 hours in support of the frontal assault on the main beach. By that time, if everything went according to plan, the Airborne group would have taken out the coastal gun batteries, the South Saskatchewan Regiment would have grabbed the west headland, and the Royal Regiment of Canada would be perched atop Pollet

1. Private Ron Beal, photographed in 2012 holding a picture of himself as a young soldier before embarking for Dieppe.

2. Ian Fleming in naval uniform, from the photograph album of Maud Russell, c. 1940.

3. Rear Admiral John Godfrey, Director of Naval Intelligence from 1939 to 1942, who hired Ian Fleming to be his personal assistant and right-hand man on intelligence matters.

4. Admiral Karl Dönitz, head of the German U-boat fleet and one of the few in the Nazi high command to suspect the British of breaking the Enigma-enciphered messages.

Großadmiral DÖNITZ

5. The naval four-rotor Enigma machine. The odds of cracking messages enciphered on the device without the aid of pinched material to speed up the process stood at a mind-boggling 92 septillion to 1.

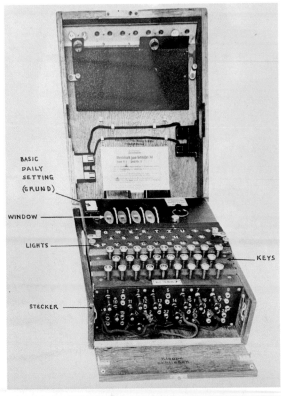

BASIC DAILY SETTING (GRUND)

WINDOW

LIGHTS

KEYS

STECKER

6. (BELOW) Used as a basis for pinch targeting, this wall chart at Bletchley Park catalogued all German wireless Morse stations, the location of their transmitters, the types of traffic they transmitted and the methods they used to communicate.

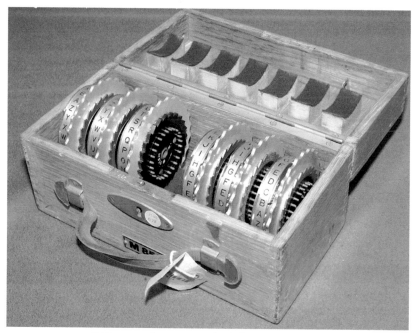

7. Two sets of spare rotor wheels for the three-wheel
Enigma machine, in their carrying box.

8. Three Enigma rotor wheels laid out on their sides. The alphabet
is visible around the edge of the top rotor wheel.

9. Frank Birch, a passionate and outspoken codebreaker who served under Admiral Reginald 'Blinker' Hall in Room 40 during the First World War. A historian by training, Birch headed the German Naval Section at Bletchley Park from 1939–45.

10. Alan Turing, 'The Prof,' an eccentric genius among codebreakers and often called the 'father of modern computing.'

11. A captured Enigma wheel, but one example of the type of naval Enigma technology targeted for 'pinch' operations by Ian Fleming's Intelligence Assault Unit in 1942.

12. British cryptanalysts Harry Hinsley, Sir Edward Travis and John Tiltman in Washington, November 1945, to hammer out agreement on American, British and Canadian signals intelligence cooperation for the post-war.

13. Major General Hamilton 'Ham' Roberts, commander of the Second Canadian Infantry Division, unfairly vilified for the failure of the Dieppe operation and its heavy loss of life.

14. Captain Peter Huntington-Whiteley, who led Ian Fleming's Intelligence Assault Unit at Dieppe at the age of 22.

15. No. 10 Platoon of X Company, Royal Marines, May 1942 – Fleming's Intelligence Assault Unit. Peter Huntington-Whiteley is in the centre; Paul McGrath is second from right in the middle row.

16. Captain John 'Jock' Hughes-Hallett, architect, lead planner and naval force commander for the Dieppe Raid.

17. Robert Edward Dudley 'Red' Ryder, who had commanded the naval force in the St Nazaire Raid, winning the VC, and would go on to lead the 'Cutting Out Force' at Dieppe.

18. (BELOW) An aerial reconnaissance photo of Dieppe harbour, showing trawlers and other small craft berthed along the Quai Henri IV. These, along with the Hôtel Moderne, were the main targets for the Royal Marine Commandos.

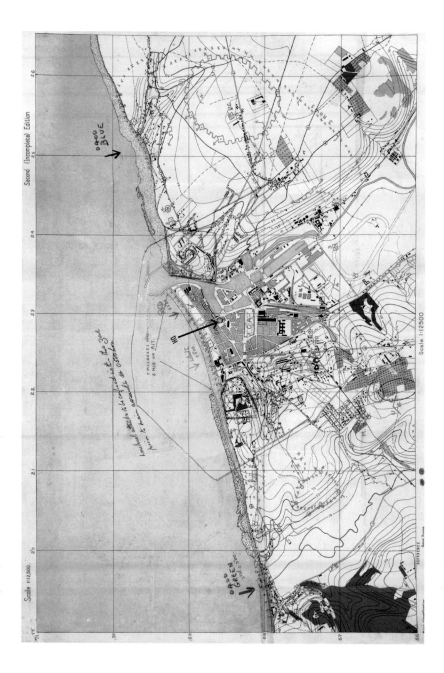

19. (OPPOSITE) One of the earliest known maps for the Dieppe Raid, produced in early May to aid the force commanders with their detailed planning. Although locations of other headquarters in and around Dieppe were known to Allied intelligence by this time, only the Hôtel Moderne (suspected to house German naval headquarters) is marked on the map (as 'HQ,' arrow added), which clearly indicates its prime importance right from the raid's inception.

20. The entrance to Dieppe harbour – the daunting route that HMS *Locust* and the Cutting Out Force were to take to reach their targets in the inner harbour.

21. Trawlers in Dieppe harbour. Until the release of classified Ultra Secret documents showing the importance of the codebooks and encrypting sheets contained in such vessels, the trawlers' significance to the raid made little sense.

22. An RAF aerial photograph showing German pillboxes and a dug-in French tank on the Dieppe harbour mole.

23. A further part of the gauntlet that the raiders would have to run to reach their targets of the Hôtel Moderne and the trawlers.

24. The Ultra Secret role of the heavily armed gunboat HMS *Locust* was long obscured in the history of the Dieppe Raid.

25. A German photo taken from atop Pollet Cliff shows the aftermath of the fighting on Red Beach, with smoke streaming from the roaring blaze in the tobacco factory that marked the shortest route to the pinch targets in the harbour.

26. An RAF aerial reconnaissance photo of the Dieppe Raid in progress. German trawlers are visible in the outer harbour, and smoke billows from the tobacco factory.

27. German propaganda photo of the carnage on Blue Beach, where the Canadians took close to 95 per cent casualties, due to German machine guns in bunkers and pillboxes on the hillside below the white house.

28. A remarkable photo included in an American report on the M4 cipher (German naval four-rotor Enigma) designed to show the lengths the Allies would go to in order to capture the material necessary to break the device.

29. Three months after Dieppe, the survivors of No. 10 Platoon take part in Operation Torch, the invasion of North Africa. Paul McGrath is second from right.

30. Paul McGrath (front row, second from right) with part of his section of No. 10 Platoon in 1945, after a series of harrowing missions in North Africa, Sicily, Normandy, Belgium and Germany had taken their toll.

31. Private Ron Beal of the Royal Regiment of Canada. In 2012, after the real reasons for the Dieppe Raid were revealed to him, he said: 'Now I can die in peace. Now I know what my friends died for.'

Cliff, with the air and naval bombardment of the main beach about to commence.

As the frontal assault went in, the *Locust* would remain on station just off the entrance to the harbour mole. From there, she would lob shells from her four-inch guns at German positions on Red Beach in support of the Essex Scottish, directed by a forward observation officer who had gone ashore with the battalion. Alternatively, if the Royal Regiment landing at Blue Beach failed to reach its objectives on the heights, the *Locust* would direct the shells towards the German guns on the east headland.

With the raid now half an hour old, the stakes on the main beach would be high, something Hughes-Hallett and Roberts clearly recognized: 'It is vital to the success of the operation as a whole,' the plan noted, 'that White and Red Beaches be in our hands with minimal delay.'[28] On the Red Beach sector, given the role that the Essex Scottish, the tanks and the engineers would play in combination with Ryder's Cutting Out Force to affect the pinch, this timing was even more pertinent. Accompanied by C Squadron from the Calgary Tanks, four companies of the Essex Scottish under the command of Lieutenant Colonel Fred Jasperson, a 42-year-old lawyer from Windsor, Ontario, were to move forward with the engineers over the beach and the promenade to the boulevard de Verdun before the Germans could gather their senses following the shock of the aerial and naval bombardment.

Once they reached the boulevard de Verdun, the four infantry companies of Jasperson's battalion would fan out and infiltrate the town through the tiny streets, with one company capturing the west bank of the inner channel, overlooking the German positions at the base of Pollet Cliff on the opposite side, while the other three made directly for the outer harbour. As this scene unfolded, combat engineers would go to work on the roadblock near the tobacco factory at the junction of the rue Duquesne, the shortest and most direct route into the outer harbour from the main beach for as the SOE liaison officer noted, 'a great deal hangs on the tank exits from the main beach of town.'[29] If the task proved impossible in the time allowed, the engineers had orders to clear the roadblocks from any street running east, to allow the tanks to proceed into the harbour to link up with the Essex Scottish. If the

Quai Duquesne route proved feasible, however, the tanks would burst into the outer harbour right onto Quai Henri IV, less than 200 yards from the trawlers on the left near the Gare Maritime, and less than 50 yards from the Hôtel Moderne to the right – both within easy range of their two-pounder cannon and Besa machine guns.

Once inside the harbour, the tanks and the Essex Scottish had orders to effect the first phase of the pinch operation – to 'destroy resistance, capture the trawlers and prevent destruction of their signals books and documents.'[30] Nearly a dozen Churchill tanks would provide mobile firepower to bring the trawler crews under a torrent of intense fire and knock out their four-inch guns, which could pose a formidable threat if not neutralized. The same would apply to any German defences in the vicinity of the Hôtel Moderne. As soon as the crews were subdued, one company of the Essex Scottish would storm on board the trawlers to kill or capture the survivors. They had instructions to tie the hands of all prisoners, to prevent them from destroying the codebooks and other documents. As one company secured the trawlers, the remaining two would knock out any resistance in the area around the Gare Maritime and the Hôtel Moderne; their specific orders were to 'capture military and naval headquarters' and to 'search for a naval codebook.'[31] These orders connect directly to the caveat the planners had earlier placed on that building: no one was to search the premises before he contacted Fleming's IAU and followed Huntington-Whiteley's instructions.

Within the environment of Combined Operations, where boldness and derring-do were prized above strict military convention, the controversial frontal assault now makes perfect sense, despite its immense challenges. First, no other route to the target was as quick or direct – a crucial element in a plan where the raiders had to close with and kill the enemy fast to take advantage of the ongoing chaos. Roberts and Hughes-Hallett hoped that their combined force of infantry and tanks, suddenly bursting into the port, would suffice to panic and subdue the German trawler crews – just as the cruisers and destroyers had done in earlier pinch operations against trawlers in the North Atlantic and Norway. Similarly, the planners' decision not to start the raid with heavy bombing now makes sense. During the detailed planning phase, various arguments were offered for scrapping the bombing. Among these were the loss of surprise, and the risk that inaccurate bombing would choke the streets with rubble, blocking the tanks from reaching the port. In response, supporters proposed using pathfinders to increase accuracy, for in their opinion, any rubble caused would be no more of an obstacle than an unblown roadblock. However, the point that won the day in favour of cancelling the high-level heavy bomber attacks came down to the need 'to avoid damage to the harbour installations' in order to 'allow HMS *Locust* and the cutting out party to perform their tasks,' as an errant bomb might sink the ships or uncontrolled fires might destroy the Hôtel Moderne – the two main targets for the mission.[32]

Once the area was secured, and the German trawler crews or the headquarters defence units were killed or captured, the Essex Scottish were ordered to 'leave the vessels and remain in observation in a position protected from fire of HMS *Locust*[,] which will engage the vessels unless it is clear that they are in [Canadian] hands.'[33] Leaving little to chance, Hughes-Hallett then called for two more contingencies, or redundancies, to ensure that the pinch came off.[34]

Regardless of whether the attack on the trawlers succeeded, stalled or failed outright, Commander Red Ryder and the Cutting Out Force would launch their strike 30 minutes after the main assault, after receiving a pre-arranged signal from the forward observation officer via radio using the code word 'trawlers' or from flares fired from any of Jasperson's companies in the outer harbour.[35] A series of green flares rising up in the sky would signify that the trawlers had been captured and German resistance overcome. Red flares would mean that the attack on the trawlers had failed and that the German defences in the harbour were still active.[36] These signals were not to denote 'stop' or 'go'; rather, they would inform Ryder of what to expect when he and his force entered the harbour – whether he would get a hot or a cold reception from the Germans. The implication is clear: whatever the colour of the flares, Ryder was to press on with his part of the plan. Come Hell or high water, the Royal Marines were going in.

First Tiger Force on the *Locust*, and then twenty minutes later Robert Force on the *chasseurs*, would move through what they hoped would be a pacified corridor in the inner channel, with the Royal Regiment of Canada on top of the eastern headland and one company of the Essex Scottish in over-watch positions in the town policing the caves at the bottom of the cliffs under the Royals. Only if heavy artillery fire persisted before they reached the entrance to the harbour mole could Ryder hold off entry – once through the mole and past the outer defences on the jetties and the northern face of Pollet Cliff, they would be on their own, and there would be no turning back. In the best 'Boy's Own' tradition as at St Nazaire, Ryder's orders called for Tiger Force and the *Locust* to be fully prepared to run the gauntlet of the inner channel, ready to take on any German positions that remained active with their deck guns and the extra mortars welded atop, as well as the rifles, sub-machine guns and the Bren guns of the Royal Marines laying prostrate on deck. To underscore the desperate and vital imperative of their mission, Mountbatten issued direct orders for the Marines to swim to their target onshore should *Locust* be sunk during its daring run towards the outer harbour. Clearly, this was anything but a 'publicity stunt.'[37]

Hoping for the best but planning for the worst, the Royal Marines had trained in Portsmouth harbour for just this scenario. Manning all of the *Locust*'s guns – her four-inch guns fore and aft, her anti-aircraft 'pom-pom' gun, her 3.7-inch howitzer amidships, and four specially mounted three-inch mortars welded to her upper deck – the Royal Marines were to lie prone on the deck, Bren guns at the ready, to 'assist in subduing enemy fire from flanks and in beating off air attacks.'[38]

Once inside the port, Ryder would fire off a message to Roberts on the *Calpe* with an inventory of pinch targets encountered inside the tight confines of Dieppe's harbour with each class of vessel accorded a code name – Dog for E-boats, Cat for R-boats, Lion for minesweepers, Bear for barges, Bull for trawlers, Pig for drifters, Horse for torpedo boats, and Cow for Siebel ferries –while *Locust* made for the island to disembark Tiger Force. Once alongside the Quai du Carénage, the men of A Company from Tiger Force would leap off and take on any unsuppressed German units in the immediate area if the guns of *Locust*, the Essex Scottish, the Calgary Tanks and the Royal Canadian Engineers had failed to subdue the guns on the trawlers and other German vessels. Once ashore, A Company would seize the swing bridges and the lock gates while No. 10 Platoon, led by Lieutenant Huntington-Whiteley

– Fleming's Intelligence Assault Unit – would go directly to their first stop, the Hôtel Moderne.[39] Equipped with their own radio set and their own code name 'Whiteley,' they sported Thompson sub-machine guns, Lee-Enfield rifles, Bren guns and grenades. In addition, each member of the fledgling IAU carried extra ammunition in bandoliers slung over his shoulders – spare Bren gun magazines and Hawkins anti-tank grenades in their pouches – along with a large haversack stuffed with explosives for demolition and smaller waterproof bags to store captured material along with a small fire extinguisher, in case the Germans attempted to destroy the desired material by fire or an errant shell ignited their target.[40]

Depending on the situation when the men arrived at the Hôtel Moderne, they would enter a building either controlled by the Essex Scottish, if all went well, or, if not, still in German hands. In the latter case, they would attempt to breach and clear the Hôtel in the quickest possible manner – meaning that they would start at the bottom of the three-storey structure and move methodically through every room, killing or incapacitating all the occupants before they had time to destroy the targeted material. It would be a nasty business, calling for speed and extreme ruthlessness in close-quarter fighting, with their Thompsons, brass knuckles, commando knives or bare hands finishing off the defenders. Then they would go on to the next room and the one after that, until the entire building was secured. Only then could the planned search begin.

Once inside, the IAU had orders to rifle through desks, filing cabinets, waste-paper baskets, fireplaces, and every nook and cranny of every room, searching for signs of the vital signals material and equipment they were after and stuffing everything useful they could find into their haversacks. If they came across the commandant's safe, where they would likely find codebooks for future issue and other potentially vital documents, they would try to open it immediately. If they failed, they would call for the 'safe cracker' attached to the IAU to blow open the door and reveal its contents.[41] Once the Hôtel Moderne yielded its expected treasures, they would move on to the trawlers seized by the Essex Scottish and the tanks in the original assault.[42] There they would collect what the Essex men had already pinched or, as Allon Bacon had done at Vaagso, conduct a detailed search of the vessels on their own.

If for some reason the Essex and tank attack did not achieve its objectives, Jock Hughes-Hallett had put a third contingency in place. Huntington-Whiteley and his men would proceed to the trawlers, aided by the guns on the *Locust* and later the French *chasseurs* carrying Robert Force. Regardless of the situation, Titch Houghton's men would follow down the narrow channel and into the port, exchanging fire, if necessary, with German guns in the caves at the bottom of Pollet Cliff, and land at the Quai Henri IV. Ideally, they would support both Tiger Force and the IAU, corralling captured vessels to be towed back to England. However, as yet another layer to ensure the pinch, Houghton received orders that 'if Tiger Force has failed to land, or if it is obvious to Commander Robert Force that Tiger is NOT moving on its objectives[,] Robert Force will seize the objectives itself, informing Tiger of its progress.'[43] To reinforce the bold and near-suicidal nature of the mission, the orders warned, 'Should any vessel be sunk before berthing, all personnel will land at the nearest steps and fight their way to Tiger HQs' located on the island, to regroup and press on to their objectives.[44]

The orders for the Royal Marine Commando also reveal why seizing both sides of the inner channel was crucial to the entire plan. Not only did it create a corridor to get into the harbour, but it also provided the pipeline to get the captured material *out*. The exit strategy had a distinct James Bond flavour to it all.

✎

In 2007, tucked away in an old, decrepit shed in the little town of Eye, in Suffolk, England, the son-in-law of Royal Marine Commando corporal Ernest 'Lofty' Coleman made a fascinating and unexpected discovery: the partially destroyed remains of Lofty's wartime experiences, which he penned in 1995 but never published. Coleman died just before I began my inquiry into Dieppe, but his son-in-law and I made contact when he reached out online to find anyone who might shed light on this remarkable memoir. His family subsequently sent it to me and have allowed me to quote it here, since the vivid quality of this unique first-person account provides revealing and compelling evidence, particularly when cross-referenced with the official documents. According to Coleman, who as an eighteen-year-old served under Huntington-Whiteley first at Chatham and later as part of No. 3 Section of No. 10 Platoon:

> As section leader, I had to have intensive training in the use of explosives and [the] art of demolition, [as] at this point I had no idea what I [had] got myself into. Further training took place at Portsmouth dockyard[;] it was at this time we were told that Portsmouth dockyard was very similar to Dieppe ... At the briefing which took place prior to the raid, I was given a most unusual job which I [was] rather looking forward to[:] the platoon were to make a landing at the Dieppe dockyard and give covering fire so that two other commandos could assist me in locating a building which was to be entered[;] within this building was a safe holding some important documents. For this operation[,] instead of the usual equipment, I was to wear a hiker's type of haversack to take the explosives in and take the documents out. When I had the documents in my possession, I was to make my way to the dockside[,] where a boat would be waiting for me to take [me] back home. My two colleagues, one a team leader, the other a crack safe breaker, had to make their way back to the platoon[,] where they were expected to collect as many invasion barges together as possible and bring them back to England[;] the rest were destroyed.

Although writing more than 50 years after the event, Coleman's recollection is extraordinarily accurate. In the plans and operational orders for the raid on Dieppe, special instructions warned all commanders of one special proviso that rose above the din of the ongoing battle: 'A unit of the R.M. Commando may be expected to bring a special report from Rutter Harbour to the HQ Ship. Any R.M. Officer or NCO giving the codeword *Bullion* is to be given priority passage in any R Boat from Rutter harbour.'[45] Although there is no indication of this code word in either set of the Royal Marine orders – and it may even have been replaced with another word at the last moment – there are special provisions in the orders for Huntington-Whiteley and his platoon to report directly to Houghton on Quai Henri IV after seizing the material. In this case, a special motor launch, specifically laid on for this purpose, would arrive in the outer harbour to whisk the designated members of the IAU and their precious haul out of Dieppe. Meanwhile, the rest of the raid would continue, with the tanks and the Essex Scottish moving south and east of the port to cover demolition teams from both the Royal Marine Commando and the Royal Canadian Engineers, who would systematically destroy targets in the port, including the Hôtel Moderne, to cover their tracks before they re-embarked on the *Locust*.

This crucial new evidence throws an entirely different light on the military plan for the Dieppe Raid: the proportion of the forces allocated to the pinch mission establishes it as a 'raid imperative,' firmly sealing it as a pinch by design rather than a pinch by opportunity. Nearly *half* the entire raiding force was involved with the pinch. Two battalions out of the five landing in the initial wave, one tank squadron, a series of engineer combat teams, Ryder's Cutting Out Force (with the 300 men of Picton Phillipps's Royal Marine Commando), along with HMS *Locust* and nearly a dozen French *chasseurs*, tugs, drifters and Eagle ships all played a direct role in creating the conditions to ensure that the pinch succeeded. Even the selection of Ryder to lead the Cutting Out Force was a calculated decision: the planners were counting on his knowledge, his experience and, above all, his leadership and guts to carry out this crucial mission.

No other aspect of the military portion of the Dieppe Raid required resources approaching this magnitude, nor did any other military forces need the level of cooperation and coordination necessary to achieve this objective. Even the design of the detailed plan features the core principles associated with the developing pinch doctrine: an emphasis on surprise, speed and shock to overwhelm bewildered defenders so that the desired material could be seized before it was destroyed. This time the operation would also include a pipeline – to get the Intelligence Assault Unit quickly to its target and out again – a luxury no other intelligence organization taking part in the raid enjoyed. These same hallmarks had been seen in previous pinch operations, though not on the same scale as in the plans for Rutter.

Finally, no other objective for the raid enjoyed the inherent redundancy of the various back-up schemes the planners built in for the pinch. In this case, if the Essex Scottish and the Calgary Tanks failed to reach their target, then Tiger Force would prevail. If Tiger Force faltered, then Houghton's Robert Force would take over. And if Robert Force failed, Major General Ham Roberts still had another, a fourth, card to play: his 'floating reserve' of the Fusiliers Mont-Royal and the remaining squadron of the Calgary Tanks was waiting offshore, ready if needed.

ᔕ

On June 1, at the inaugural meeting of the force commanders – almost a full week *before* detailed planning began for Operation Rutter with the finalization of the frontal assault and Mountbatten's invitation to the intelligence agencies to hitch their wagon to the raid – the role of the *Locust* and the Intelligence Assault Unit grabbed centre stage. Concerned about the 'political aspect' of covering the potential loss of the *Locust* in Dieppe harbour, Mountbatten suggested that they publicly pass off her role in the operation as a blockship – one specifically sunk to render the port unusable.[46] The force commanders immediately pointed out that this explanation would backfire because both this Yangtze river gunboat and the German invasion barges had flat bottoms, making them unsuitable for this purpose. Undaunted, Mountbatten suggested to Admiral Tom Baillie-Grohman, Air Vice-Marshal Trafford Leigh-Mallory and Major General Ham Roberts that, once the *Locust* ran the gauntlet through the narrow channel to the port beyond and the 'special party' disembarked, she would then return to the channel to lend fire support to forces in the bridgehead rather than remain at risk in the tight confines of the outer harbour.[47] Clearly, his request denotes not only that he had an intimate knowledge of the pinch but, even more important, that the plan for delivery of the IAU came in advance of the detailed plan. Even at this early stage, the pinch was the central driver for the entire operation.

With the military and naval plans built around the pinch, Ham Roberts, his brigadiers, and certain battalion and company commanders had to be put in 'the know' (to varying degrees) about this

261

crucial objective for Operation Rutter. Just prior to kick-off for the raid, Roberts brought his brigade commanders and their staffs together for a final conference to tie up all the essential elements for the 'party' as he called it. First on his agenda was the primary importance of security and surprise, and he reiterated the standing orders that no discussion of the operation would be tolerated in the mess or in any unsecured location. Failure to comply with this order would, he emphasized, be met with severe disciplinary action. 'If information gets out,' he warned his battle-starved subordinates, the 'party will be cancelled.'[48] Second, he reinforced the point that speed was 'very essential' for success and that 'all defences' had to be 'run over as soon as possible.' Indeed, indecision or hesitation would not be tolerated, he stressed, and the 'speedier the assault the fewer casualties' – though he quickly assured his men that casualties would be 'very few.'[49] The mounting hubris within Combined Operations had obviously trickled down and infected the Canadian commander, igniting his enthusiasm. Saving his best salvo for last, Roberts, echoing the provisions of Pound's 'in the know book,' confided to his brigadiers: 'Certain things which we are after may mean an important factor to the outcome of the war.'[50]

CHAPTER 12

All Essential Features

... within this building was a safe holding some important documents ... When I had [them], I was to make my way to the dockside, where a boat would be waiting to take me back home.
Ernest Coleman, unpublished memoir

HMS *Locust* was not designed for speed; she was likely the slowest vessel scheduled to take part in the Dieppe Raid. Part of the Dragonfly class of river gunboats designed to project and protect British imperial might half a world away in China, she had been reassigned to duties in Europe immediately after her launch in 1940. Most of her short but charmed life had been spent in operations in the Thames estuary and occasionally in the English Channel. Known as a 'happy ship' but also a lucky one, she survived a pounding from German aircraft during the Dunkirk evacuation, where Dick de Costobadie guided her 'in and out of Hell' during the harrowing departure. Two years later, all those who climbed aboard her for the raid on Dieppe hoped her legendary good fortune would continue to flow.

The *Locust* weighed in at a modest 585 tons but measured more than three-quarters the length of a football field. With her flat-bottomed hull drawing a mere five feet, her trio of rudders enabled her to navigate deftly in shallow and swift-running waters but contributed to a pronounced roll when she encountered rough weather in the open sea. She topped out at only seventeen knots – but it wasn't speed that had caught the attention of Captain Jock Hughes-Hallett. Along with her ability to manoeuvre with ease in strong currents and tight bodies of water – a useful quality for navigating the confines of Dieppe's inner harbour – firepower was her strong suit. Equipped with two four-inch guns, one at the front on the bow deck and another at the back on the stern upper platform, a 3.7-inch howitzer positioned amidships, two three-pounder guns on each side, and a multi-barrelled 40-millimetre anti-aircraft cannon known as a 'Chicago Piano' on the aft deck, the *Locust* packed a wallop.

To give extra firepower for the run down the gauntlet of Dieppe's inner channel that led to the harbour, the Marines retrofitted the ship, adding four of their three-inch mortars to the upper deck, strengthening an already potent shipboard arsenal. They knew that the *Locust*'s guns would be its only key to success: the ship was so lightly armoured that it offered little tangible protection from German guns at point-blank range. It would be kill or be killed, just as it had been for the commandos at St Nazaire, meaning that the *Locust*'s gunners had to be quick off the mark and dead on target, laying down a steady stream of fire on German gun positions in the caves to kill, suppress or incapacitate them – anything to prevent or curtail their firing on the ship. Such action required extreme skill and daring: the 51-man crew would have to pull together to support the gunners even as they kept the *Locust* steady and prevented it from running aground in the narrow channel, all the while dodging German fire from land and perhaps from the air as well.

With Dick de Costobadie now firmly ensconced in Lord Louis Mountbatten's headquarters planning pinch operations, the 54-year-old William John Stride took over as ship's captain. A mature veteran of the First World War, he was capable and popular, having worked his way up from the lower decks to command, and had experience with pinch operations. In one of the first actions of the war, Stride commanded His Majesty's Minesweeper *Tedworth*, used as a dive platform in the vain attempt to pinch Enigma-related material from the sunken *U-13*.[1] After a short time training together, Red Ryder had become a fan, sensing that Stride's 'robust' and 'unflappable' character made him an 'excellent person to have as a kind of "flag captain."'[2] In Operation Rutter, the *Locust* would be under the overall command of Ryder, as the Cutting Out Force commander with the final authority and responsibility, but Stride would control the moment-by-moment operations of the ship while in battle.

Anticipating the danger they would face once they breached the harbour mole at Dieppe, Stride took the precaution of boarding up the walls of the bridge with railway ties to provide an added measure of security – an act Ryder later admitted 'probably saved our lives.'[3] Below deck, the men, such as the nineteen-year-old seaman John Parsons, whose job it was to feed the Chicago Piano with ammunition hoisted on a conveyor, had little idea what they were about to face.[4] Ryder's appearance on the bridge alongside Stride, coupled with the Royal Marine Commando contingent on board with them, reinforced the idea among the crew that they were in for something big. Their initial excitement over having a legendary St Nazaire hero with them soon gave way to the sober realization that his previous excursion into battle had included one of His Majesty's destroyers, specially rigged as a ticking time bomb. As Parsons recalled, 'Lower deck rumour had it that he would want to blow us up in Dieppe harbour. Which did not appeal to us much!' The arrival of nearly 200 'escape kits' for use by the commandos, plus a vast collection of explosives and other specialized stores, did nothing to alleviate their growing anxiety.[5]

After carrying out one final exercise in Portsmouth harbour, the Royal Marines were confined to the Upper Chine School on the Isle of Wight, while Ryder and No. 10 Platoon (Ian Fleming's Intelligence Assault Unit) sailed across the Solent to Eaglehurst House on the English coast, where they fine-tuned their mission in the same facility where Marconi had once experimented with his wireless communications. By July 2, they were all back in the town of Shanklin Chine on the island for the final briefing before embarking for the raid.[6]

The following day, 125 men from Major Titch Houghton's Robert Force climbed aboard eight French *chasseurs* – one of them captained by the young Philippe de Gaulle, the only son of the Free French leader, now in exile in England. The remaining 172 officers and men of the

Royal Marine Commando Tiger Force boarded a thoroughly crowded *Locust*; with Lieutenant Colonel Joseph Picton Phillipps and his head-quarters staff, the Marines of A Company, No. 3 Platoon, No. 10 Platoon under Lieutenant Peter Huntington-Whiteley, and No. 1 Demolition Party, there was little room for the men to 'sling their hook' (or ham-mocks, in Royal Navy slang).[7]

Similar conditions existed on almost every ship and at every air-field now readying for departure. Across south-east England, soldiers, sailors and airmen prepared for the largest raid of the war – the biggest amphibious operation to date. The excitement in the air was palpable.

But it was not to be. Bad weather set in, forcing a postponement of the operation from July 3 to July 7. Then, after a German air raid on July 5 hit several of the raiding ships in port and lessened the chance of surprise, the continuing inclement weather led those in command to cancel the raid. The war diaries for both General Ham Roberts's Second Canadian Division and the Royal Marines noted the men's deep disap-pointment. This feeling was no doubt shared by the trio of United States Marines who had been sent to take part in the pinch operation – a story that has remained unknown until now.[8] Just how did these Americans come to be involved in the pinch?

◆

As spring moved into summer that year, the pressure on Rear Admiral John Godfrey and his Naval Intelligence Division had begun to mount in many quarters. Whether he knew it explicitly or not, he should have sensed that the clock was now ticking on his tenure as Director of Naval Intelligence. His sometimes abrasive and obstinate attitude, quick temper and blatant attempts at empire building had led to fric-tion and an increasingly frosty relationship with the other heads of intelligence who sat with him on the Joint Intelligence Committee.[9] His overbearing character and patronizing demeanour could be toler-ated as long as he continued to provide the goods, but as soon as the four-rotor crisis deepened, his welcome began to wear thin, particu-larly after the discovery that German naval intelligence had broken the British naval codes – something Section 10 of Godfrey's NID was tasked to protect.[10]

For the previous two years, as Blinker Hall had once urged, Godfrey and his indispensable fixer Ian Fleming had been working tirelessly to cultivate close liaisons with the American embassy in London and the American intelligence services in Washington. Now, finally, the early returns on both fronts looked extremely promising. First, Godfrey had courted Admiral Alan G. Kirk, the enthusiastic anglophile who served as the American naval attaché in London and enjoyed a direct line to Roosevelt and the White House. Later, when Kirk ran the Office of Naval Intelligence in Washington, Fleming tried to strengthen the bond through constant personal attention. Second, Godfrey and Fleming fostered their growing relationship with Colonel William 'Wild Bill' or 'Big Bill' Donovan, who would go on to head the new American intelligence agency, the Co-ordinator of Information (COI) – later known as the Office of Strategic Services (OSS) which served as forerunner to the Central Intelligence Agency (CIA).[11] Increasing the power and influence of this institution had been a British imperative for some time. Along with William Stephenson – the Canadian millionaire known as 'Little Bill' who ran British Security Coordination (BSC) that looked after British intelligence interests in North America* – Godfrey, SIS head Stewart Menzies and Foreign Office officials all conspired to make Donovan 'their man' in Washington.

Donovan, a Medal of Honor winner from the First World War who shared the same maverick personality and aggressive outlook on intelligence as these men, seemed the perfect candidate. He was much more malleable than the anglophobic J. Edgar Hoover, the head of the FBI, who was later described as a 'cross between a political gangster and a prima donna.'[12] Donovan, an Irish Catholic Wall Street lawyer from Buffalo, was at times brilliant, always tough and extremely cocksure.[13]

Like Roosevelt, who learned of Blinker Hall's prowess during a visit to London in 1917 while working as the under-secretary of the navy, Donovan, too, became enamoured of the dark world of British intelligence upon his first official sojourn in the UK.[14] 'To understand

---

* HS 8/818, 'Liaison with CCO – General.' Although widely known as 'Intrepid' in popular history after the war, Stephenson's official code name was the less than dramatic '48000.'

the significance of ... Donovan,' Godfrey stressed, 'one has to go back to ... 1940 when he came over at the personal request of his old friend Knox and Stimpson on an exploratory and unofficial mission.* He had a particular request from Mister Knox to establish intimate collaboration with the British Navy, both in the spheres of technical development and intelligence.'[15]

As CIA historian Tom Troy relates: 'Donovan had been much impressed with the necessity for the protection of US supplies which were then beginning to flow to Europe' and had 'stopped in London ... to get acquainted with Britain's plans and intentions ... with particular reference to the Atlantic. As he saw it, the British were taking a severe plastering on the seas, an American policy ought to be aimed at remedying this situation.'[16]

Godfrey at once seized upon Donovan as an essential conduit, advising Admiral Sir Andrew Cunningham, the Commander-in-Chief of the Mediterranean fleet: 'There is no doubt that we can achieve infinitely more through Donovan than any other individual.'[17]

Churchill, however, was sceptical and initially refused to permit Donovan into trade secrets like Ultra intelligence. But following a spirited appeal from William Stephenson, who 'impressed upon him that the latter really exercises a vast degree of influence in the administration,' and had 'Knox in his pocket,' Churchill acquiesced. Two days after 'Big Bill' arrived in London, he sat down at 10 Downing Street for lunch with the prime minister.[18]

Upon his return to the United States, Donovan approached Roosevelt with the support and urging of the British with a controversial idea for a civilian intelligence agency that would bring together research, intelligence, propaganda, subversion and commando operations under one roof – rather like a 'fourth arm' of the military services – and which would coordinate all foreign intelligence activities for the United States.[19]

As Godfrey wrote: 'The DNI placed great reliance upon this new organization as a means of redeeming US intelligence from chaos.' The picture was indeed a dark one from the British perspective, and he

---

* Secretary of the Navy Frank Knox and Secretary of War Henry L. Stimpson.

concluded that US intelligence was 'unlikely to be of much assistance for many months to come' except in particular areas such as the Pacific, North Africa and unoccupied France where, as neutrals, the Americans could maintain observers – particularly in ports. 'If they entered the war,' he wrote, 'even this usefulness would disappear' as there were no 'other US intelligence sources to fall back on and, at present, no machinery for improving them.'[20] Donovan, in Godfrey's estimation, might prove to be the machine, if he accepted 'a full measure of advice in cooperation from British intelligence.'[21]

As such, Godfrey and other members of British intelligence had shaped and supported the plan, and, realizing full well the precarious nature of the request, and that 'much depended on Colonel Donovan,' Churchill sent Godfrey, with Fleming in tow, to Washington in May 1941 to meet with Roosevelt in an attempt to get Donovan appointed as the head of the new agency, where he would act as an American 'spymaster.'[22]

When they arrived, the pair stayed at Donovan's Georgetown flat, where Fleming, under Godfrey's direction, penned a loose set of organizational requirements for Donovan's nascent intelligence service.[23] As Godfrey realized, 'It was a grandiose project, fraught with political dangers, but appeared, at any rate, a step forward.'

The timing was perfect: Roosevelt, increasingly dissatisfied with the patchy quality of the current intelligence community in the United States, proved susceptible to corrective suggestions. As Godfrey crowed later: 'Donovan's qualifications as the coordinator of intelligence were advocated to Mister Roosevelt, and Colonel Donovan was appointed. His finances were set by a secret vote, he was responsible to the president direct, and Mister Stevenson, the head of our Secret Service in New York, worked "in the closest cooperation" with him.'[24] Within days of Godfrey's meeting with the president, Roosevelt established the new office of the Co-ordinator of Information, or COI, with Donovan as its head, though the public announcement was delayed until July 11. As Troy summed up the appointment:

For the first time in eight years of the Democratic administration of Franklin D. Roosevelt, William J. Donovan, a lifelong Republican and a foe of the New Deal, but a vigorous internationalist and a close friend of the new Navy chief had in that friendship, a firm operating base in the machinery of the national government.[25]

Donovan's new organization looked impressive on paper, with its unlimited budget and presidential backing, but the British were disappointed that its mandate was not absolute. Ordered to 'collect and analyze all information and data which may bear upon the national security' for the president and those he designated, the COI was given the authority to request data from other agencies and departments, but not allowed to interfere with the duties and responsibilities of the president's military and naval advisers.[26] And that made its position precarious, particularly when the competing elements of the navy, army, State Department and FBI came together in a loosely united front to oppose Donovan's sudden bid to become an American 'intelligence tsar.' Sober to the political realities, Godfrey foresaw that 'Donovan and his party of enthusiasts,' having 'like all young intelligence services ... that urge towards the production of spectacular and dramatic results,' would 'have to go through a period of disillusionment.'[27] Nevertheless, the DNI added, 'I feel that, if we play our cards properly, we can exploit to the full the money and enthusiasm that Donovan, with the backing of the president, will throw into his new service.'[28]

Regardless of the fragile ground, the British still rejoiced in their accomplishment. As William Stephenson trumpeted to Churchill: 'I have been attempting to manoeuvre Donovan into the job of coordinating all United States intelligence ... you can imagine how relieved I am after months of battle and jockeying in Washington that our man is in position.'[29]

Mountbatten was also impressed, doubting 'whether any one person contributed more to the ultimate victory of the Allies than Bill Donovan.'[30] Like Godfrey, Mountbatten also understood the value that a US intelligence pipeline such as Donovan's might offer to his Combined Operations Headquarters. In addition, Roosevelt's son James, a Marine Corps Reserve captain, was Donovan's aide-de-camp at the COI. Mountbatten and Godfrey interpreted that appointment as an opportunity to showcase the British brand of amphibious 'commando' operations – the kind based on intelligence provided by the Inter-Services Topographical Department – and eventually to replicate that approach to pinch operations in the United States.

In theory, 'pinch' operations were nothing new to the Americans, as for years they had engaged in an 'almost hyperactive, surreptitious entry program.'[31] Everyone from the FBI to the OSS, army and ONI were 'all out stealing codes,' pinching material that dealt with Spanish, Vichy French, Finnish, Brazilian and Chilean diplomatic codes, mostly in audacious and highly risky schemes that drew the scorn of the British and raised fears of compromise unless their action could be sufficiently harnessed, channelled and refined. In one case, Hoover's FBI agents penetrated the Spanish embassy at the precise moment that Donovan's men arrived on the scene, leading to embarrassment, resentment and recrimination and the subsequent cancellation of future operations against Portugal and Turkey.[32]

In the spring of 1941, the Twelfth Naval District in San Francisco assembled a team of 'entry specialists' under the leadership of a private detective, who all proceeded to dress up like customs inspectors and board a Japanese merchantman anchored in the bay. Arresting the crew on a trumped-up drug smuggling charge, they made off with a merchant codebook only to find that the army had broken the system earlier and that their uncoordinated effort now threatened to alert the Japanese. However, as there was 'no question that codebook acquisitions jump-started the Navy in the cryptanalytic business,' pinch operations were not going away any time soon, but they required that a more professional and secure approach be found and developed.[33]

Just weeks before the Japanese attack on Pearl Harbor, Donovan had led the charge for American 'commando-styled' operations. Two weeks earlier, he had presented Roosevelt with a one-page memorandum recommending 'that there be organized now, in the United States, a guerrilla corps, independent and separate from the Army and Navy, and imbued with the maximum spirit of the offensive. This force should, of course, be created along disciplined military lines, analogous to the British Commando principle.'[34] The brief piqued Roosevelt's interest and garnered his support for action.[35] Encouraged, Donovan reached out to both the US Marine Corps and the US Army for help. The Marine

Corps created the 1st Special Training Unit (later known as the Marine Raider Battalion) in February 'for the express purpose of securing clearer insight into the operations, training and methods of the British commando organization,' while the army followed, in mid-June 1942, with the creation of the US Rangers.[36]

The road was not yet smooth, however, and obstacles soon appeared. Over the preceding months, Donovan had drawn the ire of the service intelligence departments, and in particular of General George C. Marshall, the army chief of staff, who, next to FDR, was the most powerful man in wartime America. Never a fan of the audacious or the irregular, the coolly impersonal Marshall once said: 'You can sometimes win a great victory by a very dashing action ... But often, or most frequently, the very dashing action exposes you to a very fatal result if it is not successful. And you hazard everything in that way.'[37] J. Edgar Hoover also viewed the COI with suspicion, in part because of Donovan's close association with the British and his willingness to work with their Soviet ally, and also because of the lack of professionalism he perceived in the cadres of COI agents, who he alleged came from the ranks of socialites, toughs and Hollywood stuntmen.

By early 1942, the COI, despite the open purse strings, had yet to make the impact Roosevelt had expected, and jealous rivals within the American intelligence community quickly accused it of organizational impotence. Before long, these criticisms spilled over to Donovan himself, with allegations that he had ignored a direct presidential order by running agents in South America, a traditional FBI domain – not to mention a litany of rumours of adulterous indiscretions and other personal slights designed to damage his credibility.

Like Godfrey, as long as Wild Bill Donovan delivered the goods, he remained on solid ground, but by April 1942 Churchill had received alarming news through Major General Hastings Ismay, his liaison on the Chiefs of Staff Committee, that their much-celebrated man in Washington was in trouble, with his status under review at a high level.[38]

Part of the problem stemmed from Donovan himself. Godfrey reckoned (with some irony given the perception of him on his own JIC) that he was an empire builder who 'seemed, on occasion, to think of himself not as an intelligence officer at all but rather as one who should have supremacy over the Chiefs of Staff.' Compounding the problem, the very nature and source of Donovan's power – his personal influence with the president – roused other departments to battle against him. The State Department stood rigid upon protocol; the FBI developed a bitter antagonism; the Navy Department shunned him, while the head of Army intelligence openly referred to the COI as 'Bill Donovan's Circus.' In these circumstances, 'it is plainly necessary,' Godfrey recorded, for the British 'to consider the COI from a new angle.'[39] It had become 'clear' to Godfrey 'that, so far as pure intelligence was concerned, NID might have to rely more and more on a coordination of the American service Department with the State Department and the FBI, if this coordination could be attained, and less and less on Colonel Donovan's COI.'[40]

By the middle of 1942, as the shipping crisis continued unabated, faith that COI would emerge as a first-class intelligence organization waned. 'Still it remained valuable, as it always has been, on the level of high politics,' Godfrey wrote, for 'the link through Colonel Donovan with the president had been of utmost value checkmating the Registration Bill, inspired by the State Department and sponsored by anti-British interests, which, while professedly aimed against enemy intelligence, could have been used equally to shut down British intelligence.'[41] In this realm, Donovan had 'safeguarded us here,' Godfrey confessed. 'Big Bill' could still be relied upon as a 'valuable ally in the future,' but the DNI preferred to keep 'both pots boiling' and cosy up to the services. Quickly, Godfrey dispatched liaison officers to confer with both the US Army and Navy on ISTD and SIGINT issues, as 'in the important realm of special intelligence (ULTRA),' he wrote, 'much remained to be done.'[42]

They had spent years cultivating Donovan as a prime asset in their delicate relationship with American intelligence and a direct back channel to the president. With so much invested, they had to support any feasible effort they could to legitimize and enhance Donovan's status and influence – and by extension their own.[43] The problem was apparent: if they could not reinforce Donovan's organization, now rechristened the Office of Strategic Services (OSS), all the hard work that Godfrey, Fleming and to a lesser extent Mountbatten had invested in the relationship would be for naught.

Part of increasing the profile of Donovan, COI and the Anglo-American Intelligence cooperative was to bring the US Navy into the fold to a limited degree when it came to Ultra at the apex of the *annus mirabilis* in the summer of 1941.[44] Out of this came an intelligence-sharing agreement whereby the British would concentrate their efforts on European codes and ciphers with the Americans dedicating their time to Japanese codes in the Pacific.

Fundamental to keeping this relationship well-oiled was to maintain the British supply of Ultra concerning U-boats flowing to the Americans, which it did without fail until British resources ran dry with the introduction of the four-rotor naval Enigma on February 1. Once this occurred and sinkings of American merchant vessels soared, the US Office of Naval Intelligence began to pressure the British to uphold their end of the agreement. First, the Americans reiterated a request for a captured naval Enigma machine for research purposes; but handing over a three-rotor machine would not help alleviate the losses off American shores and would reveal to the Americans – who for the moment were still in the dark about the introduction of the four-rotor – Bletchley's current impotent position. Fearing that such an admission would, in turn, encourage the Americans to unilaterally seek their own solution, the British chose to foot-drag at first, no doubt hoping that Operation Myrmidon at Bayonne or Operation Chariot at St Nazaire would restore the flow of naval Ultra and satisfy the Americans. Alas, both failed to strike gold and the British shifted gears, eventually admitting they were in trouble when it came to naval Ultra and extending an offer of cooperation in this field. With that, they fully expected to retain the lead in a burgeoning cooperative arrangement with US naval intelligence by introducing them to British pinch policy, now firmly affixed within Mountbatten's brand of combined operations.

With Rutter now in the detailed planning stages, Mountbatten extended the invitation to a small and select group of US Marines, who, as Donovan suggested, would train with the Royal Marine Commando and prepare to ride into battle with Tiger Force on HMS *Locust*. Given all the complexities over the sharing of intelligence between the two countries, what better way to deliver the pinched material than through a commando-style pinch operation involving the Americans?

Simultaneously, the British could narrow the gulf between the two sides on the cryptographic issue yet maintain their dominance in the field, display the work of the new IAU and their pinch doctrine underscored by the work of the ISTD, and pump up the vulnerable Donovan at the same time. If they could solve these pressing concerns, they would score hefty political points for all concerned. From every angle, it seemed a devilishly clever plan.

So, on June 20, a special contingent of three US Marines led by Captain Roy T. Batterton Jr, a former assistant naval attaché, was plucked from the second week of their seven-week training programme with the commandos in Scotland and inserted into Tiger Force – to train specifically with the Royal Marines on *Locust*. Although there is no indication of their attachment to No. 10 Platoon, given what is now known from their operational orders about the mission of the Royal Marines, the Americans would have been involved in some capacity. In addition, plans were made for Marine Corps colonel Franklin A. Hart, who had been attached to Mountbatten's command since the autumn of 1941 and was actively engaged in the planning of the raid, to join Commander Ian Fleming and a few other 'guests' on board one of the headquarters ships offshore to monitor the *Locust*'s role in both Operation Rutter and its remount Operation Jubilee.[45] A memo from Frank Birch at the Naval Section sheds more light on their role, for on August 1, an American liaison officer had approached Bletchley and revealed that they had been 'organizing a special pinch team' of their own and 'would welcome our experiences on this subject.'[46]

৽

In addition to the delicate situation with the Americans, the potential spread of the four-rotor Enigma machine and the deepening crisis at sea were preoccupations in the weeks leading up to Operation Rutter. By early June, in addition to learning earlier that ships in the Channel and in Norway carried the four-rotor, the British discovered that U-boat ciphers encrypted on the four-rotor naval Enigma had been introduced in the Mediterranean which threatened to complicate the crucial re-supply of Malta and Egypt, but also cast a shadow over plans for the coming invasion of North Africa that autumn. Then, as the Operation

Rutter forces sat in southern English ports waiting to launch the post-poned raid on Dieppe, another series of events shed dramatic light on the problem. It happened 800 miles to the north, not far from the Lofoten Islands, where the North Sea meets the Arctic Ocean.

One of the few ways Great Britain could provide material and political assistance to the Soviet Union in its intense struggle against Nazi Germany was by running a series of giant supply convoys through the North Sea and into the Arctic Ocean past Norway en route to the Soviet ports of Murmansk and Archangel. For over a year, these convoys had been viewed, politically at least, as essential in keeping the tenuous link with Stalin alive.

On June 27, PQ-17, the largest and most expensive convoy to date, left Iceland for its voyage to Murmansk. Comprising 33 cargo ships and one tanker, the convoy was escorted by destroyers, with a group of British and American cruisers shadowing her miles behind. Before it could reach the Soviet ports, the convoy would have to run great risks, successfully avoiding attacks by German aircraft, U-boats and large surface vessels such as the battlecruisers *Admiral Scheer*, *Lützow* and *Admiral Hipper* and the Bismarck's sister, the super-battleship *Tirpitz*. The First Sea Lord, Admiral Dudley Pound, never a fan of these political convoys, complained loudly to his American counterpart Admiral Ernest King that they were a 'millstone round our necks,' citing the 'steady attrition in both cruisers and destroyers' as one of many drawbacks in what he considered a 'most unsound operation with the dice loaded against us in every direction.'[47] King agreed, and although sympathetic, warned that 'we can only expect loud, violent repercussions on the political level originating, of course, in Russia itself' should they cease for any reason.[48] Faced with this conundrum, Pound faithfully executed his orders but chose the most conservative approach so as not to unduly risk the capital ships of Home Fleet whose loss would unhinge the delicate balance of power in the war at sea.[49]

Until this moment, Pound and the Royal Navy had effectively used the intelligence drawn from Bletchley's ability to tap into the three-rotor Enigma cipher for home waters and Norwegian message traffic. The near crystal-clear picture of any preparations to attack the convoys provided by Ultra had paved the way for insight into the actions of

Tirpitz in the same fashion that the Admiralty had harnessed SIGINT in the hunt for the *Bismarck*. In March, Bletchley Park had intercepted a series of messages that confirmed the Kriegsmarine's focus on destroying the convoys as a top priority, followed by the movement of additional aircraft, U-boats and heavy ships to Norway. They also had deciphered Dönitz's message to his submarine captains: 'The task for U-Boats is to prejudice the delivery of supplies to Murmansk. Sink everything that comes within range of your torpedo tubes; head other U-Boats on to the convoys. Your own attack should have a preference but act according to the situation. The employment of our own naval surface forces or air forces is intended should the opportunity arise.'[50]

As such, Pound had carefully choreographed the response of the Home Fleet to avoid contact when the *Tirpitz* made her first sortie from her Norwegian lair against PQ-12 in March and with the other convoys that followed.[51] In this case, Ultra proved decisive, and as Godfrey recorded: 'Admiral Pound ... was always fully conscious of the value of intelligence and once remarked to me that thanks to High-Grade intelligence (ULTRA) he would achieve the reputation of becoming the greatest sea strategist in the history of the navy.'[52] Despite the hyperbole, Godfrey remained sober in his assessment of Pound, who, in the DNI's opinion, had 'developed a flair for cover plans by which high-grade intelligence could be used without jeopardizing the source. Less patient men or one who had not the capacity or the time to listen ... would not have realized this novel responsibility or have been able to achieve it. It is a rare kind of wisdom, combined with restraint, watchfulness and discriminating memory, which does not come naturally to some naval officers.'[53]

Without air support to cover the convoy, and Pound hesitant to needlessly risk his battleships or cruisers, the Royal Navy had little choice but to place their faith in Ultra and signals intelligence to give warning of German movements and positions. Pound, who wielded final authority over PQ-17, knew long before the convoy sailed that the movements of large surface vessels such as the *Tirpitz* faced the handicap of an acute oil shortage plaguing the Kriegsmarine in Norway, but also knew that despite this handicap, the Kriegsmarine was intent on smashing the convoy. If, and when, contact occurred, Pound had but few options. If enemy aircraft and U-boats came on the scene, the best course of action would be to maintain the integrity of the convoy with its destroyer escort; if the *Tirpitz* or any of the other surface raiders appeared, it would be best practice to order the ships in convoy to scatter to avoid destruction by the large naval guns of the behemoths. Once apart, however, each vessel faced certain death from roving aircraft and U-boats. Either way, Pound knew there could be heavy losses, but at the very least, he would use Ultra to keep the capital ships from Home Fleet out of harm's way. It would be the lesser of all evils.[54]

On the night of July 4, when it appeared that *Tirpitz* had sortied from her Norwegian lair to intercept the convoy, Pound issued the highly controversial order for the convoy to scatter and for the merchant ships to try to reach the Soviet ports on their own. The result was a slaughter, and in Churchill's understated words, 'one of the most melancholy of naval episodes in the whole of the war.'[55] Only eleven of the 34 ships that left Iceland on June 27 managed to reach the Soviet Union by July 8, with the rest picked off one by one by aircraft and U-boats. More than 130,000 of the original 200,000 tons of valuable cargo was lost (430 tanks and 210 bombers, as well as 3,350 vehicles and almost 100,000 tons of ammunition), along with the lives of 153 merchant sailors.[56]

For decades, Pound's fateful decision appeared rash and defied explanation. Part of the criticism stemmed from the lack of crucial evidence linking the ever-expanding four-rotor crisis to the convoy's demise. So long as Pound could read almost every move by the Kriegsmarine in Norway and its adjacent waters, he maintained a fragile threshold of confidence that he could judiciously react to any sortie by Tirpitz – until Harry Hinsley, working overtime at the Naval Section on the overnight shift, discovered an ominous and disturbing wireless traffic pattern.

Early on the morning of July 4 – twenty hours before Pound made his decision – news broke through an upswing in wireless chatter that the *Tirpitz* might be readying to go to sea. Expecting as they did with *Bismarck* to tap into message traffic to and from *Tirpitz*, first Bletchley and then Pound were shaken to their core when suddenly all intercepted messages defied every attempt at decryption and atmospheric conditions in the Arctic rendered other sources of SIGINT near impotent.[57] Without clear insight as to her intent and without the usual means for confirmation which Naval Section and the Admiralty had relied upon for over a year, Pound held his breath, hoping the fog of war would clear via Ultra yet again. Within a few hours, his worst fears were confirmed when Hinsley announced that 'special settings' called *Neptune*, using 'specially cyphered traffic' between the German Admiralty and the Commander-in-Chief of the fleet on *Tirpitz*, had gone into effect using the four-rotor machine.[58] Stymied, all Bletchley Park could do was warn the Admiralty that this 'confirms the conjecture that a special cypher is now in force' and that from this point onwards, message traffic was now 'undecodable.'[59]

As with most commanders, and particularly the ageing Pound, who were not 'greatly interested in conjectures from the behaviour of the traffic, when the content of the signals would be known to them in a few hours time,' the hard evidence now stared the First Sea Lord directly in the face. The dearth of intelligence concerning the intentions of *Tirpitz* was not a temporary difficulty, easily remedied by other means or by further cryptographic action by the boffins at Bletchley but, for the foreseeable future, a permanent condition.[60]

Whether this information prompted him to make his decision to scatter the PQ-17 convoy or whether it merely reinforced in dramatic fashion his preconceived desire to do so remains open for debate. What it does show, however, is that, from an intelligence perspective, the four-rotor crisis was not abating but instead escalating at an alarming rate, making a revived raid on Dieppe even more crucial.

౿

There is nothing in the Dieppe story more controversial than the allegations brought against Lord Louis Mountbatten that he circumvented the proper chain of command to remount Operation Rutter after its cancellation in early July 1942. Historian Brian Villa rightly points out in his seminal 1989 work *Unauthorized Action* that no trace of a signed operational order for the remount has ever come to light – and so it continues to be.[61] However, Villa and the other Dieppe historians who attempted to tackle this issue were thwarted by the lack of access to crucial documents that remained classified when they were penning their works. With the recent releases that reveal the pinch imperative driving the raid, Mountbatten's seemingly spurious claim that he 'received special instructions from the Chiefs of Staff that only certain individuals were to be informed of the intention to re-mount the operation' can no longer be easily dismissed.[62] Initially viewed as a conspiracy, they appear legitimate now that the security instructions for Ultra Secret operations, technologies, methods and sources, in play for decades following the war, have been revealed. With the veil of secrecy now drawn aside, it is a more straightforward exercise to connect the historical dots.[63]

On July 8, after a series of postponements due to the inclement weather and much to everyone's disappointment, Admiral James, Commander-in-Chief, Portsmouth, issued the order to cancel Operation Rutter. A day later, King George VI noted in his diary: 'Dickie gave me the latest news of the COS conversation ... he is rearranging Rutter under another name for the end of August.'[64] On July 14, less than a week after the 'cancellation,' Mountbatten summoned all the lead planners from the Canadian Army and the RAF to his headquarters, where they were told that Operation Jubilee had replaced Rutter.[65] Two days later, on July 16, a month and three days shy of the Dieppe Raid's new incarnation as Operation Jubilee, Mountbatten and Major General Ham Roberts paid a visit to the headquarters of General Andrew McNaughton, the Canadian Army commander, to discuss something McNaughton mysteriously referred to at the time as 'Operation J_____.'[66] During this discussion, Mountbatten revealed that only a select few knew of the remount* and that both he and the chiefs of staff were concerned that comments made by Canadian prime

---

* This inner circle included General Sir Alan Brooke, Air Chief Marshal Sir Charles Portal and Admiral Sir Dudley Pound from the Chiefs of Staff Committee; General Hastings Ismay, their liaison to Churchill; Generals Bernard Paget and Bernard Law Montgomery, and their Canadian subordinates Andrew McNaughton, Harry Crerar and Ham Roberts along with his senior staff officers; Air Vice-Marshal Sir William Sholto Douglas and Air Vice-Marshal Trafford Leigh-Mallory from the RAF; and, among Mountbatten's own staff, Captain Jock Hughes-Hallett, assisted by Marquis 'Bobby' de Casa Maury, his intelligence officer.

minister William Lyon Mackenzie King in parliament on Dominion Day, July 1, had compromised the security of Rutter and as a result, they had requested that 'no information concerning Operation J_____ be sent to Canada.'[67] According to Hughes-Hallett, four days after this exchange, the chiefs of staff approved the revival of the operation 'by inference' without mentioning target or code name but instead authorizing 'the next-large-scale raid.'[68]

None of the files from that period, however, mention either John Godfrey or Ian Fleming in the report, but they were not left out of the loop.[69] A recently declassified Ultra Secret history of Naval Intelligence Division shows clearly that John Godfrey and, by extension, his personal assistant Ian Fleming were part of this tight group and knew about these clandestine plans to remount.[70] In the opinion of the unnamed author of this history, the silence was but 'an example of [the] extravagant security' for the whole operation.[71] At a routine daily meeting of the NID on August 14, a request from Mountbatten's headquarters for an intelligence work-up for 'Operation Jubilee' crossed the desk of one of Godfrey's staff officers who had never heard of an operation with that name, let alone been informed of its nature, the date or the target. Soon, however, he discovered that Godfrey had been 'told verbally of Jubilee' and admitted to having 'some vague knowledge of it' but that 'the rest of NID had been denied all official knowledge of the plan.'[72] Why would Mountbatten invoke such extraordinary measures to indicate that the Dieppe Raid was an improper or unauthorized action? The answer appears to lie in the primordial importance of surprise in pinch operations, Mountbatten's love of the double bluff to achieve this end, and his paranoia of spies on the Isle of Wight, the central training ground for the raiding force.

Just before the St Nazaire operation back in March, Mountbatten had chosen to employ the double bluff as a means of achieving surprise, informing the Chiefs of Staff Committee that, if the raid did not come off on the date planned, he would remount it as soon as conditions permitted for the Germans would never expect an assault on the same place once the cat was out of the bag. It was a controversial idea that raised eyebrows, but it became central to Mountbatten's standard cloak-and-dagger playbook, particularly with a pinch imperative at stake.

Although critics believed it would never achieve sanction, the evidence for Dieppe refutes that contention and shows that the remounted raid retained much more continuity with its original conception than previously thought.[73]

First, Mountbatten did not dismiss his force commanders and their staffs following the 'cancellation' of Operation Rutter, with the exception of the prickly Rear Admiral Tom Baillie-Grohman, but instead put them on alert for the remount. On July 17, the day after he met with McNaughton to discuss Operation J_____, the Combined Operations chief proposed the following entry to be included in the chiefs of staff minutes for a discussion that apparently had taken place some time between July 8 and that day:

> The Chief of Combined Operations was directed to mount an emergency operation to be carried out during August to replace Operation Rutter. It was agreed that this task should be carried out in conjunction with the military and air force commanders of Rutter and that, so far as possible, the same forces should be employed in order to cut down the time required for training. In view of the new appointments of the Naval Commander for Rutter and the dispersal of some of his naval staff, and in view of the short time available, Lord Louis Mountbatten agreed to furnish a naval staff for Operation Jubilee from the Naval Planning Section of COHQ to work in conjunction with the Commander-in-Chief, Portsmouth's staff ... They decided that the executive responsibility for the mounting and launching of the Operation will be vested in the Chief of Combined Operations working through the normal Service channels.[74]

Just over two weeks later, at the offices of the Political Warfare Executive in Woburn Abbey north of London, Peter Murphy was apprised of Operation J_____ on August 6 but not told that it was a remount. Reviewing the dossier, he expressed his concern that this 'new' plan appeared in form to be a scaled-back version of Rutter but drew the conclusion that 'Rutter and J_____, [were] not the same place.' For Murphy, hitting the same target after 'cancellation' made no sense, and he warned that the short time frame given between receipt of the plan and its launch (just ten days in his estimation) was 'too short in which a general strategic picture ... could be built-up [to] include Combined Operations raids.'[75] He then went on to further press his argument: 'It is doubtful if this one raid would lend itself sufficiently well to our purpose since it could only be treated from a new angle by making a sudden and obvious break with our angle adopted heretofore.'[76]

Harry Hinsley, who went on to chair Bletchley Park's 'pinch committee' and participate in the high-level intelligence-sharing negotiations with Canada and the US, would, after the war, become the highly respected author of the official history of British intelligence. In his seminal volume on operational intelligence published in 1981 (after the first revelation of Ultra but long before the massive release of material used in this study), he noted that on August 12, the chiefs of staff had indeed sanctioned Jubilee in a closed-door session, yet his evidence does not draw a direct line to any explicit statement in that regard.[77] This notation in the official record is still highly disputed but would appear to marry up with the Ultra Secret Security protocols. But perhaps there is no better confirmation of the continuity between the plans than that, on the night of August 18, just as Jubilee got under way, General Andrew McNaughton sent a cable to the Department of National Defence headquarters in Ottawa referencing his earlier message of July 9 – the day after Rutter II was cancelled – that informed Lieutenant General Kenneth Stuart, Chief of the General Staff (Canada), that the 'special matter of which I advised you [is] now underway.'[78]

Clearly, the continuity in the evidence demonstrates that the remount was preordained rather than an 'unauthorized action' as some critics have claimed. Perhaps more accurately, Mountbatten's machinations are indicative of a fully sanctioned 'unorthodox action,' which makes perfect sense given the desperate context of the time and the rampant 'Boy's Own' attitude of his 'inexperienced enthusiasts' at COHQ. Given that surprise formed the prime element for a successful pinch, it is more than conceivable, given what we now know, that security demands necessitated working outside the traditional channels, something the highly ambitious Mountbatten embraced with open arms.

By mid-1942 – certainly, after St Nazaire – it was widely understood that the Germans expected an upswing in raids along the French coast, particularly over the summer period at the tail end of the 'raiding season,' when environmental conditions lent themselves readily to amphibious operations. But with an information weapons system like Ultra, the British knew of the constant strengthening of their coastal defences, and that they maintained regular high alerts during times when tidal and wind conditions permitted landings. Although the Allies could not hope to surprise the Germans on the strategic level, there was nothing to prevent them from achieving tactical surprise. If the planners and the force commanders played their cards right, and secrecy was maintained in almost hermetic fashion, there was no reason, certainly in Mountbatten's mind, why they couldn't pull off a successful pinch raid.

What Mountbatten counted on above all was that after the 'cancellation' of Rutter, German intelligence would discard or downgrade Dieppe as a potential target: remounting a raid on the same target was hardly a textbook operation of war and something only a fool would try. Relying on the conventional to blind his enemy to the unconventional, Mountbatten reiterated the need for naval and air diversions (willingly supplied by both the RAF and the Royal Navy) off Boulogne to distract the Germans while the raiding force struck out undetected across the Channel in the darkness for Dieppe.

The ace up Mountbatten's sleeve in the run-up to Operation Jubilee, and of course on the day itself, was Ultra as for the time being, shore facilities and local traffic in the Channel area still used the three-rotor settings while the distribution of the new four-rotor device and its ancillary materials continued. For the moment, Bletchley Park could still read the message traffic in the Channel area, so Mountbatten and his staff could monitor German actions, inactions and reactions on any movement on land, on the sea and in the air to ensure that surprise held. With Ultra came the ability to keep an eye on the dispositions of aircraft, infantry, artillery, E-boats and even U-boats. It also provided insight into any buildup of specialized equipment, extra stores, ammunition or defensive works in the target area that might suggest compromise or interfere with the projected raid, including German convoys that routinely ran up and down the French coast and used Dieppe as a waypoint and for refuelling and resupply.

Somewhat ironically, perhaps, the entire concept of the double bluff might never have made it off the drawing board without Ultra; otherwise, it was just too risky. Yet, through these means, the OIC, NID and Godfrey, along with the planners and the force commanders, could keep tabs on any movements or developments by the enemy in the weeks and days leading up to the raid and, of course, on that one day in August as well. On August 5, Godfrey sent Mountbatten confirmation couched in language traditionally used to cover adept SIGINT analysis: 'An agent whose information is graded A0 reports that rumours were circulating to the effect that from the 18th July onwards the British are to attempt large scale landings over a wide stretch of the North coast of France, but that the German authorities are inclined to discount these rumours.'[79]

To further increase security, enhance the chances of attaining the objectives by surprise, and ensure that neither climactic nor bureaucratic forces would derail the raid, Mountbatten removed all non-essential elements that might attract the attention of German intelligence or tie up planning and lead to compromise or cancellation.[80] Knowing that resentment towards COHQ flourished at the service ministries and among the chiefs of staff, Mountbatten swapped the airborne element called for in Rutter for two veteran commando units that played lead roles in the pinch raids at Lofoten and Vaagso. Instead of running the risk of cancellation due to a stiff breeze that would scrub the airborne drops, he chose instead to land both commando units by boat on the outer flanks of the landing area to silence a pair of Kriegsmarine coastal batteries, giving the raiding force the unfettered ability to operate off the coast of Dieppe.[81] By so doing, he not only removed the need for the near-perfect weather conditions required for delicate airborne operations, but avoided the perils of bargaining for assets not directly under his control. This change in the plan also helped to maintain the vital element of surprise, by eliminating waves of troop-carrying aircraft that would light up German radar and ground defences. Their addition gave Mountbatten wider 'pinch' coverage for these two units were experienced in scrounging for anything that looked promising, and with the coastal batteries under Kriegsmarine control, there was always the possibility that they too could strike gold.*

Yet another threat Mountbatten had to consider were the daily runs, weather permitting, of German reconnaissance aircraft over the south coast of England. These flights had discovered the Rutter forces marshalling for the raid in early July, leading to the subsequent German air raid that hit two of the ships. Now, instead of concentrating the strike force in a few select ports as before, Mountbatten spread it out among many ports throughout southern England. He even disguised the troopships as coastal convoy vessels, given that they had to embark in daylight to make their rendezvous in mid-Channel, and eliminated from the raiding force any non-essential vessels that did not traditionally ply those waters.

Although it has since been posited that Pound refused to risk his capital ships in the tight confines of the Channel due to the presence of the Luftwaffe, there is no evidence that cruisers or battleships were either officially requested or promised and then stripped from the Dieppe Raid. More than likely, given the existing pinch policy, which called for suppressive rather than destructive firepower, their sudden presence would no doubt raise the alarm at the highest levels along the German-held coast of France. This, in turn, would rob the raiding force of the element of surprise and provoke a significant and no doubt spirited response from the Luftwaffe and the Kriegsmarine.

The same also applied to vessels such as tugs, drifters and Eagle ships initially assigned to Ryder's Cutting Out Force to tow the captured barges out of the port during Rutter. Normally the tugs and drifters were occupied with duties other than raiding, so their inclusion in any task force would alert German intelligence to the impending action. So Mountbatten stripped them too from Jubilee.[82] Similarly, the primary role of the Eagle ships was anti-aircraft protection in the Thames estuary, and any move from their usual operating area was

---

* Another example of the extravagant security was the fact that each of these units was given its own mission with its own code name, and neither one seems to have known that it was taking part in a larger operation called Jubilee aimed at Dieppe. No. 3 Commando's operation was code-named Flodden, while No. 4 Commando's was Cauldron.

bound to draw German interest. Mountbatten knew that if he left them in place during Operation Jubilee, they would create a false sense of 'business as usual.' To replace the extra firepower these ships would have provided, HMS *Alresford*, a lumbering First World War-vintage minesweeper, joined the French *chasseurs* in Robert Force for the Dieppe Raid.[83]

The corollary effect of Mountbatten's continued 'fat-trimming' changes for Jubilee was to underscore the primary role of the pinch. No longer were the Royal Marines concerned with towing back the mass collection of German barges, as had been called for in the first incarnation of Rutter. For Jubilee, this was abandoned, and the Royal Marines were tasked with capturing them now only as a contingency and told either to 'hot wire' the vessels and sail them back to England on their own *if* the situation presented itself or sink them as Ryder had initially suggested. In addition, the planned attack on the airfield and on German army headquarters was downgraded from definite to contingent. In short, the only significant objective from Rutter that remained firm for Jubilee was the pinch operation to be carried out by part of the Canadian raiding force and the entire Royal Marine Commando, with Fleming's IAU in the starring role.

Yet with this accomplished and the raid set to go, doubts still reigned among those not fully indoctrinated into the Ultra Secret core of the raid, as well as those in the know. Peter Murphy openly questioned the operation to his boss at PWE, arguing that the channel was 'heavily mined ... the approaches on land well-defended, and that the landing itself will be a difficult matter.'[84] When he asked Mountbatten's lead planner, Colonel Robert Neville who helped Fleming with the formation of the IAU, what he thought the chances were of 100 per cent success, the Royal Marine answered coldly: 'If we <u>get</u> there all right, and manage to land successfully, I can promise you that we shall have a complete success.'[85] Reeling from the less than reassuring answer, Murphy pressed Neville and another staff officer about the increasingly risky nature of the operation: 'I surmised and got the strong impression ... that this operation is considered very critical from the point of view of the CCO's personal career <u>and</u>, of course, all that implies in the successful prosecution of the war. If he brings

<u>this</u> off, they seemed to say, he is on top of the world and will be given complete control.'[86]

⤳

'A visit to the Ogre in his den' was how Winston Churchill's wife, Clementine, described her husband's impending visit to Moscow that began on August 12, 1942, for the first face-to-face meeting between the British prime minister and the Soviet leader, Joseph Stalin.[87] Long known for his anti-Communist stance, Churchill had been forced, after the German invasion of the Soviet Union a year earlier, to embrace 'Uncle Joe' as an ally of convenience and necessity in the fight against Nazi Germany. The urgent trip stemmed from Stalin's overt displeasure over two pressing items that appeared to threaten the fragile alliance: first and foremost, the suspension of the supply convoys following the PQ-17 disaster; and second, the oft-cited question of a 'second front' needed to alleviate the pressure on the Soviets from the German summer offensive currently cutting a swath towards Stalingrad.

For decades, Dieppe scholars have viewed the opening of a 'second front' in 1942 as the driving force behind the inception and remounting of the raid. Certainly, a cursory examination of the files gives that impression. When Stalin summoned Churchill to Moscow following the suspension of the Russian convoys, and the Allied decision to suspend Sledgehammer and open the second front in North Africa rather than France or Southern Europe, the second front indeed appears to have been the focus of his angst.

However, a detailed review of the existing evidence, coupled with material released over the last decade, does not support this long-offered contention as a fundamental driver for the remounting of the raid and, in fact, drastically reshapes the context in which we understand Dieppe.

At the same time that the planning syndicate began to lay down the outline for Rutter in late March, Combined Operations and the chiefs of staff already had two 'large-scale' raids under consideration for the summer of 1942 explicitly designed to aid the Soviets.[88] The first, Operation Sledgehammer, pushed vigorously by both the Soviets and the Americans, called for an amphibious force comprising eight divisions to land on the Cherbourg peninsula in Normandy in mid-July, where they would defend the lodgement for several weeks and possibly months, drawing German air and land reinforcements away from the eastern front, and wearing them down in a costly attritional struggle. The second, known as Operation Imperator, called for a 'large-scale raid on the continent' in August, but, unlike Sledgehammer, this raid was limited in both time and scope, and would not exceed several days or weeks. The intent behind Imperator was straightforward: 'bring about air operations under conditions advantageous to ourselves, to destroy the maximum number of aircraft,' depending upon which of three bold and bloody options the planners chose to implement.[89] Their first option called for a sizeable amphibious and airborne raid on St Omer comprising a force of two infantry divisions, supported by an armoured brigade, a parachute brigade, two tank battalions and a support battalion, along with anti-aircraft and field artillery. The second called for the capture of the large port city of Boulogne in a corps-size operation that included two infantry and one armoured division. The third and smallest, boldest and most suicidal was a plan to land a force of one motorized division supported by 60 tanks at the mouth of the river Somme near Cayeux with orders to rush to Paris, muck about, and return three or four days later to Dieppe for evacuation.[90] Each of these options for Imperator (and Sledgehammer for that matter) made the desperate actions at St Nazaire and Bayonne look rational in comparison and Rutter downright conservative.

None of the Combined Commanders, including Mountbatten, felt that either operation made much sense from a military or naval perspective. With its plan to take out 60 Luftwaffe fighters a month right from its inception in late March, Imperator drew fire from the Combined Commanders who cautioned that they would need a series of raids in the Calais area to produce these numbers, as a 'single raid will not achieve this object.'[91] By late May, their opinion had not changed. 'It is realized,' they noted, 'that none of the above projects can be classified as operations of war,' but were instead 'merely methods of achieving a political object.' Pessimistic about their chances of success, they advised the chiefs of staff that 'every effort should be made to avoid embarking on an operation which the enemy can make appear as a total defeat.'[92]

In the first week of June, Churchill learned that the planners had narrowed down their options and decided upon a raid at the mouth of the Somme that would last '2–3 days.'[93] The choice of the Cayeux area came as a compromise; originally the planners had hoped to land around Boulogne as it was the most advantageous point for fighter operations in the Channel. One quick look at the formidable beach defences around the port forced their hand, as did their requirements for the primary purpose of the raid – to draw the Luftwaffe into a fight. To ensure that the raid came well within their 'effective fighter umbrella,' they decided to adopt Cayeux for its location at the extreme southern outer marker of air cover – some 55 kilometres north of Dieppe.[94] Although they gave due consideration to a rush to Paris, cooler heads prevailed when the chairman of the chiefs of staff, General Alanbrooke, stepped in and forced the planners to scale the raid back. Instead of pushing far inland, the new plan called for more modest targets in and around the 'aerodromes and other "vulnerable locations" in the Cayeux area before what was left of the raiding force would re-embark from the same bridgehead' a few days later.[95] Satisfied with the changes, the COS duly signed off on the plan, setting D-Day for Imperator during the same tidal window in August (the 18th to the 26th) eventually selected for Dieppe.[96]

Although discussions and preparations concerning these contentious operations continued throughout May, neither received resounding support from the prime minister nor the chiefs of staff despite American and Soviet pressure. In the interim, Churchill had begun to push hard for his own 'wildcat operation' in the Arctic regions of Norway known as Operation Jupiter, and when he received the scaled-back proposal for Imperator from the chiefs of staff, he did not welcome it with open arms. Understanding that the COS had planned the operation on the premise that 'if things go bad on the Russian Front in the summer,' Imperator was to be 'the only operation' they could mount 'to aid the Soviets' and indeed, would form Britain's 'response to a "cri du Coeur" from Russia.' Unimpressed, Churchill added: 'Certainly it would not help Russia if we launched such an enterprise, no doubt with world publicity, and came out a few days later with heavy losses. We would have thrown away valuable lives and material and made ourselves and our capacity for making war ridiculous throughout the world.'[97]

When Churchill addressed the War Cabinet near noon on June 11, he underscored his talk with a set of guiding principles for British strategy concerning Russia – 'No Substantial landing in France in 1942 unless we are going to stay' and 'No substantial Landing in France unless the Germans are demoralized by failure against Russia.' He then laid out a reworked raiding programme for the summer and early autumn with Rutter, which he described as a 'Butcher and Bolt Raid' of about '24 hours duration employing some 6–7,000 men' set for mid-June. The controversial Operation Imperator, which had been 'planned as a large-scale raid to follow Rutter,' had for the moment been cancelled, with the launch of the 'on again-off again' Sledgehammer now pushed back to the late summer or early autumn but only 'if conditions proved advantageous' and 'German morale [had] started to crack.'[98] On that matter, Churchill assured his ministers that he 'had not committed us in any way' during his talks with the Soviets and that these conditions had been 'clearly explained to and understood by them,' for the last thing he wanted should Russia find herself in dire straits would be 'a nasty cropper of our own.'[99]

Churchill had, quite sensibly, steadfastly refused to yield to either American or Soviet pressure for action, and handed Vyacheslav Molotov (the Soviet foreign minister in London for discussions) a carefully crafted aide-memoire laying out western Allied strategy for the coming months that echoed and amplified his discussions with the COS. Off the top, he pledged to continue running the supply convoys to 'the best of our ability' but assured the Soviets that the RAF, with the help of the USAF, would pound German cities and industry from the skies while the Eighth Army would push Axis forces out of North Africa. To help pin down the 33 German divisions currently stationed in the west, Churchill hoped to launch a series of raids on an increasing scale throughout the summer and reiterated that he would only launch Sledgehammer if conditions allowed. As he explained, 'it would not further the Russian cause nor that of the Allies as a whole if, for the sake of action at any price, we embarked upon some operations which ended in disaster.'[100] To offset Soviet or public dismay, the British prime minister reiterated his earlier promise to commit 1 million men to the opening of a second front in Europe in 1943.[101]

By the last week of July, however, fortunes had changed as the German summer offensive had succeeded to a greater degree than originally expected, with Army Group South now poised to cut off Soviet oil resources south of Stalingrad. In the desert, Rommel's Afrika Korps had regained the upper hand by seizing Tobruk and chasing the British Eighth Army into Egypt, which spurred another no-confidence motion in Parliament – the second in just six months. Soon, the supply convoys would come to a halt due to the introduction of the four-rotor Enigma on *Tirpitz* just as sinkings of Allied merchant vessels hit an all-time high with 250 vessels, amounting to 1.1 million tons of crucial shipping, lost to Dönitz's U-boats in just June and July alone. The only bright spot in this dismal vista came with the highly successful British amphibious invasion of Madagascar (Operation Ironclad), planned and carried out by COHQ in May, that provided Mountbatten's command with genuine 'lessons learned' that they carried forward into the invasions of Sicily, Italy and Normandy later in the war and of course Operation Torch – set to hit North African shores later that autumn.[102]

For the most part, relations with the Soviets had held along the lines laid out in the aide-memoire, with no major uproar about the second front question until after the suspension of the Arctic convoys. Immediately following Churchill's July 18 note to Stalin announcing his decision to suspend deliveries, the Soviet leader sent a tersely worded message that tackled the convoy issue head-on:

> According to our naval experts, the arguments of British naval experts on the necessity of stopping delivery of war supplies to the northern harbours of the USSR are untenable. They are convinced that, given goodwill and readiness to honour obligations, steady deliveries could be effected with heavy loss to the Germans ... Of course, I do not think steady deliveries to northern Soviet ports are possible without risk or loss. But then no major task can be carried out in wartime without risk or losses ... I never imagined that the British Government would deny us delivery of war materials precisely now when the Soviet Union is badly in need of them in view of the grave situation on the Soviet-German front.[103]

With that out of the way, only then did Stalin turn his guns to the second-front issue: 'I fear the matter is taking an improper turn. In view of the situation on the Soviet-German front, I state most emphatically that the Soviet Government cannot tolerate the second front in Europe being postponed till 1943.'[104]

Despite the increasing pressure from Stalin, which Churchill and his ministers initially took as 'venting,' Churchill, supported by his War Cabinet, refused to budge on the course of action laid down in June but did agree to resume the convoys in September once climatic conditions permitted more wiggle room for the Home Fleet and a somewhat safer routing.

This juncture was the one moment where the Western Allies could have offered to placate the Russians with some form of substantial offensive action, but on the following day, both British and American chiefs of staff (in London for talks) dug in their heels and chose to cancel Sledgehammer as a scheduled action in favour of Torch, which by default pushed landings in Europe proper back to 1943.[105] As a contingency to placate Soviet angst or adapt to a fluid strategic situation on the eastern front, they pledged to keep Sledgehammer on the books for 'deception purposes' or should 'any emergencies or a favourable opportunity' arise. Sensing a sacrificial offering may be required, they also agreed to revive Imperator and rechristened it as 'Wetbob' which would, 'if urgent political considerations made it necessary, be carried out regardless of the state of German morale.'[106] Once again, the Dieppe Raid was never mentioned at all, let alone in the context of direct support or sacrifice for Stalin in the conventional sense.

In response to this less than encouraging news, Stalin summoned Churchill to meet him in Moscow 'for joint consideration of urgent matters pertaining to the war against Hitler' at the tail end of the prime minister's scheduled trip to North Africa planned for early August.

Some historical works claim that when Churchill boarded the plane in the small hours of August 1 for Moscow by way of Cairo, he went armed with the Dieppe Raid to placate Stalin. However, the evidence shows that the only sacrifices he planned to offer for the sake of the alliance came in the form of operations against Norway and (despite the reservations of the War Cabinet and the chiefs of staff) Sledgehammer, and the revived Imperator, kept ready to be mounted at a moment's notice if the political or strategic situation required. Indeed, if the Dieppe Raid was meant to be in any way sacrificial, the planners were unaware; in the intelligence and information section of the planning documents, they wrote:

> British raids have caused anxiety to the German authorities, and a number of measures have been taken to meet the situation, but there are no signs that troops are being detached from Germany or the Russian Front and sent to the west: the reverse, in fact, is the case. So long as Germany is occupied in Russia, only a threat to some vital objective would cause a reversal of this policy.[107]

Certainly, from the German point of view, the seemingly immaterial seaside port of Dieppe did not present a 'vital objective' that would demand a swift strategic response. In no way did the singular, one-day 'return ticket' nature of Rutter (and later Jubilee) offer sufficient bait to provoke that desired goal.

By the time Churchill finally touched down in Moscow on August 12 after a spirited ten days in the desert, he had learned from his Cabinet that the initial life-and-death urgency of Stalin's summons had begun to simmer. A week earlier, Anthony Eden, the secretary of state for foreign affairs, addressed in Cabinet a July 25 letter from Mr Paul Winterton, special correspondent in Moscow for the left-leaning *News Chronicle* (forerunner to the *Daily Mail*) who reported on the current mood in Russia.[108] Although 'some Red Army soldiers' complained that Great Britain and the Americans had not done enough so far, sparing their own men at the expense of the Soviets while Russia was 'going it alone,' there was no fear that tardiness in opening the second front would lead to a severing of relations. According to Winterton, repercussions would be felt in the *long, rather than short term, which 'may imperil a sound peace' once the war is over.*[109]

The issue of great urgency and ire 'at the present time,' according to Winterton, came with the cancelling of convoys which the

---

* Author's italics.

correspondent noted was 'particularly irritating' to the Russians but went to 'emphasize that all publicity on the subject here is very correct, and there is absolutely no suggestion that Russia is being badly let down.'[110]

The inference is drawn from the official minutes of the meetings in Moscow that initially described Stalin's view as 'very glum,' and had given the impression that the fate of Russia and the entire alliance was in the balance when Churchill and Stalin first shook hands. This, however, is not the case.[111]

Averell Harriman, Roosevelt's special envoy to Russia who accompanied Churchill, recorded that despite blunt retorts by Stalin in the opening hours of their initial meeting, the prime minister had managed to bring the temperature down, explaining step by step the problems confronting the Western Allies but promising to step up the bombing of German cities. As Harriman noted, Churchill's tactic satisfied Stalin's blood lust; 'the meeting broke up early' and 'in spite of the early difficulties, the relationship between the two men had reached a most friendly basis.'[112]

The files of Alexander Cadogan, the British undersecretary of state who represented the Foreign Office on the trip, declassified only in 2013, not only support Harriman but further illuminate and recalibrate our understanding of this most crucial moment in the Second World War. As Cadogan reported to his boss, Lord Halifax, Stalin's tone had changed from one of urgency and outrage, as expressed in his July cable, to something far more conciliatory in the official minutes.

According to Cadogan, after Churchill had spent some time 'explaining the impossibility of invading France this year,' Stalin never once so much as hinted that 'Well, if you can't do more than that, I don't know how much longer we can stand the strain.' Cadogan acknowledged that he was relieved and surprised when Stalin repeated several times that he was 'astounded at the spirit and determination of his [Russian] people. He didn't know them[;] he had never dreamt that they could show such unity or resolution.'[113] Indeed, the Soviet leader had come to the realization that, despite his urgings and American promises, logistically, it was not feasible to launch a second front in Europe in 1942. North Africa was, however, a different story. When Churchill mentioned this proposed invasion, the Soviet leader lit up in a way the delegation had not anticipated. Operation Torch 'seemed to have caught Stalin's fancy,' Cadogan wrote. The Soviet leader stunned all those in attendance by nodding his approval and stating, 'May God prosper this enterprise.'[114]

In their last meeting on August 15, Stalin pushed Churchill further on Torch, delighting the prime minister by telling him that 'the indirect effect on Russia will be very great. It will be a blow to the Axis powers.'[115] He then pressed Churchill concerning what would happen in France should Torch succeed. Within this context, the prime minister replied that the Germans would have to occupy southern France and Italy but would not be able to do so from troops or aircraft in the Channel area, which he had promised to pin in place in the aide-memoire in June. At that moment, knowing full well that the requirement to employ Sledgehammer or Imperator for political purposes was nil, Churchill briefed Stalin on the upcoming Dieppe Raid which was already 'in train':

> 'In order to make Germany anxious about an attack from across the Channel, there will be a more serious raid in August, although the weather might upset it. It will be a reconnaissance in force. Some 8,000 men with 50 tanks will be landed. They will stay a night and a day, kill as many Germans as possible and take prisoners. They will then withdraw. That is a reconnaissance in force. It can be compared with a bath which you feel with your hand to see if the water is hot ... as we intend to withdraw immediately after the operation ... the object is to get information and to create the impression of an invasion. Most important, I hope it will call forth a big air battle.'[116]

Again, none but the requirement to 'get information' was central in the original Rutter plan, nor in its reworked forms – Rutter II and Jubilee. The pinch imperative was the locomotive driving the raid, with the other excuses conveniently hitched to the train now set to leave for Dieppe in the coming days.

But despite his satisfaction, the suspension of the Arctic convoys remained a hot topic and Stalin continued to reiterate the vital essence of his July cable on that subject.

As Churchill knew, the Soviet leader's grumbling was not merely political bluster but an expression of the extreme fragility of the Soviet war economy. Although much has been written about the inferior types of tanks and aircraft manufactured in the United Kingdom for delivery to the Soviet Union, these armaments did, in fact, play a crucial role in the fighting: most of the cargo that was delivered went right into action once it was unloaded from the boats. The Soviets would eventually develop their own prosperous industrial capabilities and thrive, in part thanks to American Lend-Lease deliveries later in the war, but the year 1942 proved to be a most vulnerable point for the Soviet Union. Its industrial centre had been based in its western regions, and in the summer and autumn of 1941, Stalin had taken the unorthodox step of closing all the factories that lay in the path of the German onslaught and moving them thousands of miles to safety behind the Ural mountains. This transfer necessitated a complete retooling of Soviet industry, with considerable downtime – right at the worst possible moment.

In these strained circumstances, the arms deliveries from Great Britain were desperately needed to plug the gaps and buy time for the Soviet factories to start producing again. But over and above that, certain machine tools that had been lost to the Germans had to be replaced. There was no point in building a factory in a safe location if the highly specialized machine tools, castings, or vital resources (oil, rubber, aluminium alloy, industrial diamonds, phosphates, jute, special steels and chemicals, and aviation fuel) needed to produce and employ weapons of war and other industrial machinery were lacking.[117] And therein lay the value of the British convoys: a good measure of their cargo was not merely the denigrated tanks and aircraft, but the vital industrial resources needed for the core infrastructure of the Soviet war effort.[118]

Meanwhile, at home, Winston Churchill was also under great pressure. He had just undergone his second no-confidence vote in six months, handily defeating the motion as he had earlier in the year, yet the clock seemed to be ticking against him as the coalition war leader, particularly following the embarrassing loss of Tobruk in Libya to Hitler's armies. Ivan Maisky, the Soviet ambassador to the United Kingdom, who witnessed the motion, recorded: 'Churchill has won a brilliant victory in Parliament. But he shouldn't get carried away. In fact, the overwhelming majority in the House is in a very anxious and critical mood, blaming the Government for the long chain of military defeats that has ended, for now, in Libya.'[119]

Calls from the vocal left-wing minority for a 'second front now' could for the present be ignored, but the cavalier way in which the merchant seamen in the PQ-17 had been sent to their icy graves raised doubts among the industrial labourers who saw the fruits of their heavy work plummet to the bottom of the ocean.[120]

However, the ever-cautious Admiralty was not willing to risk its fleet and re-establish the convoys that August during the four-rotor blackout, when they had no way to follow the movements of the *Tirpitz* and other heavy German vessels. Until the blackout ended or environmental conditions changed to permit rerouting of the convoys to the northern Soviet ports over a less risky, even if still vulnerable, course, the Admiralty remained reluctant to reverse its decision.

When Churchill in 1950 was reviewing this turbulent period while writing his memoirs of the war, he deliberately attempted to divorce himself from the disastrous results of the Dieppe Raid – something he did not fathom when meeting with Stalin in Moscow – by feigning ignorance of the timing and intent of the raid. In a pointed witticism attributed to him years later, Churchill reportedly said: 'History will be kind to me – as I intend to write it.' And to whitewash his place in history, and to a lesser extent preserve security, he feigned ignorance over the remount of Rutter as Operation Jubilee at Dieppe. Perhaps preoccupied with his own legacy, the calculating prime minister began the process of appearing to know nothing within four months of the mission. Just before Christmas 1942, he queried Pug Ismay, his chief of staff, about the raid: 'Although for many reasons everyone was concerned to make this business look as good as possible,' he wrote, 'the time has now come when I must be informed more precisely about the military plans.' Ismay replied that Great Britain's star commander Bernard Law Montgomery, by then the beloved hero of the victory over Rommel at El Alamein, had approved the overall military plan for the Dieppe Raid. Stymied, Churchill then dropped the matter after Mountbatten defiantly suggested that, if pressed, he would demand an official inquiry.

Victory in 1945 did nothing to quell the raw emotion and stigma associated with Dieppe. By then, Mountbatten had become the apparent villain, and Churchill attempted to place the responsibility for the remount squarely on his shoulders. Reaching out to Pug Ismay once again, perhaps to suggest he toe the party line, Churchill demanded to know who had made 'the decision to revive the attack after it had been abandoned and Montgomery had cleared out.'[121] Churchill wrote:

> What we say about this is a matter for subsequent consideration, but we must at least know ourselves what the facts were – namely: did the Chiefs of Staff, or the Defence Committee or the War Cabinet ever consider the matter of the revival of the operation (a) when I was in England, (b) when I was out of England or was it all pushed through by Dickie Mountbatten on his own without reference to higher authority?[122]

Knowing full well the details of the raid, including the pinch portion, Pug Ismay must surely have suspected what Churchill was up to. Apologizing 'for being so inadequate about the Dieppe Raid,' he refused to take the bait but reminded Churchill that, 'in the vital interests of secrecy, nothing was put on paper,' thereby confirming Mountbatten's claim.[123] Then he fired the deciding salvo, telling the now-former prime minister that he 'must have approved the operation in principle,' given that he requested urgent information about the remount before he departed from Moscow.[124] This exchange apparently ended the matter because, in the Dieppe passage in his memoirs, Churchill dutifully, if reluctantly, admitted: 'I personally went through the plans with the CIGS, Admiral Mountbatten and the Naval Force Commander J. Hughes-Hallett. It was clear that no substantial change between Jubilee and Rutter was suggested, beyond substituting commandos to silence the flank coastal batteries in place of air-borne troops.'[125] This affirmation came after the fact, but confirmation appears in a series of messages exchanged between Churchill and Pug Ismay at the end of the Moscow trip.

On August 15, following a contentious round of discussions concerning the suspension of the Arctic convoys, Churchill wired

Ismay, asking: 'What is the position about the renewal of Rutter?'[126] Clearly, the prime minister, the highest authority in the land, had knowledge of the raid and had given permission to remount it, even if not through the normal channels. Ismay's reply the following day confirms that Churchill was aware not only of the remount but of the Ultra Secret objective behind the raid. He informed the anxious PM, with veiled details attached, that 'Jubilee, which is renewed Rutter *in all essential features*, is due to be carried out at first light August 18th. If weather unfavourable 18th August, operation can be launched any subsequent day up to 24th August inclusive.'[127] After a one-day delay caused by inclement conditions, Ismay cabled Churchill just after his plane touched down in Cairo on the return leg of his Russian journey: 'Weather sufficiently good – Jubilee has started.'[128]

CHAPTER 13

Of Blood and Thunder

*On that awesome day, we were baptized in the blood
and thunder of war, and those who survived the
carnage will never forget it as long as they live.*
Royal Marine Private Paul McGrath

L ate on the afternoon of August 18, a two-car convoy pulled up
to Trafalgar Gate, the main access to His Majesty's Naval Base
Portsmouth. Commander Ian Fleming, dressed in a navy peacoat,
demanded directions from a confused guard to the precise location of
the British Hunt-class destroyer HMS *Fernie*, berthed somewhere near
Lord Nelson's flagship, HMS *Victory*. Officially listed as an 'observer'
for the raid, Fleming, accompanied by several American officers,
attachés from the US embassy in London, had come to oversee the
operational combat debut of his fledgling Intelligence Assault Unit.[1] The
most prominent of his visitors, US Army brigadier general Lucian K.
Truscott Jr and Marine Corps colonel Franklin A. Hart,* who, as part

---

* One of the changes to the raid between its origins as Operation Rutter and
its implementation as Operation Jubilee had seen the air drop, scheduled to
obliterate the coastal batteries at Dieppe, replaced by an amphibious attack
carried out by two additional British Army commando units, both of which were
veterans of pinch operations in Norway. These units, Lieutenant Colonel John

of Mountbatten's staff, had taken part in the planning for Dieppe, had now come to study British amphibious techniques and to witness first-hand the combat debut of 50 members of the newly created US Army Rangers.[2]

As Fleming's entourage entered Portsmouth dockyard, the scene they witnessed resembled that in many other ports along the south coast of England. All around them, ships were making final preparations for the raid under a cover plan designed to disguise it as yet one more tedious training exercise. To maintain this 'business as usual' appearance and prevent any dockyard speculation stemming from a sudden surge in activity, ammunition and special equipment essential for the mission had been smuggled on board over several nights, and all extra rations had been cancelled. The guard's strange reaction to Fleming's request for directions confirmed that Louis Mountbatten's extreme and almost obsessive attention to secrecy and security had worked. In the days leading up to the raid, Ultra had revealed nothing to suggest that the Germans had caught on to the remount. With Captain Jock Hughes-Hallett about to sneak the largest raiding force in history across 70 miles of the English Channel, everything appeared to be going their way.

After Fleming and the Americans had presented their credentials to the guard, they soon found the *Fernie* and her sister ship, HMS *Calpe*, among the myriad destroyers, troop transports, converted Channel steamers, motor launches, anti-submarine trawlers, gunboats and landing craft in Portsmouth harbour. They were welcomed aboard the *Fernie* by first officer Lieutenant Willett – 'a young

---

Durnford-Slater's No. 3 Commando and Lieutenant Colonel Simon Fraser's (the 15th Lord Lovat's) No. 4 Commando, would now host the US Army Rangers, distributed throughout them in 'penny packets.' The Rangers had replaced the US Marine Corps, which in Rutter had been assigned to go into battle with the Royal Marine Commando on board the *Locust*. The switch was likely prompted by *Locust*'s sacrificial role in the pinch attempt – the 'political' implication that had been in Mountbatten's mind since early June. Still, with the four-rotor crisis looming and pinch opportunities opening up in the Pacific theatre to exploit their work against Japanese codes and ciphers, the Americans, in particular Colonel Hart, were still most eager to monitor the events surrounding Jubilee. (Marine Corps History Division, Reference Branch, Franklin Hart biographical file.)

public school entrant in his early 20s,' as Fleming described him.[3] Willett explained that his commanding officer, a gregarious sort with immense bravado, had run his motorcycle into an immovable object earlier in the day and would not be able to take *Fernie* into battle. Nevertheless, Willett did, and Fleming later recorded that he won respect and admiration for his handling of the ship by raid's end. Days earlier, both destroyers had undergone a special refit that transformed them from traditional submarine-hunting and convoy escort vessels to modern headquarters ships, or floating communications fortresses, for raiding operations.

Fernie and *Calpe* bristled with scores of antennae connected to hypersensitive communications and navigational gear whose settings proved so delicate that they prohibited the firing of her main four-inch gun except in emergencies. Clearly impressed by the technological array, Fleming eagerly noted at least four additional wireless teams totalling 40 to 50 operators. Positioned on deck, below deck, in wardrooms and the captain's cabin, as well as on the bridge, these wireless operators would perform a variety of communications tasks designed to keep all parts of the raiding force linked together – the two force commanders on board and those on shore – either by direct voice link or through eavesdropping on the labyrinthine radio net. Forward Observation Officers (FOOs) would control air and naval support to the troops ashore; 'Phantom' and 'J Service' personnel would monitor Allied messages from special liaison officers, and 'Headache' teams of German-speaking radio operators would scan the airwaves for German plain-language messages uttered in the heat of battle.[4] The chatter from these wireless sets would establish the backbeat for the drama about to unfold – and once the operation began, would provide Fleming and the other observers with a ringside seat at the raid.

As Chief of Combined Operations, Mountbatten knew that effective command, control and communications formed the potential key to success in this operation, and he was leaving nothing to chance. As he had planned for Operation Rutter, Jock Hughes-Hallett and Major General Ham Roberts would, respectively, call the shots for the sea and land forces from the floating command centre aboard the *Calpe*, but if something went horribly wrong there, the *Fernie* housed a complete back-up command team led by Roberts's chief of staff, Brigadier Churchill Mann. Meanwhile, an RAF liaison officer would work from the bridge of *Calpe*, with Air Vice-Marshal Trafford Leigh-Mallory orchestrating the entire air umbrella from his Uxbridge headquarters in London. In Portsmouth, Admiral Sir William James would keep tabs on every aspect of the raid from his newly constructed command bunker under Fort Southwick. Patched into all the networks, his headquarters became the relay hub: he could eavesdrop on the action from across the Channel and send on the latest intelligence provided from the Operational Intelligence Centre, working under John Godfrey's watchful eye in London.

⌒

On the Isle of Wight, close to 4,000 men from Ham Roberts's Second Canadian Division, along with 60 tanks from the Calgary Tank Regiment and nearly a dozen teams of Royal Canadian Engineers and other ancillary elements, loaded onto troopships and landing craft. Few, if any, suspected that this 'preparatory exercise' would, in fact, be the 'real deal.' Amid the scores of vehicle convoys heading to the coast were several trucks with tarpaulins drawn, carrying Colonel Joseph Picton Phillipps's Royal Marine commandos to the port of Cowes. There they would board the *Locust* and the French *chasseurs* anchored offshore.

Despite the intense security and the cover plan, suspicion had begun to grow within the ranks of the Royal Marines that something big was brewing. On August 15, Picton Phillipps and his company commanders received word that Operation Jubilee would take place on any day between August 18 and 23, weather permitting, and that they should draw up their orders for the pinch – an exact replica of Rutter but with new code names. Under strict instructions to keep the men in the dark until the last possible moment – ideally when aboard their assault craft – only the company commanders and platoon officers knew about the remount of the raid. Picton Phillipps had even initiated Operation 'Itchen,' a bogus week-long training scheme designed to conceal the nature of the preparations – particularly if inclement weather forced a day-to-day postponement, as had been the case in Rutter.[5]

However, the natural flurry of pre-raid activity, which called for the Marines to prime grenades, fill Bren gun magazines and oil weapons, only fuelled rumour and conjecture. 'The explanation given,' recalled Jock Farmer, 'was that we were going on an exercise! Even the dimmest amongst us wasn't going to buy that.'[6] By the afternoon of August 18, Picton Phillipps received word that the tanks had embarked – a sure sign that the raid was on – and he held an Orders Group that night with his officers and NCOs to go over the exact details of their mission. Following the meeting, the Royal Marine Commando jumped in the trucks bound for Cowes, and by five o'clock that afternoon, all were aboard the *Locust* and the *chasseurs* en route to Portsmouth, where they would link up with the raiding force.

For the men of Robert Force, commanded by Major Robert Houghton, speculation hit fever pitch while they waited aboard the *chasseurs*. 'After a while, no one was allowed on deck and all the NCOs were summoned for a briefing,' wrote the intrigued eighteen-year-old Bob McAlister. The anticipation rose after Commander Red Ryder arrived to discuss 'special duties,' and the men were issued with ammunition, special tools and emergency rations, along with escape instructions.[7] McAlister recalled:

> We were shown aerial 3D photographs of Dieppe and areas along the coast for two or three miles, and inland too. We were told this was the real thing. A thrill ran through everyone. This was what the lads wanted. Everyone was thrilled and excited ... the fact that we soon [would] be in action brought us closer to each other and dependent on each other. Our attitudes changed, little differences forgotten. We were brothers in arms and ready for anything.[8]

The same sentiment prevailed among the Royal Marines of Tiger Force and the IAU aboard the *Locust*. After they squeezed below deck, they received an issue of French currency, which immediately told them that this time the raid was on. According to Jock Farmer: 'It was so crowded that anybody who had hand grenades hanging from their pouches were told to fuck off, as we did not want any accidents amongst ourselves.'[9] Their orders remained the same as in Rutter, reported Corporal

Paul McGrath: 'driving into the harbour, attacking and capturing the German Naval headquarters based in a dockside hotel and extracting specified contents therefrom, and removing a number of German invasion barges for towing back to England.'[10] However, as eager and optimistic as the Royal Marine commandos were about the mission, Jock Farmer recalled that they remained quite sober, realizing that they could be embarking on a one-way ride:

> *Locust* was designed to ram any obstacle in its way; it was obvious it was not coming back. Somebody tentatively asked, 'How do we get back?' It was a question that should not have been asked. Later, when the same man offered in a jocular tone, 'Why don't we raise one of the boats we just sunk, dry it out, find out from the Germans where they kept the diesel and fill up?' only stony silence followed.[11]

Capping off the day in grand style, a motor launch approached the *Locust*, bringing Mountbatten for a visit before the raiding fleet sailed. 'We were all up on deck,' recalled Douglas Bevan, a 21-year-old specially trained in demolitions, 'the whole ship's company, all the Royal Marine Commandos, and, typical of Mountbatten in those days, he jumped up on one of the cap stands at the front of the ship. He stood up and told one of the ship's officers to stand us at ease.'[12] Standing on the bow with No. 10 Platoon, Paul McGrath was impressed too, noting that the Chief 'cut a splendid figure, in the admiral's uniform' as he gave a quick pep talk, then 'dashed off to give repeat performances on other ships.'[13] Mountbatten's visit had the desired effect: it left everyone with the distinct impression that this 'was the real McCoy, it was on definitely' – a welcome relief after the disappointment of Rutter six weeks earlier.[14]

Sergeant John Kruthoffer, the usually tough-minded 21-year-old second-in-command to Lieutenant Peter Huntington-Whiteley, found these expectations intensely moving. He wrote later that 'the unit was in prime condition – very well trained – handpicked really keen types ... with a genuine desire and anxiety to prove ourselves.'[15] August 19, 1942, would provide that chance in spades. As Paul McGrath recalled in his memoir: 'On that awesome day, we were baptized in the blood and thunder of war, and those who survived the carnage will never forget it as long as they live.'[16]

⁌

A day earlier, on August 17, Jock Hughes-Hallett and Commander David Luce, two parts of Mountbatten's syndicate that had conceived of the raid nearly six months earlier, spent the better part of the day carefully reviewing the complex plan, trying 'to imagine and anticipate all the contingencies that might arise.'[17] That night, inclement weather rolled in, putting the launch of the raid in doubt, but during a highly charged and intense three-hour meeting, Mountbatten and Hughes-Hallett took to the offensive, pressing Admiral James to push ahead despite the forecast. The Admiralty and the Air Ministry meteorologists were 'every bit as gloomy as Old Testament Prophets,' Hughes-Hallett wrote, but a local weather expert dismissed their predictions, stating that a pocket of fine weather would cover Dieppe on the morrow. With this encouraging news, Admiral James agreed to launch the raid.[18]

At 1715 hours, a warning order, followed minutes later by the code word *Tulip*, officially signalled the start of Operation Jubilee. General Andrew McNaughton quickly relayed the message to Ottawa, just as Major General Hastings Ismay sent it on to Churchill as he was returning from his visit to Stalin in Moscow.

By 1800 hours, HMS *Calpe*, with Jock Hughes-Hallett and Ham Roberts on the bridge, sailed out of Portsmouth harbour, stopping only to watch part of the burgeoning armada pass through the Spithead anti-submarine barrier 'in perfect formation.' To Jock Hughes-Hallett, the new Dieppe naval force commander who had replaced Tom Baillie-Grohman – with Mountbatten's ecstatic approval – the spectacle had 'a certain dream-like quality.'[19]

Over the previous few hours, nearly 250 ships had secretly crept out from bases in southern England and the Isle of Wight and formed into thirteen assault groups bound for Dieppe. First, though, they had to navigate through a dangerous mid-Channel minefield. Led by a few minesweepers, each group maintained its course through carefully cleared lanes marked by dimly lit dan buoys. Ploughing through at close to twenty knots to reach Dieppe under cover of darkness, there was little room for error. Although they were aided by advanced navigational gear, some borrowed from the RAF's Bomber Command, Hughes-Hallett's orders called for immediate cancellation if one of the large mother ships ferrying the infantry and their landing craft to the drop-off point, ten miles off the coast of Dieppe, succumbed to a German mine or any other enemy action. The men on the crowded ships donned Mae West life preservers, and collectively held their breath as each group took its place in the queue to slip through the danger zone.

Almost miraculously, everything went better than Hughes-Hallett had expected, and nearly all of his ships navigated the lanes on time and on target. The major exception, it is reported, was HMS *Locust*: with a top speed of only seventeen knots, compared with the brisk eighteen-to-twenty-knot pace of the rest of the raiding force, the river gunboat had apparently been given special permission to trail behind. Following it came Motor Launch 291 (*ML-291*), which most likely was the designated craft that would whisk the pinched material out of Dieppe harbour. As Hughes-Hallett recorded in his official report: 'After passing Nab Tower, *Locust* was unable to maintain speed of Group 4[,] proceeded independently ...'[20] Ryder's memoirs concur: 'Proceeding along the Sussex coast, we finally lost all contact with the main body off Beachy Head. Between Rye and Dungeness[,] neither of which were visible in the dark, we had to alter course in a South Easterly direction through a swept channel across a minefield.'[21] Except for *ML-219*, Ryder and Captain William John Stride found themselves alone, behind schedule and on the edge of what they hoped was one of the two channels through the minefield. As Ryder recalled:

> This was to have been marked by a lighted Dan buoy, but we could see no sign of it. 'Well, Skipper,' I remember saying to Stride, 'What do we do now?' 'It's usually best to take them at right angles, Sir,' he replied calmly ... we took his sound advice and plunged boldly through the minefield, breathing rather more freely when by dead reckoning we thought we were across.[22]

Whether sheer luck, the shallow draft or a combination of both saved the ship from certain destruction remains unknown, but *Locust* was now significantly behind time for its rendezvous off the main beach, where it was expected to provide fire support for the Essex Scottish as they began their landing at 0510 hours. That delay, however, was minor compared with the calamity that was about to unfold.

∽

Despite the scores of post-battle assertions from both sides of the line that the Germans knew in advance about the Dieppe Raid, nothing in any file currently in the public domain suggests that the Germans had caught on. In fact, the overwhelming weight of the evidence points to the contrary. Thanks to the constant watch kept by Ultra on the home waters key that for the moment remained enciphered on three-rotor Enigma settings, the British knew since St Nazaire that the Germans expected more attacks somewhere along the French or Norwegian coasts before climatic conditions forced an end to the 'raiding season' in the autumn. Nothing in the days leading up to Jubilee, however, gave any indication of suspicious German activity despite their continuous state of high alert during obvious raiding periods. German coastal convoys operated as usual; no extra bombers had arrived to reinforce Luftwaffe squadrons in the area; no additional infantry or tanks had moved into the Dieppe sector to bolster the defenders, and no unusual patterns in German radio traffic had arisen. As Fleming noted in his post-action account for Godfrey (who sent it straight to Mountbatten), no U-boats had flocked to the area, nor had mobile artillery been brought up to keep the fleet at bay; and no minefields had been laid on any of the approaches or along the beaches.[23]

So far, as the raiding force worked its way out across the Channel on a night that increasingly turned black as pitch, everything continued to unfold as planned. This included a most welcome message – one gleaned through Ultra – that a small German convoy of trawler-type vessels, scheduled to arrive on August 17 but delayed by bad weather, would indeed be in Dieppe harbour by early morning of the 19th.[24] These vessels were expected to house the desired signals material, and the message confirmed that when the raiding fleet arrived, their 'prizes' would indeed be ready for the taking.

At 0127 hours, just as the last ships cleared the minefield, a subsequent series of Ultra decrypts reached Admiral James's headquarters in Portsmouth. After a quick assessment, he relayed the information gleaned to the raiding fleet. It was clear that Hughes-Hallett's monumental luck was about to run out. The first decrypt, from 0100 hours, reported that a German patrol consisting of a collection of 'small craft' was operating off the tiny Channel port of Le Tréport, less than twenty miles up the coast from Dieppe.[25] Nothing at that time indicated that these craft would enter the operational area. Less than an hour later, however, a subsequent report made it clear that this was now highly probable.[26]

A flurry of further intercepts between 0212 and 0244 hours revealed that this 'patrol' was, in fact, the expected German coastal convoy, on course for Dieppe but running late. A subsequent decrypt confirmed that it consisted of a small number of armed trawlers, and was scheduled to reach the port just as the raiding force arrived off Dieppe. For the ships that received the warning, the implication was clear: Group 5 on the far left flank would collide with the German convoy out in the Channel roughly 60 minutes before H-hour.[27]

On board HMS *Fernie*, Ian Fleming stuffed his personal papers and identification into a sandbag for deposit in the captain's safe and then climbed into an armchair in the wardroom for a pre-game nap. All the while, he wondered what kind of prize that bag would make for the Germans should *Fernie* be sunk and salvaged.[28] On HMS *Locust*, meanwhile, the Royal Marines made their final checks for battle, reviewing their maps and memorizing their code words and contingency plans in case things went wrong. On the river gunboat's reinforced bridge, Ryder and Stride destroyed 'all secret documents related to the operation,' except for map tracings, photographs and communications orders.[29]

At 0347 hours, just over an hour before the landings would begin, Fleming and his American comrades were rudely awakened by the staccato sound of distant gunfire echoing off the thin walls of *Fernie*. Moving swiftly up onto the slick deck of the drab grey Royal Navy destroyer, Fleming discarded the remnants of a hand-rolled cigarette and pressed his binoculars to his eyes, adjusting the focus wheel to account for the darkness. In the distance, a series of fire-red, mushroom-shaped explosions, topped by the flickering silver glow from star shells, merged with the carnival of red, orange and green tracer fire that darted back and forth. Then came another round of machine-gun and light cannon fire, punctuated at irregular intervals by the whiplash crack of larger-calibre naval gunfire, followed by more explosions. The raid on Dieppe had indeed begun – albeit 63 minutes prematurely – with Fleming fixed on the spectacle, wondering how it would impact the vital mission of his IAU.

What Fleming and almost everyone aboard each ship in the raiding force had witnessed was the seemingly avoidable collision between Group 5 and the small German coastal convoy that Portsmouth had warned was making for Dieppe. Commander Derek Bathurst Wyburd led Group 5 from the bridge of Steam Gun Boat 5 (*SGB 5*), recently christened *Grey Owl*, with orders to shepherd twenty Assault Landing Craft (ALCs) carrying Lieutenant Colonel John Durnford-Slater's No. 3 Commando to Yellow Beach and their target – the coastal battery at Berneval.

The German convoy – three converted deep-sea trawlers outfitted for anti-submarine warfare* and five coastal motorboats, or 'flak detachments,'** indeed loaded with the desired signals materials – had appeared through the low-lying mist. The sharp, wild firefight that ensued set *Grey Owl* alight, with German fire from high-powered flak guns knocking out her main guns and shearing off her antennae. According to the official accounts, the clash took Durnford-Slater, riding on the bridge with Wyburd, by surprise. Immediately, the landing craft following behind scattered, some succumbing to heavy fire that punctured the extra petrol tanks carried on board. Through the 'tangles of wreckage' on the bridge of *Grey Owl*, Durnford-Slater could hear the 'moans of the dying.' 'A shell had scored a direct hit, and it was piled with about ten dead and wounded sailors,' he recalled. 'One badly wounded naval officer cried, "This is the end!" I was inclined to believe him ...'[30]

---

* *UJ-1404, UJ-1411* and *UJ-1410*.
** *Ost-Vlanderen, Hydra, Iris, Spes-Salutis*, and the *Franz*.

As a direct result of this 'bump,' as Durnford-Slater euphemistically termed it, Group 5 now had little hope for a successful coordinated landing on Yellow Beach.[31]

In Hughes-Hallett's carefully measured after-action report that set the narrative for accounts that followed, he portrayed the clash as a 'chance' or 'unfortunate' encounter, but this claim is far from the truth.

As early as June 11, during the planning for Rutter, Portsmouth command had warned both Admiral James and Mountbatten's headquarters that 'it is normal for enemy escorted convoys to leave Boulogne south-westwards at dusk ... and it is suggested that covering force of Rutter should be ready to deal with such vessels.' It went on to state that 'RDF (Radar) plots would, as is usual, be passed to Commander-in-Chief Portsmouth (Admiral James), for necessary action.'[32] On the day itself, messages to this effect were dispatched in timely fashion to all the ships in the raiding force warning of the approaching threat. These messages were received by Wyburd and Durnford-Slater on *Grey Owl*, Ian Fleming on HMS *Fernie* and Ryder on HMS *Locust*, as well as most of the ships in the armada. According to Hughes-Hallett, however, warning of their approach failed to reach him on board the headquarters ship HMS *Calpe*, nor apparently did it reach the destroyers *Brocklesby* and the Polish vessel *Ślązak* guarding the eastern flank.

Astonishingly, Wyburd admitted in his report that he had received the warning but had decided even before the raid began that he would fight his way through to keep the delicate timing and synchronization of his portion of the raiding fleet intact. By his own admission, the Royal Navy steam gunboat commander had intentionally disregarded a direct order, which stipulated that to maintain the essential element of surprise, Group leaders should take evasive action and avoid contact with enemy vessels during the crossing.[33] Group 1, led by Commander Peter Scott in *SGB 9*, had apparently followed those orders when informed of the approaching convoy, yet Wyburd had seemingly put the entire raid at risk by his insubordinate actions. However, when summoned aboard *Calpe* after his rescue from his floundering gunboat to meet the naval force commander for at the very least a severe dressing down, Hughes-Hallett instead lauded him for 'great gallantry and determination' and recommended him for the Distinguished Service Cross.[34]

At first blush, this action appears incongruous and inexplicable until one considers events from earlier that month that remained classified as Ultra Secret until 2014.

As early as the St Nazaire and Bayonne raids, the Royal Navy, and in particular 'Red' Ryder, had experimented with captured German call signs to increase the chance of surprise in a pinch effort. By employing low-level German codebooks and signalling procedures, they would create a false sense of security or confusion among German ships at sea or coastal fortifications controlling access to ports, buying precious time that could prevent the destruction of the material targeted for the pinch. In the wake of Chariot, where Ryder experienced some limited success along these lines, Frank Birch was livid that Naval Section at Bletchley was not apprised of this ruse beforehand as they could have offered 'precise information, which stood a better chance of foxing the enemy than the bits and pieces actually supplied.'[35]

Now, with Jubilee in the offing in early August, an approach to support operations of this kind was made to NID and Naval Section by Lieutenant Commander Peter Scott – the same highly decorated gunboat commander of SGB 9 (Grey Goose) who had obeyed orders while leading Group 1 taking Lord Lovat's commandos into Orange Beach. Scott, who had access to the Kriegsmarine Confidential Book on Very High Frequency Signalling, now wanted the visual signals most commonly used between 'E-Boats, R-Boats and unknown light craft – or to call a shore station' in particular, 'callsign titles of the Operational authorities at Cherbourg, Havre, Dieppe, Boulogne, Calais,' 'if we should want to pass signals to them?' In his estimation, 'A bogus V[isual] S[ignal] message might be used (as it has already been two or three times) to get closer before opening fire. It might also be used in the middle of an action – perhaps an even better time because of the inevitable confusion. It might be used to pacify a shore station.'[36]

Hoping to fox the enemy with the basic principles of the bluff (arouse sympathy, be aggressive and distract attention), Birch recorded that Naval Section 'duly supplied the answers' to Scott's query.[37] Yet despite the forethought, not everything came off as planned.

UJ-1404, a 435-ton former deep-sea trawler converted for anti-submarine patrols, her sister ship the UJ-1411, and two M-boats including the *M-4014* formed the German convoy escort headed for Dieppe. About ten nautical miles out in the Channel to the north of the port, the water remained remarkably calm, but a thick mist had reduced visibility despite the moonlight. At 0300, when the moon dipped, visibility worsened for the convoy, which was travelling at six knots and operating without any warning of imminent Allied naval activity. That changed abruptly moments later when the *UJ-1404*, astern of the convoy with *UJ-1411* ahead and the *M-4014* off the right flank, received an urgent message from a naval shore station that an enemy vessel was closing in from behind at 30 knots. For the next hour, nothing but faint sounds of motors off in the distance pierced the blackness, until hydrophones on one trawler picked up a contact at precisely the same moment that *UJ-1411* sighted British vessels 1,000 yards ahead.

Immediately, *UJ-1404* fired up a star shell to illuminate the area – the flare seen by Fleming and the rest of the raiding fleet – that signalled the start of what appeared to the Germans as nothing more than a 'usual S-Boat skirmish.'[38] Suspecting that British motor torpedo boats had given chase and had now caught the convoy, the German crews were surprised to see a mixture of gunboats and destroyers in addition to a 'long, heavily armed vessel' with bridge superstructure 'very far aft' that returned fire immediately with all weapons 'of heavy calibre.'[39]

Although the trawlers got the best of Wyburd's *Grey Owl*, the German convoy took a severe beating as well. The first victim, the flak-ship *Franz* (a converted trawler), was hit repeatedly by British fire and eventually limped to shore, beaching herself on the rocks just below the Berneval battery, right between the two selected landing zones for Durnford-Slater's commandos. *UJ-1404* suffered a similar fate: with engines hit by an armour-piercing shot, the converted trawler first slowed and then caught fire, forcing her crew to abandon ship, with 25 of the 44 men falling into British hands. The remaining UJs fled towards the safety of Dieppe harbour, arriving as the raid commenced, while the flakships limped back to Tréport harbour, where they augmented the port's anti-aircraft defences for the rest of the day.[40] A month later, a report on the capture of *UJ-1404*, based on interrogations of the crew along with 'supplementary' sources such as Ultra and 'pinch sources,' appeared in the files from Birch's Naval Section. Something, it seems, although not of the golden variety, had fallen into Allied hands along with the crew.[41] According to extracts from HMS *Brocklesby*'s report, the trawler was found abandoned and circling aimlessly sometime after 0530. After picking up prisoners from the water, the destroyer shelled the stricken ship repeatedly, setting it on fire until she stopped and blew up around 0645.[42] There is no mention of who boarded the vessel, when it was boarded, or exactly what was captured, despite confirmation of a pinch occurring in the Naval Section files. Part of this mystery may be solved by another report penned by the American liaison officer attached to Mountbatten's COHQ, which sheds dramatic light on the matter.[43]

United States Marine Corps Colonel Franklin Hart had served as a naval attaché in the American embassy in London until his secondment to COHQ in late 1941. From that time, not only did he serve as an instructor, but took an active part in planning for Rutter and Jubilee, specifically the integration of the United States Marines into the Royal Marine pinch force that would ride into battle on *Locust*. Although his Marine Raiders had gone off to the Pacific (replaced by US Army Rangers who went into battle with the British Army commandos instead), Hart's role in the operation had not changed by the time he rolled up to Portsmouth harbour with Fleming and Lucian Truscott earlier that night. Tasked with studying actions of the Royal Marine Commando, with an eye on pinch doctrine, he understood the role of *Locust* and remained laser-focused on her exploits throughout the raid:

> At about 0400hrs, the LSI, Glengyle, together with HMS Locust (a gunboat), and the small boats supporting No. 3 Commando ran into a German force which was never completely identified but was believed to be 5 or 6 trawlers or patrol boats. A naval engagement took place in which the LCT were dispersed, but none were damaged. The Locust was hit and suffered several casualties. Her speed was reduced for a while to 6 knots. This initial damage to Locust contributed to her failure to execute her next task.[44]

The nature of this report refutes Hughes-Hallett's claim that *Locust* just couldn't keep speed after passing Nab Tower just outside of Portsmouth harbour. It also suggests that once again, the naval force commander had massaged his post-battle narrative to cover the Ultra Secret aspects of the operation. Yet other evidence tends to support Hart's version of events. In the extract for *Locust*'s report, it states that the river gunboat only arrived at the start of the minefield at 0212 and competed her passage 33 minutes later at 0245. During that time, *Ślązak* recorded that *Locust* had taken up a position astern of Group 4, but by 0218 when the Polish destroyer had reached the exit of the minefield she noted that *Locust* 'had been left astern.'[45] Just prior to this at 0210, *Calpe*, carrying Hughes-Hallett, recorded in her navigational log that they had spotted Group 4 with all its ships 'less *Locust*' but did not speculate as to her current position.[46]

However, according to the log from HMS *Fernie* carrying Fleming and Hart, which was moving at a modest 9 knots, it noted *Locust*, in addition to the troop-carrying LSIs HMS *Queen Emma*, HMS *Princess Astrid*, HMS *Princess Beatrix*, HMS *Invicta*, a motor gunboat and a steam gunboat from Group 3 heading towards Blue Beach to deliver the Royal Regiment of Canada, overtaking her 'on the starboard' at a kilometre's distance at 0140hrs.[47] This puts *Locust* in the Channel passage pushing through the minefield far ahead of what *Ślązak* reported and no longer travelling with the ships of her assigned Group 4. More salient, however, this evidence establishes that she was not 'astern' as claimed and was at that moment clearly outpacing the armada. Fifteen minutes later at 0155, the log from *Fernie* notes that the assault ships had turned to starboard but there is no mention of *Locust*, indicating that the river gunboat had passed through the group en route for some unknown destination.[48]

What perhaps explains this came ten minutes later. As the Naval Staff battle history notes, between 0212 and 0245, 'Signals were received during passage indicating the movements of certain small craft on the French coast.'[49] Immediately following the final message in this string at 0244, *Locust* reports that Ryder ordered Stride to alter course towards their rendezvous point north of Dieppe, but there is no mention of whether this was to seek or avoid contact as per the orders for Jubilee.[50] However, Ryder's subsequent instructions to destroy by fire 'all secret documents relating to operations in the custody of Senior

Officer Cutting Out Force' clearly indicates imminent contact and demonstrates an aggressive rather than defensive posture.[51]

Following this, there is a long, unexplained gap of nearly two hours in the extracts of the message logs (which appears universal with all the ships' reports),* punctuated only by a note at 0400hrs which claims *Locust* arrived at her final waypoint after altering course earlier and had 'reduced speed to 10 knots' before they 'proceeded towards the beach.'[52] However, as *Locust* arrived at 0530 off Dieppe's main beach – twenty minutes behind schedule to participate in her next task, the bombardment of Dieppe – it makes no sense that her reduction in speed was voluntary if she had trailed behind since departure or fell out of Group 4 roughly three hours earlier.[53]

Although by no means definitive, the evidence raises the spectre that Hughes-Hallett had either decided to gamble that his raiding force could pull off the pinch well before they hit the beaches – just as Ryder had attempted at St Nazaire earlier that year – or perhaps fox the convoy and tuck in behind it, hoping to gain entry to the port of Dieppe during the ensuing confusion.

Speculative questions aside, contemporary reports that influenced the subsequent Dieppe narrative claim that this clash with the German convoy put the entire defences in the Dieppe area on high alert, stripping the raid of the precious element of surprise and leaving the men about to land on the beaches at the mercy of a prepared and waiting opponent. The facts are somewhat different. Luckily for Hughes-Hallett, none of the escaping German ships realized that they had bumped into an amphibious landing force. Instead, they mistook the gunboat and landing craft for British MTBs, which periodically ventured across the Channel to prey on coastal convoys. At first, German naval headquarters reported: 'At 0350hrs attack on our convoy by surface forces, 4 kilometres off Dieppe. Particulars not yet known. It is of

---

* One of the great problems with reconstructing events of August 19, 1942 is that Hughes-Hallett's report, and the multitude of appendices that accompany it, are extracts from the original reports written by the commanders of each vessel that participated in the raid. To this date, the originals have yet to be found (or perhaps declassified) and would likely fill in the blanks of the material left on the cutting-room floor, likely due to security concerns during the war.

the opinion of the Naval Command that it has been one of the usual attacks on convoys.'[54] Without any knowledge that amphibious craft or Allied troopships were involved, there was nothing to indicate to the Germans that they had encountered a raiding operation.[55]

Three-quarters of an hour later, less than fifteen minutes before the first boot was due to touch down on the flanks, the signal station at Dieppe observed vessels which, when challenged for a response, ignored it.[56] Again, there is nothing in the records to suggest that the Germans realized what was happening. Even after the raid began and fighting had started on the flanks, for instance, the German 15th Army, which was responsible for the land-based defence of this part of the French coast, still believed the flare-up had been nothing more than a mid-Channel squabble. All the same, they warned both the Kriegsmarine and the Luftwaffe, and ordered lookouts to intensify their efforts.[57] The same could be said for the port of Dieppe, whose jetties were fully alight to guide the way for the fleeing trawlers and whose three guard ships stood ready just outside the mole entrance to escort them to the safety of the inner harbour. Although alerted to the clash off in the distance, the German defenders of Dieppe and its environs had no clue what was about to befall them. Even if the surprise was lost, the shock of the large raiding force suddenly descending on the shore might still have had its desired effect of initially sowing chaos and despondency among the enemy.

However, what British intelligence had failed to understand throughout the planning process was that the German army in 1942 was at its peak. The soldiers defending Dieppe, despite what the assault troops may have been led to believe, were well trained, professional and extremely good at what they did best – defence. British intelligence did not so much underrate the size of the force there as they did the quality of the men defending Dieppe, along with their doctrine, training and leadership. Once the first planes lit up their radar and pounced down to attack the headlands and the beach, followed closely by the naval bombardment from the destroyers, the Germans finally realized that they were facing a raid. At that point, they turned the full might of their defences against the invaders.

∽

Despite the clash in the Channel, the surprise seemed to hold throughout the landing zones, except for one – and that was the result of plain bad luck. At precisely 0450 hours, the landings west of Dieppe, at Orange and Green Beaches, began with No. 4 Commando under Lieutenant Colonel Simon Fraser (Lord Lovat) storming ashore near their target, the coastal battery at Varengeville, while Lieutenant Colonel Cecil Merritt's South Saskatchewan Regiment landed on Green Beach at Pourville, tasked with securing the town and capturing the western headland overlooking the main beach. Lord Lovat's landing was stunningly successful; in just two hours, the sharp firefight ended with a classic bayonet charge and fierce hand-to-hand fighting that destroyed the battery guns, prompting the proud signal to Hughes-Hallett and Roberts on the *Calpe*: 'Every one of the gun crews finished with bayonet, OK by you?'

That, however, would be the only clear-cut success for the raiding force that day. Although Merritt's South Saskatchewan Regiment achieved surprise, a navigational error by the landing craft flotilla put his battalion on the wrong side of the river Scie. This mix-up delayed their advance, forcing them to fight their way across the bridge in town, a narrow bottleneck where Merritt personally led them in an act of extreme valour that garnered him the Victoria Cross. Although the regiment established a small bridgehead in the town (for subsequent landings by the Queen's Own Cameron Highlanders from Winnipeg) and captured the radar station, they could not reach the top of the western headland overlooking the main beach, and it remained in German hands throughout the raid.

To the east of Dieppe, things were worse – much worse. Because of the convoy clash, only a handful of Durnford-Slater's No. 3 Commando made it to shore at Yellow Beach, and the ones who did ended up being killed or captured as they tried to rush the openings leading to the top of the cliff. The one exception was the intrepid platoon under Lieutenant Peter Young, whose small force of commandos managed to land, climb a steep cliff and creep up close to their target – the Goebbels coastal battery. After cutting the phone lines that connected it with Dieppe, Young ordered his vastly outnumbered platoon to snipe at the battery with mortar and rifle fire from an adjacent cornfield, in the hope of drawing the Germans' attention away from other targets. They succeeded for close to three hours before they ran short of ammunition, at which point Young ordered them to beat a hasty retreat back to the boats that had brought them ashore. Although Hughes-Hallett and Roberts were out of touch with events on the east flank of the bridgehead, Young would later boast about what he believed was his greatest success on the day: 'I took 18 men ashore, did the job we had to do and brought 18 men back.'[58]

Even though the landings on the outer flank had experienced some success, as had those on Green Beach to a lesser extent, it was a different story that developed at Puys, overlooking Blue Beach, to say nothing of the slaughter about to unfold on the main beach in Dieppe itself. At Puys, Lieutenant Colonel Douglas Catto's Royal Regiment of Canada had the crucial task of seizing the eastern headland and capturing the guns on Pollet Cliff overlooking Dieppe harbour – the armaments that controlled access to and from the harbour. Unlike in other parts of the defended zone around Dieppe, the convoy clash had initially led the German commander in that sector to put his men on full alert. Not expecting anything to come from what he too suspected was a routine clash, he was moments away from calling a stand-down when his enthusiastic second-in-command had a brainwave. Seeing as his men were awake, alert and already at their guns, why not carry out an impromptu anti-raid drill? Reluctantly, the commander agreed, in complete ignorance of the scores of landing craft steaming towards Blue Beach, carrying the first wave of the Royals, who were now running seventeen minutes late and would land in daylight rather than under cover of darkness as initially prescribed in the plan.

From such lucky – or unlucky – chances are battles sometimes won or lost: arriving late on Blue Beach proved catastrophic for the Royal Regiment, and that in turn had a cascading effect on the entire plan for Operation Jubilee and the pinch itself.

Their delay, however, was due not to the convoy clash but to human error. While loading into landing craft from the converted passenger liners, *Queen Emma* and *Princess Astrid*, which acted as mother ships for the ALCs, the first wave of the Royals found themselves following the wrong steam gunboat towards Dieppe. Confusion ensued when they realized they were halfway to the Dieppe harbour mole rather than Puys. It was only when they saw the harbour lights flashing to assist the German trawlers escaping from the clash at sea that they realized their mistake, changed course and headed for Puys, now seventeen minutes behind schedule.

By that time, the pre-dawn darkness crucial for success had lifted, the early morning sun only intermittently obscured by haze. Within seconds of the landing craft coming into view of the defenders at Puys, the Germans opened fire in almost robotic fashion. The men aboard the landing craft bold enough to sneak a peek could see flashes from the cliffs ahead, announcing the projectiles that whizzed past overhead or smashed into the doors and walls of the boat. With touchdown on the beach only moments away, the tension soared, relieved only by the surge forward when the first craft contacted the chert-rock beach. As the doors swung open, the slaughter on Blue Beach began.

German small-arms fire joined the staccato machine-gun bursts, while the cadence of whining mortars and screaming artillery shells increased with each salvo. In some boats, when the ramps dropped or the doors swung open, the men exited in an orderly fashion – right rank first, left rank second and middle rank last. In other craft, swept by gunfire, a frantic scrambling ensued as the living, laden with helmets, webbing, equipment and personal weapons, stepped over the dead and the dying to rush through the tight doors of the craft or plopped over the sides into the water. Almost immediately, the water along Blue Beach frothed with a crimson hue.

Arriving in daylight, the men had no cover and no chance to take out the German defenders with the speed, dash and daring that Hughes-Hallett and Roberts had counted on.

Less than 500 yards from the beach, Private Jack Poolton's landing craft, steaming forward in the lead rank of the second wave, heard the 'bullets hitting the hull of the landing craft [which] sounded like hail on a tin roof.' Inside, one machine gun round grazed the young Royal, passing through his tunic but failing to find flesh, bone or organ. Although the men around him remained calm, Poolton could sense their rising tension as they continued onwards to Blue Beach:

I could feel the heartbeat of the man next to me. This was not from fear but anticipation of the task ahead. The second wave was to advance inland after the first had broken through the defences. However, this was to prove impossible as the first wave had run into a maelstrom ... and many were killed or wounded in the first few minutes of landing on the beach. As we landed, we were under a continuous stream of heavy machine-gun and mortar fire, and as the ramp was dropped, the firing came straight into the landing craft.[59]

For Private Ron Beal, approaching in the third wave, with German tracer fire buzzing over his head, the sights and sounds from the beach ahead recalled an ominous discussion he had overheard hours earlier with his mates aboard the *Queen Emma*. When told of their destination, one soldier asked innocently, 'How do you spell Dieppe?' He thought about it for a while before he said, 'You know, the first three letters spell *die*.' As Beal related to me years later: 'When we got there, that's exactly what we did.'[60] That exchange was foremost in his mind as his landing craft hit its mark, and the doors swung open. Sprinting over bodies of wounded, dead and dying friends, wading through severed body parts and the discarded weapons and equipment of a battalion already torn apart, he saw flashes from German machine guns buried in the concrete bunkers that climbed the cliff on the left flank. Miraculously, Beal made it up the beach, through the withering fire, and to the base of the cliff that offered the only modicum of shelter. Here, he turned to take stock. Behind him lay over 200 of his comrades, most dead, some dying, others writhing in pain, begging for aid or to be finished off. To each side of the nineteen year-old private, more men, like him, sat trapped along the seawall or under the cliff, hoping to avoid a needless confrontation with German fire from the flanks or now from above.

The Germans, sitting above on the cliff tops, watched hundreds of soldiers from the Royal Regiment clamber awkwardly out of landing craft and straight into a hail of murderous fire as they tried to scramble across 100 yards of open beach to the cliff. Only the Germans' cries for more ammunition proved louder than those of the wounded and dying below. Before long, the full weight of mortar and artillery shells added to the carnage, while Wehrmacht soldiers casually dropped grenades onto the Canadians huddled below.

At one point there was a glimmer of hope when the Royals' commanding officer, Lieutenant Colonel Douglas Catto, using a gap in the firing while the Germans brought up more ammunition, managed to get to the top of the cliff with a small band of men and pushed on towards the eastern headland. The Germans were quick to realize what had happened and resumed their deadly hailstorm that forced Beal and his comrades trapped under the cliff to surrender just a few hours after their inauspicious landing. Meanwhile, Catto, when the rest of his battalion failed to appear on the clifftop, ordered his men to hide out in a copse not far from their objective, the German gun battery atop Pollet Cliff, to await the reinforcements that never came. In the early afternoon, with the sounds of gunfire now a distant memory, he ordered them to lay down their weapons and surrender.

∽

By 0520 hours – the moment the frontal assault had been scheduled to hit the main beach, following on the heels of the carefully timed air and naval bombardment – Ham Roberts and Jock Hughes-Hallett aboard the *Calpe* had nothing to rely on but the scraps of information pouring in over the dozen or so wireless sets, augmented by an occasional glimpse of the shore through the ship's naval binoculars. Everything – from the ships at sea to the units on land and afloat, from the air force above to Leigh-Mallory's No. 11 Group headquarters at Uxbridge and Admiral James's fort in Portsmouth – was patched in to the *Calpe* and the *Fernie*, offering Fleming and those fortunate enough to eavesdrop a vivid but incomplete account of the battle.

For the historian all these years later, the message logs kept by operators to record the conversations provide a unique testimony crucial for reconstructing events. Only some of the logs have survived, unfortunately, while others collected by Hughes-Hallett for his official after-action report were never seen again in their original form, only in the extracts he released with his official account. However, some messages compiled by the 1st Canadian Corps Headquarters in England and by a few of the wireless operators on board *Calpe* and *Fernie* are available in the archives. This collection offers a unique, though partial, insight into what the force commanders faced as the raid unfolded – and, along with the contextual understanding of the pinch imperative as a driver for the operation, they provide a dramatic new understanding of decisions taken by Ham Roberts and Jock Hughes-Hallett that day.

Unlike commanders in the field, historians have the luxury of time: we can weigh and assess each message without the pressures of command or of life-and-death decisions hanging in the balance. Roberts and Hughes-Hallett, listening intently in real time to the radio chatter, were forced to play the role of coaches attempting to guide their side to victory from the remoteness of a dressing room rather than from the sidelines or behind the bench. In this case, moreover, the stakes were immeasurably higher than the outcome of a simple sporting match.*

〜

At 0500 hours, the increasing drone of dozens of RAF attack aircraft announced the start of the main beach assault, with air attacks on the headlands on each side of Dieppe and a naval bombardment of the German positions on the beach. Up to this point, everything in this sector had proceeded like clockwork, with the assault troops lowered into landing craft from the troopships *Prince Charles*, *Prince Leopold* and *Glengyle* without incident and ten miles out, beyond the range of German radar. Unlike at Blue Beach, the landing flotillas formed up successfully and departed on time, providing the men with a near-perfect view of the fireworks ashore before the low-flying Boston bombers swooped in and the destroyers turned windward to lay down a thick

---

* The camaraderie and adventuresome spirit of military men were very much on display in the message logs. The plan called for the use of the first name or nickname of the formation commander as the code name for each unit. In this case, when the South Saskatchewans hit the shore at Pourville, the *Calpe* received word that at '0450 Cecil landed.' Among the other code names were Bob (Labatt) for the Royal Hamilton Light Infantry, Fred (Jasperson) for the Essex Scottish, Ham (Roberts) for the Military Force Commander, Goose (Gostling) for the Cameron Highlanders, Doug (Catto) for the Royal Regiment of Canada, Joe (Ménard) for the Fusiliers Mont-Royal, Johnny for the Calgary Tanks, Tiger for Tiger Force, Robert for Robert Force, Bill (Southam) for the 6th Brigade and Sherwood (Lett) for the 4th Brigade.

smokescreen on the east headland and the beach ahead. The only hitch so far was the slow river gunboat *Locust*, which, arrived behind schedule – too late to participate in the Jubilee overture.

As prescribed in the plan, the landing craft slowed to a crawl about 500 yards from shore to watch attack aircraft shift their attention from the headlands to the beachfront and the buildings on the boulevard de Verdun. Swarms of fighter bombers temporarily lifted the spirits of the infantry as aerial cannons pounded away at enemy positions, followed by the 'crump, crump, crump' from sticks of bombs dropped by low-level bombers and the roar of engines at full throttle as they made good their escape over the Channel from the cascade of German anti-aircraft fire sweeping the skies. From their narrow viewpoint on the landing craft, the spectacle ahead suggested to the assault troops about to storm the main beach that the intricate Operation Jubilee was unfolding as it should. Then came touchdown.

Ordered to get off the beach and move as fast as possible over the promenade and into the town and port, they had no time to waste once the first landing craft opened its door. Captain Donald Fraser McCrae, attached to the Essex Scottish for the raid, recorded:

> At about four-thirty, some of our aircraft began attacking shore targets and almost immediately, the sea was lit up by flares and within a few minutes, we were being fired upon. It was then light enough to see a little bit and while everyone kept their heads down in the assault craft, we were able to see some of the earlier air battles and some of our bombers diving in to attack shore targets. As we continued to move in, visibility grew better and we came under fire of the shore weapons about five o'clock. The intensity of the fire increased and shells and long-range mortar bombers were bursting in the sea among the advancing craft. Some of the craft were hit and sunk, but the majority of them were able to carry on. There was no hesitation, flotillas retained their formation and despite the heavy fire, the assault wave of craft touched down on the beach at 0505hrs.[61]

Although both the Essex Scottish and the Royal Hamilton Light Infantry landing next to them on White Beach arrived on time and on target, along with the Canadian combat engineers, they were aghast to find the beach devoid of Churchill tanks. The first group of landing craft bringing the tanks was fifteen minutes behind schedule, leaving the men hopelessly exposed, with only the undulating rock beach or the low seawall for protection. Worse still, that delay gave the German defenders time to recover from the initial shock of the bombing and the naval gunfire. As McCrae continued:

> Immediately, the troops disembarked and ran up the shingle on the beach, where they were held up by the first row of barbed wire. They started to cross this immediately, some cutting a pathway through the wire to get through. The casualties were not very heavy at the first wire[,] and the bulk of the troops were able to take cover in the shingle while wire parties went on to cut the second fence of concertina wire. By this time, the enemy had begun shelling the beach very heavily with what seemed to be field artillery and heavy mortar.[62]

At first, the German fire was light, but as soon as the men crested the beach, they faced a torrent of steel and fire from carefully concealed machine-gun and sniper positions in the buildings on the boulevard de Verdun and the pillboxes and slit trenches on the promenade. Every move provoked a torrent of enemy fire and, despite the thick smokescreen wafting across the beach, German shells of all calibres began to find their mark. The engineers, essential to clear the six-foot-high, barbed-wire-crowned concrete anti-tank obstacles placed in the tiny roads that led to the port and the town, began to fall by the score while attempting to drag their explosives ashore and up the beach.

Remaining on the beach was a guaranteed death sentence; pushing ahead offered a slightly better chance of survival. But with both headlands still in German hands and the smokescreens laid down by the aircraft and the ships offshore providing only intermittent cover at best, progress meant tackling pillboxes, barbed wire entanglements and German slit trenches while simultaneously dodging bullets and shellfire pouring down from three sides. Casualties soon became horrendous in number and, given the circumstances, gruesome in nature.

Howard Large, a 22-year-old private in A Company of the Essex Scottish, tasked with storming aboard the trawlers and seizing the signals material before their crews could destroy it, wondered what kept hitting him as he sprinted over the seawall to the second belt of wire. Once he reached it, he discovered to his horror that the projectiles were the severed body parts of comrades torn to pieces by sizzling shrapnel splinters or blown apart by high explosives; all of this was followed by a pink mist that tasted of copper. As Large related, nothing was more vivid or lasting than the terrible kaleidoscope of moments on the beach. Next to him, an officer with one leg sheared off was still barking orders; another lay curled in the fetal position, his nerves fried by fear; a sergeant, writhing in pain as he tried to stuff his disgorged entrails back into his sliced abdominal cavity, was begging someone to finish him off. Further ahead, a friend, Everett McCormick, who had failed in his previous attempts to place a Bangalore torpedo to clear the barbed wire, decided instead to hold it in place as it detonated, ripping both the wire and the 38-year-old private apart. To the right, just yards away, Large watched in agony as another private, trapped in the steel labyrinth, squirmed helplessly like a macabre marionette, yelping in high-pitched tones as the phosphorus grenades clipped to his webbing ignited, eating away flesh and bone. His immolation only took seconds, but his suffering seemed an eternity to Large.[63]

At last, a quarter of an hour after the main landings went in, the Churchills from the Calgary Tanks arrived – but they struggled to get off the landing craft and up the chert-rock beach. Some, as expected, threw their tracks when the fist-sized stones clogged their sprocket holes, while others lumbered forward, attempting to make the steep grade to breach the seawall. Of the 29 tanks that eventually landed during the course of the morning, just over half made it over the seawall and onto the promenade. Lacking support from the engineers, who lay scattered with the dead and wounded of the Royal Hamilton and the Essex Scottish regiments on the beach and promenade, the 38-ton beasts could not pierce the concrete roadblocks erected by the Germans in the narrow streets near the tobacco factory or in any alternative street leading to the port. So they roamed on their own up and down the formerly grassy promenade, ripping up the turf and crushing friend and foe alike under their treads, while the crews searched in vain for any exit that would lead to the harbour, or at least off the beach.

By 0600 hours, the four companies of the Essex Scottish were pinned down on Red Beach taking heavy casualties, as were the Royal Hamilton Light Infantry on White Beach. Some of the 'Rileys' were forced to clear the casino and enter into close-quarter combat inside the walls of the dilapidated structure, including a dreaded hand-to-hand confrontation with its German defenders.[64] Right across the beach, cohesion at the battalion and company level began to break down, leaving the initiative to carry on in the hands of individual soldiers, platoons or even section-sized groups of intrepid but desperate men.

Although most of the Royal Hamilton Light Infantry remained trapped on the beach on either side of the casino, several men penetrated into the western part of the town through the walls of the local theatre (now a museum dedicated to the raid), about 30 yards beyond the boulevard de Verdun, reaching the post office, the Gestapo headquarters and Saint-Rémy church. This area was the only 'bright spot' on the main beach – the obvious place for Ham Roberts to send reinforcements should he plan to exploit the success. Unfortunately, the Essex Scottish did not share the Rileys' relative good fortune on Red Beach.

Here, on the main beach, only two small parties, including Howard Large's group, crossed the promenade at full gallop while under heavy fire and reached the boulevard de Verdun, with the survivors disappearing into the buildings nearby that separated the beach from the port. The first party, led by the company sergeant major, Cornelius Stapleton, reached their objective: the structures overlooking the trawlers where the inner channel met the Quai Henri IV. The party that included Howard Large found itself trapped in a cellar somewhere between the beach and the harbour. But having suffered more than 75 per cent casualties in little over an hour, the remnants of Lieutenant Colonel Fred Jasperson's 500-strong battalion were unable to continue organized fighting. Although they were but a stone's throw from the trawlers and less than 100 yards from the Hôtel Moderne, they could go no further. Without tank support, they did not possess the size, strength or firepower to achieve their objectives unless they received significant reinforcements.

～

When the *Locust* finally made it across the Channel to Dieppe, she was twenty minutes behind schedule and too late to contribute effectively to the Essex Scottish attack on the main beach. Given what transpired, though, it is doubtful that her four-inch guns would have made any difference. According to Jock Hughes-Hallett, not only was her lack of speed a factor but also, in the darkness, Red Ryder and her captain John Stride had her formed up behind the wrong landing group. Apparently, 'this mistake was not noticed until 0510hrs when she closed Red and White beaches at full speed arriving there about 0530hrs.'[65]

When the smokescreen cleared, the entire Dieppe panorama came into view. To Marine Douglas Bevan, shouldering a satchel of high explosives to blow the lock gates in the harbour, the scene presented a paradox he never forgot: 'It was a lovely day when we arrived there, early in the morning, beautiful blue sky. All Hell had been turned loose.'[66] Indeed, the men on board saw smoke rising from the beachfront and the headlands, aircraft twisting and turning above to avoid German flak, the whole tableau accompanied by the constant sound of explosions in the distance. Meanwhile, the Royal Marines of Tiger Force remained on the upper deck, bodies pressed prone to avoid any stray bullets or shell fragments that might be flying around, preparing for their baptism of fire.

Due to the thick smokescreen and fires raging on the beach and in the town, Ian Fleming, located not far offshore on HMS *Fernie*, was able to see little of the actual fighting on the beaches. He could, however, hear the battle raging. The noise level provided hope that things would eventually proceed as planned, although the sight of returning landing craft, some shot up and already carrying wounded, suggested otherwise. For Red Ryder and his Cutting Out Force, the clock was now ticking. From the moment the first shot was fired, the chances for a successful pinch lessened with each passing minute. Despite the prevalent notion that the German defenders' 'occidental attitude' of self-preservation would rule the day, they could still attempt to destroy the Top Secret signals material in their possession if they had enough time to recover from the initial shock.

As far as the records indicate, Ryder did not wait for the pre-arranged signal from the Essex Scottish, who in any event had more pressing issues to worry about; at 0545 hours, he decided it was time for the *Locust* to play her part. Ordering Captain Stride to steer for the harbour entrance, Ryder recorded later that they made three headlong attempts to breach the mole. On each occasion, heavy fire rained down on the gunboat from the east headland – which, according to the plan, was supposed to be in the hands of the Royal Regiment of Canada. Instead, the Royals remained pinned down on Blue Beach at Puys, out of radio contact, their wireless sets shot up or submerged in the surf.

On the first attempt, neither Ryder nor Stride could locate the out-stretched arms of the Dieppe jetties in the intense smoke, and after two near misses from large-calibre shells, Ryder ordered a quick about-face to prepare for another run. Sailing only eight feet above the waterline on the low-slung river gunboat's deck, Bevan recalled that, when the *Locust* unexpectedly turned hard following Ryder's command, the ship listed at such an angle that the men on the port side could scoop up the Channel water in their hands.[67] Below deck, Seaman John Parsons had little idea of what was happening above; all he knew was that the guns of *Locust* were blazing away, judging by the demands shouted down for a continuous stream of ammunition for the Chicago Piano and the other guns on deck.[68]

The second attempt met the same fate: the German guns were still active on the east headland, and those on the west headland were now reaching out for them too. This time Ryder asked Stride to reverse hard, backing away from the mole with all guns firing at whatever crevice tucked into Pollet Cliff belched fire and smoke at regular intervals. Undaunted, Ryder ordered yet another go at the harbour, hoping that in the intervening minutes the situation on the east headland had changed. However, in Ryder's words: 'On the third occasion, we were hit on the back of the bridge, and two men were killed. We in the forward half of the bridge being saved by Stride's railway sleepers.'[69]

Ernest Coleman, who had been designated to take the pinched material out of Dieppe on the motor launch, recalled:

We came under heavy fire from a huge gun emplacement directly on the entrance to the harbour and by other shore batteries ... the top deck of *Locust* was hit twice in quick succession ... two were killed instantly, and many more injured. I remember lying on the deck with no cover whatsoever, the speed of the shells coming over my head seemed to be parting my hair, they were that close. I saw one of the lads some short distance away from me mumbling something or possibly praying, a few seconds later I looked again, he was no longer with us.[70]

For Paul McGrath, the two hits on the *Locust* proved a pivotal moment in his young life. 'I was lying on the top deck ... belly pressed hard against the steel, rifle clutched in my right hand, my pulse at the double and waiting with others of 10 platoon ... for the moment to leap on the quayside and go about our business.'[71] Lifting his head for a brief moment before the German shells hit home, he could see:

on the right, were the cliffs overlooking the shingle beaches and prominent waterfront. To the left were the lower escarpments dominating the harbour and the crooked channel leading to the inner harbour about a quarter of a mile from the entrance. Both heights were stiff with guns whose crews, relatively safe in their concrete bunkers, kept up a savage bombardment. They were having a field day.[72]

McGrath noticed his good friend 'Ginger' Northern 'some fifteen feet away, not deigning to lie down' despite the apparent danger, while others lay prone beside him on the deck 'adrenalin pumping and primed for action.'[73] Within seconds, another shell hit the *Locust* just yards away from Coleman and McGrath. 'The noise of the explosion was gigantic,' recalled McGrath:

The shock of it blew all the fuses of my nervous system. I was petrified with such a terror it stunned my mind. I lay on the deck with a sort of premature *Rigor Mortis*, immobilized by the awful thought of immediate and terrible death. The game of war, which I had been enjoying up to that point, had suddenly turned deadly serious. Of course, I had been aware that the game had its perils, but getting killed was something that happened to other chaps. Now, for the first time, it burst like a thunderbolt upon my consciousness that my life, too, was in danger of being abruptly snuffed out. The sods were actually trying to kill ME![74]

The air 'thick with the smell of burnt explosives,' McGrath noticed Sergeant John Kruthoffer, lying motionless on the deck.

He was covered with small debris thrown up by the explosion, and at first glance, I thought he had been hit, but he grunted, stirred and expleted. He was shocked and unhurt, and like me, trying to collect his wits. Other members of the platoon lay nearby, some wounded and all in a state of shock.[75]

Not all of them escaped the wrath of the shells. Trying to collect himself, McGrath spotted the lifeless figure of Ginger Northern slumped against the bulkhead with one of the ship's crew rifling through his pockets. Prying himself from the deck, the nineteen-year-old corporal went over to enquire about this odd behaviour, only to be told by the petty officer in a gruff tone: 'He's dead ... and I'm taking his personal stuff to send back home ... orders to throw the dead overboard ... here, give me a hand.' As they dumped the body overboard, McGrath wondered if his pal was the first member of the Royal Marine Commando to die on the raid. He was, but he would not be the last.

Red Ryder was under orders not to breach the harbour mole with the *Locust* if German artillery fire was still active, and the three futile and near-disastrous attempts to charge in had dramatically reinforced the wisdom of this provision in the plan. Losing the *Locust* while running the gauntlet was acceptable – the Royal Marines on board could 'swim' to the stairs and fight on through the harbour if necessary – but nothing would be accomplished if she was sunk before reaching the inner channel. Now, having been denied on three occasions, Ryder received a direct order from Hughes-Hallett via radio at 0607 hours that the *Locust* should not 'enter until the situation at Blue Beach clears.'[76] Ryder pulled the gunboat back into the Channel but continued to exchange fire with the positions on the cliff, hoping that Catto's Royal Regiment would soon arrive from Blue Beach. For Jock Farmer, this respite was a welcome relief: 'As there was very little protection on deck we dreaded the next salvo, but luckily *Locust* was still afloat. The skipper had already put her full astern and kept going until we were just out of range – for the time being.'[77]

∽

The force commanders aboard *Calpe* never had a clear idea about what was happening at the 'sharp-end' – on the beaches. Despite all the communications technology Mountbatten had installed on both command ships, the 'fog of war' prevailed throughout the battle. Jock Hughes-Hallett and Ham Roberts were forced to make decisions based on a patchwork collection of information flowing in from numerous sources that was always incomplete, often contradictory and sometimes erroneous. The radio operators and forward observation officers tasked with relaying the events ashore had been cut down on the beach by enemy fire or had not even landed where expected. In the ensuing muddle, the commanders made some choices that, viewed through the safety of hindsight, seem wildly disconnected from reality.

By the time Hughes-Hallett ordered Ryder on the *Locust* to wait offshore, both he and Roberts knew that the landings on Orange Beach and Green Beach had scored some initial success, but they had no knowledge of the disasters on Yellow Beach and Blue Beach – only silence. With German gun positions on both headlands blazing away, they had to be aware that neither Doug Catto's Royal Regiment of Canada nor Cecil Merritt's South Saskatchewan Regiment had reached its prime objective and that the air attacks and naval bombardment had failed to deter the German gunners from raining fire down on the main beach or the seaward approaches to Dieppe. Most distressing for them was the news that the Calgary Tanks had arrived late, and that both the Royal Hamilton Light Infantry and the Essex Scottish, caught on the beach, were pinned down and reported to be taking heavy casualties. Despite the ominous news, in their view all was not yet lost.

The biggest decision for any commander in the heat of battle is whether to call in the reserve force – whether to reinforce the line or whether and when to call off an attack. There is no formula for the commander to follow in making this decision; rather, he trusts his instinct – what the Germans call *Fingerspitzengefühl*, or 'fingertip feel.' In this period of the war, some in the Anglo-Canadian high command held that commanders should not call off an attack before they had used the full extent of their force – an attitude particularly prevalent in the cocky atmosphere of Combined Operations and among enthusiastic 'thrusters' like Ham Roberts. Right from the start of the raid, Roberts and Hughes-Hallett had to weigh whether the losses incurred would justify the final result, and expectations at home were high: John Godfrey had classified the objectives of the pinch as A1 targets – targets worth incurring heavy casualties to obtain. The dilemma was straightforward: if they embarked on an attack that incurred heavy losses but in the process failed to achieve the main objective, then calling it off would be viewed as a waste of lives for no purpose; however, if they committed the rest of their force, in this case their reserves, and by so doing achieved their objective, then the extra cost would be considered worthwhile and justifiable.*[78] Despite the increasingly gloomy news pouring in over the radio, neither Ham Roberts nor Jock Hughes-Hallett would relent, and both seemed electrified by one pivotal but ultimately misleading message from the Essex Scottish. Within

---

* Lieutenant General Guy Simonds, who went on to lead the Second Canadian Corps in Normandy (and was Crerar's chief of staff at First Canadian Corps in 1942), summed up this philosophy in a speech to his officers in the summer of 1944: 'As a Commander you must consider at the outset whether the losses incurred are going to be worth the final assault. You must determine where these losses are going to be the minimum you can afford in relation to the value of the objective. We can't fight the Boche without incurring casualties and every soldier must know this. My point of view is that if I can't embark upon an operation to take a certain feature, for example, unless it will be useful to me later, the operation is not worthwhile and I call it off with 50% casualties incurred, then I have achieved nothing but a waste of lives; if I continue, and incur a further 20% casualties and bring the operation to a successful conclusion, then the operation is worthwhile. I speak of casualties in grossly exaggerated figures. In no operations yet have I participated where casualties were not between 15% and 25% and even at that, 25% is still a grossly exaggerated figure.' ('Report on the Address by Lt. Gen. G.G. Simonds, CBE, DSO, GOC 2nd Cdn. Corps, to Officers of 3 Cdn. Inf. Div. and 2nd Cdn. Armd Bde at the Château near Cairon by Major A.T. Sesia.')

minutes of Hughes-Hallett's order for Red Ryder to wait, the command team learned that the 'Essex Scottish R[egiment] crossed beaches and into houses at 604 [hours].'[79] That message marked the turning point in the Dieppe saga and started a rollercoaster ride that ended in perhaps the most controversial set of decisions ever reached in Canadian military history – and one of the greatest blunders of the Second World War. Both Roberts and Hughes-Hallett assumed from the message that the whole battalion – all four companies and 500 men, not just the remnants of two decimated and under-strength platoons – were in the town near the port and close to their targets. At this point, they decided to reinforce the Essex Scottish.

Minutes later, the news arrived that the Royal Regiment had failed to land on Blue Beach – but again, the message was erroneous. The force commanders, thinking the Royals were still afloat rather than trapped on Blue Beach, immediately switched their landing zone, ordering them to come in over Red Beach and link up with the Essex Scottish. In the interim, messages began to arrive from the Essex Scottish that the battalion was pinned down and taking grievous casualties – but Hughes-Hallett and Roberts dismissed these as the overexcited utterances of a green unit fighting its first battle. All they needed, it appeared to the commanders, was a little stiffening and reinforcement, either to consolidate their reported position in the town or to regain their momentum and push on into the port.

The force commanders also committed Lieutenant Colonel Dollard Ménard's Fusiliers Mont-Royal (FMR) to the fray. At 0640 hours, Hughes-Hallett, no doubt in conjunction with Roberts, recorded that he issued orders for the FMR to land at Red Beach near the tobacco factory, and link up with the Essex Scottish on the most direct line leading to the port and just two hundred yards from the Moderne. That too was a disaster. The landing craft bringing them to shore lost their way in the dense smokescreen and scattered, landing parts of the 500-man battalion at intervals all along Dieppe's shoreline, most of them near White Beach on both sides of the casino and at the foot of the western headland. Many of them were instantly gunned down or blown apart as they tried to cross the beach. Allegedly, a dozen men under the command of Sergeant Pierre Dubuc penetrated the town in the footsteps of the Royal Hamilton Light Infantry and made it as far as the two basins in the inner harbour.* There, they apparently stormed aboard a set of barges, hoping to hand them over to the Royal Marines, but after a short firefight with the crews, they ran short of ammunition and were forced briefly to surrender, before making their escape back to the beach.[80]

At 0645 hours, Jock Hughes-Hallett summoned Red Ryder aboard the *Calpe* for a discussion – one that resulted in the most controversial decision of the entire deadly day. He met initially with Ryder alone, he wrote later in both his after-action report and his memoirs, while Roberts continued to monitor events from the bridge. After an emotionally charged exchange, he said, 'with great moral courage, Ryder told me that he felt certain that any attempt to enter the harbour would be attended by the loss of all ships concerned, since they would have to run the gauntlet at point-blank range of batteries of medium calibre guns concealed in the caves dug into the side of the cliff.'[81] Given the fact that the orders had anticipated that result, Ryder's hesitation could have cost him his career, if not for his experience and his stature. Hughes-Hallett recorded that Ryder was 'emphatic that this part of the operation was no longer on,' and his 'very forthright advice against carrying out his part of the operation showed as much moral courage in August as he showed physical courage when he garnered the VC in March at St Nazaire. A lesser man might have felt it would be cowardly not to urge going ahead.'[82]

With Ryder's position clear, they proceeded only then 'to consult' with Roberts, who seems not to have been free to call the shots in the way Hughes-Hallett and Mountbatten would later claim. In his post-battle interpretation, Hughes-Hallett reluctantly followed Roberts's inexplicable order to commit the reserves to battle. However, in the words of the Australian journalist Wallace Reyburn, who spent hours observing the command team on board the *Calpe* during the struggle,

---

* The account given by Sergeant Dubuc and entered in the official record was dismissed by his commanding officer, Lieutenant Colonel Labatt, as 'absolutely preposterous from beginning to end.' However, the Canadian Army Historical Unit under the legendary Canadian military historian Charles P. Stacey refused to dismiss the account in its entirety, although it included, as they said, 'some embroidery.'

Roberts 'had the look of someone in an office who had been given "full authority" only to find that every time he turns around, he finds the boss looking over his shoulder.'[83] The evidence emerging in recently released documents shows that Hughes-Hallett was the main thread all through the raid – from conception to execution. This involvement, coupled with his confident and overtly ambitious personality, indicates that his account, supported in the post-war years by Mountbatten, is no more than an attempt to distance himself from the debacle by attributing their joint decision to Roberts alone. Both men, in fact, share full responsibility for the disaster that was about to unfold – what one Royal Marine called 'the sea version of the Charge of the Light Brigade.'[84]

While these decisions were being made, the Royal Marine Commando, including Ian Fleming's IAU (No. 10 Platoon), were waiting anxiously on the exposed decks of the *Locust* and the trailing French *chasseurs*. All remained blissfully unaware of what lay in store, given the fluid nature of the circumstances at play. For months they had trained intensively to run the gauntlet of Dieppe's inner channel to reach their targets in the outer harbour. Now, Red Ryder had wisely persuaded Jock Hughes-Hallett to cancel that axis of advance, but it is unclear whether he was in full agreement that they should be switched to an equally perilous course.

After this crucial meeting had finished at 0708 hours, Hughes-Hallett, who had full authority to call off any naval action at any point during the raid, issued orders for a flotilla of landing craft to form up behind the *Locust*, and then at 0731 he commanded Ryder to 'proceed as ordered.'[85] Before his return to the river gunboat, Ryder shouted via megaphone to the men from Tiger and Robert Forces on *Locust* and the *chasseurs* to transship into the landing craft forming up behind the old river gunboat.* Like the Fusiliers Mont-Royal, whose whereabouts

---

* According to Captain Hellings, a Royal Marine officer riding on the *Locust*: 'After the floating reserve had been landed there was no news, until Commander Ryder returned from *Calpe*, when he reported that Red and White beaches were clear of opposition and the General wished the Marines to go in and support the Essex Scottish through White Beach. The colonel (Picton Phillipps) gave his orders from *Locust*, the idea being to pass through the beach to the town and there, reform and report to the Colonel of the Essex Scottish, the object

were still unknown to Roberts and Hughes-Hallett, the Royal Marine Commando would go headlong onto the main beach with instructions to 'exploit into the town and report to the Colonel of the Essex Scottish Regiment.'[86] The implications of these orders are now clear: the Royal Marines would not land as 'simple reinforcements,' as many historical accounts claim. Instead, they would make one more attempt to reach their pinch targets in the harbour – albeit by different and distinctly desperate means.[87]

Within minutes of the order being issued, the men began their descent into an ad hoc flotilla of four ALCs and two tank landing craft (TLCs), some still smoking and battle-scarred from their earlier run. Once aboard the landing craft, Ernest Coleman noticed, as he recounts in his recently discovered memoir, that the battle surrounding them had whipped up to a feverish pace. 'Dog fights were going on, German planes were also dive-bombing the ships and small craft,' he recorded. 'How the cook on our boat managed to ... make us some cocoa and sandwiches I will never know!'[88]

Jock Farmer, waiting impatiently to board one of the TLCs with the rest of No. 10 Platoon, could see and hear nothing but a cacophony of 'explosions, tracer bullets and screams' from Dieppe's main beach. 'Some of the landing craft,' he noted, the half-wooden ones used by the Royal Hamilton Light Infantry, Essex Scottish and Fusiliers Mont-Royal before them, now burned 'fiercely' like 'death traps,' while larger TLCs slowly sank on the shoreline. But even before they were all on board, the German gunners spotted them forming up through the intermittent gaps in the smokescreen. 'Most of us managed to scramble aboard his craft,' Farmer recalled. 'Suddenly,' he continued, 'a couple of shells landed not far from us. The skipper of *Locust* (Stride) immediately set us adrift.'[89] Within minutes, the six landing craft were loaded and ready for their turn on Dieppe's main beach.[90]

---

of the force being to pass around the west and south of the town and attack the batteries on the eastern cliff from the south.' However, B Company Commander Captain R.K. Devereaux reports, 'I was told by Colonel Phillips that the whole force of the Royal Marine Commando was to go direct into the harbour.' (Report Operation Jubilee Royal Marine Commando, 19 August 1942, statement by office commanding B Company, Captain R.K. Devereaux, TNA ADM 1/11986.)

Meanwhile, the charnel-house battle for Red Beach continued, urgent messages flooding in from the Essex Scottish reporting that shellfire was now raining down on them from both headlands and that snipers were taking aim with machine guns from the tobacco factory and other buildings ahead. These messages were quickly followed by desperate calls for immediate evacuation.[91] Then, starting at 0742 hours, a series of messages arrived that, to the over-optimistic force commanders, made it appear as if Operation Jubilee was finally coming together. Two messages confirmed that the Royal Regiment of Canada had indeed landed on Blue Beach, though they failed to indicate that Doug Catto's unit had already been wiped out there. Ham Roberts and Hughes-Hallett concluded there was still a slim chance that the Royal Marines could take the eastern headland. A message from Hunter Force, one of the Canadian combat engineer teams, indicated that they too were alive, after being out of touch for most of the morning.

Encouraged by these fragments, the force commanders decided to send in the remaining elements of the ungainly Calgary Tanks, to assist Jasperson, bolstered by the Royal Marines, in an attempt to punch through at the tobacco factory. Still, they clung to the hope that they could grab their prime objectives in the port. In desperation, Brigadier Bill Southam, the commander of the 6th Canadian Infantry Brigade, which had just landed on the beach way behind schedule, exhorted the Essex Scottish to 'go as far towards the trawlers as possible.'[92] The final piece of this plan fell into place moments later when 'elements' of the Calgary Tanks, after spending hours trapped on the beach and the promenade, reported that they had made 'progress' in front of the tobacco factory. To the commanders on *Calpe*, it seemed that the shortest and most direct route to the harbour and the Hôtel Moderne was about to open up – a hope that trumped any discouraging and realistic reports to the contrary. At 0818 hours, with news that the situation on Red Beach was 'out of control' and – erroneously – that White Beach was firmly in Canadian hands, the Essex Scottish and the Royal Marines began their death ride towards Dieppe.

CHAPTER 14

All In on the Main Beach

Theirs not to reason why
Theirs but to do and die.
Alfred, Lord Tennyson,
'The Charge of the Light Brigade'

'We are going in!' is the cry Corporal Paul McGrath remembers from that moment. As the order was passed quickly from man to man, one young Marine turned to Peter Huntington-Whiteley, standing next to Joseph Picton Phillipps at the back of the tank landing craft, and inquired: 'For Christ sake, sir, where the fucking Hell are we?' For months the Royal Marines had trained in Portsmouth harbour for this moment, but for security reasons nobody except the officers had known the name of the port they planned to raid until the last moment; some, apparently, never knew. 'I suppose I can tell you now,' came the terse reply from the always correct lieutenant. 'That,' he said, pointing to the cloud of black smoke, 'is Dieppe – and I want to see you in my office tomorrow morning for using improper language.'[1]

Within seconds, all the boats, except for one with mechanical trouble that trailed behind, were enshrouded in a smokescreen that muffled the sound of the engines. For some reason, only repetitive refrains of 'Oh, Danny boy' raced through McGrath's mind. 'For a while,' he recalled, 'we were in an eerie, fog-bound capsule of time,' but as they drew near to the beach and the smoke cleared, shells of all calibres started to whizz overhead or fall between the craft. The closer they got to White Beach, the more intense it became, particularly from the western headland. Ernest Coleman, tucked along the starboard side of the landing craft nearest the cliffs, noted that 'the noise from the machine gun was like somebody playing a kettle drum.'[2]

For Bob McAlister, sitting with his Robert Force colleagues in a small landing craft that was following the TLC carrying members of Tiger Force, Picton Phillipps and No. 10 Platoon, the constant noise and explosions were 'terrifying.' He recalled:

I couldn't see how I could summon up enough strength to lead my section into that inferno. I had a look behind me, and what I saw gave me all the courage I needed and a great feeling of relief. The faces I looked at, including the officers sitting at the rear of the sections, were a mixture of my feelings. Their faces were white and drawn. I felt almost cheerful and could do anything.

Heading towards Dieppe at full speed, McAlister's boat was the first to be hit:

There was a terrific bang at the rear of the craft. When I looked around the flames were shooting straight up for about 40 feet, like a blow torch. One man had just cleared the hatch and went straight into the water, another was climbing out through the flames, screaming in pain. He fell in the water and continued screaming. The first officer (naval) who was in the water was shouting to us to get off the boat at once as the petrol tanks could blow up. The third chap in the engine room of the boat didn't make it. The naval chap kept shouting, 'Get clear of the boat quickly, the tanks will catch fire.' The smoke, fortunately for us, drifted across us as we piled out of the boat, hiding us from the guns on the cliff.[3]

With the German fire now increasing to fever pitch and the landing craft starting to drift apart in the smoke as they ran towards the beach, the futility of the charge began to dawn on Lieutenant Colonel Picton Phillipps, riding in the lead boat with the rest of Tiger Force and Fleming's IAU. Concluding that any effort to storm ashore would result in a useless waste of lives, the diminutive, eccentric, but thoroughly determined Royal Marine commander embarked on a selfless and heroic action of the highest order – one witnessed by all aboard the landing craft, and one they could never forget. 'The Colonel[,] realising the hopelessness of the situation,' recorded Jock Farmer in his memoirs, 'climbed on an ammunition box and, with Captain Comyn holding onto his legs as the boat was rocking heavily, put on white gloves so that other incoming craft would see him, and signalled them to turn back.' In full view of the enemy on the shore and well above the protective steel walls, exposed to enemy fire, Picton Phillipps waved off the attack. 'The next thing I noticed,' a young Marine by the name of J.J. Dwan recalled, 'was little puffs of green blanco coming off his equipment as he was being hit, then blood spurted from the left corner of his mouth, and he slumped down on to the deck of the landing craft. Nobody could have lived through that fire doing what he did. It was the ultimate act of courage.'[4]

The Intelligence Assault Unit history records that Huntington-Whiteley gave Picton Phillipps rum and comforted him in his last moments. His actions had saved some, but not all, of his Marines. Despite the signal, one or two other craft, and the TLC carrying the IAU, continued to plough their way to shore. As Paul McGrath, now standing next to the mortally wounded Picton Phillipps, recalled:

> The Sub-Lieutenant who skippered our boat seemed unaware that the action had been called off. His job was to deliver us onto the beach at the designated point, and he continued to drive forward at full throttle. The chaps at the bow were bracing themselves in the anticipation of the ramp falling in front of them, to be followed by a frantic scramble up the beach over potato-sized pebbles when, about thirty yards from the shore-line, the boat stopped abruptly. It was impaled on one of the many underwater obstacles that were submerged beneath the high tide.[5]

Then, suddenly, the vessel lurched to the starboard and righted itself.

The quick spin gave some on board a glimpse of what lay ahead for them. As Sergeant John Kruthoffer noticed, the beach was

> fire-swept ... occupied by prostrate bodies and a few desperate groups clinging to cover. A look in any direction showed only too clearly that along the whole stretch of beach, the landing of tanks and infantry had been smashed to a standstill. For those of us who could see over the side, the feeling at that moment was not of panic or unreasonable fear – but sheer amazement and disbelief. Not a logical reaction, but a short space of a few seconds when the brain tries to reject what has been fed in. 'Get out fast – spread out – and run like hell for cover.'[6]

As much as Kruthoffer wanted to get off the ship, he could not: the ramp had been jammed by the grounding as well as a direct hit from a German gun concealed in a cave in the headland. They were hopelessly exposed to German fire, which now picked up in tempo and gave no signs of abating. McGrath watched in horror as 'bombs and shells cascaded down around the boat and exploded in the sea[,] but some of the bullets struck home. There were gasps and groans and slumped bodies.' Desperate to 'get rid of us,' the young naval sub-lieutenant in charge tried 'to lower the ramp and finding it jammed, climbed up with a hammer. As soon as he showed himself he fell dead amongst us.'[7] For Kruthoffer, the whole episode proved surreal, with only 'parts of the jigsaw' clearly remembered years later:

> A group at the front trying to kick the ramp down. The CO, the crewman and others hit and falling about; a scream at the back end trying to dodge small arms fire coming down amongst them. Those looking over the shore side or trying to climb out, getting it in the head or chest and crashing back on to those behind them. Some Bren-gunners at work – one immortal bawling for full magazines – another enthusiast firing from a sitting position, threatening to shoot the head off anyone moving sideways.[8]

There was no point in any attempt to return fire, but one Marine kept hammering away with his Bren gun in what McGrath called 'a useless exercise.' Hit again and again at the rear of the boat by German shells, some Marines died instantly while others found themselves hurtled into the sky and tossed overboard into the shallow surf.

Then, according to Coleman, 'one of the naval ratings on the craft ignited a gas flare and tried to throw it over the side to give us some cover[,] but it hit the side and rebounded back into the craft.'[9] The ALC, already covered with diesel oil from the engine and petrol from extra tanks that had been punctured by shell fragments, immediately erupted in flames. An alert regimental sergeant major ordered those sitting near the ammunition box to heave it overboard, even if alight. 'We would have been blown to bits if the flames had reached it,' a thankful Paul McGrath reported. As more shells rocked the boat and the flames increased, the sergeant major, whom he never saw again, cried out, 'I'm afraid it is every man for himself, try and make it back.'[10]

But it was not easy to escape the flaming craft. 'Being unable to disembark either through the front ramp or over the shore side,' John Kruthoffer wrote,

the start of a raging fire became a deciding factor even for those who had been slow in realizing that their number was coming up. An effective smoke screen and very rapid movement meant that evacuation was carried out without many extra casualties. A quick check that those lying in the fire were dead – and then with anti-tank bombs and 36 grenades cooking and going off – instinct took over and saved the problem of planning the next move. Nobody made it ashore, except as POWs later, and the half-platoon which came back were those who were about to get out in one piece, and had the confidence to swim out towards home in the hope of being picked up.[11]

Once over the side, the survivors had a fateful choice to make: wade ashore to captivity and possible death or swim out to the Channel in the hope of being picked up before German fire or exhaustion got the better of them. For Paul McGrath and the rest of the IAU, the choice seemed obvious. 'We crowded close to the boat's hull for protection against the bullets. I quickly inflated the Mae West and, not being a good long-distance swimmer, its buoyancy encouraged me. Some voices were heard [saying] "let's go to the beach." Other voices, among them Sgt Kruthoffer's, urged "Come on, let's make for the ships."' Every man from Fleming's IAU decided to swim out to sea, hoping for rescue. Not all of them made it. The other craft that had not seen Picton Phillipps's frantic order to withdraw – the one carrying Major Titch Houghton – later landed its charges. All of them died on the beaches or fell into enemy captivity for the remainder of the war.

Ernest Coleman was now neck-deep in water, huddled, as he tells the story, with the rest of the IAU alongside the burning landing craft, the fierce fire incinerating the bodies of the dead on board. 'I was able to get around the side of the craft to get a little cover,' he recalled,

> but we had few options open to us, some of the lads decided to swim out to sea, on seeing this I decided to join them, I stripped off my clothes except for my shirt and underpants, when boarding the landing craft I was given a Mae West, I also put this on, all the time we were still under heavy fire. I finally entered the water along with my weapons, swimming long-distance for as long as possible.[12]

About 100 yards out, Coleman wrote, an explosion rendered him unconscious, and he awoke later having washed ashore. As he attempted to make a second break for the Channel, he crossed paths with two Germans, who took him prisoner.*

Paul McGrath, floating out to sea on his back and using the Mae West for support, could see the landing craft still in flames. To his left, a motor speedboat suddenly catapulted out of the harbour at a

---

* Coleman recalled in his diary: 'At the promenade I met other prisoners who had been in the water, I sat down on the grassy bank on the edge of the promenade, I was not aware until this time that I had lost my underpants, they must have come adrift when I was in the sea. ... The lads made me get in the centre of the column to save my embarrassment, I was still naked from the waist down, a bit later a Frenchman noticed me and handed me a pair of trousers, they were rather small for me but very much welcomed.'

frantic rate, in a desperate attempt to escape. Who was on it remains a mystery, but within three seconds a series of shells exploded as the Germans tried to find the range. 'One behind, one in front, and one on target which disintegrated the boat,' he noted. 'The German gunners were on form that day.'[13] Eventually, and near exhaustion, McGrath and the majority of his platoon were plucked from the English Channel and brought aboard *Calpe*, which by this time was conducting search and rescue and dodging the German bombers that were now appearing over the landing zone. Huntington-Whiteley, the man Fleming had chosen to lead what he hoped would be one of the most critical missions of the entire war, was also missing. He had disappeared into the surf, and nobody had any idea what had happened to the commanding officer.

Although there is no record of any investigation, both Mountbatten's headquarters and John Godfrey's Naval Intelligence Division probably remained uneasy until Huntington-Whiteley's fate was established. With no knowledge of Bletchley Park or cryptographic methods or procedures, Huntington-Whiteley would not have seemed a prize intelligence catch. Unless German intelligence had some reason to suspect that there was more to him and his mission than his youthful demeanour betrayed, the secret would remain airtight. However, during the retreat from the beaches, Brigadier Bill Southam and his staff were taken prisoner and, in his abandoned landing craft, the Germans discovered an almost complete set of the highly intricate operational plans for Operation Jubilee – the document that Mountbatten had ordered his brigade commanders to take ashore. Contained in the surviving portions was Appendix L – the search plan for Dieppe – the same one I used to connect Huntington-Whiteley to the Hôtel Moderne and the naval headquarters. I had the luxury of knowing who he was and what he was after, but it would not have taken the Germans long to figure that out either: the German soldiers who discovered the documents belonged to MARES – the same German intelligence commando unit on which Godfrey and Fleming had styled their own Intelligence Assault Unit.[14] Needless to say, when his interrogator plopped the captured search plan in front of him, Huntington-Whiteley would have had no place to hide. He would soon have been subjected to Nazi 'enhanced interrogation,' likely of the medieval sort.*

Fortunately for all concerned, Huntington-Whiteley did make it out of Dieppe alive. Despite the burns he had suffered during the fire on board the landing craft, he had managed to swim out to sea rather than fall into enemy hands and was picked up by a passing Royal Navy vessel, which brought him to the burn ward of the Brighton Municipal Hospital. In the description he wrote to John Kruthoffer from his hospital bed, the platoon commander explained:

> It wasn't until Saturday that I learned that most of you had got back, and you can imagine my feelings, as for the previous three days I had been absolutely certain that I was the only survivor from our ill-fated [TLC]. I was picked up by a small flak ship manned by the royals who did some splendid shooting ... I am right as rain now except for a peeling face, a couple of outsize lips and two brick-red legs which I consider very lucky remembering the amount of refuse that was flying about. I am going to write to the missing lads['] parents which will be very difficult as there is no definite news I can give them ... In fact, the only one who I am certain about is poor [Ginger] Northern who, you may or may not know, was going to be married early in September.[15]

Finally, by mid-morning, after exhausting all the reserves and cancelling the landing of the remaining elements of the Calgary Tanks on the main beach, Ham Roberts and Jock Hughes-Hallett called off the operation just after 1000 hours.**

---

* The Germans were ruthless after they found the plans, rounding up several *Dieppois*, including the local printer, who had produced copies of the German maps for the local headquarters. The Germans accused him of giving copies to the resistance, who in turn gave them to the British for targeting purposes.

** The remaining two flights of LCTs, carrying the whole of A Squadron and three troops of C Squadron – a total of 28 tanks – were never sent in. Although they did receive a signal at 0850 hours to land at White Beach, this order was countermanded ten minutes later during the approach. The two tank beach parties, instead of carrying out their planned initial tasks of directing the tanks to their objectives, spent most of their time in assisting the wounded and in organizing tank cover for the general withdrawal. ('Extract of report from the

Roberts sent a message by carrier pigeon back to England: 'Very heavy casualties in men and ships. Did everything possible to get men off but in order to get any home had to come to sad decision to abandon remainder. This was a joint decision by Force Commanders. Obviously, operation completely lacked surprise.'

On *Locust*, Red Ryder was also melancholy. Even years later, he would be weighed down by the decisions made that day. 'Coming back from Dieppe,' he wrote in his memoirs,

> I had a nagging feeling that I had not lived up to my hopes and ambitions. We had made three attempts on the harbour entrance and received an explicit signal not to continue. And yet in view of what the Canadians suffered, should I not have pressed home our attack with more resolution? We would certainly have been sunk before reaching the entrance, and one had to think of the many casualties it would have involved. It would have been a forlorn hope but might have helped others.[16]

On the *Fernie*, sitting at times just 700 yards off the main beach, Ian Fleming spent the day running between the bridge and the wardroom, trying to keep posted on the progress of the Royal Marines and his IAU. At times, according to the article he penned for the *Weekly Intelligence Report*, he peered out through his binoculars, watching *Locust* move towards the shore to take on the German guns in the eastern headland, 'pumping 4-inch shells with incredible rapidity' while the tattered landing craft went in. Off in the distance, he witnessed the British destroyer HMS *Berkeley* succumb to Luftwaffe bombs that crashed through its deck and exploded, leaving her to sink not far from Dieppe's shoreline. Then shells started to rip into the base of *Fernie*'s funnel, killing and wounding a number of sailors.

As the wounded fleet headed back to England, Ian Fleming turned to catch one last glimpse of Dieppe through the smoke. Sporadically,

---

Commanding Officer of 'B' LCT,' app. 15 to encl. 13, p. 2, John Hughes-Hallett, 'Naval Force Commander's Report No. NFJ 0221/92,' 30 August 1942, LAC, RG 24/10872/232C2 [D48].)

through gaps in the smokescreen, he glimpsed the results of some of the heaviest fighting still going on in Dieppe. On the beach, he could now make out hundreds of small figures lying motionless in an almost uniform pattern, punctuated by burning landing craft and the silhouettes of abandoned or trapped tanks. One landing craft that had ferried men and tanks to the shore only hours before was now crammed with the wounded and the bodies of the dead. The casino where he had fared poorly in his pre-war jaunts sat in near ruins. 'It was a drunken mockery of a building,' he wrote, confessing with 'unholy delight' his satisfaction at seeing the 'smile wiped off its face.' 'There was practically no movement, although heavy firing was still going on. It was a scene of utter desolation and destruction which one was glad to leave, though with a heavy heart.'[17]

～

Two days after Fleming returned to England, he sat down at his desk in Room 39 and typed up a report addressed to Wing Commander Bobby de Casa Maury, Mountbatten's Chief Intelligence Officer. When Godfrey read it, he sent it directly to Mountbatten with a note: 'I have read the attached notes by Commander Fleming who was present at Operation Jubilee in the course of his duties, and I generally agree with his remarks. I am forwarding the report personally to you as I think you may be interested to see what one of my staff has to say.' Although most of Fleming's treatise revolved around issues of security, he concluded that the Germans had no advance knowledge of Operation Jubilee.

In these candid remarks, Fleming also addressed the real reason he had been on the *Fernie*. He admitted that he was not there as a simple observer, overseeing the debut of his new IAU, as many biographical treatments maintain, but because it was his job to participate actively in the raid. 'I was accommodated in HMS *Fernie* with instructions to return to the nearest British port with any booty obtained by the IAU under the command of Lt. Col. Picton Phillipps, R.M. carried in HMS *Locust*. The IAU did not land, and in consequence, I remained in HMS *Fernie* throughout the operation and withdrawal.' Here, in one document, is Ian Fleming's confession that has sat in the archives for years, but with the exception of one account that missed its significance, it has never before been published in any writing about Dieppe.[18] Fleming was to be the anchor-man of the relay, with the Essex Scottish passing the booty to members of the IAU, who would then have Ernest Coleman whisked out of Dieppe harbour on a special motor launch to meet Fleming on *Fernie*. From there, with the battle still raging on shore, Fleming had orders to break off action and head directly to the nearest British port, bringing back what in cryptographic terms in the summer of 1942 was akin to the proverbial Holy Grail.[19]

Less than two years after he had paced the shores of England's damp Channel coast waiting for Operation Ruthless to bear fruit, Fleming, unlike his legendary literary super-agent James Bond, had been foiled again. Nothing could be clearer: this intelligence pipeline was central to the Dieppe Raid, and Fleming was the final link in the chain designed to bring the pinched material home.

Epilogue:
Recalibration

A proper evaluation is difficult because one is entirely dependent upon the British say so. If they feel that the results from a certain operation had been successful, there is little more to be said.

US Navy Report on British Procedures for Capturing
and Exploiting Enemy Naval Documents, 1944

In 1942, Ron Beal's war, like that of the overwhelming majority of the men who landed on Dieppe's beaches, was in essence 50 yards wide and 50 yards deep. As an infantry private in the Royal Regiment of Canada, he would not have been privy to the significance of the role his unit would play in relation to the overall plan. For the regular infantryman, the prevailing wisdom of the day dictated that he needed to know only just enough to get the immediate job done and nothing more. Such is the nature of military security, based on the strictest interpretation of the 'need to know' principle. Without knowledge of the planning sessions in Richmond Terrace, or the ability to eavesdrop on radio traffic during the battle, or be a fly on the wall at Bletchley Park or in Room 39, Ron Beal's initial understanding of what he went through was as narrow as his job description. However, when he returned from the war, he began his life's journey, searching for the rationale behind what he and his comrades had experienced on August 19, 1942 – something that seemed all too irrational. His quest translated into an advanced knowledge of all aspects of the raid – albeit knowledge based on the incomplete historical verdicts built up over the last 70 years.

For decades, his frustration and bitterness grew. The long litany of excuses, historical arguments and counter-arguments about what motivated the raid simply never made sense to him – or else failed to satisfy his distinctly restless soul. Like many of the others who took part in the raid – and indeed like many in the generations that followed these veterans, including many of Beal's close friends – he felt they were, as he would say, 'just thrown away.'[1] This was the Ron Beal I met with one spring morning in 2012 when I sat down to interview him for the documentary *Dieppe Uncovered*.

At first, I did not plan to reveal the findings in a detailed way to the 93-year-old veteran. However, my production partner on the film, producer/director Wayne Abbott, sensed Beal's profound angst, and so we spent the afternoon with documents in hand, taking him step by step through the story that now appears in these pages. His response was both moving and profound.

৸

Indeed, the new evidence, interwoven with the established historical record so thoroughly explored over the decades, has forced a fundamental recalibration of our understanding of Dieppe. But clearly, without that ground-breaking work of two previous generations of very talented historians, I would not have understood the potential of the initial discovery I made 25 years ago in the Public Record Office, now rechristened The British National Archives. Time too, has been on my side, as the classified archives of the various intelligence services in England, Canada and the United States have slowly made it into the public domain. Such is the collective nature of history.

As the years passed, the new evidence fell into place like pieces of a jigsaw puzzle – and there will be more to come. These new documents have made a significant contribution to the Dieppe saga, demonstrating that the search for intelligence material was not *a* driver for the raid but indeed *the* driver. At this pivotal point in time, the four-rotor crisis was the most urgent dilemma facing the NID; a conundrum that undermined the Battle of the Atlantic, the war at sea and the very centre of gravity of the war effort. More practically, the blackout and all that followed was not just a naval intelligence problem, or merely an Admiralty or 'British' problem. When the second blackout hit in 1942, it became an Allied problem, for the constant, uninterrupted flow of intelligence had been helping everyone. Everything depended upon control of the sea lanes, just as the body depends on blood in the veins to sustain life. But now a cancer had appeared, which meant that air, land, sea, industrial and domestic concerns were all at stake.

After the failure of the Dieppe pinch, however, the crisis worsened. But ten weeks later, in the final days of October, pure luck – in this case, a 'pinch by chance' from *U-559* off Port Said in Egypt by a group of heroic Royal Navy sailors – saved the day.[2] That pinch, which included the short-signal book and the weather codebook (both of which required the four-rotor machine to work on three-rotor settings for encryption and decryption), permitted the cryptanalysts to gain entry through the back door with cribs run on existing three-rotor Bombes. This was a band-aid solution without a doubt, but it provided Bletchley cryptanalysts with the ability to tread water for the first few months of 1943. By the summer, four-rotor Bombes had finally swung into action, and they read four-rotor naval Enigma-enciphered messages for the remainder of the war.[3] As the planners of the pinch raid at Dieppe knew when they sanctioned the force commanders to go 'all in' to obtain this objective, one good pinch could indeed do the trick, as had happened earlier on two occasions in Norway.

We now know too what the main targets of the raid were. Until these were revealed, and their prime, urgent importance to the war effort contextually understood, their inclusion in the planning documents made little sense. That has changed, as it is now clear that both naval headquarters and the nearby trawlers were front and centre from the raid's inception, and remained constant imperatives. The plans that Jock Hughes-Hallett and his team drew up for Dieppe – with crucial and foundational input from John Godfrey and Ian Fleming – saw all roads lead to the port housing these targets. Even with the postponements, these targets did not change; their centrality was accentuated.

The resources devoted to the pinch and their coordination in the plan also provide compelling evidence. Although the entire raiding force created the general conditions for the pinch, nearly half were allocated directly to the specific attempt – something that remained a constant in all manifestations of the plan: two infantry battalions, the Royal Marine Commando containing Fleming's specially crafted IAU, one third of the Calgary Tanks and the majority of the Canadian engineer units, not to mention the naval outlay that included 'expendable' vessels such as the *Locust*. One must also consider the choice of Red Ryder – a recently minted Victoria Cross recipient – to command the Cutting Out Force. Ryder, who had a passion for naval intelligence and would go on to command Fleming's growing IAU after Dieppe, was one of the very few men in the entire Royal Navy who possessed actual raiding experience. That rare commodity alone would have precluded risking him on a secondary or even a tertiary objective such as a publicity stunt, a theory that has been promulgated over the years.[4] If you were willing to risk losing a highly experienced and thoroughly proven combat leader like Ryder, the potential payoff had to be significant.

The plan itself, now clarified after the discovery of Royal Marine Commando orders and the record of the coordinating meeting, is revealed to have a remarkable redundancy built right into it to ensure the objective was achieved. Three waves of troops, supported by tanks, engineers, a river gunboat, a sloop and half a dozen French *chasseurs*, were tasked with carrying out the pinch: first the Essex Scottish, Calgary Tanks and Royal Canadian Engineers; then the Royal Marines, broken down into two strike forces set to spring into action twenty minutes apart. Undoubtedly, the thinking went at the time, at least one of these three groups would succeed. If not, the 'floating reserve' was standing by offshore, with the remaining Calgary Tanks and the Fusiliers Mont-Royal, which, if necessary, could form the fourth wave. No other objective in the Dieppe operation received such detailed attention or rivalled this effort in the slightest.

Compounding this evidence, the very way in which Jock Hughes-Hallett and Major General Ham Roberts handled the operation from their floating headquarters aboard the *Calpe* shows how firmly they were focused on the pinch. As the morning progressed, they continually tried to reinforce the Essex Scottish in their attempts to get to the trawlers and the Hôtel Moderne. Although more attractive opportunities for advancing inland appeared – in particular the relatively secure and tank-friendly Green Beach, and to a lesser extent White Beach after the casino fell – the commanders discounted these options. Yet each of these alternatives would have sufficed if their primary objective had been to obtain a quick victory for public relations points, to bolster sagging morale, entice the Germans to fight, draw off German resources from the eastern front, or build Mountbatten's reputation. Instead, on three separate occasions, the documents show that even when the operation did not unfold 'according to plan,' Ham Roberts, no doubt with the support of Jock Hughes-Hallett, favoured a straight run down the middle of the main beach, over the shortest, most direct route to the pinch targets in the port.[5] Following Ryder's three futile attempts to breach the harbour mole under heavy fire, and after news reached them of the Essex's precarious position, they augmented the plan on the spot, ordering the Royal Regiment of Canada to land on Red Beach in direct support when it appeared they could not land on Blue Beach at Puys. This was soon followed by orders to land the Fusiliers Mont-Royal on the main beach and then send in the Royal Marines and the remaining tanks in their wake. The key here is that all had orders to link up with and reinforce the Essex Scottish, who, although pinned down and suffering heavily, seemed within mere feet of reaching the trawlers and the Hôtel Moderne.

In aerial photos taken during the raid, we can see there were indeed German trawlers berthed in the outer harbour; and from German records, it is now known that at some point during the morning, when it became evident that the port might be overrun, the Kriegsmarine special security unit tasked with destroying sensitive documents went into action. As the battle raged, they proceeded to fill and drop into the outer harbour seven bags stuffed with Top Secret signals material to facilitate the destruction of their contents. The last bag, however, failed to sink, leading to a near-comical scene in which they resorted to hand grenades to try to scuttle the floating sack. Instead of perforating it as expected, the explosion blew it apart, showering the area with the very material they were trying to destroy.[6]

Despite the importance of the raid to the war effort, and although the commanders were operating in an atmosphere that condoned heavy casualties to achieve the pinch, by no means does the new evidence exonerate Ham Roberts or Jock Hughes-Hallett, or lessen their responsibility for the failure of the Dieppe Raid. However, it does cast their decision-making in a fresh light that now raises a new set of questions for historians, military professionals and armchair generals to consider. What must be factored in is the terrible human cost itself. In the end, it too, forms a piece of compelling evidence.

On August 19, 1942, roughly 1,000 Allied soldiers, sailors and airmen lost their lives for what appeared to be no real purpose, with approximately another 3,000 wounded or taken prisoner. What is truly striking, and what has never been considered before, is the proportion of casualties incurred with the pinch imperative. Of the 369 Royal Marines involved, 100 – over a quarter – were either killed, wounded or captured. Had it not been for the selfless sacrifice made by their commanding officer, Lieutenant Colonel Joseph 'Tiger' Picton Phillipps, that toll would have been dramatically higher. The cost to the other units involved was even more alarming. The Essex Scottish lost 530 men either killed, wounded or captured on Red Beach – 96 per cent of the total number they took into Dieppe. The Royal Regiment of Canada suffered similarly, losing 534 at Blue Beach (96 per cent), with the Fusiliers Mont-Royal losing another 513 men (88 per cent) and the Calgary Tanks 174 men and all 29 of their Churchill tanks that managed to land. In total, after factoring in the numbers from the Canadian combat engineers, the naval officers and the ratings, over 1,800 casualties were sustained in the direct pursuit of the pinch, with roughly 500 of these men listed as 'killed.' All told, this grim tally accounts for half of the deaths sustained by the entire raiding force.

In sum, the evidence is irrefutable that the pinch formed the main driver for Operation Jubilee. Even the most cynical of interpretations would have to acknowledge that, if the raid was a pinch by opportunity at its conception, it had become a pinch by design at delivery – a process that began when Rutter II was pared down to 'all essential features,' a continuum that remained and that connects it firmly with Jubilee. But the pinch was in the works from the earliest days of Rutter, not only in the outline plan but in work carried out by Godfrey's ISTD to create its broad operational framework – something they had done in earlier amphibious pinch operations conducted by COHQ.

In January, Hughes-Hallett contended that his planning syndicate responsible for those pinch raids had now considered a raiding programme for the spring and summer of 1942 and portrayed it as nothing more than 'raiding for the sake of raiding.' This impotent attempt at rationalization and justification, promoted in his heavily Ultra-sanitized memoirs, does not survive a prime facie inquiry as it would never pass muster in a time when resources were stretched to the thinnest and with the Allies reeling. War is fought on the tightest of budgets. For the chiefs of staff to approve any operation that demanded the scarcest of resources (such as landing craft and destroyers needed for anti-submarine work and convoy escort, as well as men of extreme talent and combat experience) the imperative for the raid had to be of the utmost importance to the course of the war. With that said, the ability to tap into the very heart of your enemy's most sensitive communications to discern his next moves, provided the British with an unparalleled information weapons system that promised to stretch that strained budget exponentially. In this case, raiding for pinching purposes was not only an investment in victory but also a national venture into the dawning of the information age. As such, from 1941 onwards, every sizeable raid carried out by Combined Operations came in the form of a pinch by design or a pinch by opportunity. Clearly, the ambitious technocrat Mountbatten had fully embraced the pinch imperative as the prized commodity to get his budding empire off the ground and well-positioned among the Whitehall elite. After all, why not? With the Axis powers on the offensive around the world, Combined Operations proved the only practical option to bring the desired material into range. Therefore, they could claim a monopoly on the process that delivered the golden eggs to the prime minister.

Indeed, when reports surfaced of the four-rotor's dispatch to vessels in Norway in mid-January 1942, Godfrey found himself caught between the proverbial 'rock and a hard place.' Following the 'feeding frenzy' of pinch operations in the latter half of 1941, the unbridled but incomplete success forced the DNI to impose a moratorium on pinches for fear of accelerating the spread of the device he hoped to defeat. The introduction of the four-rotor ciphers to U-boats in the Atlantic just days later on February 1 forced his hand. If Dieppe had indeed been formally selected as a target in January as Hughes-Hallett claimed in his suspect memoirs, there is no evidence whatsoever in the historical record to support this assertion at this period. Perhaps, as this came a day before Godfrey ordered a halt, any raid on Dieppe that may have been discussed informally was likely stifled *in utero*, pending a significant development. Dieppe did not appear on the radar screen in the historical sense until the two weeks following the major discovery on March 13 that minor surface vessels in the Channel carried the device. At this point, the St Nazaire and Bayonne raids were in their final stages, viewed as the immediate bid to end the blackout. However, taking no chances as the cancer had spread and would continue to spread unless they excised the tumour, it is at this point, in the last days of March, when the planning for a raid at Dieppe got really 'hot.'

This development prompted Fleming's pitch to create a permanent naval IAU explicitly devoted to that purpose, which he began to organize immediately, expecting that full sanction for its bureaucratic adoption in the order of battle would come in due course. Unimpressed with the reliability of ad hoc boarding parties, and without direct control of the Army commandos, Fleming carved out his naval Intelligence Assault Unit (which later became No. 30 Commando) from the only terrestrial combat force the Royal Navy possessed – the Royal Marines. Hoping for his fledgling unit to make its debut in Operation Sledgehammer – the large raid designed to provoke a battle of attrition on the Cherbourg peninsula – he soon discovered that it would only go in sometime in the late summer or early autumn. At this point, according to the historical evidence, Dieppe suddenly became a going concern, with planning going into overdrive immediately on a plan that cast Fleming's commandos in the starring role.

From a contextual perspective, the findings have opened up a new vista for historical research centred around pinch policy and doctrine, which, no doubt, will shed more light on the operations that did not warrant in-depth treatment in this study. Likewise, it is clear that Operation Rutter (and Jubilee that followed) was a stand-alone operation of unique design, and this does not warrant its bundling with those designed to satisfy calls for a second front or a *cri de coeur* from Stalin, to bolster morale, open a lodgement, deceive the enemy or bring the Luftwaffe to battle.

In essence, Churchill was indeed correct when he referred to Dieppe as merely 'a butcher and bolt' raid or a 'reconnaissance in force.' Unlike other invasions that followed, the architecture of the raid did not support an invasion force storming ashore, staying ashore, building up a bridgehead and then breaking out to liberate occupied lands and take the fight into Germany. Structurally, the relatively tiny port of Dieppe did not have the shipping capacity of the larger harbours of Boulogne, Cherbourg, Calais and Le Havre required to support a lodgement of the size called for in Sledgehammer or Imperator, let alone that of the Normandy invasion two years later.

As for the question of morale, there is no evidence that the raid was thrown on to bolster a war-weary Britain despite the string of negative results during the previous eight months. Peter Murphy from the PWE considered Dieppe a 'greater headache' than either the St Nazaire or Bayonne raids, particularly when Mountbatten's head-quarters approached him in the immediate aftermath to provide a 'background appreciation of the political circumstances in which the raid took place.'[7] Suspecting the COHQ commander of attempting to construct a suitable narrative to explain away the heavy cost of the raid, the report pulled no punches: 'The best thing, from a political point of view,' it concluded, 'would have been, NO RAID; the next best a sensational military success; the very least, the attainment of objectives so obviously important, and so easy to explain to the public, that no doubt could remain as to the worthwhileness of the operation.* Only the presence of one or more of these desiderata could have made the political presentation of the raid an easy matter. It is hardly too much to say, however, that none of these was present.'[8]

The disapproving tone of the report points to the nuisance factor created by the raid, something that coloured the entire document. More importantly, it betrays the fundamental lack of firm coordination within

---

* Capitalization in the original.

the tightly woven narratives planned and executed by PWE. Only now, in the wake of the raid, did Mountbatten strive to tie up talking points. As the report concluded, 'it was unfortunate that the news of the Prime Minster's interview with Stalin should have broken the very day before. This made it additionally important that the raid should no way be linked in the popular mind either here or abroad, with his Moscow visit.'[9]

To clean up the mess, the PWE expressed its immense frustration at the outlier nature of the operation, complaining how hard it was after the fact to put the best possible spin on events. 'The objectives,' it recorded, 'were not in themselves of such a nature as to provide a direct appeal to public imagination'; rather, 'more intangible objects, such as "value of experience gained" and "perfect synchronization," have to be very carefully phrased and very carefully placed if they are to carry sufficient emotional weight to counterbalance in the public mind the loss of life and material incurred.'[10]

Likewise, there is no evidence that the raid was launched as part of an elaborate deception for Operation Torch or subsequent other landings, although it was conveniently employed as such after the fact. Nor was the raid designed to intentionally draw the Luftwaffe into battle or drain reserves from the eastern front, as the plans drawn up for all incarnations of the raid did not offer the form nor the duration needed to achieve those desired results. The idea of using a raiding force to bait the Luftwaffe came after the fact when COHQ proposed Operations Coleman and Aflame, which through deceptive means, would give the impression of an expected raid without the need to risk precious assets or touch French shores.[11] Given the shortage of landing craft during the summer of 1942, this would have been the low-cost option to adopt if the primary goal was to bring the Luftwaffe out to fight.

At no time in the planning process – from inception to cancellation to delivery – did a raid on Dieppe factor into any detailed or concrete discussions among the planners, the prime minister or the chiefs of staff within any of these contexts. Instead, these larger operations proceeded on parallel lines, moving on different planes, with Rutter and Jubilee steaming ahead on a separate level, well within a dedicated and unique lane of their own.

In addition to the woefully inaccurate narrative pushed by Hughes-Hallett and championed by Mountbatten, part of the obfuscation in our understanding came down to the genuine and legitimate need to protect the Ultra Secret nature of pinch doctrine – something that only became apparent with the declassifications in 2014. To pinch effectively, the British created a doctrine or playbook to follow, which required them to take their opponents by surprise and overrun their targets quickly, grab the desired material, and then cover their tracks by dictating the narrative drawn up in advance. This meant employing over-compensation, or the 'steam-hammer to crack a nut' approach, harnessing the blanket coverage of a raid reportedly put on for larger purposes. Here, under a cloak of Ultra Secret security, they adeptly employed that tactic to deflect suspicion as to the core and intent of the raid – something that worked brilliantly not only against the Germans but generations of observers long after the war ended.[12]

∾

When I first read those two sentences at the British National Archives in 1995 – 'No raid should be laid on for SIGINT purposes only. The scope of the objectives should always be sufficiently wide to presuppose normal operational objects' – the implication was fantastic, flirting, I thought, with the realm of speculation and conspiracy theories. Would they actually mount a raid of that size and magnitude to cover a pinch? As more classified documents were released and the evidence started to build, that passage not only became central to a revolutionary new understanding of the raid's intent but also now doubles as a most fitting epitaph. The Dieppe Raid was a natural extension of the earlier pinch raids – a new form of 'special operations,' albeit on a scale never witnessed before.

Generally speaking, there are no monocausal explanations for operations of the scale and complexity of Dieppe. To get a Combined Operations raid off the ground in 1942, planners needed to have objectives that would appeal to each of the players before they would agree to participate. This, however, works on a sliding scale. For the War Office, Dieppe provided a chance to maintain its bureaucratic dominance over land operations in the Channel area in the face of the fast-rising Mountbatten and his Combined Operations empire; it was also an opportunity to take the offensive and get the Canadian Army some much-needed experience, placating their unyielding demands for action. For the Royal Air Force, the raid allowed the sampling of various untried tactics and schemes, including the harnessing of Ultra and signals intelligence as a real-time asset in air combat. Despite this, the reticent air barons remained sober as to the nature of this one-day 'butcher and bolt' raid. Although it provided a limited chance to take a swing at the Luftwaffe, they knew it fell far short of the sustained attritional campaign they demanded in the form of the still-simmering Imperator, Sledgehammer, and the embryonic Coleman. However, within the context of the air war in 1942, a limited opportunity for action was indeed better than no action at all. As such, they dutifully performed their best despite their reservations. For the Royal Navy, who provided the means to deliver the raid and who as such held de facto veto power over any operation, there were other attractions in addition to the benefits of a pinch: testing the ability to sneak a massive raiding fleet across the Channel under cover of darkness, using cutting-edge technology to deceive the enemy, foil their radar and signals intelligence capabilities, and achieve surprise. In no way, however, did they need to mount Dieppe to test their amphibious capabilities in the traditional sense. Every year for the previous quarter of a century, the staff college had spent months each year devoted to that task. Likewise, they had also achieved practical experience during the current war by launching raids in the Mediterranean and, most recently, the invasion of Madagascar, where they could truly claim to have honed their skills in this respect. As the evidence has demonstrated, none of these excuses possesses the weight of evidence necessary to support any claim of being the main – let alone the sole – driver for the raid. So, in the case of Dieppe, the overly broad and ever-malleable 'lessons learned' alibi does indeed apply to a certain degree, albeit not in the conventional sense that Hughes-Hallett and Mountbatten have led us to believe. What they were learning was how to pinch – or perhaps more fittingly in the aftermath of the disaster, how not to.

And then there is Ian Fleming, whose important position as an intelligence officer surfaced years ago but remained unconfirmed, as did the exact role he played in the Dieppe Raid. As this study clearly shows, Fleming was never 'Bond' in any of his actions. Yet, he was far from a faceless, ineffectual cog in the Naval Intelligence machinery that some sources have gone out of their way to portray. Having carried the NID liaison portfolios for MI5, MI6, Bletchley Park, the Ministry of Economic Warfare, the Political Warfare Executive, the SOE, the Joint Intelligence Committee, the Inter-Services Topographical Department, as well as the American OSS, FBI and Naval Intelligence, it is understandable why the British government did not want to discuss, let alone hint at the genuine impact he had on the course of history. There is no doubt concerning his central role in the Dieppe operation, right from its inception to its delivery. His inclusion as the anchor-man in the relay tasked to bring the pinched material home was an enormous, and in hindsight, irresponsible risk of the sort that one does not take unless the stakes are of the highest order. Even his presence on *Fernie* close by the main beach at Dieppe was either incompetent from a security perspective or a calculated roll of the dice undertaken because the potential payoff was deemed enormous and central to the Allied war effort.

The inevitable question that will arise in light of all the new evidence is whether or not Dieppe was worth it in the end. No doubt that debate will rage on. Were the deaths of nearly 1,000 men and the loss of 3,000 others worth the potential but unrealized gain? Was there a better way to go about it than this? What is clear is that with the Allied war effort in a most vulnerable state, wisely or unwisely, British authorities deemed it worth the risk. If, as in Harry Hinsley's estimation, the war was indeed shortened by two years, saving countless lives, due to the very existence of an information weapons system like Ultra, one can only imagine what the impact would have been on the course of world history had it been solved four months earlier. Conversely, perhaps the more salient question to ask is this: what if Turing and the other cryptanalysts at Bletchley had failed with the four-rotor naval Enigma? What then? Within this terrifying context, and given what was at stake, flawed method and grisly toll aside, there is no doubt that a raid on Dieppe was worth the attempt.

Perhaps the last voice on this should be that of Ron Beal, who, along with only a few comrades, not only survived the raid and German captivity but dedicated his life to finding the answer to a seemingly simple question: why?

That afternoon, after spending some time with him going through the recently declassified documents, I asked his opinion of them. At first, as could rightly be expected, all he was able to murmur was, 'I'm in shock.' On camera, he reiterated his original comment about his friends being thrown away for no reason. Then, in tears, he listed their names, apologizing for his sobbing, saying: 'You'll have to forgive an old man, but I guess I am like a lot of the other ones that carry very heavy loads about their friends that didn't make it.' The old soldier gathered himself abruptly, and after a pause to reflect, he said: 'It gave me a different perspective on why there was a Dieppe Raid ... there was a reason behind it. Despite the fact that it was never accomplished, that doesn't mean anything. There was an objective, and I know in my heart that my comrades did not die for nothing ... there was an absolute reason and purpose to the raid.'

At that point, we shut the cameras off and took a much-needed break. Ron Beal turned back towards his wife, who had stood by his side throughout his post-war ordeal. Then, as if finally liberated from shackles he had worn since that one day in August of 1942, he looked at me and uttered the line that made all the years of research worthwhile. 'Now,' he said, the tears welling up again, 'now I can die in peace. Now I know what my friends died for ...'

Abbreviations

ALC	Assault Landing Craft
CIA	Central Intelligence Agency (United States)
CCO	Chief of Combined Operations
CMHQ	Canadian Military Headquarters (London)
COHQ	Combined Operations Headquarters
COI	Co-ordinator of Information (United States)
DDNI	Deputy Director of Naval Intelligence
DNI	Director of Naval Intelligence
FBI	Federal Bureau of Investigation (United States)
GC&CS	Government Code and Cypher School
GHQ	General Headquarters
IAU	Intelligence Assault Unit
ISIS	Inter-Services Information Series
ISSB	Inter-Services Security Board
ISTD	Inter-Services Topographical Department
JIC	Joint Intelligence Committee
MEW	Ministry of Economic Warfare
MI6	Secret Intelligence Service
MTB	motor torpedo boat
NID	Naval Intelligence Division
OIC	Operational Intelligence Centre
OSS	Office of Strategic Services (United States)
PWE	Political Warfare Executive
RAF	Royal Air Force

RDF	radio direction finding
RFP	radio fingerprinting (see Glossary)
RNVR	Royal Naval Voluntary Reserve
SIS	Secret Intelligence Service (or MI6 as it is popularly known)
SIGINT	signals intelligence (see Glossary)
SOE	Special Operations Executive
TLC	tank landing craft

Glossary

BLOCK SHIP: a ship purposely sunk to render a port or waterway unusable

BOMBE: a high-speed electromechanical device designed specifically to decipher Enigma-encrypted messages, originally designed by Polish cryptanalysts in the 1930s and perfected by the British at Bletchley Park

'C': the name by which the Chief of the Secret Intelligence Service was known, his or her actual identity being Top Secret until only recently. Stewart Menzies was 'C' at the time of the Dieppe Raid.

CIPHER: a disguised writing system in which individual letters are replaced by other letters. Enigma was a cipher machine. To decipher an enciphered message requires knowledge of the cipher key. Second World War German cipher keys included *Offizier* (officer), *Stab* (staff), *Triton* (for U-boats), *Heimisch* (for German home waters; later called *Hydra*, or *Dolphin* by the British), RHV (a hand cipher) and *Werftschlüssel*, a dockyard hand cipher.

CODE: a disguised writing system in which groups of letters, or entire words, or even groups of words, are replaced by symbols (which might be letters, numbers or words). WW (*Wetterkurzschlüssel*), for example, was a weather code used by the Germans.

CRUISER: a warship that is smaller than a battleship but larger than a destroyer. Types of cruisers used in the Second World War include the heavy cruiser, the anti-aircraft cruiser and the German pocket battleship.

CRYPTANALYSIS: the process of decoding/deciphering codes and ciphers using analysis

CRYPTOGRAPHY: the process of writing or decoding/deciphering codes and ciphers. Cryptanalysis is a form of cryptography.

DIRECTION FINDING, or DFING: the process of establishing the direction from which a received signal was transmitted. Methods included HF/DF (Huff Duff), or high-frequency direction finding, and VHF/DF, or very high-frequency direction finding.

E-BAR: a type of German short signal

E-BOAT: the English name for a German motor torpedo boat, which the Germans called *S-boot* (*Schnellboot*, 'fast boat' or 'speedboat')

KRIEGSMARINE: the name given to the German navy between 1935 and 1945

MARES (*Marine Einsatzkommando*): the German naval commando unit

M-BOAT (*Minensuchboote*): large German minesweeping vessels

PINCH: a military operation in which sensitive material, such as intelligence material, is stolen (or 'pinched') from the enemy

POCKET BATTLESHIP: a form of heavily armed cruiser peculiar to the Kriegsmarine. There were only three pocket battleships: the *Deutschland*, the *Admiral Scheer* and the *Admiral Graf Spee*.

RADIO FINGERPRINTING, or RFP: a technology that was capable of identifying the particular wireless set from which a message was transmitted by photographing its wave form

R-BOAT (*Räumboote*): small German minesweeping vessels

RHV (*Reservehandverfahren*): an emergency hand cipher used by vessels as a back-up for Enigma when it broke down or on vessels not yet outfitted with the machine

S-BOAT: see E-boat

SHORT SIGNAL: a coded wireless message of fewer than 22 characters. German short signals included E-bars and Z-bars.

SIGINT: signals intelligence, which included cryptography, direction finding, radio fingerprinting and traffic analysis

SPECIAL INTELLIGENCE: see Ultra

SUPER-BATTLESHIP: an unofficial classification used to denote the very largest German battleships, such as the *Bismarck* and *Tirpitz*, as opposed to the pocket battleships

SURFACE RAIDER (also known as merchant raider): an armed military vessel disguised as a non-combatant commercial vessel

TINA: see traffic analysis

TRAFFIC ANALYSIS (code-named TINA): a form of intelligence in which the patterns in wireless communication are analysed (even if the messages themselves cannot be decrypted)

TRIBAL-CLASS DESTROYER: a type of destroyer constructed for the Royal Navy and Royal Canadian Navy before and during the Second World War, including HMS *Bedouin* and HMCS *Haida*

U-BOAT (*Unterseeboot*, 'undersea boat'): the English name for a German military submarine, specifically those used during the First and Second World Wars

UJ BOAT (*U-Jäger*, 'submarine hunter'): a German anti-submarine vessel

ULTRA: a security classification for intelligence derived from tapping into enemy communications, via cryptanalysis or signals intelligence. The cryptographic component of this was known in the Royal Navy as Special Intelligence.

WRENS: members of the Women's Royal Naval Service (WRNS)

Bibliography

DIEPPE

Atkin, Ronald. *Dieppe 1942: The Jubilee Disaster*. London: Macmillan, 1980.

Balzer, Timothy. '"In Case the Raid is Unsuccessful" ... Selling Dieppe to Canadians.' *Canadian Historical Review* 87, no. 3 (September 2006): 409–30.

——. 'Selling Disaster: How the Canadian Public Was Informed of Dieppe.' Master's thesis, University of Victoria, 2004.

Bercuson, David J. *Maple Leaf Against the Axis: Canada's Second World War*. Toronto: Stoddart, 1995.

Bucourt, Nicolas, et al. *Raid de Dieppe: 19 août 1942*. Bayeux, France: Heimdal, 2012.

Campbell, John P. *Dieppe Revisited: A Documentary Investigation*. London: Frank Cass, 1993.

Dickinson, Paul, and Terry Copp. *Dieppe*. Barnsley, UK. Pen and Sword, 2001.

Ford, Ken. *Dieppe 1942: Combined Operations Catastrophe*. Oxford: Osprey, 2003.

Franks, Norman R. *Greatest Air Battle: Dieppe, 19th August 1942*. London: William Kimber, 1979.

Greenhous, Brereton. *Dieppe, Dieppe*. Montreal: Art Global, 1992.

Hatch, Alden. *The Mountbattens: The Last Royal Success Story*. London: W.H. Allen, 1966.

Henry, Hugh. *Dieppe: Through the Lens of the German War Photographer*. London: Battle of Britain Prints, 1993.

——. 'A Reappraisal of the Dieppe Raid, 19 August 1942: Planning, Intelligence and Execution.' PhD diss., Cambridge University, 1996.

Henshaw, Peter. 'The British Chiefs of Staff Committee and the Preparation of the Dieppe Raid, March–August 1942: Did Mountbatten Really Evade the Committee's Authority?' *War in History* 1, no. 2 (1994): 197–214.

——. 'The Dieppe Raid: A Product of Misplaced Canadian Nationalism?' *Canadian Historical Review* 77, no. 2 (1996): 250–66.

——. 'The Dieppe Raid: The Quest for Action for All the Wrong Reasons.' *Queen's Quarterly* 101, no. 1 (Spring 1994): 103–15.

Leasor, James. *Green Beach*. New York: Morrow, 1975.

Lotz, Jim. *Disaster at Dieppe: The Biggest Catastrophe in Canadian Military History*. Toronto: James Lorimer, 2012.

Mahoney, Ross Wayne. 'The Royal Air Force, Combined Operations Doctrine and the Raid on Dieppe, 19 August 1942.' Master's thesis, University of Birmingham, 2009.

Mellor, John. *Dieppe – Canada's Forgotten Heroes*. Scarborough, ON: Signet, 1975.

Mordal, Jacques. *Dieppe: The Dawn of Decision*. Toronto: Ryerson Press, 1962.

Mountbatten of Burma, Louis. 'Operation Jubilee: The Place of the Dieppe Raid in History.' *Journal of the Royal United Service Institution for Defence Studies* 119, no. 1 (1974): 25–30.

Munro, Ross. *Gauntlet to Overlord*. Toronto: Macmillan, 1945.

Neillands, Robin. *The Dieppe Raid: The Story of the Disastrous 1942 Expedition*. London: Aurum Press, 2005.

Prince, Stephen. *Royal Navy and the Raids on St. Nazaire and Dieppe*. London: Taylor and Francis, 2002.

Reyburn, Wallace. *Glorious Chapter: The Canadians at Dieppe*. Toronto: Oxford University Press, 1943.

——. *Rehearsal for Invasion*. London: Harrap, 1943.

Reynolds, Quentin. *Dress Rehearsal: The Story of Dieppe*. Garden City, NY: Blue Ribbon, 1943.

Richard, Béatrice. *La Mémoire de Dieppe: Radioscopie d'un mythe*. Montreal: VLB Éditeur, 2002.

Robertson, Terence. *Dieppe: The Shame and the Glory*. London: Pan Books, 1965.

Roskill, Captain S.W., DSC, MA, RN. 'The Dieppe Raid and the Question of German Foreknowledge.' *Journal of the Royal United Service Institute* 109 (February 1964): 27–31.

Saunders, Tim. *Dieppe: Operation Jubilee*. Barnsley, UK: Leo Cooper, 2005.

Sengupta, Narayan. *Disaster at Dieppe: World War II's Little D-Day*. Kindle edition.

Souster, Raymond. *Jubilee of Death: The Raid on Dieppe*. Toronto: Oberon Press, 1984.

Vance, Jonathan F. 'Men in Manacles: The Shackling of Prisoners of War, 1942–1943.' *Journal of Military History* 59, no. 3 (July 1995): 483–504.

Villa, Brian. 'Mountbatten, the British Chiefs of Staff, and Approval of the Dieppe Raid.' *Journal of Military History* 54, no. 2 (April 1990).

Villa, Brian, and Peter Henshaw. 'The Dieppe Raid Debate.' *Canadian Historical Review* 79, no. 2 (1998): 304–15.

Webb, Daniel J. 'The Dieppe Raid – an Act of Diplomacy.' *Military Review* 60, no. 5 (May 1980): 30–37.

West, Nigel. *Unreliable Witness: Espionage Myths of the Second World War*. London: Weidenfeld & Nicolson, 1984.

Whitaker, Denis W., and Shelagh Whitaker. *Dieppe: Tragedy to Triumph*. Toronto: McGraw-Hill Ryerson, 1992.

Zuehlke, Mark. *Tragedy at Dieppe: Operation Jubilee, August 19, 1942*. Vancouver: Douglas and McIntyre, 2012.

CRYPTOGRAPHY AND BLETCHLEY PARK

Aldrich, J. Richard. *GCHQ*. London: HarperCollins, 2010.

Babbage, Charles. *On the Economy of Machinery and Manufactures*. 1832.

Babbage, Charles. *Reflections on the Decline of Science in England*. 1830.
——. *The Writings of Charles Babbage*. Houston, TX: Halcyon Press, 2009. Kindle edition.

Carter, Frank. *Breaking Naval Enigma: An Account of the Additional Problems Encountered and the Methods Used to Solve Them*. Bletchley, UK: Bletchley Park Trust, 2008.

Collier, Bruce, and James MacLachlan. *Charles Babbage: And the Engines of Perfection*. Oxford: Oxford University Press, 1998.

Copeland, Jack B. *Colossus: The Secrets of Bletchley Park's Code-breaking Computers*. Oxford: Oxford University Press, 2006.

——. *Turing: Pioneer of the Information Age*. Oxford: Oxford University Press, 2012.

Denniston, Robin. *Thirty Secret Years: A.G. Denniston's Work in Signals Intelligence 1914–1944*. Clifton-Upon-Teme, UK: Polperro Heritage Press, 2007.

Erskine, Ralph, and Michael Smith, eds. *The Bletchley Park Codebreakers: How Ultra Shortened the War and Led to the Birth of the Computer*. London: Biteback Publishing, 2011.

Haufler, Hervie. *Codebreakers' Victory: How the Allied Cryptographers Won World War II*. New York: Penguin, 2003.

Hinsley, F.H., and Alan Stripp. *Codebreakers: The Inside Story of Bletchley Park*. New York: Oxford University Press, 1993.

Hodges, Andrew. *The Alan Turning Enigma*. London: Random House, 1983.

Kahn, David. *The Codebreakers: The Comprehensive History of Secret Communication from Ancient Times to the Internet*. New York: Simon & Schuster, 1996.

——. *Seizing the Enigma: The Race to Break the German U-Boat Codes: 1939–1943*. Barnsley, UK: Pen and Sword, 2012.

Montaqim, Abdul. *Pioneers of the Computer Age: From Charles Babbage to Steve Jobs*. Monsoon Media, 2012.

Newton, David E. *Alan Turing: A Study in Light and Shadow*. Bloomington, IN: Xlibris, 2003.

Paterson, Michael. *Voices of the Codebreakers*. London: David and Charles, 2007.

Sebag-Montefiore, Hugh. *Enigma*. London: Weidenfeld & Nicolson, 2000.

Smith, Michael. *The Secrets of Station X: How the Bletchley Park Codebreakers Helped Win the War*. Hull, UK: Biteback Publishing, 2011.

Watkins, Gwen. *Cracking the Luftwaffe Codes: The Secrets of Bletchley Park*. London: Greenhill Books, 2006.

Wescombe, Peter, and John Gallehawk. *Getting Back into SHARK: H.M.S. Petard and the George Cross*. Bletchley, UK: Bletchley Park Trust, 1997.

WAR AT SEA: GENERAL

Bell, Christopher M. *Churchill and Sea Power*. Oxford: Oxford University Press, 2013.

Brodhurst, Robin. *Churchill's Anchor: Admiral of the Fleet Sir Dudley Pound*. Barnsley, UK: Pen and Sword, 2000.

Roskill, S. *War at Sea 1939–1945*. Vol. 2, *The Period of Balance*. London: HMSO, 1956.

Sutherland, Jon, and Diane Canwell. *Churchill's Pirates: The Royal Naval Patrol Service in World War II*. Barnsley, UK: Pen and Sword, 2010.

BRITISH INTELLIGENCE

Andrew, Christopher. *Secret Service: The Making of the British Intelligence Community*. London: Hodder and Stoughton, 1987.

Bennett, Gil. *Churchill's Man of Mystery: Desmond Morton and the World of Intelligence*. London: Routledge, 2006.

Boyce, Frederic, and Everett Douglas. *SOE – The Scientific Secrets*. Stroud, UK: Sutton Publishing, 2003.

Conant, Jennet. *The Irregulars: Roald Dahl and the British Spy Ring in Wartime Washington*. New York: Simon & Schuster, 2009.

Downing, Taylor. *Churchill's War Lab: Codebreakers, Scientists, and the Mavericks Churchill Led to Victory*. London: Little, Brown, 2010.

Foot, M.R.D. *Memories of an SOE Historian*. Barnsley, UK: Pen and Sword, 2008.

Hinsley, Harry, et al. *British Intelligence in the Second World War.* Vol. 3, Part 1, *Its Influence on Strategy and Operations.* London: Stationery Office Books, 1984.

Holt, Thaddeus. *The Deceivers: Allied Military Deception in the Second World War.* New York: Skyhorse, 2007.

Jones, R.V. *Most Secret War.* Harmondsworth, UK: Penguin, 2009.

Keegan, John. *Intelligence in War: The Value and Limitations of What the Military Can Learn About the Enemy.* London: Hutchinson, 2002.

Macdonald, Bill. *The True Intrepid: Sir William Stephenson and the Unknown Agents.* Surrey, BC: Timberholme Books, 1998.

Macintyre, Ben. *Double Cross: The True Story of the D-Day Spies.* London: Random House, 2012.

Mahl, E. Thomas. *Desperate Deception: British Covert Operations in the United States, 1939–44.* Brassey's Intelligence and National Security Library. Washington: Potomac Books, 1998.

Mathieson, William D. *Nine Hours: The Canadians at Dieppe – August 19, 1949.* Belleville, ON: Epic Press, 2011.

National Security Agency. *Cryptologic: The Zimmermann Telegram.* n.d.

Turner, Des. *SOE's Secret Weapons Centre – Station 12.* Stroud, UK: History Press, 2006.

NAVAL INTELLIGENCE

Beesly, Patrick. *Very Special Admiral: The Life of Admiral J.H. Godfrey.* London: Hamish Hamilton, 1980.

——. *Very Special Intelligence: The Story of the Admiralties Operational Intelligence Center 1939–1945.* Annapolis, MD: Naval Institute Press, 2006.

Gannon, Paul. *Inside Room 40: The Codebreakers of World War I.* Birmingham, UK: Ian Allan, 2010.

Ramsay, David. *'Blinker' Hall: Spymaster: The Man Who Brought America into World War I.* Stroud, UK: History Press, 2009.

AMERICAN INTELLIGENCE

Carlson, Elliot. *Joe Rochefort's War: The Odyssey of the Codebreaker Who Outwitted Yamamoto at Midway*. Annapolis, MD: Naval Institute Press, 2011.

DeBrosse, Jim, and Colin Burke. *The Secret in Building 26: The Untold Story of America's Ultra War Against the U-Boat Enigma Codes*. New York: Random House, 2004.

Fullilov, Michael. *Rendezvous with Destiny: How Franklin D. Roosevelt and Five Extraordinary Men Took America Into the War and Into the World*. New York: Penguin Press, 2013.

Smith, Bradley F. *The Ultra-Magic Deals and the Most Secret Special Relationship, 1940–1946*. Novato, CA: Presidio Press, 1994.

Stafford, David. *Roosevelt and Churchill: Men of Secrets*. London: Little, Brown, 2004.

Waller, Douglas. *Wild Bill Donovan – The Spymaster Who Created the OSS and Modern American Espionage*. New York: Simon & Schuster, 2011.

Weiner, Tim. *Enemies: A History of the FBI*. New York: Random House, 2012.

IAN FLEMING

Batey, Mavis. *From Bletchley with Love*. Bletchley, UK: Bletchley Park Trust, 2008.

Gardiner, Philip. *The Bond Code: The Dark World of Ian Fleming and James Bond*. Pompton Plains, NJ: Career Press, 2008.

Lycett, Andrew. *Ian Fleming: A Biography*. London: Weidenfeld & Nicolson, 1995.

Macintyre, Ben. *For Your Eyes Only*. London: Bloomsbury, 2008.

McCormick, Donald. *17F: The Life of Ian Fleming*. London: Peter Owen, 1994.

Pearson, John. *The Life of Ian Fleming*. London: Bloomsbury, 2011.

Playboy and Ian Fleming. *Ian Fleming: The Playboy Interview*. 50 Years of the Playboy Interview. Beverly Hills, CA: Playboy Enterprises, 2012.

Weiner, Robert G., B. Lynn Whitfield, and Jack Becker, eds. *James Bond in World and Popular Culture: The Films Are Not Enough*. Newcastle upon Tyne, UK: Cambridge Scholars, 2010.

U-BOATS, BATTLE OF THE ATLANTIC, RUSSIAN CONVOYS

Bishop, Patrick. *Target* Tirpitz: *X-Craft, Agents and Dambusters – The Epic Quest to Destroy Hitler's Mightiest Warship*. London: Harper Press, 2012.

Budiansky, Stephen. *Blackett's War: The Men Who Defeated the Nazi U-Boats and Brought Science to the Art of Warfare*. New York: Alfred A. Knopf, 2013.

Carruthers, Bob. *The Official U-Boat Commander's Handbook*. Hitler's War Machine. Henley-in-Arden, UK: Coda Books, 2011.

Cooper, Bryan. *The War of the Gun Boats*. Barnsley, UK: Pen and Sword, 2009.

Edwards, Bernard. *Attack and Sink: The Battle of the Atlantic 1941*. New York: Brick Tower Press, 1998.

——. *The Road to Russia: Arctic Convoys 1942–45*. Barnsley, UK: Pen and Sword, 2002.

——. *War of the U-Boats: British Merchantmen Under Fire*. Barnsley, UK: Pen and Sword, 2006.

Gallehawk, John. *Convoys and the U-Boats*. Bletchley, UK: Bletchley Park Trust, 1997.

Gannon, Michael. *Operation Drumbeat: Germany's U-Boat Attacks Along the American Coast in World War II*. New York: HarperCollins, 1990.

Gardner, W.J.R. *Decoding History: The Battle of the Atlantic and Ultra*. London: Macmillan, 1999.

Hoyt, P. Edwin. *The U-Boat Wars*. New York: Cooper Square Press, 2002.

Jackson, Robert. *Churchill's Channel War: 1939–45*. Oxford: Osprey, 2013.

Keeney, Douglas L. *The War Against the Nazi U-Boats 1942–1944: The Antisubmarine Command*. Lost Histories of World War II. Campbell, CA: FastPencil, 2012.

McGowen, Tom. *Sink the* Bismarck: *Germany's Super-Battleship of World War II*. Brookfield, CT: Twenty-First Century Books, 1999.

Milner, Marc. *Battle of the Atlantic*. Stroud, UK: History Press, 2011.

National Security Agency. *Battle of the Atlantic: Technical Intelligence from Allied Communications Intelligence*. Kindle edition.

Nesbit, Roy Conyers. *Ultra versus U-Boats: Enigma Decrypts in the National Archives*. Barnsley, UK: Pen and Sword, 2008.

Smith, C. Peter. *Naval Warfare in the English Channel 1939–1945*. Barnsley, UK: Pen and Sword, 2007.

White, David Fairbank. *Bitter Ocean: The Battle of the Atlantic, 1939–1945*. New York: Simon & Schuster, 2006.

Williams, Andrew. *The Battle of the Atlantic: The Allies' Submarine Fight against Hitler's Gray Wolves of the Sea*. New York: Basic Books, 2003.

Williamson, Gordon. *Kriegsmarine Coastal Forces (New Vanguard)*. Oxford: Osprey, 2009.

——. *Wolf Pack – The Story of the U-Boat in World War II*. Oxford: Osprey, 2005.

Wragg, David. *Fighting Admirals of World War II*. Barnsley, UK: Pen and Sword, 2009.

——. *Sacrifice for Stalin: The Cost and Value of the Arctic Convoys Re-assessed*. Barnsley, UK: Pen and Sword, 2005.

Zetterling, Niklas, and Michael Tamelander. Tirpitz: *The Life and Death of Germany's Last Super Battleship*. Havertown, PA: Casemate, 2009.

GERMAN NAVY

Dönitz, Karl, Grand Admiral. *Memoirs: Ten Years and Twenty Days*. New York: Da Capo Press, 1997.

Garzke, William H., and Robert O. Dulin. *Battleships: Axis and Neutral Battleships in World War II*. Annapolis, MD: Naval Institute Press, 1985.

Mallmann Showell, Jak P. *Enigma U-Boats: Breaking the Code*. Birmingham, UK: Ian Allan, 2009.

Mallmann Showell, Jak P. *German Navy Handbook 1939–1945*. Stroud, UK: Sutton, 1999.

ROYAL NAVY

Harding, Richard, ed. *The Royal Navy 1930–1990*. London: Frank Cass, 2005.

Hoey, Brian. *Mountbatten: The Private Story*. Stroud, UK: History Press, 2008.

Konstam, Angus. *British Motor Gun Boat 1939–45*. Oxford: Osprey, 2010. 456

MOUNTBATTEN

Knight, John. *The Kelly: Mountbatten's Ship*. London: John Knight, 1997.

McGeoch, Vice-Admiral Sir Ian. *The Princely Sailor: Mountbatten of Burma*. London: Brassey's, 1996.

Murfett, Malcolm H., ed. *The First Sea Lords: From Fisher to Mountbatten*. New York: Praeger, 1995.

Murphy, Ray. *Last Viceroy: The Life and Times of Rear-Admiral the Earl Mountbatten of Burma*. London: Jarrolds, 1949.

Pattinson, William. *Mountbatten and the Men of the 'Kelly.'* Wellingborough, UK: Patrick Stephens, 1986.

Roberts, Andrew. *Eminent Churchillians*. London: Weidenfeld & Nicolson, 1994.

Smith, Adrian. 'Mountbatten Goes to the Movies: The Cinema as a Vehicle for Promoting the Heroic Myth.' *Historical Journal of Film, Radio and Television* 26, no. 3 (August 2006): 395–416.

Terraine, John. *The Life and Times of Lord Mountbatten*. London: Hutchinson/Arrow, 1968/1970.

Ziegler, Philip. *Mountbatten: The Official Biography*. London: Collins, 1985.

——. *Mountbatten Revisited*. Austin, TX: Harry Ransom Humanities Research Center, 1995.

CHURCHILL

Churchill, Winston S. *The Second World War*. Vol. 4, *The Hinge of Fate*. Boston: Houghton Mifflin, 1950.

Clarke, Peter. *Mr. Churchill's Profession: The Statesman as Author and the Book That Defined the 'Special Relationship.'* New York: Bloomsbury Press, 2012.

D'Este, Carlo. *War Lord: A Life of Winston Churchill at War, 1874–1945*. New York: HarperCollins, 2008.

Gilbert, Martin. *Continue to Pester, Nag and Bite – Churchill's War Leadership*. Toronto: Random House, 2004.

Hastings, Max. *Finest Years: Churchill's as Warlord 1940–45*. London: HarperCollins, 2009.

Ive, Ruth. *The Woman Who Censored Churchill*. Stroud, UK: History Press, 2008.

Knight, Nigel. *Churchill: The Greatest Briton Unmasked*. Cincinnati, OH: David and Charles Limited, 2008.

Manchester, William, and Paul Reid. *The Last Lion: Winston Spencer Churchill: Defender of the Realm, 1940–1965*. New York: Little, Brown, 2012. 457

Nel, Elizabeth. *Winston Churchill by His Personal Secretary: Recollections of the Great Man by a Woman Who Worked for Him*. Bloomington, IN: iUniverse, 2007.

Reardon, Terry. *Winston Churchill and Mackenzie King: So Similar, So Different*. Toronto: Dundurn Press, 2012.

Reynolds, David. *In Command of History: Churchill Fighting and Writing the Second World War*. Harmondsworth, UK: Penguin Books, 2004.

Richards, Dennis. *The Royal Air Force at War*. Vol. 1, *The Fight at Odds*. London: HMSO, 1953.

Richardson, Charles. *From Churchill's Secret Circle to the BBC: The Biography of Lieutenant General Sir Ian Jacob*. London: Brassey's, 1991.

Roskill, Stephen. *Churchill and the Admirals*. London: Collins, 1977.

Toye, Richard. *Churchill's Empire: The World That Made Him and the World He Made*. London: Macmillan, 2010.

SECOND WORLD WAR: GENERAL

Alanbrooke, Field Marshal Lord. *War Diaries 1939–1945*. Berkeley: University of California Press, 2001.

Brown, Colin. *Whitehall: The Street That Shaped a Nation*. London: Simon & Schuster, 2009.

Davis, Wade. *Into the Silence: The Great War, Mallory, and the Conquest of Everest*. Toronto: Alfred A. Knopf, 2011.

Groom, Winston. *1942: The Year That Tried Men's Souls*. New York: Grove Press, 2005.

Hamilton, Nigel. *Monty: The Battles of Field Marshal Bernard Montgomery*. London: Hodder and Stoughton, 1994.

Howarth, S., ed. *Men of War: Great Naval Leaders of World War II*. London: Weidenfeld & Nicolson, 1993.

Ismay, Lord. *The Memoirs of General Lord Ismay*. New York: Viking Press, 1960.

James, Admiral Sir W.M. *The Portsmouth Letters*. London: Macmillan, 1946.

Montgomery, Bernard Law. *The Memoirs of Field-Marshal the Viscount Montgomery of Alamein, K.G.* London: Collins, 1958.

Pakenham, Simona. *Sixty Miles from England: The English at Dieppe 1814–1914*. New York: St. Martin's Press, 1967.

Roberts, Andrew. *Masters and Commanders: The Military Geniuses Who Led the West to Victory in World War II*. Toronto: Penguin, 2009.

Stubbington, John. *Kept in the Dark: The Denial to Bomber Command of Vital ULTRA and Other Intelligence Information during World War II*. Barnsley, UK: Pen and Sword, 2010.

COMMANDOS AND RAIDS

Barclay, Glen St. J. '"Butcher and Bolt": Admiral Sir Roger Keyes and British Combined Operations, 1940–1941.' *Naval War College Review* 35, no. 2, sequence 290 (March/April 1982): 18–29.

Beadle, Major J.C. *The Light Blue Lanyard: 50 Years with 40 Commando Royal Marines*. Square One Publications, 1992.

Buckley, Christopher. *Norway, the Commandos, Dieppe*. The Second World War 1939–1945: A Short Military History Series. London: HMSO, 1951.

Bull, Stephen. *Commando Tactics: The Second World War*. Barnsley, UK: Pen and Sword, 2010.

Cabell, Craig. *The History of 30 Assault Unit: Ian Fleming's Red Indians*. Barnsley, UK: Pen and Sword, 2009.

———. *Ian Fleming's Secret War*. Barnsley, UK: Pen and Sword, 2008.

Cherry, Niall. *Striking Back: Britain's Airborne and Commando Raids 1940–1942*. Solihull, UK: Helion, 2009.

Cooksey, Jon. *Operation Chariot – The Raid on St. Nazaire*. Elite Operations Series. Barnsley, UK: Pen and Sword, 2005.

Dazel-Job, Patrick. *Arctic Snow to Dust of Normandy: The Extraordinary Wartime Exploits of a Naval Special Agent*. Barnsley, UK: Pen and Sword, 2002.

DeFelice, Jim. *Rangers at Dieppe: The First Combat Action of U.S. Army Rangers in World War II*. New York: Penguin, 2008.

Dorrian, James. *Saint-Nazaire: Operation Chariot – 1942*. Battleground French Coast. Barnsley, UK: Pen and Sword, 2006.

Durnford-Slater, John. *Commando*. London: William Kimber, 1953.

Fergusson, Bernard. *The Watery Maze: The Story of Combined Operations*. London: Collins, 1961.

Fowler, Will. *Allies at Dieppe: 4 Commando and the US Rangers*. Oxford: Osprey, 2012.

Greenhous, Brereton. 'Operation Flodden: The Sea Fight off Berneval and the Suppression of the Goebbels Battery, 19 August 1942.' *Canadian Military Journal* 4, no. 4 (Autumn 2003): 47–57.

Hopton, Richard. *A Reluctant Hero: The Life of Captain Robert Ryder VC*. Barnsley, UK: Pen and Sword, 2011.

Hughes-Hallett, J. 'The Mounting of Raids.' *Royal United Service Institution Journal* 95 (Feb.–Nov. 1950): 580–88.

Lovat, Lord. *March Past: A Memoir*. New York: Holmes and Meier, 1979.

Macksey, Kenneth. *Commando: Hit-and-Run Combat in World War II*. New York: Jove Publications, 1991.

Messenger, Charles. *The Commandos 1940–1946*. London: William Kimber, 1985.

Mills-Roberts, Derek. *Clash by Night: A Commando Chronicle*. London: William Kimber, 1956.

Parker, John. *Royal Marines Commandos*. London: Headline, 2012.

Prince, Stephen. *The Blocking of Zeebrugge – Operation Z-O 1918 (Raid)*. Oxford: Osprey, 2011.

Rankin, Nicholas. *Ian Fleming's Commandos: The Story of 30 Assault Unit in WWII*. London: Faber and Faber, 2011.

Van der Bijl, Nicholas. *Commandos in Exile: The Story of 10 (Inter-Allied) Commando 1942–1945*. Barnsley, UK: Pen and Sword, 2008.

CANADIAN FORCES

Antal, Sandy, and Kevin R. Shackleton. *Duty Nobly Done: The Official History of the Essex and Kent Scottish Regiment*. Windsor, ON: Walkerville, 2006.

Brown, Kingsley, Sr., Kingsley Brown Jr, and Brereton Greenhous. *Semper Paratus: The History of the Royal Hamilton Light Infantry (Wentworth Regiment), 1862–1977*. Hamilton, ON: RHLI Historical Association, 1977.

Cook, Tim. *Clio's Warriors: Canadian Historians and the Writing of the World Wars*. Vancouver: UBC Press, 2006.

———. *Warlords: Borden, Mackenzie King and Canada's World Wars*. Toronto: Penguin, 2012.

Dickson, Paul Douglas. *A Thoroughly Canadian General: A Biography of General H.D.G. Crerar*. Toronto: University of Toronto Press, 2007.

Douglas, W.A.B., Roger Sarty, and Michael Whitby. *The Official Operational History of the Royal Canadian Navy in the Second World War, 1943–1945*. Vol. 2, part 2, *A Blue Water Navy*. St. Catharines, ON: Vanwell Publishing, 2007.

Douglas, William A.B., and Brereton Greenhous. *Out of the Shadows: Canada in the Second World War*. 2nd ed. Toronto: Oxford University Press, 1995.

Elliot, S.R. *Scarlet to Green: A History of Intelligence in the Canadian Army 1903–1963*. Toronto: Canadian Intelligence and Security Association, 1981.

English, John A. *The Canadian Army and the Normandy Campaign: A Study in Failure in High Command*. London: Praeger, 1991.

Freasby, W.R., ed. *Official History of the Canadian Medical Services, 1939–1945*. Vol. 1, *Organization and Campaigns*. Ottawa: Queen's Printer, 1956.

Goodspeed, D.J. *Battle Royal: A History of the Royal Regiment of Canada, 1862–1962*. Toronto: Royal Regiment of Canada Association, 1962.

Granatstein, J.L. *The Generals: The Canadian Army's Senior Commanders in the Second World War*. Toronto: Stoddart, 1993.

Greenhous, Brereton, et al. *The Official History of the Royal Canadian Air Force*. Vol. 3, *The Crucible of War, 1939–1945*. Toronto: University of Toronto Press, 1994.

Kerry, A.J., and W.A. McDill. *History of the Corps of Royal Engineers*. Vol. 2. Ottawa: Military Engineers Association, 1966.

Les Fusiliers Mont-Royal. *Cent ans d'histoire d'un régiment canadien-français: Les Fusiliers Mont-Royal, 1869–1969*. Montreal: Éditions du Jour, 1971.

Marteinson, John, and Michael R. McNorgan. *The Royal Armoured Corps: An Illustrated History*. Toronto: Robin Brass Studio, 2000.

Meanwell, R.W. *1st Battalion, the Essex Scottish Regiment 1939–1945: A Brief History*. Aldershot, ON: Gale and Polden, 1946.

Moir, John S., ed. *History of the Royal Canadian Corps of Signals, 1903–1961*. Ottawa: Corps Committee, Royal Canadian Corps of Signals, 1962.

Nissen, Jack, and A.W. Cockerill. *Winning the Radar War: A Memoir*. Toronto: Macmillan, 1987.

Queen-Hughes, R.W. *Whatever Men Dare: A History of the Queen's Own Cameron Highlanders of Canada, 1936–1960*. Winnipeg: Bulman Brothers, 1960.

Rickard, John Nelson. *Politics of Command: Lieutenant-General A.G.L. McNaughton and the Canadian Army, 1939–1943*. Toronto: University of Toronto Press, 2010.

Ritchie, Andrew R. *Watchdog: A History of the Canadian Provost Corps*. Toronto: University of Toronto Press, 1995.

Stacey, C.P. *A Date with History*. Ottawa: Deneau, 1982.

———. *History of the Canadian Army in the Second World War: Six Years of War*. Ottawa: Queen's Printer, 1955.

Acknowledgements

The research for two editions of this book unfolded over a period of 25 years, and I would like to begin by thanking everyone who helped to make it possible. One of the best aspects of this historical research journey has been meeting a wide range of people who have influenced my work and become colleagues – and some, lifelong friends.

Without the work of at least two generations of historians before me, this book could not have been written. Starting with C.P. Stacey's pioneering work in the days following the raid, through Terence Robertson's work in the sixties that embedded Dieppe in the Canadian consciousness, to the stellar and seminal offerings of Brian Villa and John Campbell in the late eighties, followed by historians such as Ben Greenhous, Steve Prince, Peter Henshaw, Hugh Henry, Denis and Shelagh Whitaker and more recently Béatrice Richard and Timothy Balzer, all these historians have made dramatic and lasting contributions to our understanding of the darkest day in Canadian history. Contextually, the many publications by J.L. Granatstein, David Bercuson, Holger Herwig, Desmond Morton and Terry Copp have been invaluable to my research.

In the area of cryptography, the work of Ralph Erskine continues to inspire, as do the lasting contributions by David Kahn, David Syrett, Richard Aldrich and John Ferris. Likewise, Hugh Sebag-Montefiore's excellent study on the early days of pinch operations is clearly ground-breaking, as is Nicholas Rankin's book on 30 Assault Unit, Richard

Hopton's on Robert 'Red' Ryder, Robin Neilland's on the Royal Marines, Jack Copeland's on Alan Turing, and Jock Gardner's on Ultra and the Battle of the Atlantic.

I am grateful to Dr Stephen Harris, who recruited me some twenty years ago, when I began my graduate studies, to work at the Directorate of History and Heritage in Ottawa. That appointment not only gave me a job but laid the path for a career. Likewise, there were many others at DHH who have generously helped me over the years: Serge Bernier, Alec Douglas, Bill McAndrew, Bob Caldwell, Bill Rawling, Donna Porter, Isabelle Campbell, Carl Christie, Mike Whitby, Richard Gimlett, Sean Hunter, Ken Reynolds, Michelle Litalien, Jean Morin, Greg Donahy, Bill Johnston, Yves Tremblay, Jim McKillop, Andrea Schlecht and the late Ben Greenhous, among others. This list also includes a historian's best friend – the archivist. In this case, without the support and expertise of Owen Cooke, Warren Sinclair and Valerie Casbourn at DHH and the wisdom, friendship and advice of Paul Marsden at Library and Archives Canada, this research would never have been possible.

Although he has moved on from DHH to greener pastures at the Laurier Centre for Military and Disarmament Studies in Waterloo, I must thank Dr Roger Sarty, who was a friend, mentor and boss all those years ago when I was a very small cog in the machine that created the official history of the Royal Canadian Navy in the Second World War. In addition, I would like to thank Mike Bechthold and Professor Emeritus Terry Copp at Wilfrid Laurier University.

Equally, I would like to thank Brian Villa, Peter Henshaw and Hugh Henry, whose scholarship and encouragement kept me on my toes, constantly posing a battery of salient questions throughout this process. Similarly, I am grateful to Beth Crumley (formerly of the United States Marine Corps Historical Center) for information on the USMC commitment to the Dieppe Raid. I am indebted to Ralph Erskine and, at Bletchley Park, to Bob Horner and the late Brian Oakley for their insights on British cryptography. In addition, I must thank Bob Hanyok for his generous help with the American cryptographic landscape, and Adrian Smith at the University of Southampton for his assistance with Mountbatten. This research could not have been completed without 'bird dogs' on the ground – the researchers at various archival facilities, particularly Simon Cawthorne, Bob O'Hara, Gregor Murbach, Galen Perras and Greg Hill, who fulfilled that role with remarkable skill and my former student and budding historian Ryan Pinchuk who left this world far too early to fulfil his destiny.

I would also like to thank the staff at the National Maritime Museum in Greenwich, the Imperial War Museum in London, the University of Toronto Archives (in particular Eric McGeer), the Royal Marine Commando Museum and Archives in Portsmouth, and Hugh Alexander and Mark Dunton at the British National Archives (fondly remembered as the PRO).

I am grateful to Stephen Prince and his staff at the Royal Navy's Naval Historical Branch in Portsmouth, and especially to Jock Gardner and Mark Bentinck (who put me on to Paul McGrath), for their generous help with numerous naval queries from this all too 'military' of historians. None of this could have come to fruition without the help of Tony Comer (the historian at GCHQ) who, when presented with the evidence, immediately provided key technical advice and judiciously expedited the release of key documents that helped take this research to a new level.

A special note of appreciation goes out to the veterans and their families who generously gave of their time to talk to me and granted permission to quote from their letters, diaries, journals and unpublished memoirs – all of which add to the drama and human reality of this story. They include Ron Beal, Howard Large, Ted Bennett, John Parsons, Paul McGrath, the family of Ernest 'Lofty' Coleman, Edward Peter Yard-Young and Andy Wilkinson, Simon McAlister and the family of Robert McAlister, Miles Huntington-Whiteley and Leo Huntington-Whiteley, Barry Batterton and the family of Roy Batterton Jr, David McKellar and the family of Ian McKellar, Lisle Ryder and the family of 'Red' Ryder, and David Lloyd of No. 40 Commando Association. I would also like to thank David Zelden and Jayne Poolton-Turvey for their work on behalf of veterans in Canada and their dedication to all things 'Dieppe'.

One of the bonuses of conducting historical inquiries such as this one is having a reason to visit the site in question. In this case, I was most fortunate to spend close to six months over an eighteen-month period in Dieppe. The City of Dieppe Archives proved crucial to establishing the whereabouts of the Hôtel Moderne, as were the owners of the Hôtel Les Arcades, Karine and Mathieu Leducq, who energetically joined in the search. I also want to thank Nicola Bucourt, Frederick Jeanne, Mathieu Masson, Hervé Fihue, and Heimdal publications in Caen for their help.

What took me over to Dieppe on a regular basis was the filming of the documentary *Dieppe Uncovered* for History Television in Canada and UKTV in England. Special thanks go to my 'partner in crime' in several documentary productions, the talented producer/director Wayne Abbott – who has traipsed across many a battlefield with me, from Hong Kong to Europe, in our effort to bring history to life on the small screen, and to Andrew Roberts.

Having taught history at the university, college and high school levels over 25 years, I was most fortunate to sign on with Marianopolis College in Westmount a decade ago. There, I have always received tremendous support for my research endeavours and I must thank a fantastic faculty and staff who truly value excellence and the spirit of collegiality, especially my office mate, Dr Maria Salomon, who listened with great patience as I droned incessantly about all things Dieppe. Thanks for being a friend.

To put a complex book together requires a team of experienced and talented professionals. I would like to thank the team at Icon Books, especially Duncan Heath, Sarah Balmforth, Andrew Furlow and Ruth Killick, and my British literary agent Andrew Lownie as well as my literary super-agent in Canada, Rick Broadhead, who went beyond the call of duty to ensure that everything came together and that it stayed on the rails.

To the friends and family I have put on hold during the writing period – Earl Chapman, Lionel Chetwynd, Greg Hill, Peter Berg, the boys from the Black Sox and the Knights, my former colleagues at LBP and in the Black Watch, John, Liette, Pat, Lorina, Dave, Carly, Stephanie, James and all the nieces and nephews – I thank you for your patience, understanding and friendship.

I also want to mention my mother and my late father, who, during a European trip in 1962, stopped by Dieppe to pay their respects to the many friends lost on the morning of August 19, 1942, and who filmed a 30-second segment of the harbour and Pollet Cliff with their 8 mm camera. They could never have realized the supreme irony of that moment: despite better vantage points, they chose, for whatever reason, to take the photo from the front steps of the Hôtel Moderne. Pure coincidence, of course – but history can move in mysterious ways.

Finally, to my wife, Carolyn, my children, Jessica, Andie and Kevin, and our Boxador pup Poppy, thank you so much for your support throughout this remarkable journey. I love you all.

Photo Credits

Private Ron Beal, 2012
© Jennifer Roberts

Ian Fleming in naval uniform
Ian Fleming Images/Maud Russell Estate Collection

Rear Admiral John Godfrey
© Imperial War Museums

Admiral Karl Dönitz
Bundesarchiv (Creative Commons licence CC BY-SA 3.0 DE)

The naval four-rotor Enigma machine
US National Archives and Records Administration

The 'Morrison Wall' at Bletchley Park
© Crown copyright. By kind permission of Director GCHQ

Two sets of spare rotor wheels for the Enigma machine
© Crown copyright. By kind permission of Director GCHQ

Three Enigma rotor wheels laid out on their sides
© Crown copyright. By kind permission of Director GCHQ

Frank Birch
© Crown copyright. By kind permission of Director GCHQ

Alan Turing
Public domain

The aftermath of the fighting on Red Beach
Collection H. Fihue

An RAF aerial photo of the Dieppe Raid in progress
© *The National Archives, Kew*

German propaganda photo of the carnage on Blue Beach
Department of National Defence/Library and Archives Canada

A photo included in an American report on the M4 cipher
US National Archives and Records Administration

The survivors of No. 10 Platoon in Operation Torch
Courtesy of the McGrath family

Paul McGrath with No. 10 Platoon in 1945
Courtesy of the McGrath family

Private Ron Beal of the Royal Regiment of Canada
© *Colin McConnell/Getstock.com*

Permissions

Every attempt has been made by the author to trace the copyright or permissions holders of images used or works quoted in this book. I welcome any information or clarification in the few instances where such information was untraceable or unavailable to me.

Pages 306, 329: Permission to quote from the IWM's interview with Douglas Charles Bevan (IWM 14882) is granted by permission of the Imperial War Museums.

Pages 259, 263, 330–31, 338, 342, 345, 346: Permission to reproduce from Ernest Coleman's unpublished memoirs, copyright © Ernest Coleman, 2013, is granted by permission of John Barker.

Notes

ABBREVIATIONS USED IN THESE NOTES
ADM, Admiralty; CAB, Cabinet Office (UK); CAFO, Confidential Admiralty Fleet Order; CANUKUS, Canada–UK–US; DEFE, Ministry of Defence (UK); DHH, Directorate of History and Heritage (Department of National Defence, Canada); DU, Dieppe Uncovered (Northernsky Entertainment, 2012, producer/director Wayne Abbott, for History Television in Canada and UKTV in the United Kingdom, first aired August 19, 2012); FO, Foreign Office (UK); GOD, Godfrey Papers; GRO, Baillie-Grohman Papers; HW, Government Communications Headquarters; LAC, Library and Archives Canada; MG, Manuscript Group; NMM, National Maritime Museum (Greenwich, UK); RG, Record Group; RMM, Royal Marine Museum Archives (Portsmouth, UK); TNA, National Archives (United Kingdom); NARA, National Archives and Records Administration (USA); FDR, Franklin D. Roosevelt Library (USA); CCC, Churchill College, Cambridge (UK); CMHQ, Canadian Military Headquarters

Chapter 1

1. Ronald Atkin, *Dieppe 1942: The Jubilee Disaster* (London: Macmillan, 1980), p. 252.
2. Juno Beach Centre, 'The Dieppe Raid,' http://www.junobeach.org/e/2/can-eve-mob-die-e.htm (accessed February 18, 2013).
3. Jock Gardner, 'Admiral Sir Bertram Ramsay,' in Stephen Howarth, ed., *Men of War: Great Naval Leaders of World War Two* (London: Weidenfeld & Nicolson, 1992), p. 360.
4. TNA HW 43/15 GCCS Naval Sigint History Vol. IV: The Organization and Evolution of British Naval Sigint.

5. Sir Harry Hinsley, 'The Influence of Ultra in the Second World War' (lecture, Cambridge University, October 19, 1993).

6. J.H. Godfrey, 'History of Naval Intelligence Division 1939–1942,' p. 246, TNA ADM 223/464.

7. TNA ADM 223/213 History of SIGINT Operations undertaken by 30 Commando/30AU N.D.

Chapter 2

1. Franklin D. Roosevelt Library, Hyde Park, New York (hereafter FDR Library) Cuneo Papers, 'Fleming File.' Cuneo was appointed by General Bill Donovan to work as the OSS personal liaison for Sir William Stephenson who ran British Security Coordination in New York City and J. Edgar Hoover, head of the FBI.

2. The nickname 'Blinker' came from Hall's chronic facial twitch, which caused one of his eyes to flash like a navy signal lamp, particularly when excited. Joseph E. Perisco, *Roosevelt's Secret War: FDR and WWII Espionage*, (New York: Random House, 2002) p. 8; see also Reginald Hall (with Phillip Vickers), *A Clear Case of Genius: Room 40's Codebreaking Pioneer*; David Ramsay, *Blinker Hall Spymaster: The Man Who Brought America Into World War 1* and Paul Gannon, *Inside Room 40: The Codebreakers of World War 1*.

3. Nicholas Rankin, *Ian Fleming's Commandos: The Story of 30 Assault Unit in WWII* (London: Faber and Faber, 2011), p. 29.

4. Donald McCormick, *17F: The Life of Ian Fleming* (London: Peter Owen, 1994), p. 47. Donald McCormick was a historian and journalist who served with Fleming in the NID and later alongside him as a journalist on the foreign desk of the *Sunday Times* in the post-war years.

5. Ibid., p. 48.

6. FDR Library, Cuneo Papers, 'Fleming File.'

7. Ben Macintyre, *For Your Eyes Only* (London: Bloomsbury, 2012), 231–33. Kindle edition.

8. Ibid.

9. Ibid., pp. 123–25. According to Macintyre, Ian Fleming kept a signed, framed copy of the eulogy as a personal treasure throughout his life.

10. FDR Library, Cuneo Papers, 'Fleming File.' p. 9.

11. Ibid.

12. Macintyre, *For Your Eyes Only*, pp. 160–62.

13. Ibid.

14. J.H. Godfrey, 'The Naval Memoirs of Admiral J.H. Godfrey,' Vol. V, 1947–1950 NID, Part II, 284 and 387, NMM GOD/171. Godfrey's memoirs (called 'Naval Memoirs' in these notes) and the hundreds of pages he either penned or had produced for what he hoped would eventually form a definitive history of the NID have remained in their unpublished form at several archival repositories, including the British National Archives, the National Maritime Museum and the Churchill College Archives in Cambridge.

15. William Plomer, 'Ian Fleming Remembered,' in *Encounter* (January 1965), quoted in Godfrey, 'Naval Memoirs,' p. 397.

16. FDR Library. Ernest Cuneo Papers, 'Fleming File.'

17. Plomer, 'Ian Fleming Remembered,' p. 400. Fleming had built a remarkable library of first editions of important inventions, theories and scientific discoveries of modern times – ideas that changed the course of history – which constituted one of the best collections of its genre in England. Following his death in 1964, the collection was purchased from his estate by Indiana University where it resides today. The author would like to thank Joel Silver for his kind help in sorting through the massive collection.

18. Charles Babbage, *The Writings of Charles Babbage* (Alvin, TX: Halcyon Press, 2009), Kindle edition; Bruce Collier and James MacLachlan, *Charles Babbage and the Engines of Perfection* (New York: Oxford University Press, 1999); Abdul Montaqim, *Pioneers of the Computer Age: From Charles Babbage to Steve Jobs* (London: Monsoon Media, 2012). The vast collection at Indiana University includes Babbage's 'Reflexions on the decline of science in England, and some of its causes' from 1830 and the work of Dionysius Lardner, who in 1834 penned a review of seven papers by or about Babbage's work including the Second 'Difference Engine' and one on a projected analytical machine.

19. Ibid.

20. McCormick, *17F*, p. 40.

21. Ibid., p. 41. Fleming wrote a paper on Babbage's work on cryptography for Godfrey, which apparently has never been found.

22. Ibid., p. 30.; FDR Library, Cuneo Papers, 'Fleming File.'

23. FDR Library, Cuneo Papers, 'Fleming File.'

24. Ibid.

25. NMM GOD/177, J.H. Godfrey, 'Ian Fleming.'

26. NMM GOD/161, Godfrey Papers, 10 November 1966.

27. FDR Library, Cuneo Papers, 'Fleming Files.'

28. NMM GOD/161, Godfrey Papers, 10 November 1966.

29. Godfrey, 'Ian Fleming.'

30. William Plomer, address given at the Memorial Service for Ian Fleming, 15 September 1964, NMM (Papers of Vice Admiral Sir Norman Denning 2/4).; FDR Library, Cuneo Papers, 'Fleming File.'

31. NMM GOD/93, J.H. Godfrey, 'Room 39,' 10 July 1948, 1–3,.

32. Godfrey, 'Naval Memoirs,' Vol. 5, Part II, p. 386.

33. 'Ian Fleming: The Playboy Interview,' in *50 Years of the Playboy Interview*, Kindle 2012.

34. NMM GOD/161.

35. Godfrey, 'Ian Fleming.'

36. Nigel West, *Historical Dictionary of Ian Fleming's World of Intelligence: Fact and Fiction* (Lanham, MD: Scarecrow Press, 2009), p. 67.

37. J.H. Godfrey, 'The Significance of British Naval Intelligence during WWII, and Post War Security,' 6 April 1965, NMM GOD/97; Naval Section miscellaneous papers, TNA HW 8/23.

38. NMM GOD/161. Italics are underlined in original.

39. Ibid.

40. NMM GOD/97, J.H. Godfrey to Donald McLachlan, 5 April 1965.

41. Godfrey, 'Significance of British Naval Intelligence.'

42. Godfrey, 'Ian Fleming.'

43. Robert Harling, 'Where Bond Began,' in the *Sunday Times*, 16 August 1964.

44. TNA ADM 196/92/39, Personnel file of John Henry Godfrey.

45. Patrick Beesly, *Very Special Admiral: The Life of Admiral J.H. Godfrey, CB* (London: Hamish Hamilton, 1980), p. 84.

46. NMM GOD/170.

47. ADM 196/92/39.

48. As Paul Gannon makes clear in his work on Room 40, 'Churchill was a doting stepfather to his infant cryptographic organization, giving it support and encouragement as well as providing the sustenance needed to ensure rapid early growth.'; Paul Gannon, *Inside Room 40* (Shepperton, Surrey, UK: Ian Allen, 2011), p. 39; Godfrey, 'Naval Memoirs,' Vol. 5, Part II, p. 271.

49. Paul Gannon, *Inside Room 40* (Shepperton, Surrey, UK: Ian Allen, 2011), p. 39.

50. The 'pinch' of material off the Magdeburg by the Imperial Russian Navy was the first of three (the Main naval code, the Transport code and the Merchant Transport code) captured that autumn giving the

British a decisive advantage in cryptography during the First World War. The importance of these captures, particularly the first, was not lost on Winston Churchill – then First Lord of the Admiralty. When the Main naval codebook was delivered to London by a Russian envoy, it was Churchill who personally took receipt of the valuable material. As cryptographic historian David Kahn stated, this was 'more precious than a dozen Faberge eggs ... one of the most significant moments in the long history of secret intelligence.' David Ramsay, *Blinker Hall Spymaster: The Man Who Brought America into World War 1* (Stroud, Gloucestershire, UK: History Press, 2009), pp. 32, 417.

51. NMM GOD/161/2.

52. Ibid.

53. According to David Ramsay, 'this choice proved inspired as Godfrey was the first DNI since Sinclair whose ability and dynamism was equal to Hall's.' Ramsay, *Blinker Hall Spymaster*, p. 305.

54. Godfrey, 'Naval Memoirs,' Vol. 5, Part I, p. 105.

55. NMM GOD/161/2. After leaving the service, Hall stood as the Conservative MP for the West Derby division of Liverpool and became a political confidant of Churchill with a reputation as a 'die-hard' right-winger who took a tough stance against Bolshevism. In 1926, during the General Strike, Stanley Baldwin appointed Churchill editor of the *British Gazette* and he, in turn, selected Hall to oversee operations where his 'energy and fondness for underhanded tactics' could undermine the strike and pressure the government into expelling Russian diplomats through leaks of Soviet messages intercepted by the British. Gannon, *Inside Room 40*, p. 248 and Ramsay, *Blinker Hall Spymaster*, p. 295.

56. Ibid.

57. Ibid.

58. McCormick, *17F*, p. 53.

59. NMM GOD/161/2.

60. Ibid. James worked for Hall in Room 40 and later penned a biography of his former boss entitled *The Eyes of the Navy: A Biographical Study of Admiral Sir Reginald Hall*. He then went on to have a successful naval career in the inter-war period that included service as the Admiralty representative on the nascent Joint Intelligence Committee where he reinvigorated naval SIGINT, particularly in regard to direction finding and Wireless Intercept services. Ramsay, *Blinker Hall Spymaster*, p. 304.

61. J.H. Godfrey, 'History of Naval Intelligence Division 1939–1942,' 12, TNA ADM 223/464.

62. Godfrey, 'Naval Memoirs,' Vol. 5, Part II, p. 207.

63. Ibid.

64. Ibid.

65. NMM GOD/161/2.

66. Godfrey, 'Naval Memoirs,' Vol. 5, Part II, p. 207.

67. NMM GOD/161/2.

68. Godfrey, 'Naval Memoirs,' Vol. 5, Part II, p. 387.

69. 'Madrid: the Claire Case,' TNA FO 1093/225.

70. NMM GOD 171. Quoted in Robert Harling, 'Where Bond Started,' *Sunday Telegraph* (London), August 16, 1964.

71. NMM GOD/161/2.

72. TNA HW 43/12, p. 278, NID staff and distribution of work, February 1940 in December 1940. NID 17 acted as DNI's personal staff and was responsible for bringing the most important items of intelligence, other than those of a purely operational nature, to Godfrey's attention. As the GC&CS history states: 'In 1940 its two officers were part of the personal staff of DNI, and the main duties of the two Commanders were to coordinate intelligence within the division and to ensure that any of it that affected the other services or the Foreign Office was passed on and appreciated. By May 1941, it had become known as the coordination and liaison section and had a strength of 13. In September 1942 it was still at root what it had always been – a coordinating section within NID and a link with organisations outside NID.'

73. J.H. Godfrey, 'Afterthoughts: Naval Propaganda,' p. 87, TNA ADM 223/619.

74. '[For] the outsider reviewing the organization of NID for the handling of general intelligence from sigint sources the situation is complicated by the existence of a third participant. There was the OIC (NID 8) for exploitation of operational special intelligence; there were the geographical sections (NID 1,2,3,4, 16, 20 and 23) to handle its long term implications; and there was NID 12 whose main duty was the production of what were known officially as the special intelligence summaries. But OIC also wrote summaries of intelligence based on sigint sources, and so, too, did the geographical sections. Moreover, NID 12 indulged both in long term studies and, occasionally, in operational exploitation. It is difficult, therefore, to fit NID 12 neatly into the picture, but its position will become clearer if we trace its origin in NID 17.' TNA HW 43/12, p. 277

75. Godfrey, 'History,' 146, ADM 223/464.

76. Rankin, *Ian Fleming's Commandos*, p. 106.

77. Godfrey 'History,' p. 146.
78. Quoted in McCormick, *17F*, p. 51.
79. Godfrey, 'Naval Memoirs,' Vol. 5, Part II, p. 278.
80. To a far greater degree than any of his predecessors or successors, Churchill was heavily involved in operational intelligence matters – something that started on the battlefield as a young officer in the Boer War where information he provided helped win the battle of Diamond Hill, considered a turning point in the conflict. As David Stafford wrote in his biographical work of the British prime minister, 'Churchill stood head and shoulders above his political contemporaries in grasping the importance of intelligence. Secret service with all its romance and melodrama, trickery, deception, plot and counter-plot, certainly appealed to the schoolboy within him.' Ramsay, *Blinker Hall Spymaster*, p. 34.
81. NMM GOD/170.
82. McCormick, *17F*, p. 71.
83. Quoted in ibid., p. 55.
84. Alan N. Scheider, 'Ian and I,' *Naval Intelligence Professionals Newsletter* (Fall 1987).
85. 'Ian Fleming, 007 – James Bond,' TNA Sefton Delmer Archive (accessed online August 11, 2013).
86. McCormick, *17F*, p. 96.
87. Donald McLachlan, 'Room 39: Top Secret Birthplace of Bond,' quoted in Godfrey, 'Naval Memoirs,' Vol. 5, Part II, p. 394.
88. TNA HW 8/15 Report on British Procedures for Capturing and Exploiting Enemy Naval Documents, p. 15. As the author writes: 'It is quite clear that at the start of the war in both the British army and Navy the arrangements made for capturing and exploiting enemy documents were not satisfactory. Fundamentally this was because nobody had any conception of the importance which intelligence was destined to assume in the conflict, and in particular the great role that ULTRA information was going to play period. It is hardly surprising, therefore, that there was little understanding of what the capture of enemy documents might contribute both to general intelligence and to ULTRA.' p. 26.

Chapter 3

1. NMM GOD/161.
2. TNA HW 43/15, pp. 213-15.
3. Naval Section GC&CS, memo, 7 September 1940, TNA HW 25/18. According to Mavis Batey, a gifted nineteen year-old cryptanalyst on

Knox's team, her boss 'would have explained to Fleming what they already knew without capturing the actual Enigma machine – the wireless transmitting routine, manual instruction books, frequencies and message indicators and how it was the document with the daily key settings, and not the actual Enigma machine, a model of which they had been given by the Poles, that was required for the breakthrough.' Mavis Batey, *From Bletchley with Love* (Bletchley, UK: Bletchley Park Trust, 2008), p. 4.

4. Note by P.R. Chambers ADI, 17 October 1940, TNA AIR 20/5238.

5. 'Air Ministry Instructions for Operation "Ruthless,"' 17 October 1940, p. 3, TNA AIR 20/5238.

6. J.H. Godfrey, 'History of Naval Intelligence Division 1939–1942,' p. 263, TNA ADM 223/464.

7. Ibid.

8. Winston Churchill, speech to House of Commons, 21 January 1941.

9. *Old Mersey Times*, 'Loss of the *Athenia* 1939,' http://www.old-merseytimes.co.uk/ATHENIA.html (accessed August 12, 2013).

10. Godfrey, 'History,' p. 264.

11. Ibid. TNA HW 43/11, pp. 257–58. As Frank Birch recorded: 'As early as December 1939, Commander A.G. Denniston then head of GCCS, had informed DNI that there was '"little hope of breaking the deadlock, reached by the cryptalaysts in their wrestling with Enigma, unless we have outside assistance, namely by capture of the machine and certain documents."'

12. TNA HW 43/15 GC&CS Naval Sigint Volume IV: The Organisation and Evolution of British Sigint by Frank Birch. Part 3: The Use of Sigint.

13. 'CANUKUS Joint Services SIGINT discussions held in Washington, 6–17 April 1942,' HW 14/46.

14. TNA HW 43/17 GC&CS Naval Sigint Volume VII : The German Navy's Use of Special Intelligence and Reactions to Allied Use, p. 153.

15. Jak P. Mallmann Showell, *Enigma U-Boats: Breaking the Code* (Birmingham, UK: Ian Allan, 2009), 86. Kindle edition.

16. The original Enigma machine, used by the German army and air force, offered only five wheels.

17. B. Jack Copeland, *Turing: Pioneer of the Information Age* (Oxford: Oxford University Press, 2013), 644–46. Kindle edition.

18. According to Mahon's 'History of Hut 8': 'In order to decode a message one has then to know wheel-order, clips, starting position of message, and Stecker. Any three of the eight wheels may be chosen – 336 possibilities. There are 17,000 possible clip combinations and 17,000 possible starting

positions – in the 4 wheeled machine half a million. The number of possible Stecker combinations is in the region of half a billion. In fact the number of ways the machine may be set up is astronomical.' Complicating matters further, the wheel order and clips on most keys were changed every two days while the Stecker and Grundstellung normally changed every 24 hours. A.P. Mahon, 'History of Hut 8,' p. 5, TNA HW 25/2.

19. David Kahn, *The Codebreakers: The Story of Secret Writing* (London: Macmillan, 1966).

20. 'History of Hut 8,' p. 18, TNA HW 25/2.

21. TNA HW 25/1, p. 19. As Alexander writes: 'Turing first got interested in the problem for the quite typical reason that "no one else was doing anything about it and I could have it to myself."'

22. Batey, *From Bletchley with Love.*

23. Copeland, *Turing*, pp. 976–80.

24. TNA HW 25/1, p. 22.

25. I.G. Good, 'From Hut 8 to the Newmanry,' in B. Jack Copeland, *Colossus: The Secret of Bletchley Park's Codebreaking Computers* (New York: Oxford University Press, 2006). Kindle edition.

26. Godfrey, 'History,' p. 264. According to the author of the US Navy's Report on British Procedures for Capturing and Exploiting Enemy Naval Documents: 'Since all sorts of communications equipment must be widely distributed, there is a definite practical limit on the amount of security which can be achieved against the capture of communication material. Thus pinching is not the only one of the basic means of breaking into the enemy communications, it is also the means whose importance has been growing as the war has progressed.' TNA HW 8/103 Report on British Procedures for Capturing and Exploiting Enemy Naval Documents, pp. 1–2.

27. Head of Naval Section to Denniston, 19 October 1940, TNA HW 8/46.

28. Godfrey, 'History,' p. 264; TNA HW 43/15, p. 210. As Birch would later write: 'Naval section's campaign, initiated in the autumn of 1940, was prompted by disappointment at the unexpected inability of the crypt analysts to exploit further their early successes in the spring. The traffic of a few days then decrypted had proved conclusively that practically all German intelligence eggs were kept in the Enigma basket. Therefore, Enigma must be broken.' See also TNA HW 43/10, p. 110.

29. GC&CS, 'The Handling of Naval Special Intelligence,' app. B to ch. XIII 'Activities of German Naval Units in the Channel,' 10 September 1940, TNA HW 8/46.

30. Ibid.

31. Ibid.

32. Ibid., 5 December 1940.

33. TNA HW 43/22 GC&CS Naval Sigint volume XII: General intelligence. 'The importance of this service lay in the fact that the continued availability of lower grade decrypts increased at all times the chances of breaking into German naval enigma through the encipherment of texts common to both types of systems.' p. 211.

34. Ibid; TNA HW 43/15, pp. 214–15.

35. Birch to Denniston, 21 December 1940, TNA HW 8/22.

36. Ibid.

37. Ibid.; Birch to Denniston, 27 December 1940, TNA HW 8/22.

38. TNA HW 43/15, p. 216.

39. GC&CS, 'The Handling of Naval Special Intelligence,' app. B to ch. XIII 'Activities of German Naval Units in the Channel,' 10 September 1940, TNA HW 8/46. HW 11/18 GC&CS Naval History Vol V: The German Navy Organization – Appendices P-Z: Technical Establishments and Dockyards; HW/19 GC&CS Naval History Vol VI: Communications.

Chapter 4

1. TNA ADM 223/464. J.H. Godfrey, 'History of Naval Intelligence Division 1939–1942,' p. 246.

2. Dönitz had 'absolute commitment to victory, absolute belief in his men and the force he commanded, absolute hatred of the enemy creed, indeed of the enemy, absolute commitment to his own country and creed. He was a convinced Nazi.' P. Padfield, 'Grand Admiral Karl Dönitz,' in S. Howarth, ed., *Men of War: Great Naval Leaders of World War II* (London: Weidenfeld & Nicolson, 1993), p. 178.

3. Lord Hankey, *Diplomacy by Conference: Studies in Public Affairs 1920–1946* (London: E. Benn, 1946), p. 148.

4. Bernard Edwards, *Attack and Sink: The Battle of the Atlantic 1941* (New York: Brick Tower Press, 2006), 80–81. Kindle edition.

5. TNA HW 50/95. 'Evidence as to the Use of SIGINT in certain Naval Operations.'

6. Ibid. According to Mavis Batey, Knox and his counterpart William 'Nobby' Clarke (who handled operational intelligence at Bletchley Park) circumvented normal channels to deal directly with Cunningham 'through Godfrey, to speed up the process without revealing the secret source ... It is not clear how they had managed to by-pass the usual Admiralty

requirements for dissemination of intelligence from Bletchley Park to the commanders in the field, but Dilly (Knox) is on record as saying that if the normal procedure had been carried out "it would have lost us the battle of Mediterranean." Godfrey, who, like his guru Admiral Hall, was an arch-conspirator, later brought Admiral Cunningham down to Bletchley Park to celebrate with Dilly's section.' Mavis Batey, *From Bletchley with Love* (Bletchley, UK: Bletchley Park Trust, 2008), pp. 11, 421.

7. Christopher M. Bell, *Churchill and Sea Power* (Oxford: Oxford University Press, 2013), 203. Kindle edition.

8. TNA HW 43/15 GC&CS Naval Sigint Volume IV: The Organisation and Evolution of British Sigint by Frank Birch. Part 3, The Use of Sigint, p. 22.

9. Bell, *Churchill and Sea Power*, p. 215.

10. TNA ADM 223/88. 'Admiralty Use of Special Intelligence in Naval Operations,' p. 56.

11. Ibid.

12. Ibid.

13. TNA DEFE 3/1 Intelligence from intercepted German, Italian and Japanese radio communications, ZTP 819 (2355 hours, 25 May 1941), ZTP 820 (1925 hours, 25 May 1941), ZTP 822 (0111 hours, 26 May 1941).

14. 'Admiralty Use of Special Intelligence,' p. 66.

15. Tom McGowen, *Sink the Bismarck: Germany's Super-Battleship of World War II* (Brookfield, CT: Twenty-First Century Books, 1999).

16. William H. Garzke, Jr, and Robert O. Dulin, Jr, *Battleships: Axis and Neutral Battleships in World War II* (Annapolis, MD: Naval Institute Press, 1985).

17. 'Admiralty Use of Special Intelligence,' p. 76.

18. Marc Milner, *Battle of the Atlantic* (Stroud, Gloucestershire, UK: History Press, 2011).

19. TNA HW 43/23. 'Technical Intelligence and the Processing of Captured Documents,' p. 56.

20. Grand Admiral Karl Dönitz, *Memoirs: Ten Years and Twenty Days* (New York: Da Capo Press, 1997).

21. TNA HW 8/103.

22. TNA HW 43/16 GCCS Naval History. The Organization and Evolution of British Naval SIGINT Vol 4; Ibid.

23. TNA HW 8/46 'Handling of Naval Special Intelligence,' p. 171; HW 8/103 'Report on British Procedure for Capturing and Exploiting Captured Enemy Naval Documents,' p. 2.

24. 'German Ciphering Machines Quoted in Handling of Naval Special Intelligence,' CAFO 1544, 184, TNA HW 8/46.

25. TNA ADM 223/213. History of SIGINT Operations undertaken by 30 Commando/30AU N.D.

26. TNA HW 8/103.

27. MM Godfrey Papers GOD 177, 'Churchill and People' by J.H. Godfrey, April 1965.

28. TNA HW 8/46.

29. 'Technical Intelligence and the Processing of Captured Documents,' p. 65, TNA HW 43/23.

30. NAUK HW 43/15, p. 216.

31. J.H. Godfrey, 'Churchill and Combined Operations,' MM/GOD/161.

32. 'Handling of Naval Special Intelligence,' TNA HW 8/46.

33. Ibid.

34. TNA HW 43/15, p. 217.

35. Operation Claymore, TNA CAB 121/447.

36. Most Secret memo to the Prime Minister, Operation Claymore, from Colonel Hollis, 27 January 1941, TNA CAB 121/447 and HW 25/1.

37. Godfrey, 'History,' p. 163.

38. Ibid.

39. TNA DEFE 2/142. As an example of the type of report that appeared in Allied papers, the *Singleton Argus* from New South Wales, Australia, ran the headline: 'Ten German ships sunk: effective raid on Lofoten Island on Friday, March 7, 1941.' In the short article that followed, they stressed the ship sinkings, the destruction of the fish-oil plant, the rescue of Norwegian patriots and the capture of prisoners.

40. 'Handling of Special Naval Intelligence,' p. 175, TNA HW 8/46. The list included: Sachsenwald, Muenchen, Coburg, Ostmark, Sachsen, August Wriedt, Lauenburg, Hohman. Naval Section used broken Enigma messages to track down and pinpoint their positions. They were thought to carry naval Enigma on Home Area Keys, Weather Cipher in *Wetterkurzschlüssel* that used a page and table reference, and the Short Signal Book which was introduced in April to ships operating in the mid-Atlantic. Seizure of these vessels would a) deprive the enemy of valuable weather reports; b) remove a potential source of information concerning British fleet and shipping movements; c) offer an opportunity for obtaining ciphers including the Short Signal Book (extensively used by German raiders and supply ships) in the case of those ships in mid-Atlantic, as well as d) do something to remove German confidence in their ability to sail infested seas.

41. TNA HW 43/12, GC&CS Naval Sigint Vol III: The Organization and Evolution of British Naval Sigint by Frank Birch, p. 101. 'Finally, in January 1941 DNI himself – Rear Admiral John Godfrey – took the initiative, and the new experiment proved a great and lasting success.' The job Godfrey handed Haines was twofold: 'he will visit BP frequently to facilitate cooperation between NID and BP and will be responsible to DNI for the coordination of the results of the work of the naval section at BP and for the action taken by NID on the material provided by BP. He is authorised to communicate, when necessary, direct with the heads of naval subsections of GC&CS and similarly heads of Naval subsections are each to communicate with DNI via ADIC on matters of intelligence, technical wireless questions will be dealt with by DSD9, as previously, and the existing direct contact between the naval sections and OIC in operational matters will continue.'

42. TNA HW 8/46, p. 175.

43. Ibid.

44. TNA HW 43/15, p. 320.

45. TNA HW 8/46, p. 175.

46. Ibid., p. 261.

47. Ibid.

48. Ibid.

49. TNA ADM 1/11133; ADM 1/11382; ADM237/33.

50. U-boat archive, http://www.uboatarchive.net/U-110A/U-110-3rdEscort GroupLTBalmeReport.htm.

51. Stephen Roskill, *The Secret Capture: U-110 and the Enigma Story* (Seaforth Publishing, Kindle Edition).

52. Ibid.

53. Donald McLachlan, *Room 39: Naval Intelligence in Action, 1939–45* (London: Atheneum, 1968), p. 275. McLachlan claims quite incidentally that *U-110* was indeed towed back to a British port during the summer of 1941 but the ultimate fate of the U-boat still remains uncertain. It is possible however, that McLachlan, writing so long after the fact, has mistaken *U-570* which was captured and later recommissioned as HMS *Graph*, for *U-110*.

54. TNA HW 8/46. 'Handling of Special Naval Intelligence,' p. 175.

55. Ibid., p. 176.

56. David Kahn, *Seizing the Enigma: The Race to Break the German U-Boat Codes, 1939–1943* (Houghton Mifflin, 1991), p. 173.

57. TNA HW 8/46. 'Handling of Special Naval Intelligence,' p. 177.

58. Ibid.

59. TNA HW 8/46.175. 'Handling of Special Naval Intelligence,' p. 177.

60. TNA KV 4/187. Diary of Guy Liddell. Note that this passage was omitted from the published version of his diary that was edited by Nigel West. See also HW 8/46, p. 225.

61. TNA HW 8/46. 'Handling of Special Naval Intelligence,' p. 177.

62. TNA HW 8/23 Naval Section Misc. Papers 1941.

63. TNA HW 8/46. 'Handling of Special Naval Intelligence,' p. 177.

64. J.H. Godfrey, 'The Naval Memoirs of Admiral J.H. Godfrey,' Vol. V, 1947–1950 NID, Part II, MM GOD/170.

65. Although no current financial statements have been made public, it is a long-held view that GCHQ, the successor to GC&CS, maintains the largest budget of all the intelligence services in Great Britain, something echoed in the United States with the NSA and in Canada with the CSEC.

66. TNA HW 43/12, p. 170.

67. TNA HW 43/17. GC&CS Naval Sigint Volume VII: 'The German Navy's Use of Special Intelligence and Reactions to Allied Use,' by Lt Cmdr K.W. McMahon, USNR, p. 171.

68. Ibid.

69. TNA HW 43/15, p. 262.

70. TNA HW 43/15, p. 263.

71. TNA HW 43/15, p. 262.

72. TNA HW 43/15, p. 262.

73. TNA HW 43/17, p. 153.

74. TNA HW 43/17, p. 153. The 'jamming' inlay came in the form of fillers in the code and cipher tables that were printed in regular ink which, as the actual table was washed away, would be left in an attempt to deceive the enemy.

75. HW 43/17, p. 174. 'The German Navy's Use of Special Intelligence and Reactions to Allied Use.' The German document quoted is: Seekriegsleitung B.Nr. Skl/Chef MND 1760/41 Gkdos, Berlin, 24/7/41.

76. Ibid.

77. Ibid.

78. TNA HW 43/17. GC&CS Naval Sigint Vol VII: 'The German Navy's Use of Special Intelligence and Reactions to Allied Use,' p. 175.

79. TNA HW 43/17, p. 168.

80. TNA HW 43/15, p. 282.

81. TNA HW 43/17, p. 168.
82. TNA HW 43/17, p. 169.
83. TNA HW 43/15, p. 263. GC&CS Naval Sigint Vol IV: 'The Organisation and Evolution of British Naval Sigint,' by Frank Birch.
84. TNA HW 43/17, p. 168.
85. TNA HW 45/17, 'German Reactions to Allied Use of Special Intelligence,' p. 177. Dönitz noted in his war diary: 'nevertheless, in a series of examples set forth, I do not regard U-Boat transmissions as the occasion for appropriate enemy reaction, but on the contrary, either known or presumed causes.'
86. TNA HW 43/17, p. 178. *Stichwort* was a procedure that 'consisted of the application to the daily machine settings of a fixed alteration, easily memorable by means of a mnemonic word. This provided a sufficient safeguard against the straightforward use of captured memorandum, but no protection at all against Allied cryptanalytic methods, which made practically no a priori assumption about the machine settings.' However, *Stichwort* proved little more than a nuisance for the cryptanalysts. Instead of tackling an improved machine or a new encryption system, the *Stichwort* additive required the cryptanalyst at Bletchley to run only eight wheel orders and 26 plugboard connections rather than 336 wheel orders and trillions of plugboard combinations to solve the puzzle. See p. 153.
87. TNA PREM 3/196/1. *U-570* was taken in tow to Iceland and eventually back to England where she was repaired and recommissioned in the Royal Navy as HMS *Graph*.
88. TNA HW 43/15, p. 262.
89. Ibid.
90. TNA HW 43/17. GC&CS Naval Sigint Vol VII: 'The Germany Navy's use of Special Intelligence and Reactions to Allied Use,' p. 182.
91. TNA HW 43/17, p. 185.
92. TNA HW 43/17, p. 186. The sinking of surface raider *Schiff 16* on November 22 and the refuelling vessel *Python* on December 1 while in their respective rendezvous positions with U-boats by Royal Navy cruisers, did nothing to ameliorate this problem. Nonetheless, although they could not pinpoint the source, it is clear from the GC&CS history that 'German fears during 1941 had been provoked by the inexplicable conduct of British Forces at sea.'
93. TNA HW 43/17, p. 194.
94. TNA HW 8/158. Memorandum No. 3, Schlüssel M (Form M4).

Chapter 5

1. Ralph Erskine, 'Naval Enigma: The Breaking of Heimisch and Triton,' *Intelligence and National Security* 3(1) (1988): pp. 162–83.

2. 'History of Hut 8,' p. 74, TNA HW 25/2; and Schlüssel M (Form M4) *c.*22 January 1942, HW 8/24.

3. In fact, the 'four-rotor' did not have a fully functioning fourth wheel but rather a set half-wheel that did not move with the others when the machine was in operation. Although this restriction theoretically reduced the machine's efficiency, it still massively increased the odds against decryption.

4. Miller, Dr. A. Ray, The Cryptographic Mathematics of Enigma. Center for Cryptologic History, National Security Agency, 2019.

5. TNA HW 25/1, p. 11. As Alexander wrote: 'Three wheel bombe will test all 17,576 possible positions of the Wheel Order for a three rotor Enigma in about 20 minutes. With 336 possible wheel orders on the three rotor it would take 112 Bombe hours or five bombes working together for 24 straight hours to break the key.'

6. GCHQ Archives. Letter from Nigel De Grey to Brigadier John Tiltman, January 4, 1950. While preparing his history of Hut 8, De Grey wrote to Tiltman: 'The reason I want to get the low down on this particular subject is that if baldly stated that we knew from about May 1941 that the 4 wheel machine was threatened & that we did not get appropriate machinery to deal with it into action until about April 1943 it would look as if something had gone badly wrong. In fact I think there were many contributory causes but I didn't myself come into the picture till Feb '42 & there is nothing written down to go upon. It is not a question of vamping up excuses but of explaining the circumstances & difficulties that the same may not occur again.'

7. TNA HW 43/15 GC&CS Naval Sigint Volume IV: 'The Organisation and Evolution of British Sigint' by Frank Birch. Part 3, 'The Use of Sigint,' p. 64. As Birch writes: '"Cover" for the operations against the other seven ships, whose whereabouts were known from Special Intelligence (ULTRA), was obtained by use of DF bearings and by ordering cruisers to operational patrol areas. This presented no great difficulty or risk to security. There was, however, a grave risk in the cumulative effect of sinking in a short space of time <u>all</u> the eight ships whose positions were known from Special Intelligence (ULTRA),' p. 62 (underlining is original).

8. TNA HW 1/118; HW 1/122.

9. Ibid.

10. Ibid; TNA HW 43/11, pp. 214–15.

11. TNA HW 25/1, p. 10. To speed up the process, a 'Crib' – knowledge of the exact decode of all or part of a message. BP got these from routine messages whose form and partial substance they could predict – such as a weather message that began the same way each day. The second was re-encodements – messages that would be sent out to a general audience were enciphered on three-rotor Enigma machines AND four-rotors. In this case, as BP could still read the three-rotor, they were able to obtain a crib of the identical message that was sent to U-boats in northern waters and the Atlantic although enciphered on separate keys and machines. This is the reason why they could not afford to lose the three-rotor as they needed it for cribs, hence the need for heavy cover for pinch operations. Also, with the bigram tables read, the cryptanalysts could adopt another test – this one mathematical. Banburismus examined the effect of encoding the indicator at the Grundstellung (earlier method using the K-book). Note: the common denominator was that they both required pinched material.

12. RHV was 'used regularly by Harbour Defence Vessels in Norway and the Channel Area which are not yet fitted with Enigma, or which it is not intended to fit, with Schlüssel M (Enigma).' TNA HW 8/15.

13. Short signals used a codebook to make up messages that were then enciphered on Enigma. There were three editions of the book. Edition 1: 1939–20 January 1941, indicator taken from first letter of transmitted message. Edition 2: 20 January 1942–10 March 1943, indicating tables used: Weimar 20 January 1942–25 October 1942, Eisenach 25 October 1942–11 January 1943, Naumburg 11 January 1943–10 March 1943. Edition 3: 10 March 1943–8 May 1945, indicating tables changed on the first of every month.

14. TNA HW 8/15 Naval Section Memorandum: 'A survey of "Werftschlüssel,"' 23 November 1941.

15. TNA HW 8/23. Naval Section memorandum. The Short Signals became even more important to the cryptographic effort with the introduction of the four-rotor for a very particular reason. According to Mahon's 'History of Hut 8': 'All printed indicator tables for Short Signals were destined for use on Dolphin, Shark and other keys, and only gave three wheel settings for messages. These were converted into 4 wheel settings by an order saying that the reflector wheel was to be placed at A. This order was in force until November 1944 and throughout this period the clip on the

Reflector Wheel was kept at A. All Short Signals therefore were effectively enciphered in a 3 wheel machine – and menus based on them were 3 wheel jobs.' TNA HW 25/2. 'History of Hut 8,' p. 64.

16. TNA HW 8/15 Naval Section Memorandum, 'A survey of 'Werftschlüssel,'" 23 November 1941.

17. TNA HW 8/23 Naval Section Misc. Papers. Supplement No. 4, 30 November 1941. As Naval Section noted: 'WS 47 went out of force on 17th December. The new WS numbered 49 became currently readable from about December 29th. Cribs into Enigma have again been provided. The indicator system is now known and will expedite the decoding at later states in each period.' TNA HW 8/24 Naval Section Misc Papers 1942. Supplement No. 5, 31 December 1941.

18. Adrian Smith, *Mountbatten: Apprentice Warlord* (London: IB Tauris, 2010). Kindle edition.

19. *Life* magazine, 17 August 1942, p. 64.

20. TNA ADM 196/93/0/56; ADM 196/123/0/346; ADM 196/147/0/425.

21. Mountbatten's alleged bisexuality was a source of constant debate before and after his assassination in 1979. His most recent biographer, Adrian Smith, has found no direct proof of any homosexual relations between the Chief of Combined Operations and Coward or any of the other openly gay men whom he kept as friends. Smith states categorically that 'no correspondence held by the University of Southampton contains any obvious suggestion of a homo-erotic relationship,' though he does caution that 'this is scarcely surprising as any intimate letters would remain firmly under lock and key at Broadlands [Mountbatten's home].' Smith, *Mountbatten*, p. 23.

22. Elizabeth Nel, *Winston Churchill by His Personal Secretary: Recollections of the Great Man by a Woman Who Worked for Him* (Bloomington, IN: iUniverse, 2007), 1045–46. Kindle edition.

23. Donald McLachlan, *Room 39: Naval Intelligence in Action, 1939–45* (London: Atheneum, 1968), p. xi.

24. TNA ADM 196/93/0/56; ADM 196/123/0/346; ADM 196/147/0/425.

25. McLachlan, *Room 39*, p. xi.

26. Quoted in David Reynolds, *In Command of History: Churchill Fighting and Writing the Second World War* (Harmondsworth: Penguin Books, 2005), 12528–29. Kindle edition.

27. 'Brigade 115 Force Operation Order 1,' 6 December 1941, TNA ADM 202/352.

28. For Anklet, see TNA CAB 121/455; ADM 116/4381; ADM 202/351; ADM 202/352.

29. For Operation Archery, see TNA WO 231/5; WO 199/3057; AIR 20/1050; WO 32/10535.

30. John Durnford-Slater, *Commando: Memoirs of a Fighting Commando in World War Two* (Barnsley, UK: Greenhill Books, 2006), p. 86.

31. Ken Ford, *Operation Archery: The Commandos and the Vaagso Raid 1941* (Oxford: Osprey Publishing, 2011), p. 18.

32. Hugh Sebag-Montefiore, *Enigma* (London: Weidenfeld and Nicolson, 2000).

33. Ibid.

34. Ibid.

35. *London Gazette*, 16 August 1940.

36. John Hughes-Hallett, *Before I Forget*, Hughes-Hallett Papers, LAC MG30-E463.

37. Lieutenant Commander A. de Costobadie, DSC, RN, 'Report on Operation Archery,' in Niall Cherry, *Striking Back: Britain's Airborne and Commando Raids 1940–1942* (Solihull, UK: Helion & Co., 2010), app. XIII.

38. Ibid.

39. Ibid.

40. Ibid.

41. Ibid.

42. 'Handling of Naval Special Intelligence,' p. 177, TNA HW 8/46.

43. Ibid.

44. Ibid.

45. Durnford-Slater, *Commando*, p. 88.

46. Ibid.

47. Ibid.

48. Ibid.

49. Naval Section Memorandum No. 12, 'State of Work Report, February 1942,' 3 January 1942, Naval Section Miscellaneous Papers, TNA HW 8/24.

50. William Manchester and Paul Reid, *The Last Lion: Winston Spencer Churchill: Defender of the Realm, 1940–1965* (New York: Little, Brown, 2012), 10408–10. Kindle edition.

51. TNA ADM 205/19 'Future British Naval Strategy.'

52. TNA 205/19.

53. TNA ADM 205/19. Notes on Warship Production and Supply Situation 20 December 1941 by British Supply Representative.

54. TNA ADM 205/19. Disposition of British Naval Forces. Memorandum by Admiral Dudley Pound, c.5 January 1942.

55. TNA HW 43/15, p. 107.

56. Naval Section memorandum, 9 March 1942, Naval Section Miscellaneous Papers, TNA HW 8/24.

57. Naval Section Memorandum No. 6, 31 January 1942, TNA HW 8/24.

58. Naval Section Miscellaneous Papers, TNA HW 8/24.

59. Schlüssel M (Form M4), c.22 January 1942, HW 8/24.

60. 'History of Hut 8,' 74, TNA HW 25/2; and Schlüssel M (Form M4) c.22 January 1942, HW 8/24. The date of the message referring to the outfitting of two destroyers was 14 January 1942.

61. According to Mahon in his 'History of Hut 8': 'It was clear that it was the policy of the German Navy to distribute the new machine to all units, starting with those most often involved in major operations.' 'History of Hut 8,' p. 62, TNA HW 25/2.

62. TNA HW HW 8/158 Memorandum No 3 Schlüssel M (Form M4). BP knew in January 1941 through captured documents that Naval Enigma Machine M2802 was a Four -Rotor Enigma and that in July of that year they captured material related to M4 with the serial number M3172. The conclusion reached was that by July 1941 910 M4s were in existence.

63. TNA HW 8/24.

64. Naval Section Miscellaneous Papers, 20 January 1942, TNA HW 8/24.

65. J.H. Godfrey, 'History of Naval Intelligence Division 1939–1942,' p. 46, TNA ADM 223/464.

66. Cavanaugh Report, p. 7, TNA HW 8/103.

67. Ibid., pp. 16–17.

68. Ibid., p. 8; and Schlüssel M (Form M4), TNA HW 8/24.

69. A glossary of German naval technical terms was also of paramount importance. When the cryptanalysts managed to break into the German messages, they were confronted by the plain-language technical terms that could be almost as daunting as a cipher itself.

70. Cavanaugh Report, p. 8, TNA HW 8/103.

71. Ibid. According to the historian at GCHQ, these cards were destroyed at the end of the war as they were considered 'ephemeral' and therefore not for historical preservation.

72. TNA HW 43/24, p. 275.

73. Ibid.

74. Ibid.

75. Godfrey to Mountbatten, 13 May 1942, University of Southampton Mountbatten Papers, MB1/B15.

76. Mountbatten to Godfrey, 15 May 1942, University of Southampton Mountbatten Papers, MB1/B15.

77. Frank Birch, 'Our Intentions,' 11 April 1942, TNA HW 8/24.

78. Ibid.

79. TNA ADM 196/93.

80. Baillie-Grohman to Mountbatten, September 14, 1942, NMM GRO/29.

81. Ibid.

82. Mountbatten to Baillie-Grohman, 17 September 1942, NMM GRO/29; TNA ADM 196/93. A further assessment of Hughes-Hallett from 1942 related that 'he had a forceful personality and much self-confidence and is generally right, but not quite always.'

83. Hughes-Hallett, *Before I Forget*, p. 117.

84. Ibid.

85. Ibid., p. 106.

86. TNA ADM 196/149/615.

87. Hughes-Hallett, *Before I Forget*, p. 118.

88. COHQ, 'War Diary, Operation Bludgeon,' TNA DEFE 2/2.

89. Hughes-Hallett, *Before I Forget*, p. 117; 'Operation Myrmidon,' TNA DEFE 2/366.

90. Hughes-Hallett, *Before I Forget*, p. 117.

91. Ibid., p. 118.

92. Ibid.

Chapter 6

1. Grand Admiral Karl Dönitz, *Memoirs: Ten Years and Twenty Days* (New York: Da Capo Press, 1997), p. 202.

2. Gudmundur Helvason, 'U-109,' http://uboat.net/boats/u109.htm (accessed August 11, 2013).

3. The Wrecksite, 'SS *Tacoma Star*,' http://www.wrecksite.eu/wreck. aspx?31352 (accessed August 11, 2013).

4. U-boat Archive, 'Report of 4th War Patrol *U-109*,' http://www. uboatarchive.net/U-109/KTB109-4.htm (accessed August 11, 2013).

5. Guðmundur Helgason, 'Tacoma Star,' https://uboat.net/allies/ merchants/ship/1307.html (accessed August 11, 2013).

6. U-boat Archive, 'Report of 4th War Patrol *U-109*.'

7. Ibid.

8. Ibid.

9. TNA ADM 223/284. 'U-Boat Tracking and Anti-U-Boat Warfare' NID 8S, p. 3.; ADM 223/284 John Godfrey, NID 8S 'U-Boat Tracking,' 24 April 1947.

10. TNA ADM 223/284. 'U-Boat Tracking and Anti-U-Boat Warfare' NID 8S, p. 3; The potential danger with Ultra or any high level intelligence which comes 'straight from the horse's mouth' is that it may appear 'complete' when it is not. Even the appearance of it being 'wholly complete' compared to other sources like direction finding, traffic analysis, radio fingerprinting, radar, aerial reconnaissance, etc. whose results are 'doubtful' in comparison, tend to spur human nature to accept and expect its infallibility. In the short term (i.e. one or two messages) it could be problematic but where ULTRA paid huge dividends was in the constant building up of the contextual picture of the German response to the vagaries of the war at sea. In this case, as Birch writes: 'You will get cumulatively day after day on all subjects in all areas ... a very complete picture and a very comprehensive knowledge. This is your background; it is solid and reliable, and it grows more so. Your foreground on its own, will continue to be sketchy and incomplete. But, if your background accumulation is properly recorded and thoroughly analyzed, it will bridge the gaps in the foreground's continuity, increase currency by cribbing, unravel the incomprehensible jargon of decrypts and gauge the accuracy of the enemy's statements. In short, background interprets, buttresses and fills the gaps in the foreground. It is intelligence research that puts a stranglehold on the enemy.' TNA HW 43/15.
GC&CS Naval Sigint Volume IV: The Organisation and Evolution of British Sigint by Frank Birch. Part 3: The Use of Sigint, p. 17.

11. Ibid. 'The ideal situation from the Tracking Officer's viewpoint is one in which the dispositions, position and future movements of all enemy U-boats are established and continuously maintained. In other words, the Tracking Room endeavours by means of available intelligence to reproduce as nearly as possible the operations room of the enemy. Needless to say, the ideal situation is not attainable. However, due to the ability of the US and British cryptographic sections in breaking the enemy's cipher, at times the ideal has been approximated.' TNA HW 50/95. U-Boat Tracking: Admiralty and United States Fleet F-21 (Atlantic Section of Combat Intelligence, Headquarters Commander-in-Chief, United States Fleet) War Report.

12. TNA HW 43/22, p. 307. 'The quality that made German naval Enigma quite outstanding as a source of information was its comparative completeness. Whereas neither German air nor army Enigma were at any time considered to provide more than a partial picture of the enemy's communications on any subject, there were periods of the war when German naval communications relating to a definite theatre were not only interpreted in their entirety, but were also 100% decrypted.'

13. TNA HW 25/2. 'History of Hut 8.'

14. Ibid., p. 65.

15. Michael Smith, *The Secrets of Station X: How the Bletchley Park Codebreakers Helped Win the War* (London: Biteback, 2011), 2624–29. Kindle edition.

16. Ibid., pp. 2666–69.

17. Jim DeBrosse and Colin Burke, *The Secret in Building 26* (New York: Random House, 2004).

18. 'U-Boat Tracking and Anti-U-Boat Warfare.'

19. TNA HW 43/11 GCCS Naval Sigint Vol II: The Organization and Evolution of British Naval Sigint by Frank Birch, p. 114.

20. TNA HW 43/11 GCCS Naval Sigint Vol II: The Organization and Evolution of British Naval Sigint by Frank Birch, p. 73. As Birch revealed, HF/DF (Huff Duff) began to be fitted in destroyers and escort vessels in 1941 and 'its value was considerable,' for a U-boat that sighted a convoy would announce that fact to 'home' the others in on the target. If, of course, they knew the frequency in advance then they could give a location of the U-boat that was precise to within about 50 miles. Many times it was crypt that gave them the frequencies to listen for or alerted them that U-boats may be in the path of the convoy.

21. TNA HW 11/19, p. 92. Difficulties with long-range wireless communications with U-boats: 'High frequency which is audible in one area can, owing to the skip or local conditions, be quite inaudible in another; high frequencies are also easily affected by atmospheric and ionospheric conditions. The German U-boat communication system was entirely governed by the distance in which boats were operating and by the seasonal changes affecting these conditions. In order to maintain contact with U-boats and surface craft operating in distant waters, however, it was necessary to issue schedules of frequencies with routine plans indicating the times of the day during which certain frequencies were to be used, and to revise the schedules according to the seasons of the year and prevailing atmospheric and ionospheric conditions in many parts of the world.'

22. TNA ADM 223/294. Naval Intelligence Division and Operational Intelligence Centre, Intelligence Reports and Papers. Operational intelligence: ULTRA monographs, TNA HW 8/98. The Naval Y Service in Wartime: An account of the growth, equipping, training and control of the Royal Navy's sigint interception organisation during WWII by Commander G.E. Hughes, p. 11.

23. TNA ADM 223/464; TNA HW 8/24 Memorandum No. 65, RFP and TINA, 8 September 1942; TNA HW8/24 Naval Section Analysis of RFP/TINA on U/B W/F, July–August 1942; RFP and TINA (RFP recognizes the transmitter, and TINA recognizes the signature of the wireless operator) got off to a good start in early 1941 and looked quite promising. By the end of the year, however, it had not lived up to that promise: 'RFP Classification of ships, and of U-Boats in particular, had not lived up to the expectations that were hoped for, or the promise shown by the proportion of correct results obtained and proved in the early part of the year.' TNA HW 43/11 GCCS Naval Sigint Vol II: The Organization and Evolution of British Naval Sigint by Frank Birch, p. 86.

24. TNA ADM 223/285. Godfrey to Rear Admiral Willis, 19 January 1942.

25. Ibid.; TNA ADM 223/464. RFP was considered to be 'still at the stage where it can make correct identifications only when the characteristics of the transmitters in question are well defined or where the number of possibilities are limited. German transmitters do not have well-defined characteristics as a rule.' Success with U-boats was 'very limited.' TNA HW 43/11 GCCS Naval Sigint Vol II: The Organization and Evolution of British Naval Sigint by Frank Birch, pp. 87–88.

26. TNA ADM 223/285. Godfrey to First Sea Lord and Vice Chief Naval Staff (VCNS), 9 June 1942.

27. Ibid.

28. TNA ADM 223/464; Hervie Haufler, *Codebreakers' Victory: How the Allied Cryptanalysts Won World War II* (New York: New American Library, 2003), 1488–90. Kindle edition.

29. Naval Air Requirement, 27 February 1942, ADM 205/15; T.D. Statistical Section, 'Note on Annual rate of loss of Merchant tonnage (Required for the First Lord),' 18 March 1942.

30. Naval Air Requirement, 27 February 1942, ADM 205/15.

31. TNA ADM 205/15 'Merchant Shipping Losses (Including Tankers) since 1939.'

32. Naval Air Requirement, 27 February 1942, ADM 205/15; T.D. Statistical Section, 'Note on Annual rate of loss of Merchant tonnage (Required for the First Lord),' 18 March 1942.

33. Ibid. According to Dönitz, the success achieved by what he considered only a 'small number of U-boats' was 'extraordinary' in the first six months of 1942. During this period, his U-boats managed to sink 585 ships for an average of 97.5 ships a month that totalled over 3 million tons of Allied shipping while only losing four U-boats per month. Grand Admiral Karl Dönitz, *Memoirs: Ten Years and Twenty Days* (New York: Da Capo Press, 1997), p. 223.

34. TNA ADM 205/14. First Sea Lord's Records 1939–1945, 'Merchant Tonnage Sunk by Enemy Action as Reported up to 22nd December 1942' (Thousands gross tons).

35. TNA ADM 205/15. 'Requirements in Aircraft to Regain Command at Sea,' *c.* October 1942.

36. TNA CAB 65/27/14 War Cabinet 98th Conclusions July 28, 1942.

37. TNA CAB 195/1 W.M. (42) 98th Meeting July 28, 1942.

38. Ibid.

39. Ibid.

40. William Manchester and Paul Reid, *The Last Lion: Winston Spencer Churchill: Defender of the Realm, 1940–1965* (New York: Little, Brown, 2012), 10935–44. Kindle edition.

41. DeBrosse and Burke, *Secret in Building 26*, Prologue.

42. TNA ADM 205/15 T.D. Statistical Section, 'Note on Annual rate of loss of Merchant tonnage (Required for the First Lord),' 18 March 1942.

43. Churchill College Cambridge (CCC), CHAR 9/184B, Secret Session of Parliament, April 23, 1942.

44. Ibid.

45. Ibid.

46. Hansard. Quoted in House of Lords Debates: Conduct of the War, July 2, 1942.

47. Ibid.

48. Ibid.

49. Ibid.

50. Ibid.

51. Ibid.

52. ADM 205/15. Director of Plans, 'Memorandum: Sea and Air Power in Future Developments,' 27 February 1942. In addition to the intelligence blackout, a captured U-boat revealed that 'it was built,' as Churchill wrote, 'of a steel stronger and much more flexible than anything we have used for warships, and that explosions which crack and hole our armour merely

dented the German craft.' TNA CAB 101/242 Churchill to Lord Cherwell, 16 February 1942.

53. Naval Air Requirement, 27 February 1942, ADM 205/15.

54. Ibid.

55. ADM 205/14. 'Imports into United Kingdom 1942.'

56. TNA ADM 205/20 'Memo for First Sea Lord,' 25 June 1942.

57. Ibid.

58. TNA ADM 205/15 Director of Plans, 'Memorandum: Sea and Air Power in Future Developments,' 27 February 1942; ADM 205/15 'Requirements in Aircraft to Regain Command at Sea,' *c.* October 1942; ADM 205/15 Naval Air Requirement, 27 February 1942.

59. Laurence Paterson, *2nd U-Boat Flotilla* (Annapolis, MD: Naval Institute Press, 2003), p. 139.

60. Elizabeth Nel, *Winston Churchill by His Personal Secretary: Recollections of the Great Man by a Woman Who Worked for Him* (Bloomington IN: iUniverse), 1403–11. Kindle edition. Churchill's love affair with SIGINT was evident as early as the First World War when, while serving as First Lord of the Admiralty, he demanded direct delivery of raw material from Room 40 and kept an updated map based on the latest SIGINT developments. David Ramsey, *Blinker Hall Spymaster: The Man Who Brought America into World War 1* (Stroud, Gloucestershire, UK: History Press, 2009), pp. 47–48.

61. TNA ADM 205/15 Naval Air Requirement, 27 February 1942.

62. TNA ADM 205/15 Sir Dudley Pound to Vice Chief Naval Staff (VCNS) et al., 24 February 1942,; Christopher M. Bell, *Churchill and Sea Power* (Oxford: Oxford University Press, 2013), 259. Kindle edition.

63. Martin Gilbert, 'Churchill and Bombing Policy' (Fifth Churchill Center Lecture, Washington, D.C., 18 October 2005).

64. CAB 66/ 26/ 41WP (42) 31 WSC memorandum, 'A Review of the War Position,' 21 July 1942, p. 1, quoted in Bell, *Churchill and Sea Power*, p. 385.

65. ROSK 7/ 210. Tovey to Pound, 7 June 1942, quoted in Bell, *Churchill and Sea Power*, p. 262.

66. National Security Agency, Early Papers Concerning UK–US Agreements, 'Aide Memoire for the President,' July 8, 1940.

67. Ibid.

68. Herbert Osborn Yardley, *The American Black Chamber* (New York: Bobbs-Merrill, 1930).

69. TNA HW 8/49. 'History of Liaison with OP-20-G (Washington),' p. 4.

70. Robert L. Benson, 'Origins of British-American Intelligence Cooperation (1940–1941),' US National Security Agency web page.

71. David O'Keefe interview with Professor Sir Harry Hinsley, Cambridge University, Cambridge, 13 February 1996.

72. Ibid.

73. Ibid.

74. Benson, 'Origins of British-American Intelligence Cooperation.' TNA HW 57/9. In 1942, these messages were relayed by an Ultra Secret radio link code-named 'Hydra' at a specially built facility, commonly known as 'Camp X,' located just outside Toronto, Canada.

75. NMM GOD/68. J.H. Godfrey to Ted Merrett, 19 February 1965.

76. TNA HW 57/10. Message for C.S.S. from Tiltman Washington, 27 November 1941.

77. TNA ADM 223/285. Godfrey to Hastings, 23 January 1942; Message for Naval Attaché, 5 March 1942. In March 1942, the British had yet to deliver upon their promise to provide a captured naval Enigma to OP-20-G. With the Ultra pipeline now dry and unable to aid in reducing the slaughter off the eastern seaboard, the US Navy fired off a message direct to its naval attaché in London that not only violated proper channels and normal protocol but reinforced Britain's two greatest fears concerning American insecurity and impatience: 'Urgently desire the Admiralty furnish Navy Department one captured German Naval Enigma Cipher Machine, even if damaged and inoperative, plus all available keys, even though out of date. This in accordance (with) agreement (on) mutual exchanges (of) all cryptographic information of Axis Powers under which U.S. Government furnished Japanese Purple Machine and other Japanese naval and diplomatic codes and ciphers to British Government. Also request all available captures or solutions of weather report, contact report, and other minor systems.'

78. Quoted in Stephen Puleo, *Due to Enemy Action: The True World War Two Story of USS Eagle* (San Francisco: Untreed Reads, 2013), p. 56.

79. TNA HW 57/10.

80. DeBrosse and Burke, *Secret in Building 26*.

81. NSA. Brigadier John Tiltman: A Giant Among Cryptanalysts, 2007, p. 5.

82. TNA HW 57/9. 'Enigma Policy,' 5 May 1942.

83. Ibid.

84. Colin Burke, 'Agnes Meyer Driscoll vs. the Enigma and the Bombe,' http://userpages.umbc.edu/~burke/driscoll1-2011.pdf (accessed March 27, 2013).

85. DeBrosse and Burke, *Secret in Building 26*, ch. 4.

86. Burke, 'Agnes Meyer Driscoll.'

87. NSA. Brigadier John Tiltman: A Giant Among Cryptanalysts, 2007, p. 29.

88. Ronald Lewin, *Ultra Goes to War* (Barnsley, UK: Pen and Sword Books, 2008), p. 144.

89. TNA HW 57/9. Tiltman to Travis, 6 April 1942.

90. Parker, Frederick D., *A Priceless Advantage: U.S. Navy Communications Intelligence and the Battles of Coral Sea, Midway, and the Aleutians*, 2nd edition, 2013.

91. TNA HW 57/10. Message from Captain Geoffrey Stevens to Commander Travis, September 15, 1942.

92. TNA HW 57/10. Captain Geoffrey Stevens, the GCCS Liaison officer in Washington, informed Travis on September 15, 1942 on an informal discussion he had with Commander Joseph N. Wenger, the head of Op-20-G and one of the most important figures in American cryptographic history, as follows:

1) When Colonel Tiltman was in Washington it was agreed that the United States was to know all about the bombe and was to form a second line in case of damage or other causes putting BP out of action. The United States Navy agreed that it would not attempt to work with the bombe on any E problem provided that it was supplied by us with the results of our work or the explanation why there were no results.

2) It was not specifically stated that the explanation had to be reasonable or acceptable to the United States: this was understood, at least by US Navy.

3) Since January there have been no results from U-boat traffic. The explanation offered is that we have neither time nor machines to do it.

4) When Tiltman was here it was thought that the first fast bombe would be ready at the beginning of June. Eli reports that he has now been told that there may be some bombes ready in 6 to 8 months sometime about February 1943.

5) The explanation for there being no results might be satisfactory were it impossible for the US to produce bombes, or even were they not now vitally interested in the U-boat situation.

6) As it is, they see the situation like this: a) the failure to read U-boat traffic is due to a lack of fast bombes. b) they can produce, they say, 300 plus bombes partly electronic in 4 months from the word go. c) Op-20-G cannot say they are doing all they can for all that is necessary when in point of fact they are doing nothing and we're

not providing them with the answer. d) The U-boat situation is becoming a public issue which it was not at the time of Tiltman's visit. e) They cannot be an effective second line as agreed during Tiltman's visit unless they do make at least some machines. At the time of the original agreement it was not appreciated here that an effective second line would require more than a few machines. Now it is evident that to be really effective and not suffer from the old story of too little too late, even a second line must have machines in very large quantities. f) That for one party to insist on sticking to the letter of an agreement when the situation demands an alteration of it for the benefit of both parties is just plain crazy.

7) US realizes that security is very vital in this matter and, when only the life of G(reat) B(ritain) depended on it, were prepared to take a back seat. Now that their own life depends on it too, and they see no results, they are not prepared to sit idly by. They point out that between us we have arrived at the position of a man who has a secret weapon which is so secret that he dare not use it in case the enemy finds out!

8) Unless someone could persuade somebody very high up to call off the whole business, pressure will be applied to OP-20 G and they will have to proceed with the work regardless of agreements. But one must remember that in this extremely Democratic democracy everybody from the president down is subject to pressure particularly on a public matter like the sinking of US ships by U-boats.

9) The press asks, the Senate and the Congress ask, what is our Navy doing about the submarine menace? FDR sends for Knox, who sends for King, who sends for DNC who sends for Wenger, and if Wenger says 'nothing,' somebody in the trail back to FDR with that answer is going to stop it and say 'well do something and do it mighty quick or there are going to be some people out of a job around here!'

10) In other words, sooner or later, the United States Navy is going to tackle the U-boat traffic whether we like it or not.

Chapter 7

1. Originally known as NID6.
2. MM, Godfrey Papers GOD 37. Letter to Bassett from Godfrey, January 17, 1961.
3. MM, Godfrey Papers GOD 37. NID Policy, November 7, 1942.
4. Godfrey to Menzies, 13 January 1942, TNA ADM 223/285.

5. Obituary of Margaret Godfrey, *Independent* (London), November 1, 1995.

6. J.H. Godfrey, 'The Naval Memoirs of Admiral J.H. Godfrey,' Vol. 5 1947–1950 NID, Part II, 284, MM GOD 171.

7. Ibid.

8. Ibid.

9. Ibid.

10. J.H. Godfrey, 'Churchill and Strategy,' 16 June 1966, NMM GOD 177.

11. J.H. Godfrey, 'Working with Churchill,' 1966, NMM GOD 177.

12. Godfrey, 'Naval Memoirs,' Vol. 5, Part II, p. 288.

13. Ibid., 284. As Godfrey himself noted years later, the concept was truly profound and displayed foresight that he later argued served as a basis for the creation of the modern MOD structure in the United Kingdom.

14. J.H. Godfrey, 'Afterthoughts: 'Total Intelligence,' the ISTD and Geographical Handbooks,' 87, TNA ADM 223/619; Patrick Beesly, *Very Special Admiral: The Life of Admiral J.H. Godfrey* (London: Hamish Hamilton, 1980).

15. Godfrey, 'Naval Memoirs,' Vol. 5, Part II, p. 211.

16. 'Inter-Services Topographical Department – The Early Days,' TNA ADM 223/466.

17. Ibid.

18. Godfrey, 'Naval Memoirs,' Vol. 5, Part II, p. 285.

19. Nicholas Rankin, *Ian Fleming's Commandos: The Story of 30 Assault Unit in WWII* (London: Faber and Faber, 2011).

20. Bassett and Wells, 'Inter-Services Topographical Department'; Beesly, *Very Special Admiral*, p. 205.

21. Beesley, *Very Special Admiral*, p. 205.

22. Godfrey, 'Naval Memoirs,' Vol. 5, Part II, p. 286.

23. Ibid.

24. Ibid.

25. TNA WO 252/469.

26. Godfrey, 'Naval Memoirs,' Vol. V, Part II, p. 383.

27. C.E. Lucas Phillips, *The Greatest Raid of All* (London: Heinemann, 1958); and *Jeremy Clarkson: Greatest Raid of All Time* (BBC television documentary, 2007).

28. This dry dock had been specially built to service the passenger liner *Normandie*, hence its name.

29. Interestingly, Charles Lambe, the deputy director in the Plans Division and, after March 1942, the director, was one of Mountbatten's trusted confidants. Earlier, in 1936, Mountbatten had used his connections to

secure Lambe an appointment as a royal aide-de-camp, partly as a career boost for his old friend, but primarily to ensure that the Royal Navy was permanently represented inside Buckingham Palace. In 1959, Lambe succeeded Mountbatten as First Sea Lord and Chief of the Naval Staff.

30. TNA DEFE 2/131.

31. Winston S. Churchill, *The Second World War*, vol. 4, *The Hinge of Fate* (Boston: Houghton Mifflin, 1950).

32. J.H. Godfrey, 'History of Naval Intelligence Division 1939–1942,' 56, TNA ADM 223/464.

33. TNA CAB 121/364. Although the citation has March 25 noted on it, this date is a mistake. According to Alan Brooke's diary, the meeting to discuss the outline plans for the raids took place on the morning of February 25. On March 25, he wrote, 'no points of great importance' occurred. Considering that Chariot went in on March 28 and Myrmidon a week after that, there is no way that an outline plan for an operation of this size could gain approval and move into full operation in such a short space of time.

34. 'Myrmidon Outline Plan,' n.d., TNA DEFE 2/367.

35. 'Myrmidon Summary,' 22 February 1942, TNA DEFE 2/367.

36. Minutes from COS meeting, 25 February 1942, TNA CAB 121/364.

37. 'Naval Orders Operation Myrmidon,' TNA DEFE 2/367.

38. Ibid.

39. Ibid.

40. Ibid.

41. When Frank Birch learned of the raid he wrote: 'Had we known that it was hoped to fox shore batteries ... we could have supplied precise information, which stood a better chance of foxing the enemy than the bits and pieces actually supplied.' After the war as Birch noted, Captain Colpoys reflected on the mindset at NID: 'It is a pity we did not arm the expedition with more signalling defence gambits,' but 'at the time we were most reluctant to make use of this knowledge for security (of source) reasons. In this particular case, a hazardous inshore expedition, we had to be prepared for any craft to be captured and ransacked by the enemy. People taking part in these hazardous enterprises will write things down for fear they forget them and the good intentions of destroying a list cannot be carried out by a dead man.' TNA HW 43/15, p. 324. GC&CS Naval Sigint History Vol IV: The Organization and Evolution of British Naval Sigint, by Frank Birch.

42. Ken Ford, *St. Nazaire 1942: The Great Commando Raid* (Oxford: Osprey Publishing, 2001), p. 63.

43. Richard Hopton, *A Reluctant Hero: The Life of Captain Robert Ryder VC* (Havertown, PA: Casemate Publishers, 2012), 4253–54. Kindle edition.

44. This road, however, was not without its bumps. On March 5, Godfrey sent a message that can only be described as a 'rocket' to Mountbatten, complaining about a comment he had made at a Chiefs of Staff Committee meeting in which Mountbatten claimed they did not have sufficient intelligence in the Bayonne area for Operation Myrmidon. 'Actually, our intelligence on this part of the world is not at all bad and could easily be worked up ... I do suggest in common fairness that it would be better to bring us into the picture as early as possible and, of course, you will appreciate how discouraging it is for my junior intelligence officers to see such a remark when they are simply longing to do all they can to help you and, incidentally, working very hard on our behalf. I am sure you won't mind my calling your attention to this, but Intelligence is a two-way traffic business. One's got to push and pull and not be content to sit down and let the stuff come to him.' (Godfrey to Mountbatten, 5 March 1942, TNA ADM 223/90.)

45. Quoted in Philip Ziegler, *Mountbatten: The Official Biography* (London: Collins, 1985), p. 170.

46. 'Confidential Report on Operation Myrmidon,' 9 April 1942, TNA DEFE 2/366.

47. Jock Gardner, 'Admiral Sir Bertram Ramsay,' in Stephen Howarth, ed., *Men of War: Great Naval Leaders of World War Two* (London: Weidenfeld & Nicolson, 1992), p. 360.

48. Mountbatten to Major General F.H.N. Davidson, Director of Military Intelligence, 14 May 1942, TNA DEFE 2/366.

49. Quoted in Ziegler, *Mountbatten*, p. 165. The actual motto was 'United We Conquer.'

50. On the occasion of Ryder's investiture, Mountbatten wrote: 'I have never had more pleasure in writing to congratulate anybody than in writing to you for your grandly earned Victoria Cross. Alas, so few of the V.C.s of this war have been given to living people and it is essential for the younger officers and men coming along to have a few heroes to look up to who are still in the land of the living. I consider your V.C. will have achieved a double purpose: firstly, it is the greatest compliment that could be paid to the whole of your force; secondly, it will centre round it all the enthusiasm for the fighting spirit which is only awaiting an outlet in this country.' (Hopton, *Reluctant Hero*, pp. 4372–77.)

51. Hopton, *Reluctant Hero*, p. 4399.

52. Phillips, *Greatest Raid of All*, p. xvii.

Chapter 8

1. 'History of 30 AU,' TNA ADM 223/500.
2. The only time the commandos came under Mountbatten's control was when they were attached to his headquarters for operational purposes by the War Office under orders from the chiefs of staff.
3. TNA HW 8/103. Report on British Procedures for Capturing and Exploiting Enemy Naval Documents, p. 13.
4. After Dieppe, the title for A Commando was changed to No. 40 Royal Marine Commando.
5. Dr Anthony King, 'The Ethos of the Royal Marines: Precise Application of Will' (report, Department of Sociology, University of Exeter, May 2004).
6. Ibid.
7. *Globe and Laurel*, August 1942, 75, quoted in King, 'Ethos of the Royal Marines.'
8. No. 40 Royal Marine Commando, 'War Diary,' TNA ADM 202/87.
9. Jock Farmer, *JOCK of 40 Royal Marine Commando: My Life from Start to Finish* (Shanklin Chine: Shanklin Chine Publishers, 2007).
10. R.E.D. Ryder, unpublished memoirs, courtesy of Mr Lisle Ryder.
11. Farmer, *JOCK*.
12. Ibid.
13. Ibid.
14. Ibid.
15. Robin Neillands, *By Sea and Land* (Barnsley, UK: Pen and Sword, 2004), p. 20.
16. Ibid.
17. King, 'Ethos of the Royal Marines.'
18. 'A History of 30 Commando (Latterly Called 30 Assault Unit and 30 Advanced Unit),' TNA ADM 223/214, ch. 2; Paul McGrath interview for *DU*.
19. Farmer, *JOCK*.
20. John Kruthoffer to Robin Neillands, 25 March 1986, Robin Neillands Papers, RMM.
21. I.G. Aylen, 'Recollections of 30 Assault Unit,' *Naval Review* 65, no. 4 (1977): 318.
22. 'Proposal for Naval Intelligence Commando,' 20 March 1942, TNA ADM 223/500.

23. The unit was also known during the war by several cover names, such as the Special Engineer Unit, No. 30 Commando and 30 Advanced Unit.

24. 'Proposal for Naval Intelligence Commando.'

25. Ibid.

26. 'A History of 30 Commando (Latterly Called 30 Assault Unit and 30 Advanced Unit),' ch. 2, TNA ADM 223/214. TNA WO 204/7322. A report entitled 'Special Engineering Unit' from January 1945 confirms that: 'This unit was started in March 1942 as an experimental unit with a function roughly similar to that of the Abwehrkommando employed by the Germans to serve their parallel intelligence interests. The capacity of such a unit is its ability: 1) to operate with, or in front of, the foremost elements during offensive operations, whether land, sea or airborne, and to exploit these operations for the collection of intelligence; 2) to attack previously selected intelligence targets of a "long range" nature; 3) to achieve a variety of clandestine objectives in enemy occupied territory.'

27. 'Proposal for Naval Intelligence Command,' 20 March 1942, TNA ADM 223/500; 'A History of 30 Commando (Latterly Called 30 Assault Unit and 30 Advanced Unit), ch. 2, ADM 223/214.

28. 'A History of 30 Commando.' What the report missed was that this unit was part of a larger group of intelligence commandos that the Germans had employed since the invasions of Poland and later France, where they scored great success capturing material left behind by the fleeing Allied armies in Paris and in naval facilities all along the coast.

29. It was Godfrey's successor, Admiral Edmund Rushbrooke, who coined this telling phrase. Memo 'No. 30 Commando,' 4 November 1942, TNA ADM 223/500.

30. Both the Myrmidon naval force commander Captain A.H. Maxwell-Hyslop and the Captain of HMS *Badsworth*, Lt. Gordon Thomas Seccombe Gray, argued for the formation of a specialized unit. Gray, whose ship carried two of the four special boarding parties, remarked that 'there does seem to be a case for forming a specially trained body of seamen if such combined operations are to continue. In this particular case, the special boarding parties might well have been called on to display considerable seamanlike ability, and it is evident that we can no longer expect to find prime season in our Depots.' He went on to argue that none of the men selected for the boarding parties had any experience in the type of operation they were about to carry out. None had knowledge of explosives and were drawn from a Care and Maintenance party who were

now expected to work alongside highly trained commandos. TNA DEFE 2/367 'Myrmidon.'

31. 'Proposal for Naval Intelligence Command.'

32. Ben Macintyre, *For Your Eyes Only* (London: Bloomsbury, 2012), 259. Kindle edition.

33. 'A History of 30 Commando.'

34. TNA ADM 223/500 'Note from Godfrey for Fleming,' 23 March 1942.

35. Adrian Smith, *Mountbatten: Apprentice Warlord* (London: IB Tauris, 2010). Kindle edition.

36. Casa Maury to Fleming, 1 April 1942, TNA ADM 223/500.

37. Godfrey to Campbell, Drake and Fleming, 13 April 1942, TNA ADM 223/500.

38. In 1945, the author of the Report on British Procedures for Capturing and Exploiting Enemy Naval Documents sang the praises of the 30 AU for their effectiveness and their large-scale impact: 'The 30 A.U. have more than justified themselves. Their captures of communications intelligence material have been of the greatest value. In addition, they have brought back technical material which would hardly have been acquired in any other way, but these direct achievements are no more significant than their indirect accomplishments. Pinching is, by its very nature, haphazard and unpredictable. To be successful throughout the Navy as a whole, all personnel must be made conscious of its importance and procedures must be established which will make it possible for the captured material to be sent back to the intelligence centres at maximum speed. The 30 A.U. have played a major part in this essential work of indoctrination and organization. The dramatic character of their activities and the backing they have received from high military and naval authorities have focused attention on the importance of capturing enemy materials, and in particular communications intelligence materials. Their constant efforts to bring their more valuable captures back to Admiralty at top speed has not only emphasised in the minds of all concerned the importance of haste, but has also created the very channels to make such haste possible. The fact that they have been active in several naval commands has enabled them to spread these two doctrines through a large part of the Navy.'

Chapter 9

1. There is no evidence of the Gare Maritime in Dieppe today; it was demolished in 1995 to make way for a promenade and a series of quayside restaurants and cafés.

2. The streets were named in honour of First World War field marshal Ferdinand Foch, who commanded the French army at the end of the war, and Verdun, the site of a ten-month bloodletting battle of attrition in 1916 that had a profound effect on France and its culture.

3. TNA ADM 223/107. J.H. Godfrey, 'Formation of the Situation Report Centre of the JIC,' 18 August 1942; ADM 223/466 'Geographical Handbooks and Interservice Topographical Department.'

4. Ibid.

5. TNA ADM 223/475. Combined Operations Intelligence Procedure.

6. Robin Neillands, *The Dieppe Raid: The Story of the Disastrous 1942 Expedition* (Bloomington and Indianapolis: Indiana University Press, 2005), p. 103.

7. TNA HW HW 8/158. Memorandum No 3 Schlüssel M (Form M4) *c*. January 20, 1942.

8. TNA HW 8/103. Report on British Procedures for Capturing and Exploiting Enemy Naval Documents, p. 7. Of course to a certain degree the same would go for vessels hemmed into the confines of a port who could not readily flee from attackers as they could in the open sea.

9. TNA HS 8/819. Liaison with CCO November 1941–March 1942. Although the SOE were called in to provide intelligence on Dieppe for Operation Rutter at its inception – an operation they code-named Knotgrass/Traveller – they were not asked to provide forces to take part in the raid until mid-June.

10. TNA HW 8/158. Naval Section Memorandum No. 75 'State of Work,' 25 September 1942.

11. TNA HW 18/13; HW 18/35; ADM 223/94.

12. FDR Library, Map Room Collection, Box 35. Although not used primarily as a U-boat base, British intelligence had learned that at least on one occasion in 1941, Dieppe housed fifteen U-boats for a two-day period in March, confirming that the signals material desired would likely be found in the French seaside port. Telegram from Lord Halifax in London to President Franklin Roosevelt in Washington, Report on Military Situation, March 20, 1941.

13. TNA ADM 223/93, ADM 223/3.

14. TNA HW 8_103 US Navy Report on British Exploitation of Captured Documents, p. 8.

15. Ibid.

16. Ibid.

17. TNA HW 11/19, p. 18. Vol. VI, 'The German Navy – Communications' by Miss M.E. Coles; edited by Lieutenant Commander L.A. Griffiths, RNVR. Each Communications Equipment Division controlled one or more communications equipment depots, located at smaller ports. On p. 10: 'The final responsibility for naval communications, as in all German naval matters, rested with the Supreme Command of the Navy, which was similar in function to the British Admiralty.' Responsibility for communications was, by 1942, divided into the following sections: The Development Div for research and experimentation; The Fitting-Out Div for procurement and supply; Group for planning and installations; Group for Central communications affairs (personnel and admin); The Division for Land-Line Equipment; responsible for the supply and installation of land-lines for naval use.

18. TNA DEFE 2/550. Although 'NID' (Naval Intelligence Division) appears at the top of the document, subsequent messages make reference to 'DNI' (Director of Naval Intelligence) as the originator of the message. Given the fact that both are acronyms, I assumed that the latter was a mistake until subsequent documents spelled it out in no uncertain terms. In other words, the Director of Naval Intelligence – in this case Godfrey, or Fleming on his behalf – was the author of the special inquiry. See DEFE 2/542.

19. Addendum No. 1, TNA DEFE 2/550. Although this document lists the originator as NID, a subsequent mention spells out that it came from the 'Director of Naval Intelligence,' precluding any typographical confusion over DNI/NID.

20. TNA AIR 8/896. Addendum No. 9.

21. LAC RG 24, vol. 20, 488. 'Naval Commander Channel Coast: First Report on Dieppe Operation,' 20 August 1942.

22. Ibid.

23. LAC RG 24, vol. 20, 488. 'Intelligence Control Station France: Evaluation of Dieppe Operation,' 12 September 1942.

24. Combined Operations, Intelligence Section, Report CB 04157 F (I) Addendum No. 9, TNA AIR 8/896.

25. 'Minutes of a Meeting Held at Combined Operations Headquarters at 1100 hrs 14/4/42 to Discuss Operation Rutter,' TNA DEFE 2/546. For Haydon, see TNA WO 373/93. The map in question is contained in AIR 16/747 and appears to have originated early in the planning process – certainly during the outline planning stage and before the force commanders began detailed planning in May.

26. TNA DEFE 2/542.

27. Battle Summary No. 33: 'Raid on Dieppe, August 19th 1942' (1946), 2, TNA ADM 234/354.

28. Ibid.

29. Ibid.

30. Built in 1938 in Scotland, the vessel was commissioned in spring 1940 and went straight into battle with De Costobadie at the helm during the Dunkirk evacuation, an action in which he earned the Distinguished Service Cross for bravery.

31. Lord Alanbrooke, *Alanbrooke War Diaries 1939–1945: Field Marshal Lord Alanbrooke*, Orion Publishing Group, Kindle Edition. Entry for May 13, 1942.

32. TNA ADM 223/479.

Chapter 10

1. Shane B. Schreiber, *Shock Army of the British Empire: The Canadian Corps in the Last 100 Days of the Great War* (Santa Barbara, CA: Praeger, 1997).

2. Mountbatten to Guy Simonds, 4 February 1969, LAC Hughes-Hallett Papers.

3. Ibid; Two meetings were then held on March 6, 1942, following a series of discussions between Harry Crerar (Commanding 1st Canadian Corps) and BLM Montgomery South-East Army Commander and the DGIGs A.E. Lye. Five days before, on March 1, Crerar met with CIGS Field Marshal Alanbrooke who agreed to the importance of Canadians being employed in future raids and a meeting between Crerar and Mountbatten to discuss ways and means. The first meeting was held at the Naval and Military club at 1315 on March 6 with Crerar, Lye, Mountbatten and Simonds. Lye supported the views of Crerar that the Canadians should get into action now that the threat of German invasion had waned. 'Commodore Mountbatten said that the proposal to use a wholly Canadian detachment for raiding operations ran counter to the policy which he had settled upon and agreed with Paget. Mountbatten, however, appreciated the special position of Canadian Corps and agreed to make an exception to policy in favour of a purely Canadian enterprise, limited in scope (no more than 100 men) providing Paget would also agree.' DHH or NAC Note from meeting by Guy Granville Simonds.

4. Peter Henshaw, 'The Dieppe Raid: A Product of Misplaced Canadian Nationalism?' *Canadian Historical Review* 77, no. 2 (1996): 250–66;

John Nelson Rickard, *The Politics of Command: Lieutenant General A.G.L. McNaughton and the Canadian Army, 1939–1943* (Toronto: University of Toronto Press, 2010); Paul Douglas Dickson, *A Thoroughly Canadian General: A Biography of General H.D.G. Crerar* (Toronto: University of Toronto Press, 2007); Dean Oliver, 'Historiography, Generalship and Harry Crerar,' in Lieutenant Colonel Bernd Horn and Stephen Harris, eds., *Warrior Chiefs: Perspectives on Senior Canadian Military Leaders* (Toronto: Dundurn Press, 2001); J.L. Granatstein, *The Generals: The Canadian Army's Senior Commanders in the Second World War* (Toronto: Stoddart, 1993).

5. The Canadians, however, were not Louis Mountbatten's first choice to take part in the Dieppe Raid, nor had he seriously considered them for the operation until the political realities of coalition warfare forced his hand. His original preference was his favourite, the Royal Marine Division, the infantry arm of the Royal Navy. 'I was anxious to use troops that had amphibious knowledge,' he wrote years later, 'and had some actual active services experience. There were enough of the Royal Marines and certainly in the Commandos to qualify them for such a description.' 'Notes on a Conference Held on 6 Mar 42,' LAC RG 24, vol. 10,765; Crerar to Lieutenant General B.L. Montgomery, 5 February 1942; 'Memorandum on Visit of Lt-Gen B.C.T. Paget, GOC, SE Command, to Comd Cdn Corps, at 1500hrs, 6 Sept 1941,' LAC RG 24, vol. 10, 765.

6. Terence Robertson, *Dieppe: The Shame and the Glory* (London: Pan Books, 1965), p. 55.

7. Wade Davis, *Into the Silence: The Great War, Mallory, and the Conquest of Everest* (Toronto: Knopf, 2011). Mallory's body remained undiscovered for 75 years, until 1999, when an expedition that had set out to search for the climbers' remains found clothing they could identify on a slope 800 vertical feet from the summit. Whether Mallory and his climbing partner, Andrew 'Sandy' Irvine, reached the summit before they died remains a subject of continuing speculation.

8. TNA ADM 196/92.

9. Adrian Smith, *Mountbatten: Apprentice Warlord* (London: IB Tauris, 2010), 207. Kindle edition.

10. Baillie-Grohman to Mountbatten, 14 September 1942, NMM GRO/29.

11. Memo from Baillie-Grohman to Mountbatten, 10 July 1942, NMM GRO/29. Unfortunately, there is nothing in the files so far released to confirm or dispel the suggestion that Baillie-Grohman was indeed referring to Ian Fleming.

12. Dickson, *A Thoroughly Canadian General*, p. 203.

13. Granatstein, *The Generals*, p. 32.

14. Admiral William James, *Portsmouth Letters* (London: Macmillan, 1946), pp. 173–74.

15. John Hughes-Hallett, *Before I Forget*, p. 155, Hughes-Hallett Papers, LAC MG30-E463.

16. Ibid., p. 135.

17. CMHQ Report No. 159, 'Operation Jubilee, The Raid on Dieppe, Aug. 19: Additional Information on Planning,' 4, DHH.

18. CMHQ Report No. 100, 'Operation Jubilee, Part I: Preliminaries of the Operation,' DHH.

19. Ibid.

20. Ibid.

21. George Ronald, interview with General Hamilton Roberts, *c.*1962, George Ronald Papers, LAC MG30-E507.

22. Battle Summary No. 33: 'Raid on Dieppe, August 19th 1942' (1946), 5, TNA ADM 234/354.

23. CMHQ Report No. 101, 34, DHH.

24. Richard Hopton, correspondence with author, August 2012.

25. R.E.D. Ryder, unpublished memoirs.

26. Ibid.

27. Ibid.

Chapter 11

1. J.H. Godfrey, note, '30 AU,' 5 September 1970, TNA ADM 223/214.

2. Rear Admiral Godfrey DNI to Brig. Kirkman, AVM Medhurst, Brig. Menzies, Brig. Petrie with copy to JIC, 2 June 1942, TNA ADM 223/500.

3. Ibid.

4. Ibid. The pinch aspect of Operation Rutter was in place right from the start and his request in this letter was not of an operational but, rather, an administrative nature. In other words, the wheels were already in motion to include a force like this one on the raid as an 'experiment.' Godfrey was looking for official 'logistical' sanction to create a standing unit, and his request should not be confused with one for an operational nod.

5. 'A History of 30 Commando (Latterly Called 30 Assault Unit and 30 Advanced Unit),' ch. 1, TNA ADM 223/214.

6. Ibid. Very little, if anything, is known of these units except for a brief passage that appears in this history.

7. 'RM Commando Exercise Operational Order No. 8,' 22 June 1942, No. 40 Royal Marine Commando War Diary, TNA ADM 202/87.

8. Ibid.

9. Paul McGrath, *The Dieppe Raid, Wednesday 19th August 1942: Recollections of W.P. McGrath DSM*, self-published.

10. 'RM Commando Exercise Operational Order No. 8.'

11. 'History of 30 AU,' Part II, Section 3, Intelligence Briefing and Planning for 30 Commando/30 Assault Unit, TNA ADM 223/500. Although the Royal Marine Commando was known only as A Commando at this time, it was re-designated as No. 40 Royal Marine Commando immediately after the raid – a name it still has today. Thereafter, all paperwork, war diaries and references to A Commando were changed to reflect its new name, No. 40 Royal Marine Commando, although technically it did not exist as such at the time.

12. TNA ADM 358/2436. According to Paul McGrath, who discovered Huntington-Whiteley's body in a gutter a day later, the young Royal Marine officer was killed as he accepted the surrender of German prisoners on the outskirts of Le Havre. Apparently, while the surrender was in progress, another German unit, annoyed at their brethren's attempts to capitulate, opened fire on the entire group, killing friend and foe alike, including Huntington-Whiteley. (Interview with Paul McGrath for *Dieppe Uncovered*.)

13. TNA, HW 8/103 Report on British Procedures for Capturing and Exploiting Enemy Naval Documents. Enclosure No 4: No. 30 Assault Unit – Target List for Operations Overlord and Ranking Case C: 'Priorities' by Commander Ian Fleming. 6 May 1944, p. 9.

14. On the fiftieth anniversary of the Dieppe Raid, McGrath wrote a short memoir about his exploits for the Royal Marine Association. He later self-published it under the title *The Dieppe Raid, Wednesday 19th August 1942: Recollections of W.P. McGrath DSM*.

15. McGrath, *Dieppe Raid*.

16. No. 40 Royal Marine Commando, 'War Diary,' February 1942, TNA ADM 202/87.

17. Miles Huntington-Whiteley, interview for *DU*.

18. Paul McGrath, interview for *DU*.

19. 'History of 30 AU,' Part II, Section 3.

20. 'Technical Intelligence and the Processing of Captured Documents,' pp. 67–68, TNA HW 43/23.

21. Godfrey Edward Wildman-Lushington to Chiefs of Staff, 8 June 1942, TNA CAB 121/364; TNA HS 8/819. The first indication that the Force Commanders had of any attachment of SOE agents to the raid came on June 17, 1942.

22. TNA HS 8/819. 'CCO/SOE Liaison Officer's Report No. 78 date 4/5/42 0900hrs.'

23. TNA HS 8/819. June 8, 1942.

24. Search Plan, app. L, TNA WO 252/108.

25. 'Considerations affecting Operation Rutter and the Clarification of this plan to be known as Rutter II,' 7 July 1942, LAC RG 24, vol. 10, p. 750.

26. Ibid.; 'Raids 2nd Canadian Division RUTTER II: Considerations affecting Operation Rutter and the Modification of this plan to be known as Rutter II,' LAC RG 24, vol. 10, p. 750.

27. LAC RG 24, vol. 10, p. 872, file 252C2 (D37), Rutter – Generally. 'Notes on a Conference of Navy, Essex Scot, Tanks, Engrs and RM Commando 28/06/42.'

28. 'Notes on Meeting Held Inf[orming] Bde [Brigades] about Forthcoming Operation "Rutter,"' 27 June 1942, LAC RG 24, vol. 10, 872, File 252C2 (D37) Rutter – Generally.

29. TNA HS 8/818 CCO/SOE Liaison Officer's Report No. 78 date 4/5/42 0900hrs. On May 8 the SOE gave Rutter their own internal code name called 'Knotgrass/Traveller' and immediately set about working in close cooperation with the Royal Canadian Engineers of Ham Roberts's Second Canadian Division on the issue of tank obstacles. This came not long after they helped train the one platoon of Royal Marine Commandos tasked with carrying out the pinch and a select team within that platoon assigned with 'safe-cracking.'

30. 'Operation Rutter Detailed Military Plan Phase IIB Attack on Trawlers,' LAC RG 24, vol. 10, p. 765.

31. 'War Diary Essex Scottish,' August 1942, app. VI, LAC RG 24, vol. 17, p. 513.

32. TNA ADM 199/1079 Operation Jubilee: Raid on Dieppe Lessons Learned, p. 43.

33. 'Operation Rutter Detailed Military Plan Phase IIB Attack on Trawlers.'

34. TNA AIR 16/760. Operation Rutter: 'Minutes of a meeting Held June 25th, 1942.' Roberts was fully aware of the pinch imperative of the raid from the time he began the detailed planning for Rutter. In fact, so entwined in their operations was he that he was called to a meeting by

Godfrey on June 25 to help settle a tempest in a teapot with IAU's role in the operation in connection with that of the Army's Field Security Section who normally carried out pinches ashore.

35. LAC RG 24, vol. 10, p. 872, file 252C2 (D37), Rutter – Generally. 'Notes on a Conference of Navy, Essex Scot, Tanks, Engrs and RM Commando 28/06/42.'

36. Ibid.

37. TNA ADM 1/11986. Royal Marine Commando Operational Order No. 9. August 15th, 1942. Sadly, I never had the pleasure of discussing this or any other of my findings with historian and former Royal Marine Robin Neillands before his death in 2006. Needless to say, the new evidence would have answered the questions that he raised in his work on Dieppe and as a retired Royal Marine, I am sure he would have been equally shocked by and proud of the central role that his arm was slated to play in the raid.

38. 'Royal Marine Commando Operational Orders No. 8 Operation Rutter June 30 1942 and No. 9 Operation Jubilee August 15 1942,' TNA ADM 1/11986.

39. Ibid.

40. D. O'Keefe interview with Paul McGrath, October 25, 2010.

41. Ibid.

42. TNA ADM 1/11986. 'Royal Marine Commando Operational Orders No. 8, Operation Rutter, June 30, 1942 and No. 9, Operation Jubilee August 15, 1942.'

43. 'Royal Marine Commando Operational Orders No. 8 Operation Rutter June 30 1942 and No. 9 Operation Jubilee August 15 1942,' TNA ADM 1/11986.

44. Ibid.

45. 'Operation Rutter: Section III – Special Instructions June 22, 1942,' TNA ADM 179/220. This portion, hastily pencilled in, called for the R-boat to rendezvous with *Calpe*, but this seems to be an error for *Fernie*.

46. 'Operation Rutter, Minutes of 1st Meeting of the Combined Force Commanders at Combined Operations Headquarters on June 1st 1942.' TNA DEFE 2/546.

47. Ibid.

48. 'Notes on Meeting Held Inf[orming] Bde [Brigades] about Forthcoming Operation "Rutter."'

49. Ibid.

50. Ibid.

Chapter 12

1. TNA HW 3/137 Historical Memorandum No. 33: History of Naval Section VI (Technical Intelligence), p. 7. The Kriegsmarine suspected the possibility of compromise by the U-boat sunk in shallow waters and laid on a bombing raid to destroy the submarine. Their suspicions bore fruit for when the planes arrived, they spotted the marker buoys laid down by the Royal Navy which indicated that salvage operations had either begun or were about to begin. The air raid failed, and British divers recovered a box of documents from the submarine, but no Enigma-related material was captured in the haul. Hugh Sebag-Montefiore, *Enigma* (Orion Publishing Group). Kindle edition, location 1933. Kindle edition.

2. R.E.D. Ryder, unpublished memoirs.

3. Ibid.

4. Parsons, correspondence with author.

5. Ibid.

6. TNA ADM 179/225. Exercise Pompey.

7. TNA ADM 202/87; Parsons, correspondence with author.

8. Beth Crumley, 'A Roomful of Military Historians,' Marine Corps Association & Foundation, courtesy of the author.

9. TNA ADM 223/285 Special Intelligence Part II 'Letter from Godfrey to Admiral Dudley Pound,' August 15, 1942.

10. MM Godfrey Papers GOD/38 'Special Intelligence to JSM Washington,' September 8, 1942.

11. TNA ADM 223/491 As Godfrey wrote: 'On the advice of Admiral Hall, I had already made a point of getting into personal touch with Mister Kennedy, the US ambassador, who gave the name and telephone number of one of his confidential secretaries to whom I could communicate anything of special naval significance, and seek a personal interview, which, both with Kennedy and Winant, was never refused. I established the same sort, in fact far better, relationship with Winant, saw him frequently and he often dined with me in my flat in Curzon St. This special relationship with Donovan and Winant was a great help during my first mission to the United States in the summer of 1941 before Pearl Harbour, the object of which was to coordinate the arrangements for the exchange with the United States of all forms of intelligence.'

12. 'Brit spymaster reveals tensions with "gangster" Hoover in WW2,' *Windsor Star*, October 27, 2012, https://www.pressreader.com/canada/windsor-star/20121027/282200828172832 (accessed August 13, 2013).

13. Ibid.

14. David Stafford, *Roosevelt & Churchill: Men of Secrets* (London: Thistle Publishing, 2013), 1296–99. Kindle edition.

15. TNA ADM 223/491. Anglo-US Naval Collaboration by Admiral John Godfrey. May 7, 1947.

16. Troy, Thomas F., 'The Coordinator of Information and British Intelligence: An Essay on Origins.' *Studies in Intelligence* 18, no. 1-S (Spring 1974), p. 61.

17. Joseph E. Persico, *Roosevelt's Secret War: FDR and World War II Espionage* (New York: Random House, 2001), 1648–51, Kindle edition; TNA ADM 223/491. As Godfrey recorded: 'In addition, he (Donovan) urged full intelligence collaboration and the placing at our disposal of reports by US consular officers, especially in French ports, direct liaison between myself, and the USDNI, and the establishment of secret indirect methods of communication. In the sphere of technical material Donovan said he would be able to smooth out difficulties, as he had among his clients and his client's relatives such a large number of industrialists of all sorts many of whom were carrying him contracts for the British government.'

18. Troy, Thomas F., 'The Coordinator of Information and British Intelligence: An Essay on Origins.' *Studies in Intelligence* 18, no. 1-S (Spring 1974), p. 63.

19. Center for the Study of Intelligence, Central Intelligence Agency, 'COI Came First,' https://www.cia.gov/library/publications/intelligence-history/oss/art02.htm (accessed August 12, 2013).

20. TNA ADM 223/491.

21. Ibid.

22. Ibid.

23. Ibid. As Godfrey recorded: 'I discussed my dilemma with Mister Stevenson, who had brought in Sir William Wiseman, a British businessman in New York. Wiseman did in 1914 to 1918 what Stephenson did between 1940 and 1946. They told me that the only person who could handle this with any hope of success was the president, and that somehow I must meet Mister Roosevelt. The actual way that it was arranged was that Wiseman spoke to Sultzberger, the editor of the *New York Times*, who I had met, saying that it was important that I should meet the president, but not saying why. Sultzberger rang up Mrs. Roosevelt , asked her to ask me to dinner and make sure that I have an hour with the president afterwards. All went according to plan and as a matter of fact he gave me one and a half hours and, on the recommendation of Winant, who had been brought into the picture, Donovan was appointed to the job within

three weeks. How it all worked out is described in my reports in NID dockets in the bound volume. Although we didn't get a great deal out of the "Donovan set up" in terms of intelligence, we benefited greatly by having such a good friend occupying a key position and I hardly like to think of the chaos, had we had to deal with separate authorities in regard to SIS, psychological warfare.'

24. TNA ADM 223/491.

25. NOTE on page 13 of Troy, Thomas F. 'The Coordinator of Information and British Intelligence: An Essay on Origins.' *Studies in Intelligence* 18, no. 1-S (Spring 1974).

26. Thomas F. Troy, 'Donovan's Original Marching Orders' (originally published 1973), Center for the Study of Intelligence, Central Intelligence Agency, https://www.cia.gov/library/center-for-the-study-of-intelligence/kent-csi/vol17no2/pdf/v17i2a05p.pdf (accessed August 12, 2013).

27. TNA ADM 223/491.

28. Ibid.

29. Sig Rosenblum, *Spymaster: 'Wild Bill' Donovan, Father of the CIA* (Hampton Hill, 2008), 639–43. Kindle edition.

30. Ibid., 1414.

31. Johnson, Thomas R. 'The Sting – Enabling Codebreaking in the Twentieth Century' in *Cryptologic Quarterly*, Vol. 23, Spring/Summer 2004, p. 51.

32. Johnson, Thomas R. 'The Sting – Enabling Codebreaking in the Twentieth Century' in *Cryptologic Quarterly*, Vol. 23, Spring/Summer 2004, p. 51.

33. Johnson, Thomas R. 'The Sting – Enabling Codebreaking in the Twentieth Century' in *Cryptologic Quarterly*, Vol. 23, Spring/Summer 2004, p. 47.

34. Crumley, 'A Roomful of Military Historians.'

35. Ibid.

36. Ibid.

37. Thomas E. Ricks, *The Generals: American Military Command from World War II to Today* (New York: Penguin Press, 2012), 26. Kindle edition.

38. Telegram from Joint Staff Mission Washington to General Ismay, 9 April 1942, TNA DEFE 2/908.

39. TNA ADM 223/491.

40. Ibid.

41. Ibid.

42. Ibid.

43. Ismay to Mountbatten, 9 April 1942, TNA DEFE 2/908.

44. TNA ADM 223/491.

45. TNA HW 8/103. Report on British Procedures for Capturing and Exploiting Enemy Naval Documents, p. 2. As the author points out: 'As regards the immediate importance of pinching to the American Navy, two points should be emphasized: our relative inexperience, and the fact that we are encountering in the Pacific Theatre situations which the British have already faced in the Atlantic.'

46. Birch to DD(s), 1 August 1942, TNA HW 57/9. Although the pinch at Dieppe failed to materialize as hoped, the inter-Allied cooperation came together just a few months later during Operation Torch – the invasion of North Africa. Here, Fleming's 30 Assault Unit, comprised of Dieppe pinch veterans from No. 40 Royal Marine Commando, would strike gold – albeit not when it came to the four-rotor Enigma problem which was solved in late October through a pinch by chance. Unlike at Dieppe where Fleming stood offshore, he was now forced to remain in Whitehall while Commander Dunstan Curtis took them into battle. According to Curtis, 'Ian was immensely excited. You would have thought he was the one who was going on the trip. It was an adventure for him. He must have given an extraordinary amount of thought to this particular show. He had organised air pictures and maps and models to show exactly where we would land and what to go for. He knew where enemy HQ was. He told us what troops were there, what they were up to and what we ought to find.' The results were exactly what Fleming hoped for when, outside Algiers, 30 Assault Unit in cooperation with the Americans captured a high-grade multi-turnover *Abwehr* machine used for a link that had yet to be broken by Dilly Knox's section at Bletchley. The capture resulted in their ability to read six weeks' traffic dealing with German relations with Vichy France. Mavis Batey, *From Bletchley with Love* (Bletchley, UK: Bletchley Park Trust, 2008), p. 31.

47. TNA ADM 205/19. Message from Admiral Pound to Admiral Ernest J King USN, May 18, 1942.

48. TNA ADM 205/19. Letter from King to Pound, May 21, 1942. According to Godfrey, Admiral King was 'a man of commanding ability, self assurance, drive, and vision. He saw how the situation could be redeemed and the War won and he rode it through opposition. As a Commander in Chief of the US Navy and Chief of Operations he held the powers vested in the British First, Third and Fourth Sea Lord very nearly those of the whole board of Admiralty. He reported his actions to the Secretary of the Navy Department, but was responsible only to the president, as

Commander in Chief of all armed forces of the United States, and he
enjoyed President Roosevelt's complete confidence. Off duty Admiral
King was a man of geniality and charm; "on service" his manner changed.
He was brusque, outspoken and overbearing to anyone from Admiral
Leahy, the president's naval advisor (and probably the president himself)
downwards. He knew that he had to fight a long defensive war while
simultaneously building a new American Navy and bringing the personnel
of all ranks up to the pitch of war efficiency which the situation required.
He realised that a heavy hand was needed.' ADM 223/491.

49. Right after the PQ 17 dispersal a person named S.M.B. (Mr Bruce) wrote:
'The developments in connection with the present Russian convoys
are of the most profound importance,' and went on to write later, 'The
passing of these northern convoys is vital.' Pound replied, 'You remark
that the passing of these Northern Convoys is vital but I am sure you will
agree that this is much less vital than our control of sea communications,'
adding: 'If we unreasonably risk the Home Fleet, and to send them into
the Barents Sea is an unreasonable risk, we risk having our vital sea lines
cut, whereas if the Tirpitz was sunk it would affect Germany's position
hardly at all.'

50. TNA ADM 223/3. 'OIC and NID Summaries Naval Section German Effort
Against North Russian Convoy Routes.'

51. TNA ADM 223/470. Special Intelligence Monographs, 'Convoys to
Northern Russia' 1941–1945; HW 43/15, p. 298. As Birch wrote: 'The
handling of it (ULTRA) operationally was, therefore, a comparatively
new technique when, in March of that year, Tirpitz made a sortie from
Trondheim to operate against Convoys PQ 12 and QP 8.' The same could
be said of the 'Channel Dash' when the battlecruisers *Scharnhorst* and
Gneisenau along with the Heavy Cruiser *Prinz Eugen* and ancillary craft,
ventured out from Brest and moved up through the English Channel
making for Norwegian waters in early February. HW 43/15, p. 74.

52. TNA ADM 223/466. Naval Intelligence Monographs, 'The Influence of
Admiral Pound as First Sea Lord & Phillips as VCNS.'

53. Ibid.

54. In a post-war letter, Admiral Andrew Cunningham agreed with
Godfrey's assertion that Pound was 'very narrow' and 'had not any
thought beyond naval affairs.' Sympathetic to his plight, Cunningham
continued: 'Pound had a lot to put up with from Winston who I think
took advantage of his deafness and liability to forget. When I came
home in 1942 to go to Washington, I found Pound in great distress. He

asked me if I thought he ought to resign and I said certainly not. He also told me that Winston was thinking of getting rid of him and putting Mountbatten in as First Sea Lord!! Naturally I told him to glue himself to his chair, but he was much worried about it.' MM GOD 62. Cunningham Letters, May 17, 1956.

55. Winston S. Churchill, *The Second World War*, vol. 4, *The Hinge of Fate* (Boston: Houghton Mifflin, 1950), p. 237.

56. David Wragg, *Sacrifice for Stalin: The Cost and Value of the Arctic Convoys Re-assessed* (Casement Publishers), Kindle edition, locations 3219–3222. Casemate Publishers. Kindle edition. The statistics were devastating. Twenty-four ships out of 36 had been lost, with the numbers evenly divided between eight ships sunk by U-boats, eight by aircraft, and another eight damaged by aircraft and finished off by U-boats, more than 142,000 tons of shipping altogether. The war effort had lost 430 tanks and 210 bombers, as well as 3,350 vehicles and almost 100,000 tons of ammunition. In the circumstances, it was perhaps surprising that just 153 lives were lost.

57. TNA HW 43/24, p. 16. 'The first problem arose with the German advance into Norway in April 1940 and the establishment of German radio stations along the Norwegian coast. Not more than 50% of the total traffic from this area could be received in the United Kingdom. Ionospheric disturbances, frequent in polar regions, made reception of radio fingerprints difficult and medium frequencies were rarely audible owing to the distance. In an effort to improve the position, tests were carried out in Iceland, but no better results were obtained. Interception, however, was important because North Norway provided bases for both surface warships and U boats. And, with the regular reading of Enigma and the German invasion of Russia, the safety of British supply convoys to Murmansk became dependent to some extent as well on its completeness ... but this cumbersome method of communications, aggravated by ionospheric conditions which occasionally made wireless contact impossible for as long as 48 hours at a time, caused such delay in the receipt of messages that they were seldom of tactical or immediate analytic value.'

58. Hinsley to OIC, 'Comments on ZTPG Series of German Naval Messages 0115hrs 04/07/42,' HW 18/158.

59. Ibid.; and Hinsley to OIC, 'Comments on ZTPG Series of German Naval Messages 0305hrs 04/07/42,' HW 18/158.

60. TNA HW 43/24, p. 143.

61. Brian Loring Villa, *Unauthorized Action: Mountbatten and the Dieppe Raid*, 2nd edn (Oxford: Oxford University Press, 1994).

62. Extract from COS (42) 355, 23 December 1942, TNA ADM 223/299.

63. In 1975, following the release of Fredrick Winterbotham's book *The Ultra Secret* which revealed the systematic penetration of the Enigma systems of the German Army, Navy and Air Force, the British government conducted a systematic review of 'sensitive material' released to the British National Archives, known at that time as the Public Record Office. They concluded that they would allow the release of what they deemed 'sensitive' material into the public domain but would retain 'Really Sensitive Material' which applied to: 'Material comprising details of intelligence activities carried out against neutrals or allies, details of still applicable methodology such as techniques of cryptanalysis, and details of personnel or operational matters which are still sensitive.' TNA CAB 163/255. 'War History: WWII.'

64. Andrew Lownie, *The Mountbattens* (Chelsea Harbour, London, UK: Blink Publishing, 2019), p. 139.

65. LAC RG 24 Vol 10, 708. 'Operation Jubilee – Papers.'

66. 'Memorandum of meeting for Operation J_____ on July 16, 1942,' 25 July 1942, LAC RG 24, vol. 10, 584.

67. LAC RG 24 Vol 13, 611 Memorandum by General Andrew McNaughton, July 21, 1942.

68. DHH CMHQ Report 159. 'Operation Jubilee, August 19, 1942. Additional Information on Planning,' p. 3.

69. Ibid.

70. At the time, the security classification for this history read Ultra Secret, which included not only signals but also the histories written after the war. They all came under one great Ultra umbrella.

71. 'Naval Intelligence Division History, 1939–1942,' Manuscript II, Royal Navy Historical Branch, Portsmouth, UK.

72. Ibid.

73. Churchill expressed his surprise over this strategy which was gaining momentum at the upper levels. 'How do we "deceive" the enemy,' he said to Brigadier Hollis, the Secretary of the Chiefs of Staff, 'if we lead them to believe that we are going to do something which, in fact, we are going to do? Do we want them to know and be fully prepared to meet us? There would be point in this if we decided against Sledgehammer.' (101/242 Churchill to Hollis, 23 March 1942). TNA CAB. Records from the chiefs of staff meeting the following day, attended by both Godfrey

and Mountbatten, noted that 'the success of Operation Chariot depended very largely on the success of the diversion created by air bombing. He was anxious for a ruling as to whether or not the Operation should be postponed if the force had sailed and it was then found that air action was impossible on account of adverse weather. There was nothing to indicate that the force was part of a combined operation and he considered that the secrecy of a "repeat" operation was unlikely to be compromised by the early return of the force after it had sailed.' (79/19 94th Meeting of the Chief of Staff Committee, 24 March 1942, TNA CAB 101/242).

74. TNA AIR 8/883. Appendix to report: 'Operation Jubilee,' July 17th, 1942.

75. TNA FO 898/345.

76. Ibid.

77. F.H. Hinsley, *British Intelligence in the Second World War*, Vol II (HMSO Official Histories Book 2). HMSO. Kindle edition; TNA CAB 79/22, COS (42) 234th Meeting, 12 August 1942.

78. Message from McNaughton to Stuart, 18 August 1942, LAC RG 24, vol. 10, 584.

79. University of Southampton, Mountbatten Papers, Letter from DNI to CCO, August 8, 1942.

80. For an excellent treatise on the bureaucratic manoeuvring by Mountbatten, see Stephen Prince, *The Royal Navy and the Raids at St. Nazaire and Dieppe* (London: Frank Cass, 2002).

81. Durnford-Slater recalled that when he visited Second Canadian Division Headquarters shortly after his Commando Unit came aboard for Jubilee, he was greeted by much enthusiasm as they wanted to 'hear of our Vaagso experiences.' John Durnford-Slater, *Commando: Memoirs of a Fighting Commando in World War Two*, (Barnsley, UK: Greenhill Books, 2006), p. 102.

82. Originally Eagle ships were introduced into Rutter to provide anti-aircraft protection for the landing craft and to carry troops for subsequent transfer to R-boats for landing ashore. According to the record of a meeting between the Military and Air commanders in mid-July, it was the Admiralty who objected to their inclusion as 'they would much prefer to dispense with the Eagle Ships, and there is little doubt that from the point of view of secrecy their employment is most undesirable, since their movement from the Thames to the south coast could hardly fail to be observed and to excite the curiosity of the German command.' Military and Air Commanders Meeting: Suggested Points for Decision *circa* July 16 1942, DHH 78/492.

83. Ibid.

84. TNA FO 898/345 Murphy, Peter 'Special Problems Arising from Circumstances of Jubilee' August 6, 1942. Underscored words are in the original.

85. Ibid.

86. Ibid.

87. Martin H. Folly, 'Seeking Comradeship in the "Ogre's Den": Winston Churchill's Quest for a Warrior Alliance and his Mission to Stalin, August 1942' (research paper, Brunel University, 2007), http://bura.brunel.ac.uk/handle/2438/5738 (accessed May 1, 2013).

88. Field Marshall Lord Alanbrooke, *War Diaries 1939–1945* (Orion Publishing Group), Kindle edition. On March 10, Field Marshal Alanbrooke, the chairman of the Chiefs of Staff Committee, confided in his diary: 'Long COS with Mountbatten attending for the first time. We discussed the problem of assistance to Russia by operations in France, with large raid or lodgement. Decided only hope was to try to draw off air forces from Russia and that for this purpose raid must be carried out on Calais front.'

89. TNA WO 199/306. Combined Commanders Meetings (42) 5 May 20, 1942.

90. Ibid.

91. TNA CAB 121/368. Special Information Centre Offensive Operations, 1942, Report by CinC Home Forces, AOC-in-C Fighter Command and Chief of Combined Operations. March 27, 1942.

92. TNA WO 199/306. Combined Commanders Meetings (42) 5, May 20, 1942.

93. TNA CAB 121/368. Special Information Center, Memorandum from Colonel Price to the Prime Minister, June 7, 1942.

94. Ibid.

95. Ibid.

96. Ibid.

97. TNA CAB 121/368. Special Information Center, June 1, 1942.

98. TNA CAB 65/30/20. June 11, 1942.

99. Ibid.

100. Ibid.

101. Ibid.

102. TNA DEFE 2/320. 'Operation Ironclad': a sizeable force of one battleship, two aircraft carriers and six cruisers, 22 destroyers, six corvettes and a bevy of minesweepers escorted five assault vessels and two troopships

in the attack. Altogether, COHQ landed a reinforced division and then supported it ashore (including launching subsidiary amphibious strikes) for the next six months until the Vichy French finally surrendered in early November of 1942.

103. TNA PREM 3/463, no. 57. Sent on July 23, 1942: MESSAGE FROM PREMIER STALIN TO PRIME MINISTER CHURCHILL. Joseph Stalin, *Correspondence between the Chairman of the Council of Ministers of the USSR and the Presidents of the USA and the Prime Ministers of Great Britain during the Great Patriotic War of 1941–1945* (Prism Key Press). Kindle edition.

104. Joseph Stalin, *Correspondence between the Chairman of the Council of Ministers of the USSR and the Presidents of the USA and the Prime Ministers of Great Britain during the Great Patriotic War of 1941–1945* (Prism Key Press). Kindle edition.

105. TNA WO 199/3006. Memorandum by COS, July 24, 1942.

106. TNA WO 199/3006. Meeting of the Combined Commanders, July 25, 1942.

107. TNA DEFE 2/544. Operation Rutter.

108. TNA CAB 66/27/19 WP (42) 339 August 5, 1942, Memorandum by the Secretary of State for Foreign Affairs for the War Cabinet. This is a cable to the Editor of the *News Chronicle*.

109. Ibid.

110. Ibid.

111. TNA CAB 66/28/3 WP (42) 373 Prime Minister's Visit to Moscow, August 23, 1942.

112. Foreign Relations of the United States: Diplomatic Papers, 1942, Europe, Volume III.

113. Alexander Cadogan to Lord Halifax, 'War: Soviet Union. Account of Stalin/ Churchill Meeting in Moscow,' 29 August 1942, TNA FO 1093/247.

114. Ibid.

115. TNA PREM 3/76A/12 Record of the Cairo and Moscow Conferences, August 1942.

116. Ibid.

117. David Wragg, *Sacrifice for Stalin: The Cost and Value of the Arctic Convoys Re-assessed* (Havertown, PA: Casemate), 1105–6. Kindle edition.

118. Alexander Hill, 'British Lend-Lease and the Soviet War Effort June 1941– June 1942,' *Journal of Military History* 71, no. 3 (July 2007): 773–808. Upon his departure from Moscow, Churchill signalled Clement Attlee (the

deputy prime minister) to fill him in on his meetings with Stalin. Churchill told Attlee that he received a 'full account' of the Russian position from the Soviet leader and that Stalin spoke with 'great confidence of being able to hold out until the winter.' What really worried Stalin at this juncture was the convoy issue and the two discussed a limited 'wildcat' invasion of Norway (Operation Jupiter) to remedy the situation. According to Churchill, the land route through Iran was 'only working at half what we hoped' and was insufficient to keep the Soviets supplied with crucial material and technologies like aluminium and trucks, which Stalin considered to be more important than tanks to the success of his armies. 'On the whole,' Churchill relayed, 'I am definitely encouraged by my visit to Moscow. I am sure that the disappointing news I brought could not have been imparted except by me personally without leading to really serious drifting apart. It was my duty to go. Now they know the worst, and having made their protest are entirely friendly; this in spite of the fact that this is their most anxious and agonising time. Moreover, M[arshall] Stalin is entirely convinced of the great advantages of Torch and I do trust that it is being driven with super-human energy on both sides of the ocean.' Churchill to Attlee, Reflex Telegram No. 112, TNA CAB 120/69.

119. Ivan Maisky, *The Maisky Diaries: Red Ambassador to the Court of St James's, 1932–1943* (Yale University Press), Kindle edition, locations 9732–9738.

120. The question of the second front in public opinion in Britain remained one of practicality during the summer of 1942, much to the contrary of what has been written in various studies. According to the Cabinet reports on home opinion over that span, there was considerable optimism following the Soviet counteroffensive in the winter and the pledge from the Western Allies to open the second front in Europe in 1943. By late July, however, confidence in a quick victory on the eastern front had waned and the war was once 'again expected to be a long one' and although most found the idea desirable and inevitable, public opinion was that a second front should only be opened at the time and in the manner sanctioned by those with expert knowledge. By the end of August, the possibility of Soviet collapse loomed large in the mind of the British public, with much sympathy for the Soviets. However, there was 'nothing in the nature of an agitation for this front to be opened immediately' as the 'hard realities of our positions have sunk in.' TNA CAB 195/1 Cabinet Secretary's file 15 June 1942; TNA CAB 66/26/28 War Cabinet Report on Home Opinion, 17 July 1942; CAB 66/28/15 War Cabinet Report on Home Opinion, 28 August 1942.

121. CHUR 4/25A/21–3.

122. David Reynolds, *In Command of History: Churchill Fighting and Writing the Second World War* (Harmondsworth: Penguin Books, 2005), 7422–24. Kindle edition.

123. Ibid., 7426–27.

124. Ibid.

125. Winston S. Churchill, *Memoirs of the Second World War* (Boston: Houghton Mifflin, 1959), p. 636.

126. TNA CAB 120/66.

127. TNA CAB 120/69 (italics added).

128. Ibid.

Chapter 13

1. 'Anonymous member of Special Branch, Newhaven–Dieppe,' *Weekly Intelligence Report* [NID] no. 129, 28 August 1942, pp. 11–20, DHH; Fleming to Casa Maury, 21 August 1942, DEFE 2/333.

2. Memorandum for CCO from Brigadier Truscott, n.d., *c.* Aug.–Sept. 1942, TNA DEFE 3/335.

3. 'Anonymous member of Special Branch,' p. 11.

4. TNA WO 215/20. Assault Squadron J Section May–December 1942, Operation Jubilee, Dieppe Raid. Phantom Report by Lt. Fane landing with Main Force: 'The plan was to land at the same time as 4th Brigade on Red Beach. 4th Brigade was chosen because information about the demolitions was coming into the Brigade in question and these forward battalions had the docks and armed trawlers as an objective, and would receive the information of HMS *Locust*'s attack. The policy was then to go to 6th Bde HQ and get reports about the capture of the aerodrome at St. Aubin and the 210 in HQ in Arques by the forward battalion of the Brigade. Brigadier Southam would then conduct the withdrawal and leave the shores last.'

5. No. 40 Royal Marine Commando, 'War Diary,' TNA ADM 202/87.

6. Jock Farmer, *JOCK of 40 Royal Marine Commando: My Life from Start to Finish* (Shanklin Chine: Shanklin Chine Publishers, 2007), p. 59.

7. 'Memorandum on interview at Navy Office of Canada, on October 14th with Sto. I Pearson, V10685, and Ldg. Stm Cline,' N.W., LAC RG 24, vol. 3951.

8. McAlister memoirs, courtesy of the McAlister family and Phillip Lloyd of No. 40 Royal Marine Commando Association.

9. Farmer, *JOCK*, p. 59.

10. Paul McGrath, *The Dieppe Raid, Wednesday 19th August 1942: Recollections of W.P. McGrath DSM*, self-published, p. 1.

11. Farmer, *JOCK*, p. 59.

12. Douglas Charles Bevan, interview, Imperial War Museum (IWM 14882), 1995.

13. McGrath, *Dieppe Raid*, p. 1.

14. Bevan, interview.

15. John Kruthoffer to Robin Neillands, 25 March 1986, Robin Neillands Papers, RMM.

16. McGrath, *Dieppe Raid*, p. 1.

17. John Hughes-Hallett, *Before I Forget*, p. 177, LAC Hughes-Hallett Papers.

18. Ibid.

19. Ibid., p. 178.

20. Jock Hughes-Hallett, 'Naval Force Commander's Narrative,' Hughes-Hallett Papers, DHH 78/492.

21. R.E.D. Ryder, unpublished memoirs.

22. Ibid.

23. TNA DEFE 2/333, Fleming Report, August 21, 1942.

24. ZIP/ZTPG 68844 and ZIP/ZTPG 68845, DEFE 3/187.

25. Battle Summary No. 33: 'Raid on Dieppe, August 19th 1942' (1946), 13, TNA ADM 223/354.

26. Ibid.

27. ZIP/ZTPG 68850, TNA DEFE 3/187.

28. Fleming to Casa Maury, 21 August 1942, DEFE 2/333.

29. Enclosure 13 'Extract of Report from HMS Locust,' app. 20, LAC RG 24, vol. 10,872; NMM GRO/24.

30. Quoted in Tim Saunders, *Dieppe: Operation Jubilee – Channel Ports* (Battleground Europe), Pen & Sword Books. Kindle Edition.

31. Brereton Greenhous, 'Operation Flodden: The Sea Fight Off Berneval and the Suppression of Goebbels Battery, 19 August, 1942 in *Canadian Military Journal*, Autumn 2003, pp. 47–57.

32. TNA ADM 179/220, Operation 'Rutter': outline plan, with orders and charts relating to the appointment of force commanders: reports on planning, June 11, 1942.

33. NHB Battle Summary No. 33, Raid on Dieppe: Naval Operations, 1959, p. 18.

34. Supplement to the *London Gazette*, October 2, 1942.

35. TNA HW 43/15, p. 324.

36. Ibid., p. 326.

37. Ibid., p. 325.
38. DHH SGR II 283. Dieppe Operation: Combat Report of Boat M4014, August 1942.
39. DHH SGR II 283. Dieppe Operation: Combat Report of Boat M4014, August 1942.
40. 'Combat Report of four Coastal Motor Ships,' 22 August 1942, DHH Steiger Papers SGR II/285.
41. DHH Hughes-Hallett Papers Naval Force Commander's Report on Jubilee Appendix 27 to Enclosure No. 13. 'Extract of Report by Commanding Officer HMS 'Brocklesby' At 0530hrs she parted company with Ślązak to investigate a burning ship in position about 4 degrees bearing 340 from Berneval. She was a German armed trawler ... and was still underway steaming in circles and abandoned by her crew who were in the water. 20 survivors were picked up and the vessel was shelled until burning from end to end and stopped. She was later seen to blow up at about 0645.'
42. TNA ADM 199/1079. Appendix 20 to Enclosure 13, 'Extract of Report from HMS *Brocklesby*.'
43. TNA HW 18/13. POW Information Regarding *UJ1404* with supplementary material from 'Z' and 'Pinch' sources. September 24, 1942.
44. USMC Historical Center. Naval Attaché London England, Narrative Report on the Dieppe Raid, August 19, 1942 as Observed by Colonel Franklin Hart USMC, August 27, 1942. The author would like to thank Beth Crumley for providing a copy of this report. According to the Naval Staff History No. 33, *Locust* moved as part of Group 4 along with HMS *Glengyle*, *ML291*, *MGB 326*, HMS *Duke of Wellington*, HMS *Prince Leopold*, HMS *Prince Charles*. Appendix A, p. 47.
45. TNA ADM 199/1079. Dieppe Reports, Appendix 20 to Enclosure 13, 'Extract of Report from ORP Ślązak.'
46. TNA ADM 199/1079. Dieppe Reports, Appendix 20 to Enclosure 13, 'Navigational Log HMS Calpe.'
47. TNA ADM 199/1079. Dieppe Reports, Appendix 20 to Enclosure 13, 'Extract of Report from HMS Fernie.'
48. TNA ADM 199/1079. Dieppe Reports, Appendix 20 to Enclosure 13, 'Extract of Report from HMS Fernie.'
49. TNA ADM 199/1079. Dieppe Reports, Appendix 20 to Enclosure 13, 'Extract of Report from HMS Locust.'
50. TNA ADM 223/354. Dieppe Battle Summary, No. 33, 1946, Version P.13. A warning signal was sent by C-in-C Portsmouth at 0127: 'Small craft apparently patrolling approximately 350 degrees Treport 15 Miles

at 0100.' There was so far nothing at this point to show that these craft were likely to enter the operational area, but fresh reports showed that this was very possible, so at 0244 a further message was sent to the Naval Force Commander: 'Two Craft 302 degrees Treport 10 miles, course 190 degrees, 13 knots at 0226hrs.'

51. TNA ADM 199/1079. Dieppe Reports Appendix 20 to Enclosure 13 'Extract of Report from HMS Locust.'

52. Ibid.

53. USMC Historical Center. Naval Attaché, London, England, Narrative Report on the Dieppe Raid, August 19, 1942 as Observed by Colonel Franklin Hart USMC, August 27, 1942.

54. Battle Summary No. 33.

55. Ibid.

56. Dieppe Operation Naval Commander Channel Coast, 'Lessons Learnt August 30 1942,' DHH Steiger Papers SGR II/280.

57. Ibid. 'According to information from 81st Army Corps, one of our convoys has been attacked by fast British ships at 0400hrs, at about 20 kilometres off the port of Dieppe. Troops have intensified their lookout. Navy and Air authorities have been advised.'

58. Robin Neillands, *The Dieppe Raid: The Story of the Disastrous 1942 Expedition* (London: Aurum Press, 2005), p. 129.

59. Jack A. Poolton, *Destined to Survive: A Dieppe Veteran's Story* (Dundurn, Kindle edition).

60. Interview with author for *DU*, 3 March 2011.

61. 'Action of the Essex Scottish (Red Beach), Statement by Capt D.F. McCrae,' TNA DEFE 2/339.

62. Ibid.

63. Author's interview with Howard Large for *DU*, 3 October 2011.

64. Denis W. Whitaker and Shelagh Whitaker, *Dieppe: Tragedy to Triumph* (Toronto: McGraw-Hill Ryerson, 1992), p. 253.

65. Jock Hughes-Hallett, 'Naval Force Commander's Narrative,' Hughes-Hallett Papers, DHH 78/492.

66. Bevan, interview.

67. Ibid.

68. John Parson, correspondence with author.

69. R.E.D. Ryder, unpublished memoirs.

70. Ernest Coleman, unpublished memoirs, courtesy of John Barker.

71. McGrath, *Dieppe Raid*, p. 5.

72. Ibid.

73. Ibid.

74. Ibid., p. 6.

75. Ibid.

76. Naval Force Commander's Narrative, encl. no. 5, 'Operation Jubilee List of Important Signals,' LAC Hughes-Hallett Papers.

77. Farmer, *JOCK*, p. 60.

78. LAC RG24, vol. 17, 506.

79. Naval Force Commander's Narrative, encl. no. 5.

80. 'Operation Jubilee: The Raid at Dieppe 19/08/42, Part II: The Execution of the Operation, Section 2, The Attack on the Main Beaches, Report Battle Account of St. Pierre Dubuc, Fusiliers de Mont-Royal,' DHH CMHQ 108.

81. Hughes-Hallett, *Before I Forget*, p. 185.

82. 'Lord Mountbatten's Comments on Dieppe Chapter,' *c.*1970, LAC Hughes-Hallett Papers. In this case, it is Mountbatten quoting Hughes-Hallett back to Hughes-Hallett.

83. Wallace Reyburn, letter to the editor, *Sunday Telegraph* (London), 17 September 1967, LAC Hughes-Hallett Papers.

84. Quoted in Neillands, *Dieppe Raid*, p. 238.

85. Naval Force Commander's Narrative, encl. no. 5, 'Operation Jubilee List of Important Signals,' LAC Hughes-Hallett Papers.

86. 'Report Operation Jubilee Royal Marine Commando 19/08/42,' TNA ADM 1/11986; Capt. P.W.C. Hellings RM DSC, 'Report on Events of 19/08/42 off Dieppe of A Coy Royal Marine Commando,' TNA ADM 1/11986.

87. Ernest Coleman, unpublished memoirs.

88. Ibid.

89. Farmer, *JOCK*, p. 61.

90. Naval Force Commander's Narrative, encl. no. 5. Hughes-Hallett's only response was to order Ryder, who had remained on *Locust*, to pick up the wounded on the beach once the Royal Marines landed.

91. Naval Force Commander's Narrative, encl. no. 5.

92. Hugh G. Henry, 'The Planning, Intelligence, Execution and Aftermath of the Dieppe Raid, 19 August 1942' (Ph.D. dissertation, St. John's College, University of Cambridge, October 1996).

Chapter 14

1. Paul McGrath, *The Dieppe Raid, Wednesday 19th August 1942: Recollections of W.P. McGrath DSM*, self-published, p. 1.

2. Ernest Coleman, unpublished memoirs.

3. McAlister, unpublished memoirs.

4. J.J. Dwan to Neillands, November 7, 2002, Robin Neillands Papers, RMM.

5. McGrath, *Dieppe Raid*, p. 9.

6. Kruthoffer, quoted in Robin Neillands, *By Sea and Land* (Barnsley, UK: Pen and Sword, 2004), p. 29.

7. McGrath, *Dieppe Raid*, p. 8.

8. Kruthoffer, quoted in Neillands, *By Sea and Land*, p. 29.

9. Ernest Coleman, unpublished memoirs.

10. McGrath, *Dieppe Raid*, p. 9.

11. Kruthoffer, quoted in Neillands, *By Sea and Land*, p. 29.

12. Ernest Coleman, unpublished memoirs.

13. McGrath, *Dieppe Raid*, p. 11.

14. 'A History of 30 Commando (Latterly Called 30 Assault Unit and 30 Advanced Unit),' Ch. 2, TNA ADM 223/214; 'Camp 020 Interim Report on the case of Erich Pfeiffer,' TNA KV 2/267.

15. Huntington-Whiteley to Sergeant Kruthoffer, n.d., *c.* 26 August 1942; quoted in Neillands, *By Sea and Land*, pp. 33–4.

16. R.E.D. Ryder, unpublished memoirs.

17. *Weekly Intelligence Report* [NID] no. 129, August 28, 1942, DHH.

18. The exception was John Campbell's masterful *Dieppe Revisited*, in which he cites the document but fails to understand its true significance. Rather, he focuses on the security issues and on Fleming's veiled references to his own Ultra indoctrination.

19. TNA DEFE 2/333, Fleming Report, August 21, 1942.

Epilogue

1. *DU.*

2. David Kahn, *Seizing the Enigma: The Race to Break the German U-Boats Codes, 1939–1943* (1991).

3. According to Mahon's 'History of Hut 8,' 'The capture of the complete indicator tables and codebook for WWs was of vital importance,' for it enabled *Shark* to be broken operationally for the first time since the blackout started in February of 1942. The method was used with great success as the next 88 out of 99 *Shark* days were read until March 10, 1943, when the Germans changed the WW books creating another 'mini-blackout.' Eventually that was solved by the use of B-bars to gain entry through the back door of *Shark*. 'History of Hut 8,' 77, TNA HW 25/2.

4. Mountbatten to Godfrey, 29 August 1942, BNA DEFE 2/955. As Mountbatten would later tell Godfrey after the DNI petitioned for the

VC winner's services to head the new 30 Assault Unit following Dieppe: 'I know you will agree it will not be much use having the most perfect Intelligence Assault Unit unless the operations on which they are sent are properly planned and carried out.'

5. Of course, if Jock Hughes-Hallett did not agree, he had the power as naval force commander – not to mention the cocksureness – to call off any attempts to land further reinforcements simply by refusing to provide the boats or by turning for home. Despite their difference in rank, for the raid Roberts and Hughes-Hallett were equals, masters of their own military and naval domains respectively.

6. Intelligence Control Station France, 'Evaluation of Dieppe Operation,' 14 September 1942, LAC RG 24, vol. 20, 488. According to the German report, the last bag that did not sink consisted of the following which went missing during the raid:

   a) 10 special panels for exterior ... Inserted star signal boards.

   b) 1 telephony camouflage board for ship registration and field service at frenz. Coast. Valid

   c) 6 radio signal booklets for harbor protection boats in the area of Command Admiral France – edition November 1941 – m.dv. No. 423/ pr. pfr.n.r. 75 to 80. valid until 7/31/42.

   d) 1 radio signal booklet for harbor protection boats in the area of the Komd. Adm. France with associated key group boards and distribution plan for key group boards for the H.S. Radio signal booklet France, Edition June 42 M.Dv. No. 423/Fr. 104 – Valid from 1.8.42.

   e) 1 special print of the marine list of the signal book – M. Dv. No. 150 a – Rev. No. 519th.

   f) gkdo's (geheime Kommandosache) letter book 1941/42.

   g) 1 collection go.N.T.B. 1942 (until early August).

   h) 1 collection belonging to T.B.Marbef.Kanal Canal 1942 (until early August).

   i) collection of gas protection orders 1942.

   j) 1 collection of fortress orders 1942.

   k) 1 file gkdos 1941/42.

7. TNA FO 898/345. Letter from Peter Murphy to Brigadier R.A.D. Brookes, September 13, 1942.

8. Ibid.

9. TNA FO 898/345. The Part of Political Warfare In the Combined Operations Raid on Dieppe. August 22, 1942.

10. Ibid.
11. TNA AIR 20/4529. Operation Coleman: Proposals for Combined Operation Air Battle on the French Coast, October 1942; AIR 16/762. Operation Aflame.
12. TNA HW 57/9. Memorandum for Admiral King by K.A. Knowles. Knowles, who headed the US U-boat Tracking Room, noted after discussions concerning the production of an official naval history: 'Such a history can be made available to all Naval officers for proper study, whereas a "true" history which incorporated special intelligence must, by its nature, be limited in the dissemination to the high command alone.'

Index